ReFocus: The Films of John Hughes

ReFocus: The American Directors Series

Series Editors: Robert Singer, Frances Smith, and Gary D. Rhodes

Editorial Board: Kelly Basilio, Donna Campbell, Claire Perkins, Christopher Sharrett, and Yannis Tzioumakis

ReFocus is a series of contemporary methodological and theoretical approaches to the interdisciplinary analyses and interpretations of neglected American directors, from the once-famous to the ignored, in direct relationship to American culture—its myths, values, and historical precepts. The series ignores no director who created a historical space—either in or out of the studio system—beginning from the origins of American cinema and up to the present. These directors produced film titles that appear in university film history and genre courses across international boundaries, and their work is often seen on television or available to download or purchase, but each suffers from a form of "canon envy"; directors such as these, among other important figures in the general history of American cinema, are underrepresented in the critical dialogue, yet each has created American narratives, works of film art, that warrant attention. *ReFocus* brings these American film directors to a new audience of scholars and general readers of both American and Film Studies.

Titles in the series include:

ReFocus: The Films of Preston Sturges
Edited by Jeff Jaeckle and Sarah Kozloff

ReFocus: The Films of Delmer Daves
Edited by Matthew Carter and Andrew Nelson

ReFocus: The Films of Amy Heckerling
Edited by Frances Smith and Timothy Shary

ReFocus: The Films of Budd Boetticher
Edited by Gary D. Rhodes and Robert Singer

ReFocus: The Films of Kelly Reichardt
E. Dawn Hall

ReFocus: The Films of William Castle
Edited by Murray Leeder

ReFocus: The Films of Barbara Kopple
Edited by Jeff Jaeckle and Susan Ryan

ReFocus: The Films of Elaine May
Edited by Alexandra Heller-Nicholas and Dean Brandum

ReFocus: The Films of Spike Jonze
Edited by Kim Wilkins and Wyatt Moss-Wellington

ReFocus: The Films of Paul Schrader
Edited by Michelle E. Moore and Brian Brems

ReFocus: The Films of John Hughes
Edited by Timothy Shary and Frances Smith

edinburghuniversitypress.com/series/refoc

ReFocus:
The Films of John Hughes

Edited by Timothy Shary and
Frances Smith

Edinburgh University Press is one of the leading university presses in the UK. We publish academic books and journals in our selected subject areas across the humanities and social sciences, combining cutting-edge scholarship with high editorial and production values to produce academic works of lasting importance. For more information visit our website: edinburghuniversitypress.com

© editorial matter and organisation Timothy Shary and Frances Smith, 2021, 2023
© the chapters their several authors, 2021, 2023

Edinburgh University Press Ltd
The Tun—Holyrood Road
12 (2f) Jackson's Entry
Edinburgh EH8 8PJ

First published in hardback by Edinburgh University Press 2021

Typeset in 11/13 Ehrhardt MT by
IDSUK (DataConnection) Ltd

A CIP record for this book is available from the British Library

ISBN 978 1 4744 4902 1 (hardback)
ISBN 978 1 4744 4903 8 (paperback)
ISBN 978 1 4744 4904 5 (webready PDF)
ISBN 978 1 4744 4905 2 (epub)

The right of the contributors to be identified as authors of this work has been asserted in accordance with the Copyright, Designs and Patents Act 1988 and the Copyright and Related Rights Regulations 2003 (SI No. 2498).

Contents

List of Figures and Tables	vii
Acknowledgments	ix
Notes on Contributors	x
Film and Television Work by John Hughes	xiv

1. Introduction: Refocus on John Hughes   1
   Timothy Shary and Frances Smith

Part I Hughes in the Industry

2. John Hughes as Auteur: History, Hagiography, Historiography   24
   Elissa H. Nelson

3. "Becoming John Hughes": Regional Production, Hyphenate Filmmaking, and Independence within Hollywood   44
   Yannis Tzioumakis

4. *Ferris Bueller* vs. *Parker Lewis*: "Adapting" *Ferris Bueller's Day Off* for Television   64
   Stephen Tropiano

Part II Reconsidering Youth

5. "Life moves pretty fast": Mobility, Power, and Aesthetics in John Hughes's Teen Films   84
   Christina G. Petersen

6. "When Cameron was in Egypt's land": The Queer Child of Neglect in John Hughes's Films   102
   Barbara Jane Brickman

7 We Need to Talk About Kevin McCallister: John Hughes's
   Careless Parents and Abandoned Children   118
   Melissa Oliver-Powell

Part III Family and Fatherhood

8 Brand Name Vision: Props in the Films of John Hughes   142
   Leah R. Shafer

9 Domesticating the Comedian: Comic Performance, Narrative,
   and the Family in John Hughes's 1980s Comedian Films   161
   Holly Chard

10 Fatherhood and the Failures of Paternal Authority in
   the Films of John Hughes   179
   Alice Leppert

Part IV Contested Identities

11 Bizarre Love Triangle: Frankensteinian Masculinities
   in *Weird Science*   202
   Andrew Scahill

12 "You look good wearing my future:" Social Class and
   Individualism in the 1980s Teen Films of John Hughes   221
   Robert C. Bulman

13 The Unbearable Whiteness of Being in a John Hughes Movie   236
   Frances Smith

Other Films and Television Shows Cited in This Collection   250
Bibliography   255
Index   267

Figures and Tables

FIGURES

1.1	John Hughes in the 1980s, his defining decade	1
1.2	Autographed picture of John Hughes with the cast of *Pretty in Pink*	5
1.3	Six teen films that Hughes wrote and/or directed in the 1980s, which became epochal for a generation of youth	10
1.4	Family matters in Hughes's stories, as in *Vacation* and the sequels that followed	12
1.5	*Home Alone* was Hughes's biggest financial success, but his subsequent projects yielded diminishing returns	15
3.1	Generic playfulness and visual gags: not exercising	56
3.2	A humanized geek! John Hughes gives a much-maligned teen archetype full characterization	58
3.3	Opposite teen archetypes in harmony: the restrained hunk and the hyperkinetic geek	59
4.1	Television's Ferris Bueller and his nemesis, Principal Ed Rooney	70
4.2	Parker Lewis and his nemesis, Principal Grace Musso	72
5.1	Ted takes control of the frame in *Sixteen Candles*	88
5.2	Older brother Chet controls the frame in *Weird Science*	90
5.3	The high school class system in *The Breakfast Club*	92
5.4	Glass as a barrier in *Ferris Bueller's Day Off*	96
6.1	Cameron's traumatized isolation on the diving board represents an iconic moment in Hughes's oeuvre of neglect	104
6.2	Cameron, alone, initially dwarfed by Seurat's pointillist masterpiece	110

6.3	Cameron's imploring eyes	111
6.4	The abstraction of the extreme close-up brings us into the existential quest	112
8.1	Clark asleep at the wheel	148
8.2	Jim Dodge and mannequin watch TV	154
8.3	Kevin's battle plan	155
8.4	Pershing missile	156
10.1	Clark Griswold flirts with the Girl in the Red Ferrari in *Vacation*	184
11.1	Gary and Wyatt become spectacles to the female gaze	204
11.2	Lisa is fittingly created on an altar of heteronormativity: Milton Bradley's Game of Life	211
11.3	Gary takes up the gun to conquer the toxic hypermasculinity of Hollywood cinema	216

TABLES

3.1	Top five films targeting explicitly youth (children, teen and young adult) audiences, 1980–83	51

Acknowledgments

We thank our series editors, Robert Singer and Gary Rhodes, for inviting us to contribute this second volume to their *ReFocus* series, and for motivating collaboration between us that has lasted almost a decade now. At Edinburgh University Press, we once again give thanks to our commissioning editors Gillian Leslie and Richard Strachan; our desk editor Eddie Clark; our cover coordinator Bekah Day; and our copyeditor Anita Joseph. Thanks as well to our anonymous reviewers, who obviously cannot be named but who nonetheless were quite helpful in guiding our production of this collection. And naturally this would not be a collection without our great contributors, all distinguished figures in the field, whom we thank for their insights and hard work, as well as their patience through the unexpected delays we faced during the global pandemic of 2020.

Frances would like to acknowledge the supportive colleagues in Film Studies at the University of Sussex, and students taking American Teen Cinema. She thanks her family and the ever-enthusiastic Mr. Metcalf.

Tim acknowledges the teenage friends who accompanied him when he first saw John Hughes movies over 35 years ago—David Amanullah, Paula Hostler, and Paul Hawkins—as well as the friends who have since continued to discuss the films herein, including Chris Boucher, Richard Brown, Devin Griffiths, and Tom Scully. He dedicates this study to the most stylish and sophisticated teenager in the world, whom no movie could endeavor to represent, his wonderful daughter Olivia Xendolyn.

Notes on Contributors

Barbara Jane Brickman is Associate Professor of Media and Gender Studies at the University of Alabama. Her research interests are in girls' studies, feminist film theory, gay and lesbian studies, and American popular culture. Her work has appeared in *Camera Obscura*, *Discourse*, and *Journal of Popular Music Studies*. Since the publication of her first book, *New American Teenagers: The Lost Generation of Youth in 1970s Film* (2012), she has written a volume on the film *Grease* (2017) for the Cinema and Youth Cultures series from Routledge and co-edited *Love Across the Atlantic* (with Deborah Jermyn and Theodore Louis Trost, 2020) for Edinburgh University Press. She is also the founder and director of the Druid City Girls Media Program in Tuscaloosa, AL.

Robert C. Bulman is a professor of sociology at Saint Mary's College of California. He received his BA in sociology from U.C. Santa Cruz in 1989 and his PhD in sociology from U.C. Berkeley in 1999. His sociological areas of expertise include education, adolescence, film, and stratification. He has published a book on the depiction of high schools and adolescents in Hollywood films, *Hollywood Goes to High School: Cinema, Schools, and American Culture*. The second edition (revised and updated) was published in 2015.

Holly Chard is Senior Lecturer in Contemporary Screen Media at the University of Brighton. Her research focuses on the American media industries from the 1970s onwards, with an emphasis on Hollywood cinema. Her monograph, *Mainstream Maverick: John Hughes and New Hollywood Cinema* (2020), examines the career and films of John Hughes, focusing in particular on his teen movies and family films. Her other recent publications include an article in *Film Studies* on John Hughes's use of seriality and a co-authored journal article in the *Journal of Cinema and Media Studies* on Hulk Hogan and professional wrestling stardom.

Alice Leppert is Associate Professor of Media and Communication Studies at Ursinus College. She is the author of *TV Family Values: Gender, Domestic Labor, and 1980s Sitcoms* (2019). Her work has appeared in *Cinema Journal*, *Television and New Media*, *Celebrity Studies*, *Genders*, and several edited collections. She serves as the book review editor for *Film Criticism*.

Elissa H. Nelson is an associate professor in the Communication Arts and Sciences Department at Bronx Community College, City University of New York. She has published work on 1980s Hollywood, digital distribution, soundtracks, and teen films, and her current research focuses on the media industries, genre studies, and representations of youth. She is the author of *The Breakfast Club: John Hughes, Hollywood, and the Golden Age of the Teen Film* (2019), part of the Cinema and Youth Cultures series from Routledge. Her work has appeared in journals and anthologies including *Cinema Journal*, *Creative Industries Journal*, and *Connected Viewing: Selling, Streaming, and Sharing Media in the Digital Era*.

Melissa Oliver-Powell is a lecturer in the English and Film Studies at the University of Exeter, where she teaches on film and critical theory. She has also taught within film, literature, and gender studies at University College London, where she received her PhD in 2018, with a dissertation on motherhood in British and French film in the 1960s and 1970s. Her research focuses on issues of mothering, politics, and social justice in film, and she has published on topics including representation of abortion, mothering subjectivities, and mothering, migration, and racism in British, French, Senegalese, and American film.

Christina G. Petersen serves as Christian Nielsen Associate Professor and Chair of Film Studies at Eckerd College. Her work on the American race film industry, the history of the youth film as a modernist genre, and the phenomenon of youth spectatorship in the United States has appeared in *Film History*, *Rhizomes*, and *Mediascape*. Her book, *The Freshman: Comedy and Masculinity in 1920s Film and Youth Culture*, was published in 2019.

Andrew Scahill is an assistant professor in the Department of English at the University of Colorado, Denver. He has served as Coordinating Editor for *Velvet Light Trap* and Assistant Editor for *Literature/Film Quarterly*. He has been published in multiple journals, such as *Cinema Journal*, *Girlhood Studies*, *Flow*, *Jump Cut*, and *Postscript*. He is the author of *The Revolting Child in Horror Cinema: Youth Rebellion and Queer Spectatorship* (2015) and is featured in the documentaries *Scream, Queen!: My Nightmare on Elm Street* (2019) and Shudder Network's *Queer Horror* (2020).

Leah R. Shafer is an associate professor in the Media and Society Program at Hobart and William Smith Colleges, where she has taught courses in film, television, and new media since 2008. She holds a PhD from the Department of Theatre, Film and Dance at Cornell University. Her research focuses on the comic, the banal, the amateur, and the commercial. Her work has appeared in *Film Criticism* and *Flow: A Critical Forum on Television and Media Culture*. She has chapters in *A Companion to the War Film* (2016) and *The 25 Sitcoms that Changed Television: Turning Points in American Culture* (2017).

Timothy Shary has published extensively on aging representation in cinema, both young and old. His work on teen cinema has included *Generation Multiplex: The Image of Youth in Contemporary American Cinema* (2002; revised 2014) and *Teen Movies: American Youth on Screen* (2005), as well as *Youth Culture in Global Cinema* (2007), edited with Alexandra Seibel. On the other end of the age spectrum, he co-authored *Fade to Gray: Aging in American Cinema* (2016) with Nancy McVittie. He has also edited *Millennial Masculinity: Men in Contemporary American Cinema* (2013) and is the co-editor with Frances Smith of *ReFocus: The Films of Amy Heckerling* (Edinburgh University Press, 2016). He more recently authored *Boyhood: A Young Life on Screen* (2017), a volume on the 2014 Richard Linklater film, and his edited collection *Cinemas of Boyhood* will appear in 2021.

Frances Smith is Lecturer in Film Studies at the University of Sussex. She is the author of *Rethinking the Teen Movie* (2017), and the co-editor (with Timothy Shary) of *Refocus: The Films of Amy Heckerling* (2016), both published by Edinburgh University Press. Alongside book chapters and articles on female authorship and genre in film and television, she recently published a monograph on Céline Sciamma's *Bande de Filles* (2020) in Routledge's Cinema and Youth Cultures series.

Stephen Tropiano is the author of several books on popular culture: *Rebels and Chicks: A History of the Hollywood Teen Movie* (2005), *The Prime Time Closet: A History of Gays and Lesbians on Television* (2002), *Saturday Night Live FAQ* (2013), and *TV Finales FAQ*, co-written with Holly Van Buren (2015). He has also written books on the film musicals *Cabaret* (1972) and *Grease* (1978) for Limelight Editions' Music on Film series. He was editor of the *Journal of Film and Video* between 2002 and 2018, and is currently Professor of Screen Studies at Ithaca College Los Angeles.

Yannis Tzioumakis is Reader in Film and Media Industries at the University of Liverpool. He is the author of five books, including *American Independent Cinema* (Edinburgh University Press, 2nd edition 2017) and, most recently, *Acting Indie* (co-authored with Cynthia Baron, 2020). He is also co-editor of six collections of essays, most recently *United Artists* (2020), and he co-edits two book series: the Routledge Hollywood Centenary and Cinema and Youth Cultures. For the latter, he is currently co-authoring the volume *Rock Around the Clock: Exploitation, Rock 'n' Roll and the Origins of Youth Culture*.

Film and Television Work by John Hughes

AS DIRECTOR

Sixteen Candles (Universal Pictures, 1984)
The Breakfast Club (Universal Pictures, 1985)
Weird Science (Universal Pictures, 1985)
Ferris Bueller's Day Off (Paramount Pictures, 1986)
Planes, Trains & Automobiles (Paramount Pictures, 1987)
She's Having a Baby (Paramount Pictures, 1988)
Uncle Buck (Universal Pictures, 1989)
Curly Sue (Warner Bros., 1991)

AS WRITER

Delta House (written by) (TV series, 5 episodes) (ABC, 1979)
"The Matriculation of Kent Dorfman" (written by)
"Campus Fair" (written by)
"The Deformity" (written by)
"The Lady in Weighting" (written by)
"The Shortest Yard" (written by)
The Secret Life of Nikola Tesla (co-writer) (Zagreb Films, 1980)
[*National Lampoon's*] *Class Reunion* (written by) (ABC Motion Pictures, 1982)
At Ease (creator) (TV series, 14 episodes) (ABC, 1983)
National Lampoon's Vacation (screenplay, based on short story "Vacation '58") (Warner Bros., 1983)
Mr. Mom (written by) (Twentieth Century Fox, 1983)

Savage Islands aka *Nate and Hayes* (screenplay) (Phillips Whitehouse Productions, 1983)
Sixteen Candles (written by) (Universal Pictures, 1984)
The Breakfast Club (written by) (Universal Pictures, 1985)
National Lampoon's European Vacation (screenplay/story) (Warner Bros., 1985)
Weird Science (written by) (Universal Pictures, 1985)
Pretty in Pink (written by) (Paramount Pictures, 1986)
Ferris Bueller's Day Off (written by) (Paramount Pictures, 1986)
Some Kind of Wonderful (written by) (Paramount Pictures, 1987)
Planes, Trains & Automobiles (written by) (Paramount Pictures, 1987)
She's Having a Baby (written by) (Paramount Pictures, 1988)
The Great Outdoors (written by) (Universal Pictures, 1988)
Uncle Buck (written by) (Universal Pictures, 1989)
National Lampoon's Christmas Vacation (written by) (Warner Bros.. 1989)
Home Alone (written by) (Twentieth Century Fox, 1990)
Career Opportunities (written by) (Universal Pictures, 1991)
Dutch (written by) (Twentieth Century Fox, 1991)
Curly Sue (written by) (Warner Bros., 1991)
Beethoven (written by – as Edmond Dantès) (Universal Pictures, 1992)
Home Alone 2: Lost in New York (written by) (Twentieth Century Fox, 1992)
Dennis the Menace (written by) (Warner Bros., 1993)
Baby's Day Out (written by) (Twentieth Century Fox, 1994)
Miracle on 34th Street (screenplay) (Twentieth Century Fox, 1994)
101 Dalmatians (screenplay) (Walt Disney Pictures, 1996)
Flubber (screenplay) (Walt Disney Pictures, 1997)
Home Alone 3 (written by) (Twentieth Century Fox, 1997)
Reach the Rock (written by) (Gramercy Pictures, 1998)
Just Visiting (screenplay) (Gaumont, 2001)
Maid in Manhattan (story – as Edmond Dantès) (Revolution Studios, 2002)
Drillbit Taylor (story – as Edmond Dantès) (Paramount Pictures, 2008)

CHARACTERS CREATED

Mr. Mom (TV movie) (ABC, 1984)
Ferris Bueller (TV series; 13 episodes) (NBC, 1990–91)
Uncle Buck (TV series; 18 episodes) (CBS, 1990–91)
Home Alone (video game) (1991)
Home Alone 2: Lost in New York (video game) (1992)
Beethoven's 2nd (as Edmond Dantès) (Universal Pictures, 1993)
Weird Science (TV series; 88 episodes) (USA Network, 1994–98)
American Adventure (TV movie) (Fox, 2000)

Beethoven's 3rd (video) (as Edmond Dantès) (Universal Home Entertainment, 2000)
Beethoven's 4th (video) (as Edmond Dantès) (Universal Home Entertainment, 2001)
Home Alone 4: Taking Back the House (TV movie) (Twentieth Century Fox Television, 2002)
Beethoven's 5th (video) (as Edmond Dantès) (Universal Home Entertainment, 2003)

POSTHUMOUS CREDITS

Hotel Hell Vacation (video short) (original characters) (Hungry Man Productions, 2010)
Beethoven's Christmas Adventure (video) (original characters) (Universal Pictures, 2011)
Home Alone: The Holiday Heist (TV Movie) (original characters – uncredited) (Fox Television, 2012)
Beethoven's Treasure Tail (video) (original characters) (Universal 1440 Entertainment, 2014)
Vacation (characters) (New Line Cinema, 2015)

AS PRODUCER

The Breakfast Club (producer) (Universal Pictures, 1985)
Pretty in Pink (executive producer) (Paramount Pictures, 1986)
Ferris Bueller's Day Off (producer) (Paramount Pictures, 1986)
Some Kind of Wonderful (producer) (Paramount Pictures, 1987)
Planes, Trains & Automobiles (producer) (Paramount Pictures, 1987)
She's Having a Baby (producer) (Paramount Pictures. 1988)
The Great Outdoors (executive producer) (Universal Pictures, 1988)
Uncle Buck (producer) (Universal Pictures, 1989)
National Lampoon's Christmas Vacation (producer) (Warner Bros., 1989)
Home Alone (producer) (Twentieth Century Fox, 1990)
Career Opportunities (producer) (Universal Pictures, 1991)
Only the Lonely (producer) (Twentieth Century Fox, 1991)
Dutch (producer) (Twentieth Century Fox, 1991)
Curly Sue (producer) (Warner Bros., 1991)
Home Alone 2: Lost in New York (producer) (Twentieth Century Fox, 1992)
Dennis the Menace (producer) (Warner Bros., 1993)
Baby's Day Out (producer) (Twentieth Century Fox, 1994)

101 Dalmatians (producer) (Walt Disney Pictures, 1996)
Flubber (producer) (Walt Disney Pictures, 1997)
Home Alone 3 (producer) (Twentieth Century Fox, 1997)
Reach the Rock (producer) (Gramercy Pictures, 1998)
New Port South (executive producer) (Touchstone Pictures, 2001)

HUGHES'S APPEARANCES

The Making of Home Alone 2: Lost in New York (TV documentary, Fox Television, 1992)
A Menace Named Dennis (TV documentary, ABC, 1993)
Hal Roach: Hollywood's King of Laughter (TV documentary, ABC, 1994)
Biography (TV series documentary): "To John with Love: A Tribute to John Candy" (ABC, 1995)
E! True Hollywood Story (TV series documentary): "Sixteen Candles" (E!, 2001)
Who is Ferris Bueller? (documentary short, Paramount Pictures, 2006)
The Making of Ferris Bueller's Day Off: Production Stories (documentary short, Paramount Pictures, 2006)
Getting the Class Together: The Cast of Ferris Bueller's Day Off (documentary short, Paramount Pictures, 2006)
Teen Spirit: Teenagers and Hollywood (TV documentary, Arte, 2009)
The 82nd Annual Academy Awards (TV special, ABC, 2010)
The Greatest 80s Movies (TV documentary, Channel 5, 2014)
Drunk Stoned Brilliant Dead (documentary, 4th Row Films, 2015)
The Movies (TV series documentary): "The Eighties" (CNN, 2019)
The Movies That Made Us (TV series documentary): "Home Alone" (Netflix, 2019)

UNCREDITED CAMEO APPEARANCES

Class Reunion (ABC, 1982): "Girl" with Paper Bag on Head
The Breakfast Club (Universal Pictures, 1985): Brian's Father
Ferris Bueller's Day Off (Paramount Pictures, 1986): Guy Running Between Cabs

CHAPTER 1

Introduction: Refocus on John Hughes

Timothy Shary and Frances Smith

"It's hard for me to understand how John [Hughes] was able to write with so much sensitivity, and also have such a glaring blind spot."[1] Thus considers Molly Ringwald, one of the principal stars of John Hughes's teen films in the mid-1980s, and often credited as the writer-director-producer's muse.[2] It is precisely this question with which the various authors in this volume

Figure 1.1 John Hughes in the 1980s, his defining decade.

have wrestled, wondering how exactly the soulful scribe of *The Breakfast Club* (1985), which affirms that "when you grow up, your heart dies," squares up with the cynical humor he peddled elsewhere, often at the same time. Those elements that Ringwald rather charitably describes as "blind spots" include persistent undercurrents of sexism and racism. They also include the reification of gender stereotypes and a blasé attitude toward sexual assault, often directed towards Ringwald herself. For her part, Ringwald describes Hughes as a highly supportive director and mentor, without whom her career would never have taken off. At the same time, though, she paints a picture of a powerful figure who was quick to take offense, and who harbored grudges. As Ringwald herself explains, she came to experience Hughes's wrath when she suggested a rewrite of a prospective film project, after which the two never spoke again. John Hughes, then, was undoubtedly a complex character, whose highly popular work has yet to be fully reckoned with. Providing an interdisciplinary assessment of a wide range of Hughes's works, this volume demonstrates the multiplicity and complexity of his well-known and much-admired portrayals of childhood, adolescence, and family life.

Like many contemporary viewers, Molly Ringwald is struck by the disparity in cultural values between the mid-1980s, when she worked with Hughes, and the present day. She cites scenes from *Sixteen Candles* (1984), in which a male character boasts about the possibility of raping an unconscious girl, and from *The Breakfast Club*, in which John Bender (Judd Nelson) harasses and sexually assaults Ringwald's character, Claire, in full view of the other detentionees, who largely tolerate Bender's behavior as a mild nuisance. While Andrew (Emilio Estevez) provides some ineffective opposition to Bender in the equally dubious name of chivalry, these actions go largely unchallenged. On the contrary, Bender is rewarded with a romance with Claire in the film's closing scenes. To be sure, it's highly unlikely that either of these scenes would make it to the final cut of a teen film made today, at least not without punishment, or commentary from other characters within the diegesis. Yet in reviews of the film from the 1980s, the incidents that Ringwald describes are not mentioned, with critics preferring to dwell on the dialogue, and the performances.[3] These differences in norms are at the heart of Ringwald's enquiry into Hughes's legacy, and questions of how we might evaluate his work in the present day. As editors, we attempt to take Hughes's works on their own terms, and ground his representations of adolescence and family life within the periods in which they are set.

Hughes's "blind spots" have been especially glaring in the wake of the #MeToo and #TimesUp online movements, which themselves took off after the arrest and subsequent conviction of the influential film producer Harvey Weinstein for sexual assault in 2017. These movements aimed to demonstrate the extent of sexual harassment in a variety of environments, both within and beyond the entertainment industry. As Ringwald points out, though, despite elements in Hughes's films that remain problematic by contemporary standards, his work nevertheless endures, and continues to find new audiences. While Hughes seemed to fall into directing as a means of exerting greater control over the film scripts that he penned, he was swiftly identified as a distinct voice in American cinema. The task of this book will be to examine what made Hughes's work so distinctive, and the extent to which his legacy holds up.

Of course, there is a certain fallacy in evaluating the life of artists only through their works, and when we step back to consider the background that Hughes brought to his movies, we learn much more about the man, as well as the context of their making. For example, Hughes was born in the second month of the 1950s (on February 18, 1950), a decade that would behold enormous changes in the American way of life after the trying years of financial depression and wars that afflicted previous generations. He started life in the middle of the century and the middle of the United States, growing up in Michigan until his family moved to the suburbs of Chicago, Illinois when he was barely a teenager. This relocation as an adolescent likely inspired some of his most prominent and successful films as a writer and director, because the young characters he created not only lived in or near Chicago, they also faced tensions about alienation and upheaval.

The veneer of prosperity and calm that American culture promoted after World War II was often ridiculed or outright exploded in Hughes's satirical stories of the 1980s. While his childhood was framed by the expanding economy of the 1950s and the slowly boiling upheavals of the 1960s, Hollywood movies were drifting away from the constraints of the studios' codes and began confronting the darker dimensions of supposed social evolution. During the course of his high school years alone, the industry moved from relatively silly (if suggestive) party movies such as *Bikini Beach* (1964) and *Pajama Party* (1964) to explicit escapades such as *Candy* (1968) and *Three in the Attic* (1968), while also releasing an increasing number of movies about youth dealing with adult dilemmas, as in *A Patch of Blue* (1965), *Inside Daisy Clover* (1965), *The Graduate* (1967), and *The Heart is a Lonely Hunter* (1968). Youth discovering the potential liberations and limitations of adulthood would become a key feature of Hughes's films, along with amiable critiques of the American family that struggled to cope with children growing up.

In terms of Hughes's adolescent life itself, little has been recorded, and the private auteur was distinctly reluctant to say much about his formative years. Biographer Kirk Honeycutt offers the most detailed account of Hughes's early life, describing how the young writer eagerly recorded the curious quirks of his daily experiences in notebooks he constantly carried, starting around the time his family moved to the Chicago area. Later in high school, Hughes "developed his lifelong antipathy for teachers and other school authority figures"[4] that would factor into his teen films, though he still ventured as far as the University of Arizona in the late 1960s for two years of college. As Honeycutt claims, Hughes left his heart back in Illinois, where he had fallen in love with classmate Nancy Ludwig before graduating from high school, and he returned to marry her in 1970 at the wise old age of 20.[5]

In this new decade, Hughes rose through the ranks of advertising agencies but soon enough grew disenchanted with the business, and by 1979 he had become an editor at *National Lampoon* magazine, pursuing his interests in comedy writing. After writing a few TV episodes of *Delta House*, a series based on the *Lampoon* hit *Animal House* (1978), Hughes wrote his first *Lampoon* screenplay, *Class Reunion* (1982), which reflected on high school experiences from a decade into adulthood. That film was a failed comedy/thriller hybrid that indicated little of the depth he would soon bring to more appealing scripts in *Mr. Mom* and *National Lampoon's Vacation*, which both appeared the next year.

Hughes was thus well into his thirties when he started writing and directing the films that would later make him famous, and unlike the "film school brats" of the '70s—Scorsese, Spielberg, Lucas—who had gained notoriety for award-winning fare that pleased both audiences and critics, Hughes did not progress into the industry with great ambitions. Rather than chronicles of mean city streets or spectacles of outer space, Hughes was captivated by the quotidian delights of suburban families, which he had come to know well from his youth in the Chicago suburbs of the '60s.

The success of *Mr. Mom* and *Vacation* in 1983 gave Universal Pictures the confidence to allow Hughes to direct his script for *Sixteen Candles* the next year, which wrestled with teenage torments beyond the prevailing pabulum of the time, using both crass humor and sincere characterizations. This well-received debut further augmented Hughes's notoriety, and he quickly developed and directed an earlier script meant to be an exposé of the high school caste system, *The Breakfast Club*, as well as an absurdly riotous fusion of teen sex and science fiction, *Weird Science*, both of which came out in 1985. By this point, his recurring actors were cynically labeled the "Brat Pack" in press coverage, and became the most recognizable young stars of the decade: Molly Ringwald, Emilio Estevez, Anthony Michael Hall, Judd Nelson, Ally Sheedy.

Hughes continued to pound out scripts with remarkable efficiency even though he could not direct them all into features. His next script, *Pretty in Pink*, debuted in the spring of 1986 to warm praise under the direction of his protégé Howard Deutch, while Hughes was himself busy directing an even bigger hit that would appear a few months later, *Ferris Bueller's Day Off* (by which point he had already abandoned his recurring troupe of young performers). After the Paramount studio ordered Deutch to recut the ending of *Pretty in Pink* to please test audiences—so that the heroine ends up with the rich boy rather than her quirky friend—Hughes soon responded with the corrective

Figure 1.2 Autographed picture of John Hughes with the cast of *Pretty in Pink* (1986).

script *Some Kind of Wonderful*, which Deutch directed in 1987. He switched the genders, so that the working-class protagonist became a boy . . . who finally realized that he was better off with his gal pal from the *same* side of the tracks.

While Hughes productions up to this point had offered some refreshing level of empowerment to youth confronting gender and class conflicts, he moved away from teen films thereafter, even though many of the films he continued to write and/or direct featured younger children in prominent roles, such as *Uncle Buck* (1989), *Curly Sue* (1991), *Dennis the Menace* (directed by Nick Castle, 1993), and the comedy phenomenon *Home Alone* (Chris Columbus, 1990). Despite the occasional success of some of his later scripts, such as *101 Dalmatians* (Stephen Herek, 1996) and *Flubber* (Les Mayfield, 1997), Hughes never regained his previous fame; the cloying nature of *Beethoven* (Brian Levant, 1992) had even motivated him to write under a pseudonym borrowed from *The Count of Monte Cristo* (1844), Edmond Dantès. In 2001, he produced *New Port South* with a script by his son James, yet even its teenage characters and suburban Chicago setting generated scant attention for the erstwhile auteur of '80s teen cinema. The same indifference befell other films he worked on at the turn of the century, which included his writing of *Reach the Rock* (William Ryan, 1998), a low-budget flop that only played in three theaters, and his script assist on *Just Visiting* (Jean-Marie Gaubert, 2001), an American remake of a French comedy to which Hughes applied some comic elements for its Chicago setting.

He did have mild success with the story for one more film, *Maid in Manhattan* (Wayne Wang, 2002), and had only one more story turned into a movie thereafter, *Drillbit Taylor* (Steven Brill, 2008), both of which he wrote as Edmond Dantès. After relative seclusion for over a decade, John Hughes died in Manhattan on August 6, 2009, from a sudden heart attack, at just 59 years old. He was buried in Chicago soon thereafter, and despite a very rare honor at the Academy Awards telecast in 2010 (for a man who never earned a single Oscar nomination), he was otherwise denied the reflective celebration of his influential work that most long-term industry artists enjoy in their waning years.

Whatever the merits or flaws of his work, John Hughes was undeniably prolific. He took on various roles in the filmmaking process, sometimes writing, other times writing and directing, writing and producing, or in some cases writing, producing, and directing, altogether some 33 films between 1980 and 2008. Reportedly, Hughes would work on up to ten scripts at a time, and could churn out a screenplay in the space of a weekend.[6] While he was a writer first and foremost, Hughes was not at all keen on editing his work, relying instead on his instinctively crafted first drafts. This is not to say that Hughes was not conscious of the quality of his scripts. Rather than edit them, Hughes preferred instead to foist what he determined to be lower-quality scripts onto other, less-tested directors, as he did with his scripts for *Pretty in Pink* and *Some Kind of Wonderful*, which are otherwise two of Hughes's best treatments of social class difference in teen cinema. Another such script was for *Home Alone*; though directed by Chris Columbus, it became Hughes's most commercially successful film. By the time he wrote *Beethoven* in 1992, portraying the effect of a lovably massive St. Bernard on ordinary family life, he had stopped directing films altogether.[7] These often curious decisions paint a picture of a creative professional who took decisive action alone, without the consultation or assistance of others. Richard Lalich's unflattering profile of the filmmaker likewise suggests that Hughes was often a difficult figure to work with, despite his undoubted talents.[8]

Although his record shows some notable missteps in judgment, Hughes's feeling for the marketplace was largely astute, garnered from his early career spent writing advertising copy. Hughes talks self-deprecatingly about using young and unknown actors in his first directorial projects because they would be less likely to see that he was an amateur.[9] It was for the same reason that Hughes largely remains in a single location throughout *The Breakfast Club*. Hughes was certainly fortunate to begin his career in teen film when the market conditions were apt for a widespread blossoming of films aimed at a teenage audience. Timothy Shary argues that the advent of the multiplex cinema, often attached to a shopping mall, was significant to the development of teen cinema in the 1980s.[10] Through the myriad of screens offered by the multiplex, studios created a range of different films that targeted particular teen interests, be they in "gory horror, dance musicals, or sex comedies."[11] *Fast Times at Ridgemont High* (1982), directed by Amy Heckerling and adapted from Cameron Crowe's documented experiences pretending to be a high school student on behalf of *Rolling Stone* magazine, perhaps best demonstrates the centrality of the shopping mall complex, and the multiplex cinema, to the lives of the teenagers it portrays. It was into this marketplace, hitherto dominated by slasher films, such as *Halloween* (1978) and *Friday the 13th* (1980), and lurid sex comedies in the likeness of *Private Lessons* (1981) and *Porky's* (1981), that John Hughes's teen films emerged. The films advocated by the multiplex mentality exemplify Adrian Martin's claim that the basic narratives of teen cinema, the "syntax," in Rick Altman's influential theorization of genre,[12] are always derived from elsewhere.[13] Hughes's work would note a growing teen audience, but provided a rather different take on teenage life.

In contrast to the exaggerated material encountered elsewhere in the 1980s, Hughes's first venture into teen cinema, *Sixteen Candles* in 1984, was resolutely undramatic. As is typical of Hughes's high-concept fare, the narrative is easily explained in a single sentence: a girl's family has forgotten her sixteenth birthday. Hughes's distinction, then, was to focus on the everyday experiences of ordinary teenagers. Far from the outrageous or terrifying adventures encountered elsewhere, sending teenagers variously to outer space (*The Last Starfighter*, 1984), to war (*Birdy*, 1984), or into the path of a deranged serial killer so they could be picked off one by one (*A Nightmare on Elm Street*, 1984), Hughes's trick was to convey the undramatic, bordering on the mundane. What is more, Hughes was at pains to take the everyday concerns of teenagers seriously. "Seriously" meant not only giving the space of a feature film to seemingly small matters such as the choice of a prom date, which loom so large to teenagers themselves; it also meant recruiting actors who were roughly proximate in age to the characters portrayed on screen. As Elissa Nelson notes, Hughes benefited from a ready supply of young actors coming of age in the 1980s.[14] What is more, Freeman observes that Hughes was keen to approximate the fashions, vernacular, and musical tastes of the 1980s teenager, often canvassing his young cast for insider tips.[15] Hughes's decision to take the teenage marketplace seriously has arguably been his most significant legacy.

This is not to say that Hughes's attention to the marketplace was all in aid of a soulful portrait of adolescence in the mid-1980s. In an interview with the *New York Times* in 1991, Hughes demonstrated his particular understanding of teenage patterns of consuming media, and the second life that films increasingly enjoyed as home entertainment. He shrewdly ensured that he released a film every year in quick succession between 1984 and 1987. As he says, "*Sixteen Candles* will come out on videocassette as *The Breakfast Club* is opening [in 1985] [. . .] And every four years there's a whole new crop of teenagers. And then again in 20 years, it's going to be their nostalgia."[16] Hughes's assessment of the role of his work for his audience 20 years hence was remarkable, particularly given that, in 1991, few teen movies had acquired the nostalgic gloss that much of his work currently enjoys in the 2020s. It appears that Hughes had long understood the power of his teen representations, and the enduring relationship that adults might possess with the films they first viewed as teenagers.

Whether Hughes knew it or not, he can reasonably claim to have contributed to the creation of the teen film as a recognizable category. Of course, representations of adolescence on screen go back substantially further than the 1980s. However, films that portray teenagers that are intended to be consumed by an audience of teenagers are considerably more recent. Thomas Doherty identifies the collapse of Hollywood's vertically integrated studio system, alongside the growth in American youth culture after World War II, as the principal catalysts for the industry's orientation towards the teen market in the 1950s.[17] He argues that the resulting "juvenilization" of the Hollywood film industry is such that all films, to a greater or lesser degree, are marketed towards teenagers. Despite Doherty's compelling arguments, it was only in the 1980s, with the advent of Hughes's films, that "films oriented towards teenagers" crystalized into a distinct form. No longer would the teen film be a mere reiteration of already established film categories with a teenage cast, but a specific form with traits all its own.

John Hughes provided the essential blueprint for the teen movie as it exists in its current form. As Ann De Vaney points out, Hughes was able to draw on distinct archetypes, which he was able to reuse in his other works.[18] "The brain, the princess, the athlete, the basket case and the criminal," shorthand for the principal players in *The Breakfast Club*, are a case in point. These archetypes show up throughout Hughes's teen oeuvre and, perhaps owing to the films being released in quick succession, came to be an expectation of the teen genre.

Such ready classifications of teenagers and high school tribes has become a staple of the genre, coalescing, in cinematic terms, in what has become termed the "anthropology shot," wherein these different groups of students, and the rules of engagement with each, are explained to a neophyte student who stands in for the audience.[19] The anthropology shot is found notably in *Clueless* (1995), *Ten Things I Hate About You* (1999), *Mean Girls* (2004), and *The DUFF* (2015) among others, attesting to its longevity. The resulting description of various teenage tribes had the canny effect of introducing the audience to its particular set of characters, as well as contributing to the sense that the film tapped into the everyday lives of contemporary teenagers.

Hughes's innovations were not confined to his mobilization of teen archetypes. Perhaps surprisingly, given Ringwald's comments earlier in the chapter, Hughes's films were novel in regard to their representation of girlhood. As Jonathan Bernstein points out, girls in Hughes's 1980s teen films were the exception to the norm. The majority of girls in teen films were tasked with displaying "good-natured tolerance in the face of stalking, voyeurism, or fumbled attempts at seduction."[20] Ringwald rightly notes that some of these elements remain present in Hughes's films. Yet it should be acknowledged that Hughes also, especially in those films in which Ringwald starred, positioned teenage girls, and their concerns, front and center. What is more, when Hughes examined social class in his teen films, arguably one of his most significant contributions to the genre, it was teenage girls who provided the point of identification for the audience, and who served as that central lightning rod for the rapidly evolving disparity in social class and wealth that occurred during the Reaganite 1980s.

Teenage girls, and Ringwald in particular, were central to Hughes's articulation of class-consciousness in the 1980s teen film. The "charismatic normality" that Ringwald brought to her roles allowed her to embody the conflicted class-based feelings and vulnerability of teenage girls.[21] Anthony C. Bleach describes the films that Ringwald and Hughes made together in the mid-1980s, that is, *Sixteen Candles*, *The Breakfast Club*, and *Pretty in Pink*, as the "Ringwald–Hughes cycle."[22] While *Sixteen Candles* does not especially dwell on the social class of Ringwald's character, Samantha, it is central to the articulation of prospective prom queen Claire Standish in *The Breakfast Club*. In both cases, Hughes makes telling use of consumer goods as his camera cranes from the BMW logo of her father's car and notices his Burberry patterned scarf when he drops off his daughter for detention. Claire, of course, is the consumer *par excellence*, punished for skipping class in favor of shopping, while Bender revels in informing Claire that he can see her growing into a fat adult, a physical embodiment of her tendency towards consumption and excess. This is not to say that Claire is solely portrayed as a vapid shopper. Hughes and Ringwald together succeed in demonstrating Claire's vulnerability, not only in terms of parental neglect, but also in her evident reliance on peer approval at the expense of her own judgment and agency.

In *Pretty in Pink*, arguably a star vehicle for Ringwald, she portrays a working-class girl, Andie, positioned literally at the wrong side of the tracks in the film's opening scenes. She rightly objects to the obnoxious "richies" at her school, best embodied by a fabulously oleaginous Steff (James Spader). Yet at the same time, she develops a romance with Steff's friend, Blane (Andrew McCarthy), and drives around the wealthy suburbs fantasizing about living in such luxury herself. Andie's conflicted feelings about class are perhaps best encapsulated by her "volcanic" dress sense, which sees the character don the norms of upper-class femininity of the past, such as pearls and floral prints, though she does so in excess. As Frances Smith has argued, such an invocation of respectability is intended to have the effect of ironic mimicry that "denaturalizes norms of middle-class dress" rather than straightforward imitation.[23] Andie is at once ashamed of her working-class status, and certainly desires to improve her circumstances. But at the same time, she is contemptuous and mocking of the upper-class mores to which she ostensibly aspires. Hughes was not only unusual in exploring social divisions within and outside the high school but in choosing a teenage girl to represent these concerns. His decision to do so arguably presages the more recent cycle of dystopian teen films, the majority of which center around a teenage girl.[24]

Figure 1.3 Six teen films that Hughes wrote and/or directed in the 1980s, which became epochal for a generation of youth.

There is no doubt that John Hughes's films changed the teen film category. What is more, though, in taking teenagers seriously, he unwittingly set the stage for the development of the genre's academic study. With Hughes centering on concerns of "coming of age" that are distinct to teenagers, no longer could it be claimed that teen film merely provided established film genres in a teenage guise. Rather, Hughes became readily identifiable as an auteur, the resulting cachet conferred by the label transferred at least in part to the genre with which he is most associated. Many histories of the teen film consequently begin in the 1980s, coinciding with Hughes's films.[25]

Hughes's legacy is certainly substantially associated with the teen film. It is the teen film on which the *New York Times* obituary of the filmmaker lingers, suggesting that this is the category for which Hughes is best remembered, with his ability to "capture the lives of 1980s teenagers."[26] Nonetheless, he did not remain long in the genre, and it was in fact the films made in the 1990s that scored his biggest commercial, if not always critical, successes. So it was that following *Some Kind of Wonderful* in 1987, Hughes returned to his original preoccupations with masculinity and its fallibilities. His early screenplay for *National Lampoon's Vacation* (1983) had seen those weaknesses cheerfully embodied by comic actor Chevy Chase. In *Planes, Trains and Automobiles* (1987), Hughes employed John Candy's and Steve Martin's considerable talents in the service of portraying uptight Neal (Martin) whose journey home for Thanksgiving is marred by boisterous salesman Del (Candy). Candy was to become a recurring presence in Hughes's films, notably in his star vehicle, *Uncle Buck* (1989), in which Candy served as the eponymous stand-in parent. As in his teen films, Hughes demonstrated a considerable talent for casting, and working with the established personae of comic actors.

Hughes's films were able to tap into the sense that, in the 1980s and 1990s, models of masculinity were in flux. Stars such as Arnold Schwarzenegger, Sylvester Stallone, and Bruce Willis appeared to embody the body-building culture and increased valorization of muscularity in blockbuster action films. These figures served to reify the physical differences between men and women. In contrast, that same era also celebrated the so-called New Man, who sought greater participation in traditionally feminine-coded childcare roles, and took more command of the domestic sphere. Hughes's antiheroes are everyday men grappling with these competing expectations of masculinity; they at once strive to embody patriarchal dominance, and yet, in their various forms of ineptitude, demonstrate that they were never well suited to those roles themselves, and also betray the very absurdity of the expectations that propel them in the first place. In these ways, Hughes's characters raise questions as to the changing roles of the male breadwinner, and of fatherhood, that were well underway in the aftermath of second-wave feminism.

As Deborah Lupton and Lesley Barclay note in their book-length study of mediated fatherhood, fathers are portrayed as nurturing and emotional, thereby serving to question some of the norms of hegemonic masculinity. Yet they are nevertheless required to define themselves principally through the roles they occupy outside the home.[27] Such difficulties are evident in one of Hughes's first screenplays, *Mr. Mom* (1983), which deals with precisely the issues discussed by Lupton and Barclay, since it features Jack (Michael Keaton) grappling with fatherhood once he has been laid off from his former employment. Of course, the very title of the film prefigures Jack's difficulty with embodying this nurturing, domestic role, since it is labeled as essentially a female position. Elsewhere, in *Vacation*, Hughes satirizes Chevy Chase's hapless father figure, Clark Griswold, who valiantly attempts to embody the gender and class norms of White, middle-class masculinity, but evidently fails to do so. On one occasion, when Clark attempts to buy a car, the salesman tries to fob him off with an alternative to the model he requested, and the father's assertion of his rights as a consumer does not present itself as assertive, yet results in his previous car being crushed on the forecourt. Clark is aware of the masculine role he is required to fulfill as the Griswold *pater familias*, but he is unable to do so.[28]

Hughes's attention to the family is part of a broader wave of films about, and sometimes for, the family in the 1980s and 1990s. As Estella Tincknell observes, the aftermath of second-wave feminism and the advent of postfeminism during this period brought with it an increased focus on the role of fatherhood.[29] Here we can situate Hughes's output among other films such as *Look Who's Talking* (1989), *Parenthood* (1989), *Honey, I Shrunk the Kids* (1989), *Father of the Bride* (1991), and *Mrs. Doubtfire* (1993). These films all stage the reclamation and relocation of fatherhood that had taken place once second-wave feminism had encouraged and facilitated women's re-entry into the economic sphere, to

Figure 1.4 Family matters in Hughes's stories, as in *Vacation* (1983) and the sequels that followed.

be, as Stella Dallas put it, "something else besides a mother." Tincknell identifies two principal responses to men's newfound familial role. In "laddism" she sees the rejection of traditional masculine responsibilities and the resulting prioritization of male friendships, and patterns of behavior previously befitting much younger men. The New Man, by contrast, challenged traditional forms of masculinity by affirming his own abilities to be nurturing. However, in so doing, the New Man paradoxically demonstrates that those abilities are not a conventional part of the masculine arsenal. Hughes's films about families can be regarded as representative of this conflicted era in rethinking and reaffirming the nuclear family in American culture.

John Candy is a key figure in the articulation of caring masculinities in John Hughes's films. Though Canadian, Candy often stands in for a sympathetic American everyman in Hughes's works. As Del Griffith in *Planes, Trains and Automobiles*, he is the antidote to Neal's uptightness. Likewise, in *Uncle Buck*, the straight-talking Buck is able to get to the heart of the issues encountered by the children for whom he is caring, despite his unconventional parenting style. We see how the softness connoted by Candy's oversized frame allows him to embody the focus on care embodied by the New Man figure. At the same time though, that large size allows him nevertheless to present a credible, physical threat, as he does to Tia's (Jean Louisa Kelly) boyfriend Bug (Jay Underwood), whom he threatens with a small axe and the possibility of abduction. Buck is not presented as an attractive figure recuperating the hegemonic role of masculine fatherhood, in the same way that, say, Bruce Willis is in *Die Hard* (1988), but it is striking how frequently Candy serves in these similar roles for Hughes, as an embodiment of likeable, everyday masculinity who embodies the changes underway in male roles.

While the changing role of the father is undeniably key to understanding Hughes's family films, his most commercially successful films place the role of the mother as paramount. In both *Home Alone* and its sequel, *Home Alone 2: Lost in New York* (1991), the father, Peter McCallister (John Heard), barely features in the stories, except as an absent-minded income source for his young son, Kevin (Macaulay Culkin), who is left to fend for himself. Instead it is Kate (Catherine O'Hara), Kevin's mother, who first realizes that her son is not present, and makes every effort to return to the family home in Chicago (in the first installment), and to locate him in the streets of Manhattan (in the second). What is more, on both occasions, Kate relies not on rational calculation, but on gut instinct, and on appealing to others to help her in her quest to return to Chicago not out of mere altruism but "as a mother." It is also by her instinctive understanding of her son that she intuits that Kevin will have headed for Rockefeller Center as the location of the city's largest Christmas tree, and secures the aid of Gus (Candy again) who transports her home. Even in Hughes's script of the much later sequel,

Home Alone 3 (Raja Gosnell, 1997), it is Alex's mother (Haviland Morris) who has to work out how to balance her job with the demands of her sick child. In these instances, the mother, and maternal love, are at the forefront, and serve to reaffirm the mother's essential role as the primary caregiver.[30]

The affirmation of the mother in the various iterations of *Home Alone* stands in contrast to the mother's absence found in much of Hughes's other work. In *Pretty in Pink* for instance, needy father Jack (Harry Dean Stanton) seems to have taken on sole care of his daughter owing to a mother that has left the family some years earlier. Writing in 1991, Tania Modleski discussed the curious absence of women from the emergent wave of family films in the late 1980s, arguing that films such as *Three Men and a Baby* (1987), in which three men predictably take on the role of looking after a baby, work to marginalize the role of women in the domestic sphere. Rather than reckon with the changes in men's and women's roles alike in the nuclear family, Modleski argues that these films simply cut women out of the picture entirely.[31] Instead, the child is reaffirmed as the center of family life. Such a recentering of the child is arguably of a piece with Hughes's continued railing against figures in a position of power, which is a running feature throughout his oeuvre.

What is clear in Hughes's films is that his scripts largely favor a high-concept structure. Richard Lalich lampoons Hughes's technique, providing a short tableau of bare-bones Hughes plots, that run as follows: "There's trouble in . . . because . . . but really because . . ."[32] Lalich then provides some stock characters and plot lines frequently deployed by Hughes, such as "absent relatives, bureaucrats who are corrupt/lack compassion," alongside "stuffed shirts" and "indigents" who frequently get their comeuppance. Although Lalich's list is intended to be humorous, he does nevertheless succeed in highlighting some of Hughes's principal concerns that persist, regardless of the filmmaking tradition in which he is working. Hughes is particularly critical of those who wield their authority without compassion, while his sympathies for the working and middle classes over their wealthy counterparts likewise stands out in an industry in which unspoken wealth continues to present itself as the norm. His concern for the outsider in his films, or the marginalized party, is likewise striking. Throughout Hughes's work, whether as a writer, director, or producer, he has succeeded in granting prominence to not only previously marginalized categories of film, but also, to those who remain marginalized within those categories themselves.

This collection is not intended to canonize John Hughes as a cinematic figure, although the dozen essays that we have gathered here simultaneously celebrate and criticize the messages and receptions of his films. In seeking to assess Hughes from an academic perspective, we sought out scholars who could consider not only his depictions of youth and families, but who would also offer some context to the social and industrial conditions in which his films were made. In all cases, we turned to established researchers who had previously written on youth cinema, yet

Figure 1.5 *Home Alone* (1990) was Hughes's biggest financial success, but his subsequent projects yielded diminishing returns.

not merely as a genre or in historical terms. We asked them to consider Hughes's films from perspectives that each author found particularly trenchant, resulting in the diverse array of analyses that follow.

The first section takes on Hughes as a figure within the Hollywood industry, one who rapidly found himself transformed from a fledging screenwriter to a comedy virtuoso within the span of a single decade. The first chapter by Elissa Nelson, reflects on how Hughes has himself been the subject of a certain mythology following the success of his films, yielding a somewhat questionable folklore. Thereafter, Yannis Tzioumakis examines the industrial location of Hughes's early films, paying particular attention to his relationship with powerful Hollywood executive Ned Tanen. Then Stephen Tropiano considers the Hughes style in relation to a television adaptation of *Ferris Bueller's Day Off*, revealing specific aspects of Hughes's appreciation for teens and film that were unique to his sensibilities.

The next section focuses on the topic most often associated with Hughes, his writing and directing of films about youth in the 1980s. The first chapter in this section, by Christina Petersen, considers Hughes's important teen works of the '80s in terms of their power dynamics, particularly related to class. Thereafter, Barbara Brickman examines the intersection of neglect and heteronormativity in Hughes's youth films. Finally, Melissa Oliver-Powell evaluates the roles of parents in the Hughes films that featured younger children, questioning just who "comes of age" in these stories.

The third section expands upon themes about youth by considering how Hughes represented the American family. Here we open with a chapter by Leah Shafer, which details how Hughes used props in his family films in the service of his commentary on cultural conditions. The subsequent chapters focus more on fatherhood, as Holly Chard surveys the many male comedians who embodied the domestic tensions that Hughes so often mined for humor, and Alice Leppert follows with a study of the many failed or failing fathers across Hughes's films.

The closing section is perhaps our most confrontational, tackling more knotty aspects of Hughes's stories and characters such as sexuality, class, and race. The first entry is Andrew Scahill's close look at one of Hughes's most outrageous comedies, *Weird Science*, to consider how its myriad messages about masculinity are manifested. Robert Bulman then reflects on social conditions in the Hughes films set around high schools, calling attention to a distinct working-class sensitivity. The concluding chapter in the collection is by Frances Smith, who takes Hughes to task for the racial representations within his films, which were supported by a problematic construction of dominant White culture.

The book concludes with a filmography and bibliography to facilitate further studies of Hughes, because this slim volume is certainly not comprehensive. We are aware that the chapters here say little about his work after the early 1990s, and that numerous other nuances of his stories and characters are worthy of further examination. For an artist who remains remembered primarily for his work within a mere decade, John Hughes is nonetheless an enduring figure in cinema history, one whose films brought numerous insights to a culture in need of being entertained about its own insecurities, whether about childhood, fatherhood, or familyhood. We hope that further academic work will yield additional critical perspectives on his films, and that future audiences will continue to appreciate how those films helped us to understand—and laugh at—some of American life in the late twentieth century.

NOTES

1. Molly Ringwald, "What about *The Breakfast Club?* Revisiting the Movies of My Youth in the Age of #MeToo," *The New Yorker*, April 6, 2018, https://www.newyorker.com/culture/personal-history/what-about-the-breakfast-club-molly-ringwald-metoo-john-hughes-pretty-in-pink.
2. See Hadley Freeman, *Life Moves Pretty Fast: The Lessons We Learned from Eighties Movies (and Why We Don't Learn Them from Movies Any More)* (London: Simon and Schuster, 2015), 81. Freeman quotes *New York Times* film critic A. O. Scott: "Molly Ringwald was for Mr. Hughes what Jimmy Stewart was for Frank Capra: an emblem, a muse, a poster-child and an alter-ego," 81.

3. See for instance, Janet Maslin, "John Hughes's *Breakfast Club*," *New York Times*, February 15, 1985; Roger Ebert, "The Breakfast Club," *Chicago Sun-Times*, February 15, 1985.
4. Kirk Honeycutt, *John Hughes: A Life in Film* (New York: Race Point, 2015), 26.
5. Honeycutt, 29.
6. See Richard Lalich, "Big Baby," *Spy*, January 1993, 66–73.
7. There are as many films in the *Beethoven* film series (nine including the spin-off television series) as there are symphonies by Ludwig van Beethoven.
8. Lalich provides a number of examples, among which Hughes's spurning of John Candy's friendship, and another that recalls Kevin McCallister's (Macaulay Culkin) tantrum when he wishes his family would disappear, in which Hughes's beloved "plain cheese" pizza is unexpectedly substituted for one containing sausage, 70.
9. Bill Carter, "Him Alone," *New York Times*, August 4, 1991, 31.
10. See Timothy Shary, *Generation Multiplex: The Image of Youth in American Cinema Since 1980*, 2nd edn (Austin: University of Texas Press, 2014).
11. Shary, 6.
12. Rick Altman, "A Semantic/Syntactic Approach to Film Genre," in *Film Genre III*, ed. Barry Keith Grant (Austin: University of Texas Press, 2003), 27–41.
13. Adrian Martin, *Phantasms: The Dreams and Desires at the Heart of our Popular Culture* (Melbourne: McPhee Gribble, 1994), 14.
14. Elissa Nelson, *The Breakfast Club: John Hughes, Hollywood and the Golden Age of the Teen Film* (London: Routledge, 2019).
15. Freeman, 66.
16. Hughes quoted in Carter, 34.
17. Thomas Doherty, *Teenagers and Teenpics: The Juvenilization of American Movies in the 1950s* (Philadelphia: Temple University Press, 2002).
18. Ann De Vaney, "John Hughes Reinscribes Daddy's Girl in Homes and Schools," in *Sugar, Spice and Everything Nice*, eds Murray Pomerance and Frances Gateward (Detroit: Wayne State University Press, 2002), 204.
19. For further delineation of the anthropology shot, see Roz Kaveney, *Teen Dreams: From Heathers to Veronica Mars* (London: I. B. Tauris, 2006), 56.
20. Jonathan Bernstein, *Pretty in Pink: The Golden Age of Teen Movies* (New York: St. Martin's Griffin, 1997), 173.
21. Pauline Kael, "The Current Cinema," *The New Yorker*, 1986, 73.
22. Anthony C. Bleach, "Postfeminist Cliques? Class, Postfeminism and the Molly Ringwald-John Hughes Films," *Cinema Journal*, 49, no. 3 (2010), 24.
23. Frances Smith, *Rethinking the Hollywood Teen Movie: Gender Genre, Identity* (Edinburgh: Edinburgh University Press, 2017), 74.
24. These include *The Host* (2013), *Warm Bodies* (2013), *Tomorrowland* (2015), *The 5th Wave* (2016), *The Darkest Minds* (2018), and both *The Hunger Games* (2012–15) and *Divergent* (2014–19) franchises.
25. One such example is Roz Kaveney's *Teen Dreams*. Though Kaveney's book appears to begin with *Heathers* (1989), which follows Hughes's teen films, she rightly identifies Lehmann's film as a reaction to the sentimentality of Hughes's work. Bernstein's *Pretty in Pink* makes the bold case that the 1980s were the "golden age" of the genre, and at least two other books argue for the epoch-making nature of the decade's cinema: *Brat Pack America: A Love Letter to '80s Teen Movies* by Kevin Smokler (Los Angeles: Vireo, 2016) and *The Ultimate History of the '80s Teen Movie* by James King (New York: Diversion, 2019).
26. Michael Cieply, "John Hughes obituary," *New York Times*, August 4, 2009, 20.

27. See Deborah Lupton and Lesley Barclay, *Constructing Fatherhood: Discourses and Experiences* (London: Sage, 1997).
28. In her review of *Uncle Buck*, Rita Kempley adroitly assessed how "the paterfamiliarization of 20th-century man" was evident in the "pop cycle" of the time that contained many films by Hughes: *Washington Post*, August 16, 1989, https://www.washingtonpost.com/wp-srv/style/longterm/movies/videos/unclebuckpgkempley_a0c9a1.htm.
29. Estella Tincknell, *Mediating the Family: Gender, Culture and Representation* (London: Hodder Arnold, 2005).
30. One of his less notable scripts of the '90s, *Baby's Day Out* (Patrick Read Johnson, 1994), also focused on the mother's role as the caregiver and primary parent to the child of the title.
31. Tania Modleski, *Feminism Without Women: Culture and Criticism in a "Postfeminist" Age* (London: Routledge, 1991).
32. Lalich, 70.

PART I

Hughes in the Industry

John Hughes was not a conventional filmmaker for the 1980s. He never attended film school and was not a Hollywood player like so many of the more familiar names that populated the credits of blockbusters. However, his background in advertising did give him a certain perspective on how to sell appealing ideas, and he evidently had a penchant for honoring the mundane absurdities of American life. While the industry of the early '80s was responding to the threat of movies moving to home video by expanding to multiplex cinemas, and capitalizing on the success of late '70s hits like *Rocky* (1976), *Star Wars* (1977), and *Superman* (1978) with an endless supply of surefire sequels, Hughes was quietly adapting his comedic stories about families into scripts that studios found easy to cast and inexpensive to produce.

He rode into the Hollywood realm on the success of his *National Lampoon* association, yet the timing of his arrival was fortuitous in the social context. After Ronald Reagan became president in 1981, the country seemed poised to move away from tumults in the previous decade (the Vietnam War, Watergate, disco music) and toward a soothing reassurance that global matters—such as the Cold War that threatened nuclear apocalypse—were less important than the simple pleasures of home, specifically family. Hughes's early assignments from *Lampoon* that became TV and film scripts (the *Delta House* TV show in 1979 and *Class Reunion* in 1982) were destined to be less compelling than the story he adapted from his family's vacation in 1958, which became the basis of *Vacation* in 1983. As in *Mr. Mom* that same year, he showed Americans that the in(s)anity of family life was precious and worth celebrating, a sentiment that audiences and executives embraced.

Of course, Hughes would become more of a household name with his teen films in the mid-'80s, and that is where our first chapter begins. In "John Hughes as Auteur: History, Hagiography, Historiography," Elissa Nelson traces the tradition that Hughes rapidly established with his teen films through placing his work within the sphere of the emergent teen genre of the time. Hughes may not have set out with an agenda to change the representation of youth for an entire generation, but in many ways his six scripts about teens from 1984 to 1987 accomplished what no other Hollywood writer or director had ever done: he humanized and humorized the adolescent experience in tones that youth found comforting and not condescending. As he consequentially became known as the leading "auteur" of the teen genre in that decade, his films nonetheless promoted a rather homogenous (middle-class, White) and limited (if only to Chicago and its suburbs') perspective on American youth. While many of these films featured young female protagonists, they were also locked into a sexist privileging of masculine attitudes that largely went unchecked in the decade that defeated the Equal Rights Amendment for women, nearly sixty years after it was first introduced.¹ As Nelson goes on to point out, the increasingly self-critical '90s would not offer the same opportunities for Hughes, and his star indeed lost its luster.

The subsequent chapter by Yannis Tzioumakis, "'Becoming John Hughes': Regional Production, Hyphenate Filmmaking, and Independence within Hollywood," takes an even closer look at Hughes within the movie industry, evaluating the place of his modest hits within the scope of '80s cinema. Tzioumakis finds that Hughes's independence as a filmmaker—before the model of "indie cinema" would emerge more prominently in the early '90s—effectively positioned him against the Hollywood machinery of the era, allowing him to advance his modestly quirky projects that may have otherwise been overlooked for their lack of "high concept" credentials. Working with producer Ned Tanen, the writer Hughes became the director Hughes, developing his scripts with increasing creative control despite his unusual shooting methods and insistence on filming in the Chicago area. This latter aspect not only afforded Hughes a certain amount of regional expertise, it led to an association of Hughes with his home city that further distinguished his stories.

The closing chapter in this section, "*Ferris Bueller* vs. *Parker Lewis*: 'Adapting' *Ferris Bueller's Day Off* for Television" by Stephen Tropiano, takes us from the broader evaluations of Hughes to the specific, and across media from film to television. The hit 1986 film featuring Matthew Broderick as the title character marked a departure for Hughes, being the last film focused on teenagers that he would direct (the fourth in two years), and without any of the original Brat Pack cast that he had brought to fame in the previous three. Aside from writing a handful of TV episodes for the *Animal House* spin-off *Delta House* in 1979 and creating the military sitcom *At Ease* in 1983, both short-lived series were Hughes's only forays into the television medium, though that industry would attempt to exploit some of his film projects. After an oddly duplicative TV movie of *Mr. Mom* was made in 1984, producers in 1990 took up both *Uncle Buck* (1989) and *Ferris Bueller* as episodic series, and neither lasted beyond their initial season. As Tropiano points out through a comparison with the more successful series *Parker Lewis Can't Lose* (1990–93), which was essentially an imitation of *Ferris Bueller*, the duality of high school as a site of teenage oppression and a site of teenage rebellion against adult authority figures only made for sustained comedy when the characters could evolve beyond their initial incarnations.

Perhaps like the other characters Hughes created during the '80s, Ferris Bueller and his cohort were fixed in time, and could not adapt to the '90s youth who would be branded Generation X as they embraced skepticism beyond their years. Indeed, aside from a few obscure made-for-TV movies based on characters in his *Vacation* and *Home Alone* films, the small-screen industry only pursued one other Hughes concept, the *Weird Science* cable sitcom, which was surprisingly durable on the USA Network for five seasons (1994–98), perhaps owing to the channel's small quirky market. Hughes himself stayed away from television and focused instead on adapting previous family hits (*Miracle on 34th Street* [1994], *101 Dalmatians* [1996], *Flubber* [1997]) into reliable studio features. The adolescent sensibilities of Hughes's '80s teens were sorely dated by the '90s, and their films were destined to remain beloved relics of a less-critical and cynical era.

NOTE

1. The original Equal Rights Amendment (ERA), written by Alice Paul in 1921, was proposed as House Joint Resolution 75 to Congress on December 13, 1923, reading in its entirety: "Men and women shall have equal rights throughout the United States and every place subject to its jurisdiction. Congress shall have power to enforce this article by appropriate legislation." Despite reintroduction of the ERA over the next five decades, Congress did not approve voting on ratification until 1972. Though 35 of the 38 states required to amend the Constitution voted to approve, by 1982 the deadline for ratification passed and thus nullified the effort. Recently, three more states have voted to ratify, yet these results are resisted by conservative forces. See Lila Thulin, "The 97-Year-History of the Equal Rights Amendment," *Smithsonian Magazine*, November 13, 2019, https://www.smithsonianmag.com/history/equal-rights-amendment-96-years-old-and-still-not-part-constitution-heres-why-180973548/.

CHAPTER 2

John Hughes as Auteur: History, Hagiography, Historiography

Elissa H. Nelson

John Hughes quickly earned his reputation as a filmmaker in tune with the popular and profitable youth market. Soon after coming to Hollywood, Hughes became known as an auteur for the teen films he made in the 1980s. Indeed, a *New York Times* article in 1986 (O'Connor),[1] released just two years after his directorial feature film debut, bestowed the "auteur" label upon him. Although Hughes wrote over 30 films, produced over 20, and directed eight, he is most widely known for the six teen films he wrote and produced in rapid succession (the last two of which were directed by Howard Deutch): *Sixteen Candles* (1984), *The Breakfast Club* (1985), *Weird Science* (1985), *Ferris Bueller's Day Off* (1986), *Pretty in Pink* (1986), and *Some Kind of Wonderful* (1987). His auteur status was cemented by his easily recognizable style of writing, seemingly from a teen perspective, that connected with youth audiences, as well as by his frequently cast young stars like Molly Ringwald and Anthony Michael Hall, and by the similar stories he tackled about social hierarchies in American high schools.

Hughes and his teen films have gone through a number of critical reassessments since the 1980s. Most of his films were successful at the box office upon release and in the home entertainment market soon thereafter. The response from critics, however, was more mixed. For example, reviews of *The Breakfast Club*, one of his most celebrated films, either praised the film as "a breath of cinematic fresh air"[2] (from fellow Chicagoan Gene Siskel) or skewered it by saying "the movie is about a bunch of stereotypes who complain that other people see them as stereotypes"[3] (from *New Yorker* critic Pauline Kael). In the 1990s, after Hughes's popularity waned, historian Robert Sklar questioned whether his status as a filmmaker would rise as more time passed.[4] After Hughes died in 2009, there were outpourings of articles and interviews, as well as a special (and highly rare) Oscar tribute to him, lauding the influence he had on teens and teen films, on popular culture more generally, and on individual lives more specifically. Subsequently, in 2018, Molly Ringwald wrote an editorial for *The New Yorker* in the wake of #MeToo, a movement that brought to light rampant and pervasive sexual harassment.[5] Reflecting on her past work with Hughes, she questioned some of the more troubling relationships depicted in his teen films, including the particularly abusive way her character was treated by Bender (Judd Nelson), her presumed love interest in *The Breakfast Club*, and how Jake Ryan (Michael Schoeffling), her supposed dreamboat crush in *Sixteen Candles*, let his incapacitated girlfriend be raped by a virtual stranger. While Hughes's films have variously been praised for their depictions of teen life and for addressing class differences, they have similarly been derided for the way they deal with diversity, sexuality, and gender (as other chapters in this collection demonstrate).

This chapter proceeds by looking at John Hughes and his films in three different time periods. The first section, "History," roughly corresponds to his time making teen films in the 1980s. The analysis in this part considers the content of the teen films he made and their context of production, as well as some of the discourse surrounding them, borne out in reviews and articles that were written at and about that time. The next, "Hagiography," approximately matches the period when he stopped making teen films and subsequently started to retreat from Hollywood. Certain articles written during this period illustrate how people were wondering why and to where he disappeared and were pining for the types of films that he made. This time is replete with accolades and mentions of his far-reaching influence even in his absence, but a few noticeable queries were also starting to arise about some of the problematic content in his films. The following section, "Historiography," begins a few years after his death. It deals with more contemporary readings of Hughes and his films, especially in light of the current political and social landscape that raises awareness of racist and misogynistic behavior and calls it out as such. Conduct that was once deemed par for the course and even humorous has since become more widely understood as inappropriate and injurious.

One of the interesting features of this periodization structure is that it also has a corresponding relationship to different facets of the auteur theory. When the French critics of *Cahiers du Cinéma* first came up with the *politique des auteurs*[6] after World War II, and when Andrew Sarris adapted it as the auteur theory for American readers in the 1960s,[7] they were trying to accomplish more than just the bestowing of a label. One of the aspects that led these critics to develop the auteur theory is that they noticed recurring styles and themes in certain filmmakers' work. They realized that regardless of the subject matter, an auteur was someone who made his (the directors glorified were almost always male) discrete mark. As such, in this chapter's history section, we can look at Hughes films and discern what those recurring elements are, and what they might mean. Another motivating force of the critics was to lionize the status of the newly deemed auteur filmmakers, thereby extolling their films as well. These filmmakers were not just turning out assembly-line products from a factory. Rather, saying they were auteurs elevated the status of their films to the level of art. Indeed, as evident in the hagiography portion, John Hughes helped advance the idea that teens and teen stories were important and should be taken seriously, and should not just be tossed aside as insignificant because of the characters' and the primary audience members' youth. Still another position of the auteur theory was to re-evaluate and reassess films from the recent past. The French *Cahiers du Cinéma* critics had been restricted from seeing Hollywood films during World War II embargoes, so when they were finally able to view them, they noticed patterns and artistry that many other audiences without sufficient critical distance had missed. Hence, the historiography segment looks at how certain elements of the past are more clearly visible with the passage of time and are highlighted depending on concerns in the present. As a celebrated filmmaker who tapped into contemporary culture, Hughes and his films are thus subject to continuing review and are worthy of serious study.

This research seeks to interrogate how auteur status is granted, how it can have multiple connotations, how it can hide troubling issues behind the veil of talent, and how even important work for which we hold tender memories needs to be re-examined. The implications of these reassessments speak to larger concerns about how we can analyze the oeuvre of lauded yet problematic art and artists by focusing specifically on Hughes as a teen film auteur and on the ways valuations of him and his films have changed over time. It would be remiss to diminish the way Hughes has influenced the teen film genre, just as it would be remiss to ignore the troubling cultural and personal politics of his films. Considerations and judgments of him and his films, as well as a discourse analysis of these evaluations, need to be historically contextualized with attention to ideological shifts. What emerges from these analyses is a more nuanced overview of his films, their varying interpretations, and Hughes as a filmmaker.

HISTORY

Studying history is not simply the recalling of facts, but concerns learning about the past; it is about "making meaning of historical events . . . suggest[ing] the possibility of better understanding ourselves in the present, by understanding the forces, choices, and circumstances that brought us to our current situation."[8] Reviewing Hughes's films, as well as the context of their production and how they were received, offers a textual analysis of content in conjunction with insight into the films' contemporary environment. As some of the established cultural anthropological foundations of film and media studies posit, because films represent ideology, or the ideas and beliefs of the time and place they are made, we can look at the films and the discourse surrounding them to learn about contemporary culture. Moreover, as these analyses reveal ideological beliefs, we can also look to the films to say something about the author who created them. In this way, by examining some of the recurring styles and themes in Hughes's work, predominantly the teen films that were responsible for bestowing upon him the status of auteur, we can start to get a sense of what his work reveals about him, as well as what it says about the 1980s more generally.

Hughes's teen films are commendable for many reasons. Notably, he took teens and their concerns seriously. In interviews around the time his films were in production, Hughes would express how important it was to him to foreground the significance of the teen experience, and was quoted as saying "there's a general lack of respect for young people now"[9] and that "it's wrong not to allow someone the right to have a problem because of their age."[10] Indeed, while still giving time for teens to have fun, as in *Ferris Bueller's Day Off*, Hughes also focused on some of the serious problems teens face (even within the same film), such as debilitating pressure from parents and peers. Even if the problems seem small to people who are older, Hughes recognized that they are monumental to the people going through them. Accordingly, he would try to tell stories from a youthful point of view; Anthony Michael Hall, who was a teen during the time the films were produced, said Hughes's screenplays "know exactly what it's like to be a freshman in high school."[11] Hughes focused on particularly astute and relatable teenagers from all echelons of the social groups in high schools, and gave comparable screen time to many of them, like the ensemble of *The Breakfast Club*. By focusing on and labeling as such the archetypical characters found in both high schools and teen films, he was able to call attention to ingrained stereotypes and then show that teens could actually be quite complex.

Hughes also depicted numerous quintessential teen film elements, but he did so particularly effectively and cohesively. Like many entries in the teen film genre, his stories focused on the conflict between generations, helping to codify different dynamics by variously depicting authority figures who were absent or harmful (such as parents who are out of town when parties take place and all the adults except for the janitor in *The Breakfast Club*), or well-meaning but clueless (Sam's father in *Sixteen Candles* and Ferris Bueller's parents in *Ferris Bueller's Day Off*). In line with ongoing contemporary concerns about class, Hughes also did not shy away from pointing out how popularity in high school is often aligned with wealth as antagonistic relationships played out between the haves and have-nots in a microcosm of larger societal struggles. Additionally, his films would often take a female perspective, and as Hadley Freeman points out, the young women would be characters unto themselves instead of there to further male characters' development.[12] He made insightful comments about youth and sex in *The Breakfast Club*, including when Allison (Ally Sheedy) voiced the trenchant line about the confounding "double-edged sword" of female sexuality: "If you say you haven't, you're a prude. If you say you have, you're a slut. It's a trap. You want to, but you can't, and when you do, you wish you didn't." Meanwhile, some of the appeal of the male characters in his films is that they are often interested in romantic relationships. Even when the two teen boys in *Weird Science* "create" Lisa (Kelly LeBrock), the Barbie doll come to life, the plot is somewhat redeemed when they are more interested in learning what she can teach them about life instead of having sex with her. Furthermore, all these films were set to keenly attuned character-, story-, and mood-defining songs. His non-mainstream musical stylings, which helped to popularize New Wave music in the US,[13] comprised soundtracks that got so much recognition, he even got his own record label, eponymously called Hughes Music, at MCA in 1987.[14]

Although these complimentary characteristics are certainly notable, some writers, in trying to elevate Hughes's status, point to the idea that no one was really making films like Hughes was, and that 1980s teen films were primarily sex romps in the style of *Porky's* (1981) or slasher films modeled after *Halloween* (1978).[15] Actually, though, there were a number of successful teen films at the time that variously took teen problems seriously, tackled issues of class, or told stories of women and outsiders, and resonated with youth audiences. For example, consider a few top-grossing or well-known teen films from the first part of the decade, before Hughes's influence could affect works in production: *Little Darlings* (1980), *Fast Times at Ridgemont High* (1982), and *Valley Girl* (1983) were primarily about young women (the latter two directed by women and captured a distinctive teen argot); *The Outsiders* (1983), *The Karate Kid* (1984), and *Better Off Dead* (1985) depicted social hierarchies, some based on class; *Footloose* (1984) and *Back to the Future* (1985) featured generational conflict and disappointing authority figures; and 15 teen films had top-10 soundtrack albums on *Billboard* charts over the course of the decade.[16] Additionally, as multiplexes sprang up in shopping malls and changed the geography of cinema-going,[17] and as declining ticket sales, largely stemming from the competing forces of cable and home video, affected industry-based production and distribution decisions,[18] Hollywood wanted to entice its largest and most reliable market segment to come back to the theaters. As a result, the studios purposefully targeted the youth demographic with a broad range and large number of teen films. Hughes was in the right place at the right time, and even though his contributions to the teen film are immense, he was far from acting alone in making the teen film one of the defining genres of the 1980s.

One of the things that sets Hughes's work apart from these other films, though, was his auteur label. This label conspicuously and effectively raised the profile and status of his films. It was granted because of his signature and recognizable style, combined with the very visible element of having recurring big-name teen talent (Ringwald and Hall) starring in his films. His autobiographical storytelling, as well as his prolific and profitable output as a writer and often director or producer of his own films, were also factors in bestowing this label. While his films treated teen issues seriously and often had articulate awkward characters full of both insecurity and confidence, the specific ways these stories were told further indicated a personal authorial style. All of his teen films feature triangles with two people who end up together (or two couples in *The Breakfast Club*) and one person left out (even in *Weird Science*, although Gary [Hall] and Wyatt [Ilan Mitchell-Smith] are not romantically linked, they continue being close friends as Lisa goes off on her own). They almost all take place in suburban middle America in communities containing multiple socio-economic strata (although hardly any ethnic diversity), they're full of annoying siblings representative of typical American family dynamics, and their adult characters are often thinly drawn to keep the focus on the youth protagonists and perspectives. These patterns indicated his paradoxical concerns for simultaneously depicting realistic teen life and outlooks with fantastical fairy-tale endings. Even if in real life the mismatched couples might not end up together, in the make-believe, family-values oriented Hughes world of Shermer, Illinois, they did. Differences could be overcome, inner turmoil could finally be understood, and teens could gain the self-confidence necessary to weather the storms of adolescence, stand up for themselves, and get what they need, if not always what they want.

The autobiographical nature of the storytelling also signposted a personal style well matched to the auteur label. Hughes mined his life for his teen tales, telling Molly Ringwald when she interviewed him in *Seventeen* magazine that he wrote what he knew and cared about, and that he saw himself in characters as varied as Samantha (Ringwald in *Sixteen Candles*), Allison (in *Breakfast Club*), and Ferris (Matthew Broderick), each of them embodying different parts of his personality and experiences.[19] Later biographies of Hughes would tell of how his values were rather conservative,[20] that he wanted to be an artist, grew up poorer than other families in his wealthy neighborhood, and that he had a high school girlfriend (whom he married soon after graduating) but that they were often accompanied by a third wheel[21]—all facets of a life visible in different iterations on screen. Hughes would also mine his young actors for their input[22] and recruited teenage consultants like Sloane Tanen, daughter of famed studio executive Ned Tanen who helmed his first films, to ensure his updated versions of teen life were accurate.[23] The formula worked. Most of Hughes's films were money-making theatrical successes because of both their popularity and relatively small budgets, as the following list, which includes titles and domestic year-end box-office rankings according to BoxOfficeMojo.com, indicates: *Sixteen Candles* (44), *The Breakfast Club* (16), *Weird Science* (38), *Ferris Bueller's Day Off* (10), *Pretty in Pink* (22), and *Some Kind of Wonderful* (60).[24]

While box office is a barometer of commercial success, it is certainly not indicative of critical success. Additionally, whether Hughes's distinctive style is seen as provocative meditations on recurring themes or as symptomatic of formulaic repetition, as keen commentary or as pandering, depends on the critic, the film, and the time. Even contemporary reviews labeling him an auteur of sorts were mixed about whether this tag was complimentary. Some were glowing, as when *Time* magazine featured Molly Ringwald on the cover and declared that the Hughes movies she starred in were distinctive, "finely crafted and boasting spectacular ensemble acting."[25] Others were not, as when a review for *Pretty in Pink* in the *Chicago Reader* claimed that "John Hughes had become an industry, farming out his formulaic projects to hired hacks"[26] (establishing what was well known: that even when someone else directed his teen screenplays, Hughes's authorship was most apparent). Although Janet Maslin in the *New York Times* had panned some of his previous films, she praised *Some Kind of Wonderful*, saying that "at long last, the John Hughes method has paid off."[27] However, interspersed with her comments about him as "king of an entire genre," were qualifications, specifically, that since the genre was the teen film, it didn't matter much because the genre itself was "inconsequential and small."[28] For some critics, "auteur" did not carry the esteem originally intended partly because of their opinions about the films, but also because the genre itself was unjustly denigrated and derided.

Interestingly, many of the negative reviews of Hughes and his films focused on the supposedly meaningless trivialities of youth but largely ignored many of problematic aspects that are so glaring in retrospect. Blatant racism is on display with the character of exchange student Long Duk Dong (Gedde Watanabe) in *Sixteen Candles*: he is a pan-Asian stereotype and a non-diegetic gong rings every time his name is spoken. Black actors are almost nonexistent in his films but are disparaged nonetheless when Samantha and her friend declare that a fantasy birthday includes a black Trans Am, not a Black guy. And in both *The Breakfast Club* and *Weird Science*, White actors do impersonations of Black characters, most notably when Anthony Michael Hall does impressions of Richard Pryor. Although these send-ups were meant to be imitation as a form of flattery,[29] and Gary (in *Weird Science*) ends up looking the fool, when seen in hindsight it has the effect of mockery. There was still more in *Sixteen Candles*: Ginny's (Blanche Baker) Italian future in-laws are offhandedly deemed mafiosos; homophobia is flagrant when the epithets "fag" and "faggot" are used indifferently; and ableism is on display with the slur "retarded" and with a character in a neck brace who appears solely for providing sight gags. While some critics at the time pointed out "there are some notably unfunny ethnic jokes,"[30] others wrote, "Gedde Watanabe as the exchange student . . . elevates his role from a potentially offensive stereotype to high comedy."[31] These elements are currently perceived as contemptible, yet were then mostly overlooked by critics, suggesting both Hughes's prejudiced personal sense of humor as well as contemporaneous biases.

Perhaps most excruciatingly exhibited are Hughes's and 1980s gender norms and values. In both *The Breakfast Club* (Allison) and *Pretty in Pink* (Iona [Annie Potts]), female characters with unique styles undergo makeovers and become more traditionally feminine to appeal to male suitors. That they each first attract a popular boy and a stable adult, respectively, because of who they were originally does not seem to matter; changing to fit into conservative patriarchal conventions is what seals the deal. Correspondingly, Ferris Bueller's sister, Jeanie (Jennifer Grey), naturally just needs a boy's attention to transform from frigid to agreeable. Furthermore, in *Sixteen Candles*, the Geek (Hall) keeps harassing Samantha even after she clearly and expressly tells him to stop, and in *The Breakfast Club*, Bender is viciously abusive to Claire (Ringwald), even physically assaulting her under the table when he's hiding from Vernon (Paul Gleason), the "Dean of Students."[32] Yet, their ultimate coupling becomes the culmination of the romantic storyline feeding into the dangerous ideas that a boy is being mean to a girl because he likes her, that women need to earn men's approval, and that bad boys are cool and will be rewarded for their browbeating behavior.

While the makeovers and the harassment are certainly disturbing, the foremost appalling storyline is when Jake Ryan becomes an accomplice to rape in *Sixteen Candles*. He is framed as the idealized boyfriend, the handsome, sensitive one who is interested in a romantic relationship with regular Samantha (conveniently after he intercepts a note where she says that she's a virgin but would have sex with him). Even though he's dating Caroline (Haviland Morris), the most beautiful and popular girl in school, he's lost interest in her because she just wants to party; when she displays self-confidence and confronts him about his flagging interest in her, Jake gaslights her and tells her she's crazy. And when Caroline is passed out drunk, he declares that he could "violate her ten different ways" if he wanted to, to which the Geek incredulously asks, "What are you waiting for?" Jake's reason for abstaining is because he has shifted his attention to the virtuous Samantha. In line with the treatment of women like chattel (two popular boys offer to trade their girlfriends for Lisa in *Weird Science*; Hardy [Craig Sheffer] calls his girlfriend, Amanda [Lea Thompson], his property in *Some Kind of Wonderful*), Jake makes a deal with the Geek to trade Samantha's underwear for a human being. He helps put Caroline in his father's car and tells the Geek to "have fun." The Geek takes trophy photos of her at his friends' house, and then it is assumed that the two of them have sex even though they were both too drunk to remember and so could not legally consent. Fortunately, the next morning everything is fine because she had a good time. Caroline even comforts a wounded Jake when he comes upon her and the Geek kissing the next morning, telling him she'll leave the decision about what to do about their relationship up to him. The entire storyline is played as funny, and Jake is made out to be the dream guy who rescues Samantha from a bad birthday. Women are pigeonholed into two camps in Hughes's films: the ones like Samantha and Sloane (Mia Sara in *Ferris Bueller's Day Off*) who are variously chaste, loyal, nurturing, and thus desired; and Caroline and Benny (Kate Vernon in *Pretty in Pink*) who are variously slutty, assertive, bitchy, and thus disposable. Hughes may have depicted strong principal female characters, but only a certain type of "good girl" gets the favorable treatment, leading to an interpretation of his work upon further inspection as hostilely misogynistic and regressive.

However, just as Hughes's films' commendable qualities need to be qualified by the context in which they appeared, so do the more deplorable ones. These depictions of women were actually in line with some other films of the time that also played abuse and degradation for laughs. *Porky's* (1981) and *Revenge of the Nerds* (1984) depict scenes of men spying on undressed women. In addition, in *Revenge* the nerds engage in "revenge porn" when they use a naked picture of one of the opposing fraternity members' girlfriends to sell pies, and one of the lead nerds disguises himself as a cheerleader's boyfriend to trick her into having sex with him (aka rape), but it all allegedly turns out well because of course she liked it. Meanwhile, when a character in *Animal House* (1978) decides not to rape an underage, passed-out drunk girl, the devil on his shoulder calls him a "fag." The legacy of such behavior and attitudes is lengthy; enshrined in the canon of classic Hollywood films is *Gone With the Wind* (1939), where Rhett (Clark Gable) forcibly carries a resisting Scarlett (Vivien Leigh) upstairs, and the next morning she awakens in bed with a contented sigh. The message put forward is that it is an accepted norm that women are objects for predatory behavior, and that they just need and want to be dominated by men because it's ultimately good for them and wrong or weak for men not to take advantage.

The rape culture (or cultural practices that excuse, tolerate, ignore, trivialize, or humorize assault[33]) on display in popular comedies from the time was not something that would have been named as such then. Although apparent now, using the word "rape" to describe something other than a violent act perpetrated by a stranger was uncommon in the 1980s. In fact, the term "acquaintance rape," which describes "forced, nonconsensual penetration involving people who know one another," wasn't even used until the 1970s.[34] Surprising as it may be now, a UCLA study from 1981 revealed that "54 percent of the boys and 42 percent of the girls thought forced sexual intercourse was acceptable under certain circumstances,"[35] providing a radically different context for understanding plotlines condoning such attacks. Even famous advice columnist Ann Landers sympathized with men who raped women if they had been drinking and physically intimate beforehand,[36] clearly indicating dated cultural perceptions about sanctioned behavior. This was all part of a resistance against women's rights that became acceptable in the 1980s. Called a "backlash"[37] for the misogynistic treatment of women, these negative attitudes found their way into popular culture as evidenced by some of the content in Hughes's films and in others. Notably, no available published review from the time *Sixteen Candles* was released mentions anything about rape. As one of the dominant filmmakers in the 1980s, Hughes contributed to this backlash by both reflecting and shaping popular culture; his humor was also considered funny at the time.

HAGIOGRAPHY

There are two main definitions of the word "hagiography." One refers to writing about the lives of saints or people who are venerated; another has to do with writing that is excessively adulatory and "without sufficient criticism."[38] Indeed, like many discourses surrounding John Hughes, both as a filmmaker and a person, there is often both acclaim and criticism, usually at the same time. Hughes's reputation in Hollywood was legendary as someone who could crank out mostly successful scripts at lightning speed, but some of his films were praised and some panned; he was known to be close to the people with whom he worked and also to turn on them in an instant; his presence was felt in Hollywood as media makers would cite him as an influence, but after he decided to leave filmmaking, he never came back.

Hughes stopped making teen films after *Some Kind of Wonderful* in 1987, effectively graduating from the genre in the same four years it takes to finish high school. He had a strategy to age his films along with his audience and so moved on to young adults in subsequent stages of their lives with *She's Having a Baby* (1988).[39] It was another highly autobiographical film featuring an ad man who marries young and wants to be a writer (all from Hughes's own life), but it wasn't very successful. Because he was always mindful of giving the populace what it wanted—saying, "I have no interest, none whatsoever, in doing something for myself instead of for the audience"[40] and would readily rewrite endings if test screenings didn't go well[41]—when his young adult formulae stopped working, he tended to make films that were more family-oriented. Over the next few years, these included films such as *The Great Outdoors* (1988), *National Lampoon's Christmas Vacation* (1989), and *Uncle Buck* (1989), which still featured teens in prominent, although not primary, roles. In 1990, he wrote and produced, but didn't direct, the phenomenally profitable *Home Alone*, which led to his transition towards younger, child-centered films like *Curly Sue* (1991) and *Dennis the Menace* (1993). By 1994, he had 27 films produced in about a dozen years with a total box office gross of over $1.3 billion,[42] making him "the most credited, most bankable scriptwriter" of the time.[43]

Continuing with the contradictory impressions Hughes left, while he was bankable, he was also labeled a testy, "standoffish box office superman"[44] for his irascible behavior. More than that, articles at the time eviscerated him for his unreasonable demands, reigns of terror, and stonewalling of people he had once praised because he was so easily offended. Coworkers who refused to be named on record said he was "volatile, impetuous, and spoiled,"[45] and a "crazed, scary, capricious bully . . . total maniac screamer."[46] There was a lengthy feature in *Premiere* in 1999 celebrating "Teen Days that Shook the World" that primarily focused on the impact of *The Breakfast Club* and was only *edited* to appear as though he was talking with his former stars.[47] They spoke about how collaborative he was, how he would listen to their suggestions, how they spent time together listening to music, and how they cherished working with him. However, as Molly Ringwald and Anthony Michael Hall revealed in a piece the former wrote after Hughes died, he actually cut off all contact with both of them in the 1980s after they had told him they wanted to branch out and work with other filmmakers.[48] He never spoke to either one of them again.

Although he continued filmmaking into the 1990s, his mark as an auteur was most strongly felt with his teen films, so much so that while the two teen films directed by Deutch are clearly recognized as Hughes productions, his later authorial mark is not as readily apparent. The presence of the teen films he made continued to have an impact even though he was no longer making them. Already by the mid-1990s, *The Breakfast Club* was coming out on top of "best films of the '80s" lists,[49] and the late 1990s resurgence in teen film production had the effect of highlighting the profound influence he had on the genre. Specific films would obviously label different social cliques just as his films had (*Clueless* [1995]) while others would use direct parody and even have cameos from his teen film actors (*Not Another Teen Movie* [2001]). Over the next decade, articles were released discussing the influence he had on Hollywood and on specific filmmakers, with people like Judd Apatow saying his ideas were "all there first in John Hughes' films," and Kevin Smith claiming, "He's our generation's J. D. Salinger . . . If it weren't for him, I wouldn't be doing what I do. Basically my stuff is just John Hughes films with four-letter words."[50]

In Hughes's absence, his aura only grew, and much of what was written about him was highly complimentary. It was in this time that he became more firmly enshrined as an auteur, and in the process, the status of the teen film genre in which he worked was boosted as well. There were exaltations claiming to "revere him" for being a filmmaker able to connect with his audience, "for being the only movie person to capture what it was like to be an adolescent in the '80s,"[51] while *The Breakfast Club* was called an "enduring, timeless classic" and Hughes "the auteur of adolescence."[52] Using the theme song from *The Breakfast Club* as their invocation, articles asked what happened to him,[53] books talked about his influence,[54] and documentaries such as *Don't You Forget About Me* (2009) searched for him, but it was all to no avail. Hughes said in an interview, "When I've lost my voice, I'll know when to go. I'll disappear in a puff";[55] he did just that.

But a question remains as to how Hughes and his films continued to be received during the 1990s and 2000s in terms of their problems, the largest of which in retrospect include a lack of diversity and an abundance of misogyny. The character of Jake Ryan is particularly illustrative when simultaneously praising and qualifying Hughes's impact, especially when highlighting how few mainstream authors even found something about this character to criticize. In 2009, after he died suddenly at the age of 59 from a heart attack, Hughes's esteem grew exponentially, although there were some marginal criticisms in the tributes as well. The *New York Times* obituary reported that he was able to realistically capture what it was like as a teenager in the 1980s, that Hughes was an auteur whose "place in the pantheon cannot be denied."[56] An extended feature in *Vanity Fair* called him a "Sweet Bard of Youth," noting that even though he was a baby boomer he paradoxically became the "Teen Laureate of the 1980s" with his films speaking to Generation X, the generation coming of age at the time, and that "nearly the whole of movie-watching America" was in mourning after he died because of how many lives he touched with his films.[57] However, the same articles described how difficult he was to work with, as well as some of the problems in his films, notably the absence of any Black characters, the racist stereotypes of Asians and Italians, and how the films smooth over harsh realities. Neither of these reflections on Hughes mentioned anything about his depictions of gender and sexuality.

There were some hints as to the criticisms that would come. Following similar analyses of the ways Hughes reinscribes the patriarchal concept of "Daddy's Girl,"[58] an article in *Cinema Journal* about characters in John Hughes films examined the postfeminist, neoconservative politics of the films, and called out both the description of Caroline as an object and Hughes's repeated premises that what women really want is to conform.[59] A quick quip by one of the authors writing about what Hughes's films meant to him growing up called what happened to Caroline in *Sixteen Candles* "rape,"[60] one of the first published descriptions to label it as such. I had also labeled the incident as rape while writing my dissertation[61] in the late 2000s, and there were doubtless many others who referred to it this way too, but it was not until 2009 that a piece in *Salon*—literally titled "The *Sixteen Candles* Date Rape Scene?"—contained one of the first published extensive missives analyzing the sexual politics of Hughes's teen films.[62] The author compliments the way Hughes addressed class issues, but also mentions some of the films' racial problems and makes perceptive comments about his less-than-progressive sexual politics. However, it attributes these faults mostly to reflections of "some of the prejudices of their time."[63] The phrase "of their time" to refer to the 1980s is suspect, though; just five years earlier in 2004, the *Washington Post* ran an extended feature on the front page of the Style section titled "Real Men Can't Hold a Match to Jake Ryan of 'Sixteen Candles'"[64] detailing how dreamy the character still is to women who pine for a relationship with someone so wonderful.

Before Hughes died, a 2009 review of *Sixteen Candles* by prolific critic James Berardinelli summed up the 20-year period from approximately the late 1980s to the late 2000s both cogently and myopically. Berardinelli states that the film had good parts and bad, that it was a watershed moment, and that it was "one of the best and most honest representation of '80s high school"; however, while he realizes the Geek could either be considered a "lovesick puppy or a psycho stalker," the same consciousness doesn't extend toward Jake Ryan, whom he still labeled "far too good to be true."[65] During this time, Hughes's representations became firmly entrenched as realistic depictions of teen life and he was extolled as an astute observer of both the time in life and the time period. He was consecrated as both the voice of Generation X and as an auteur for illustrating and codifying the rules of a genre, and his teen films endure. But the reception of his films would continue to change.

HISTORIOGRAPHY

Like "hagiography," the word "historiography" also has the root "graph"—to write—but historiography is about studying how history is written, and which histories are written; it is about realizing that when we document the past we are writing histories "of the present too"[66] by concentrating on modern-day concerns and their roots. Additionally, as Michel de Certeau notes in *The Writing of History*, the word itself points to a paradoxical relationship "between the real and discourse."[67] What all this together means is that when examining history, more than just the past is investigated; the conversations that have developed around events are also analyzed, and we realize that the lenses of our contemporary focus influence the very things we choose to study. The power of historiography is apparent in the changing ways John Hughes is evaluated and in the varying ways his films, either in part, whole, or summation of his oeuvre, are judged.

In this last time period, encompassing over a decade since Hughes died to the present, there were additional pieces of praise and criticism, just as in the two prior periods. One of the interesting facets of some of these discourses, though, is in seeing how these assessments have changed and been qualified. For example, during the 30th anniversary celebrations for *The Breakfast Club*, Kirk Honeycutt, reviewer for the *Hollywood Reporter*, explained that he was wrong about his original assessment of the film, noting that "he failed it" but that because it really was a good film, he was able to change his mind.[68] Other critics questioned how they could have ever liked *Sixteen Candles*, not being able to believe on rewatching how misogynistic it was, with one declaring, "nostalgia is a sneaky bitch."[69] Along similar lines, fans of the films would try to come to terms with "Loving John Hughes Movies While Black,"[70] with author Maulud Sadiq ultimately deciding that, yes, there were parts that were offensive and that were in line with popular culture at the time, but then almost pragmatically and resignedly stating that these were the storms minorities and marginalized people had to weather: "You had to have a thick skin growing up in the '80s. And maybe that's why these films don't bother me. They were like the dojo for what I had to deal with eight hours a day."[71] The positives were that at least they could identify with Hughes's characters because of how well he depicted the outsider experience. Even interviews he gave and elements from his films that seemed positive at first can take on different meanings. His stated focus on romance in his films,[72] and view that pin-up poster images were silly and vacant, can be read on the one hand as being sensitive to women and not just viewing them as sex objects; on the other, it can be seen as being against female expressions of sexuality. The multiple views depend on interpretation, context, and perceived authorial intention.

One of the biggest shifts in this period notably came about in light of the #MeToo Movement. The movement gained momentum with the Harvey Weinstein exposés in 2017 that accused him of gross sexual misconduct spanning decades, and it triggered a domino effect as others from across multiple strata in America exposed their experiences with sexual assault. However, authors and activists had actually started these conversations in the years leading up to the tipping point. Again, just in terms of how Hughes's films have been reassessed, in "A Diamond and a Kiss" in 2016, Soraya Roberts writes that "Hughes's attempt to divest *The Breakfast Club*'s characters of their stereotypes did not extend to gender" and that ultimately Claire gives her harasser what he wants "to make his fantasy come true."[73] And earlier in 2017, Hughes's films started making lists of "15 Movies You Didn't Realize Were Sexist."[74] In the wake of the #MeToo Movement, and especially with contentious Supreme Court nominee Brett Kavanaugh defending his high school behavior by referring to some of the comedies that were popular in the early 1980s (although Hughes films were not directly mentioned), additional articles tried to make sense of how the rape storyline in *Sixteen Candles* could ever have been filmed. Notably, in an insightful article for *Vox*, Constance Grady explains that it was possible because of different perceptions and the lack of acknowledgement of rape culture, saying, "the cultural understanding of rape in the 1980s was fundamentally different from how we understand it today," evident because popular films from the time contain "supposedly hilarious sequences that portray what in 2018 would be unambiguously considered date rape."[75]

Perhaps some of the pieces written by Hughes's muse Molly Ringwald are most illustrative of the way assessments evolve with the passage of time and a revisionist lens. Ringwald has written and spoken extensively about her work with Hughes since the 1980s, but there are two pieces in particular from this specific time period that point to shifting discourses. In 2014, she discussed viewing *The Breakfast Club* with her daughter. She was nervous about the sexual content at first, but this turned out not to cause the most distress at the time; the bigger issue that arose was that her daughter shared how she felt pressured academically by her parents. Ringwald was taken aback and started to realize that as an adult watching the film, she "felt for the parents" while also appreciating how the film was so useful for opening up lines of communication.[76] However, it was not until a few years later in 2018 when Ringwald realized the extent of sexual harassment and misogyny evident in Hughes's work. Writing in *The New Yorker*, she stated that there is much she loves about the films, that they gave her a career, and were so important to her generation. However, with hindsight she realized, with surprise and some embarrassment because of how long it took her to become aware, how much is so offensive, including the ways both Claire and Caroline are treated. Ultimately, she remains torn, knowing that to embrace the films entirely "feels hypocritical," and questioning, especially because she helped create them, "How are we meant to feel about art that we both love and oppose?"[77]

While Ringwald and others reassess Hughes, it is not clear what, if anything, Hughes himself would say about his work now if he were still alive and had the chance or the inclination to reflect publicly. He had previously disavowed parts of his work, saying in the 1980s that he no longer wanted to acknowledge some of the stories he wrote for *National Lampoon*. Yet, in the same interview, he said the humor magazine taught him "the value of being honest, to reach deep into myself and pull out things that other people were also thinking."[78] He also later conceded that *Weird Science* was a "dopey-assed comedy" and that the dance sequence in *The Breakfast Club* was dated and "an extraordinarily bad idea."[79] It is not clear, however, if he was disavowing the quality or the content of his previous work. Did he think his jokes in *National Lampoon* pieces like "Sexual Harassment and How to Do It!" were no longer funny because they were not well written, or did he think they were offensive? Yes, it was satire, but women in the workplace were also objects of the ridicule. Did he have shots of naked women in his films (*Sixteen Candles* and *Weird Science*) only because it was a popular trend at the time? In *Ferris Bueller's Day Off*, did Cameron (Alan Ruck) get away with surreptitiously watching Sloane undress because "boys will be boys"? Would Hughes have changed his films to suit his audience as he had done before, or did he realize his views were no longer in line with what was popular and so he walked away? There is no way to know what his real intentions were, or how much of the films represented his own views compared to how much was him trying to appease an audience; we only have what is left in the texts. Further examination of the rest of his body of work, as other chapters in this collection indicate, may be able to provide more answers.

CONCLUSION

Recurring authorial tropes in Hughes films demonstrate positive aspects when they emphasize that teens and their lives are worth taking seriously, and his films helped solidify the status of the teen film as a genre worthy of study. However, other tropes in the same films indicate problematic turns and questionable personal values, and illustrate cultural insensitivities. Although present-day analyses bring to light troubling aspects that we cannot unsee, they do not negate the significance and magnitude of his impact. Instead of seeing only good or bad, we need to account for the concepts of context and complexity.

To more fully understand media, we have to historically contextualize who made it, as well as when and where it was made in order to gain an understanding of the ideological foundations. Even if we get a sense of Hughes's politics and personality through films and interviews, we also have to consider the limitations of the time and place in which he was working. What becomes helpful here is acknowledging the roles of history, hagiography, historiography, and future interpretations yet unknown. Indeed, as we reconsider Hughes's work, we have to be careful of thinking that we are so enlightened now, of falling into a trap of seeing progress without also acknowledging present-day shortcomings. We do not know what our current blind spots are, and we may only get an idea of some of them with critical distance and the passage of time. What historiography underscores is that the present moment will be some future's past, and that the past will live on in the present in mutable ways.

In addition to recognizing the role of context in interpretation, it is also beneficial to consider complexity. Instead of just totalizing appraisals of all good or all bad, there is a middle ground. If the commendations of his films are not qualified, we are in danger of appearing to condone their troubling narrative components. But if we only criticize, then we are potentially cutting out a piece of history, kept from recognizing the films' myriad merits, and denied the enjoyment of engaging with the films at all. The films are not sacrosanct; we can and do criticize them even if we like them. They are also not evil incarnate; watching and enjoying them does not mean viewers are racist, misogynist, or are in ideological alignment with the complete text. Explaining the problems in Hughes's work does not mean excusing them; it means not going to the disadvantageous extreme of a complete dismissal and of understanding multi-layered interpretations and implications.

Hughes's teen films are recommended viewing, even if those endorsements come with caveats. And we do not just view his films because they are important, although even admitting that they are important as teen films is a leap from certain critics' views. We also watch them because we derive some enjoyment from them, because there are many positive aspects to them that should not be erased despite the problematic elements. Ultimately, we arrive at a place of realizing that John Hughes's teen films can be both more and less than a product of their time and of their component parts, that both criticism of and fondness for his films can exist together in a web of complexity and memory. Wholesale dismissal and complete aggrandizement close off paths toward productive analyses and contextual understandings. They also shut down what might be some of the most important aspects of critical reassessments of an auteur's work: that we open a dialogue and have ongoing conversations about the changing role of important films and filmmakers in our culture and in our lives.

NOTES

1. Thomas O'Connor, "John Hughes: His Movies Speak to Teen-Agers," *New York Times*, March 9, 1986, http://www.nytimes.com/1986/03/09/movies/john-hughes-his-movies-speak-to-teen-agers.html.
2. Gene Siskel, "Teenage Life Gets Touching New Portrayal," *Chicago Tribune*, February 15, 1985, http://articles.chicagotribune.com/1985-02-15/entertainment/8501090715_1_breakfast-club-sixteen-candles-film.
3. Pauline Kael, "The Breakfast Club," in *5001 Nights at the Movies* (New York: Henry Holt and Company, 1985), 99.
4. Robert Sklar, *Movie-Made America: A Cultural History of American Movies, Revised and Updated* (New York: Vintage Books, 1994), 347.
5. Molly Ringwald, "What About 'The Breakfast Club'?: Revisiting the Movies of My Youth in the Age of #MeToo," *The New Yorker*, April 6, 2018, https://www.newyorker.com/culture/personal-history/what-about-the-breakfast-club-molly-ringwald-metoo-john-hughes-pretty-in-pink.
6. Francois Truffaut, "A Certain Tendency of the French Cinema" (1954), in *Movies and Methods: Volume I, an Anthology*, ed. Bill Nichols (Berkeley: University of California Press, 1976), 224–36.
7. Andrew Sarris, *The American Cinema: Directors and Directions 1929–1968* (Boston: Da Capo Press, 1996), 25–38.
8. Daniel Little, "Philosophy of History," in *The Stanford Encyclopedia of Philosophy*, 2017 edn, ed. Edward N. Zalta, https://plato.stanford.edu/archives/sum2017/entries/history/.
9. Quoted in Molly Ringwald, "Molly Ringwald Interviews John Hughes," *Seventeen*, March 1986, 239.
10. Ringwald (1986), 238.
11. Quoted in Roger Ebert, "John Hughes: When You're 16, You're More Serious than You'll Ever Be Again," RogerEbert.com, April 29, 1984, https://www.rogerebert.com/rogers-journal/john-hughes-when-youre-16-youre-more-serious-than-youll-ever-be-again.
12. Hadley Freeman, *Life Moves Pretty Fast: The Lessons We Learned from Eighties Movies (and Why We Don't Learn Them from Movies Any More)* (New York: Simon and Schuster Paperbacks, 2016), 68.

13. Susannah Gora, *You Couldn't Ignore Me If You Tried: The Brat Pack, John Hughes, and Their Impact on a Generation* (New York: Three Rivers Press, 2010), 160.
14. Patrick Goldstein, "John Hughes in the Pink at MCA," *Los Angeles Times*, March 1, 1987, http://articles.latimes.com/1987-03-01/entertainment/ca-6707_1_john-hughes.
15. O'Connor; Andrew McCarthy quoted in Gora, 2.
16. "The '80s Soundtracks," *Billboard*, December 23, 1989, D-24.
17. Timothy Shary, *Generation Multiplex: The Image of Youth in American Cinema since 1980* (Austin: University of Texas Press, 2014), 7.
18. Elissa H. Nelson, "The New Old Face of a Genre: The Franchise Teen Film as Industry Strategy," *Cinema Journal*, 57, no. 1 (2017), 125–33.
19. Ringwald (1986), 228.
20. Michael Weiss, "Some Kind of Republican," Slate, September 21, 2006, http://www.slate.com/articles/arts/dvdextras/2006/09/some_kind_of_republican.html.
21. Kirk Honeycutt, *John Hughes: A Life in Film* (New York: Race Point Publishing, 2015), 24–9; David Kamp, "Sweet Bard of Youth," *Vanity Fair*, March 2010, http://www.vanityfair.com/hollywood/features/2010/03/john-hughes-201003.
22. Honeycutt, 73–5.
23. Gora, 188.
24. Statistics are from BoxOfficeMojo, domestic box office grosses for in-year releases: Domestic Box Office for 1984: https://www.boxofficemojo.com/year/1984/?grossesOption=totalGrosses; Domestic Box Office for 1985: https://www.boxofficemojo.com/year/1985/?grossesOption=totalGrosses; Domestic Box Office for 1986: https://www.boxofficemojo.com/year/1986/?grossesOption=totalGrosses; Domestic Box Office for 1987: https://www.boxofficemojo.com/year/1987/?grossesOption=totalGrosses.
25. Richard Corliss, "Well, Hello Molly!" *Time*, May 26, 1986, http://content.time.com/time/subscriber/article/0,33009,961447-1,00.html.
26. Dave Kehr, "Pretty in Pink," *Chicago Reader*, 1986, https://www.chicagoreader.com/chicago/pretty-in-pink/Film?oid=1686089.
27. Janet Maslin, "Film View; Marching toward Maturity," *New York Times*, March 15, 1987, 21.
28. Maslin, 21.
29. Hall quoted in Terry Keefe, "The Hollywood Interview: Anthony Michael Hall," The Hollywood Interview, November 30, 2008, http://thehollywoodinterview.blogspot.com/2008/11/anthony-michael-hall-hollywood.html.
30. Janet Maslin, "'16 Candles,' A Teen-Age Comedy," *New York Times*, May 4, 1984, https://www.nytimes.com/1984/05/04/movies/screen-16-candles-a-teen-age-comedy.html.
31. Roger Ebert, "Sixteen Candles," RogerEbert.com, May 4, 1984, https://www.rogerebert.com/reviews/sixteen-candles-1984.
32. Considerable ambiguity surrounds the title of Mr. Vernon. In the special features of the recent Criterion Collection DVD, actor Paul Gleason recites a poem he has written about his character, calling himself the Dean of Students. (See *The Breakfast Club* [1985; The Criterion Collection, 2018], DVD). However, the script simply refers to him as "a teacher," and no character within the film refers to him by a title. (See http://www.dailyscript.com/scripts/breakfast_club.html.)
33. Shannon Ridgway, "25 Examples of Rape Culture," Everyday Feminism, March 10, 2014, https://everydayfeminism.com/2014/03/examples-of-rape-culture/.
34. Peggy Reeves Sanday, *A Woman Scorned: Acquaintance Rape on Trial* (Berkeley: University of California Press, 1997), xii.
35. Rachel Reynolds and David Jefferson, "The Crime Few Victims Will Report; Rapes Committed by Acquaintances Called Epidemic," *San Diego Union-Tribune*, August 26, 1985, A-1.

36. Ann Landers, "The Problem of 'Date Rape' Is an Ambiguous One," *San Bernardino Sun*, July 29, 1985, https://cdnc.ucr.edu/cgi-bin/cdnc?a=d&d=SBS19850729.1.12&e; Ann Landers, "A Male Viewpoint on Date Rape," *St. Louis Post-Dispatch*, August 4, 1991, 11C.
37. Susan Faludi, *Backlash: The Undeclared War Against American Women* (New York: Crown Publishers, Inc., 1991).
38. "Hagiography," Oxford Reference, 2003, https://www.oxfordreference.com/view/10.1093/acref/9780192800947.001.0001/acref-9780192800947-e-2899.
39. Bill Carter, "Him Alone," *New York Times*, August 4, 1991, http://www.nytimes.com/1991/08/04/magazine/him-alone.html.
40. Carter.
41. John Hughes, "Vacation '58/Foreword '08," *Zoetrope: All-Story*, 12, no. 2 (2008), https://web.archive.org/web/20080806191040/http://www.all-story.com/issues.cgi?action=show_story&story_id=389.
42. Tim Appelo, "John Hughes' View from the Top," *Entertainment Weekly*, December 2, 1994, http://ew.com/article/1994/12/02/john-hughes-view-top/.
43. Carter.
44. Appelo.
45. Appelo.
46. Richard Lalich, "Big Baby," *Spy*, January 1993, 68.
47. Sean M. Smith, "Teen Days that Shook the World," *Premiere*, December 1999, 69–79, 145–7.
48. Molly Ringwald, "The Neverland Club," *New York Times*, August 12, 2009, http://www.nytimes.com/2009/08/12/opinion/12ringwald.html.
49. Matthew Rettenmund, *Totally Awesome 80s: A Lexicon of the Music, Videos, Movies, TV Shows, Stars, and Trends of That Decadent Decade* (New York: St. Martin's Griffin, 1996), 79.
50. Quoted in Patrick Goldstein, "John Hughes' Imprint Remains," *Los Angeles Times*, March 24, 2008, http://www.latimes.com/entertainment/news/movies/la-et-goldstein25mar25,0,3535882.story.
51. Maura Kelly, "John Hughes: The Films He Created in the Decade of Greed Made Adolescent Angst Funny and Bearable Without Romanticizing It," Salon, July 17, 2001, http://www.salon.com/2001/07/17/john_hughes_2/.
52. Sarfraz Manzoor, "More than a Quintessential Eighties Teen Film," *The Independent*, March 24, 2004, http://www.independent.co.uk/arts-entertainment/films/features/more-than-a-quintessential-eighties-teen-film-65704.html.
53. Adam Wahlberg, "Don't You Forget About John Hughes," *Today*, March 17, 2008, https://www.today.com/popculture/don-t-you-forget-about-john-hughes-wbna23677561.
54. Jaime Clark, ed., *Don't You Forget About Me: Contemporary Writers on the Films of John Hughes* (New York: Simon Spotlight Entertainment, 2007).
55. Quoted in Appelo.
56. A. O. Scott, "An Appraisal: The John Hughes Touch," *New York Times*, August 8, 2009, http://www.nytimes.com/2009/08/08/movies/08appraisal.html?fta=y.
57. Kamp.
58. Ann De Vaney, "Pretty in Pink? John Hughes Reinscribes Daddy's Girl in Homes and Schools," in *Sugar, Spice, and Everything Nice: Cinemas of Girlhood*, eds Frances K. Gateward and Murray Pomerance (Detroit: Wayne State University Press, 2002), 201–16.
59. Anthony C. Bleach, "Postfeminist Cliques? Class, Postfeminism, and the Molly Ringwald-John Hughes Films," *Cinema Journal*, 49, no. 3 (2010), 22–44.
60. Tod Goldberg, "That's Not a Name, that's a Major Appliance: How Andrew McCarthy Ruined My Life," in *Don't You Forget About Me: Contemporary Writers on the Films of John Hughes*, ed. Jaime Clarke (New York: Simon Spotlight Entertainment, 2007), 93.

61. Elissa H. Nelson, "Teen Films of the 1980s: Genre, New Hollywood, and Generation X," dissertation, University of Texas at Austin, 2011.
62. Amy Benfer, "The 'Sixteen Candles Date Rape Scene?'" Salon, August 11, 2009, https://www.salon.com/2009/08/11/16_candles/.
63. Benfer.
64. Hank Stuever, "'Real Men Can't Hold A Match to Jake Ryan Of 'Sixteen Candles,'" Washington Post, February 14, 2004, C01, https://www.washingtonpost.com/archive/lifestyle/2004/02/14/real-men-cant-hold-a-match-to-jake-ryan-of-sixteen-candles/df1fc4ca-bfba-4396-8a4b-345498840759/.
65. James Berardinelli, "Sixteen Candles (United States, 1984)," Reelviews, May 16, 2009, http://www.reelviews.net/reelviews/sixteen-candles.
66. Popular Memory Group, "Popular Memory: Theory, Politics, Method," in *Making Histories: Studies in History Writing and Politics*, eds Richard Johnson et al. (Minneapolis: University of Minnesota Press, 1982), 205.
67. Michel de Certeau, *The Writing of History*, trans. Tom Conley (New York: Columbia University Press, 1988), xxvii.
68. Quoted in Christopher Borrelli, "'The Breakfast Club' 30 Years Later: Don't You Forget About Them," *Chicago Tribune*, February 17, 2015, http://www.chicagotribune.com/entertainment/movies/ct-the-breakfast-club-30th-anniversary-20150217-column.html.
69. Stephanie Rogers, "'Sixteen Candles,' Rape Culture, and the Anti-Woman Politics of 2013," Btchflcks, July 8, 2013, http://www.btchflcks.com/2013/07/sixteen-candles-rape-culture-and-the-anti-woman-politics-of-2013.html#.XUdkW-hKiM8.
70. Maulud Sadiq, "Loving John Hughes Movies While Black," Medium, January 23, 2017, https://medium.com/the-brothers/loving-john-hughes-movies-while-black-1c4acba2e628.
71. Sadiq.
72. Ringwald (1986), 227.
73. Soraya Roberts, "A Diamond and a Kiss: The Women of John Hughes," Hazlitt, July 5, 2016, http://hazlitt.net/longreads/diamond-and-kiss-women-john-hughes.
74. Loretta Donelan, "15 Movies You Didn't Realize Were Sexist," Bustle, January 22, 2017, https://www.bustle.com/p/15-movies-you-didnt-realize-were-sexist-30553.
75. Constance Grady, "The Rape Culture of the 1980s, Explained by Sixteen Candles," Vox, September 27, 2018, https://www.vox.com/culture/2018/9/27/17906644/sixteen-candles-rape-culture-1980s-brett-kavanaugh.
76. Quoted in Ira Glass, "Is This What I Look Like?" This American Life, May 23, 2014, https://www.thisamericanlife.org/526/is-that-what-i-look-like.
77. Ringwald, (2018).
78. Jack Barth, "Kinks of Comedy," *Film Comment*, June 1984, 46.
79. Quoted in Smith, 145; 74.

CHAPTER 3

"Becoming John Hughes": Regional Production, Hyphenate Filmmaking, and Independence within Hollywood

Yannis Tzioumakis

From the very start of his career as a writer-director and soon after as writer-director-producer, John Hughes has enjoyed immense creative freedom and has controlled most aspects in the production of his films. What is more, he did not achieve this level of freedom by working as a low-budget independent filmmaker making idiosyncratic films at the margins of the Hollywood film industry. He did it by embracing a more institutionalized form of independence that did not preclude direct or indirect collaboration with the Hollywood studios and by making genre films that targeted primarily the teen and family markets. And even though in 1987 he did launch the Hughes Entertainment production company away from Hollywood in his native Illinois, his geographical distance from the epicenter of American cinema did not necessarily mean a stronger embrace of independence or the espousal of filmmaking with a strong regional identity. It did mean, however, a further enhanced ability to control his productions and instill them with a regional sensibility that often contributed to their distinctiveness in the marketplace.

While the staggering success of *Home Alone* (1990), which Hughes wrote and produced, added further to the clout he already had in Hollywood, it may not be as clear how the filmmaker achieved the level of power he enjoyed before that film, starting from the very first production he wrote and directed, *Sixteen Candles* (1984). Prior to *Home Alone*, his work, commercially successful as it had been, had never reached the heights of 1980s blockbusters such as *Beverly Hills Cop* (1984), *Top Gun* (1986), and *Batman* (1989). *Ferris Bueller's Day Off* (1986) was the biggest commercial success of all Hughes films in the 1980s with just over $70 million at the North American theatrical box office. Such a figure located the film in 10th place among the domestic box office champions for the year.[1] With all his other films proving mostly modest successes, and even with some failures under his belt (especially *She's Having A Baby* [1988] and *Curly Sue* [1991]),[2] one wonders how Hughes managed to secure a place in the Hollywood elite. This is especially intriguing given his popular image and brand identity as a filmmaker of sensitive and intelligent films that understand teenagers, who enjoys collaborating with and empowering young talent in an industry traditionally dominated by older (male) executives.

Even more intriguing, his meteoric rise took place within the very specific corporate culture, structures, and climate of Hollywood cinema in the '80s that was predominantly characterized by an emphasis on excessive, synergy-driven, high-concept film productions. How can Hughes's clout be accounted for critically when his approach to making films did not fit this mold? How can his power be explained when his work was not as commercially successful as the work of other filmmakers that dominated 1980s cinema such as Steven Spielberg and Ivan Reitman, or producers such as Don Simpson and Jerry Bruckheimer?

In debating these questions, this chapter argues that John Hughes benefited immensely from a particular configuration of factors that enabled him to exercise control in his films from the start of his career as a filmmaker. These factors include: a very specific form of "independent" film production that helped him keep studio executives at arm's length; a distinct articulation of regional filmmaking, which together with his independence imbued his films with a particular artistic sensibility; Hughes's early adoption of multiple roles in the filmmaking process (also known as hyphenate filmmaking) which allowed him to control several aspects of the production process; and the interaction of all the above with the relatively low-stakes (and low-budget) teen genre film production in Hollywood. This combination of factors helped place Hughes and his films both inside and outside of the dominant mode of film production that characterized Hollywood in the mid-'80s. At the same time, it enabled him to develop practices that supported a distinct filmmaking vision that, arguably, needed some form of distance from Hollywood in order to materialize.

INDEPENDENT AND REGIONAL FILM IN 1980S AMERICA: DEGREES OF FREEDOM AND AUTHENTICITY

In his extensive examination of the field of independent film production in the US in the 1980s, Justin Wyatt provides a much broader and more inclusive picture of what could count as independence than most subsequent studies that focused on a narrower field,[3] which could be summarized as the commercially distributed and theatrically exhibited low-budget narrative fiction feature film. Taking as a starting point the types of companies that might be responsible for the production and distribution of independent films, Wyatt differentiates between four potential arrangements that could lay legitimate claim to the independent label: a) companies "unaffiliated with a major studio"; b) "a studio classics division operating in relative autonomy from the commercial dictates of the larger studio"; c) "a production company attached to a major"; and d) "an individual production, without distribution, financed independently of the majors altogether."[4]

Taking this taxonomy into consideration, it is clear that the majority of "American independent cinema studies" that blossomed in the 2000s and 2010s consciously focused on a very particular iteration of independence that was mostly related to films produced (and distributed) from configurations that fall under Wyatt's categories b) and d). This is because films made within contexts described under categories a) and c) tended to be relatively big and expensive productions, benefiting from often extremely well-capitalized companies that, among other things, attracted established talent.

However, these companies did not only make these kinds of films. Their slates included all types of productions, ranging from cheap exploitation fare to relatively low-budget quality auteur films that can easily be considered as part of the "independent film scene" of the era, despite the fact that their respective companies rarely are (for instance, David Lynch's *Blue Velvet* [1986] was made by the De Laurentiis Entertainment Group). The same principle also applies to companies belonging to category c), which use their "attachment" to a major studio to produce films that tend to be commercially oriented and big-budgeted. Wyatt provides the example of Imagine Entertainment and its association with Universal that commenced in the late '80s with box office hits such as *The 'Burbs* (1989) and *Parenthood* (1989). However, one can also see Imagine credited as producer for *Cry-Baby* (1990) by key independent filmmaker John Waters.

In this assessment one can also add the major Hollywood studios that have managed to maintain their proximity to independent film through other means, from supporting the Independent Feature Project and the Sundance Institute to occasionally producing and releasing films that are considered independent because they are made with "an economy of means" and therefore are eligible for independent film awards.[5] It is clear then that Hollywood and independent cinema have been enjoying a strongly symbiotic relationship, despite the fact that rhetorically they seemed to occupy opposite ends. Indeed, by the mid-'80s, "independence" in American cinema had been firmly institutionalized, operating in the margins of the industry but also taking opportunities to influence and be influenced by the Hollywood majors in productive and creative ways, as in the case of *Dirty Dancing* (1987), a teen film made by independent company Vestron for less than $5 million but routinely perceived as part of Hollywood's flurry of teen films in the mid-'80s.

Under these circumstances, locating independence—in the '80s and subsequently—becomes less associated with identifying a particular body of work that shares a number of characteristics. Instead, it aligns more with identifying particular practices that can take place within a great variety of industrial and institutional arrangements and which can enable innovative and distinctive approaches to filmmaking. In such a broad plateau, there is always a dominant independent film discourse that gets to define particular periods and, as I have argued elsewhere,[6] in a period roughly coinciding with the '80s, this discourse tended to privilege low-key, low-budget quality fiction films and some feature documentaries by a relatively small number of auteur filmmakers. However, there were several other discourses that circulated around the same time (as Wyatt's work shows) but did not receive as much attention and support from institutions involved in defining independence as did the dominant discourse, while elements of the dominant discourse can also be found outside its key players, agencies, and institutions, including in the studios.

The case of John Hughes brings together both secondary discourses of independence and elements of the dominant discourse, and so I focus on practices that enabled him to work with the kind of freedom associated with independent filmmakers, even though all his films were produced with major Hollywood studio support. Indeed, Hughes was routinely called an "independent filmmaker," with the *New York Times* calling him "the most prolific independent film maker in Hollywood history" and the *Guardian* using the same phrase as the subheading for Hughes's obituary in 2009.[7] As I suggested above and will elaborate, industrial and institutional arrangements often align in such ways that enable even the most novice of filmmakers to work with a level of creative freedom not normally associated with the Hollywood studios. John Hughes was one such filmmaker who exploited a very particular constellation of factors and managed to maintain control of his work from a very early stage in his career.

Alongside discourses of independence, the '80s also ignited debates about regional film production, some of which were also intricately linked to questions of independence. Driven by a staggering increase in the number of state and city film bureaus,[8] regional filmmaking started becoming a reality for a country that until the mid-'70s had almost all its production clustered either in Los Angeles on the west coast, or New York and New Jersey on the east. However, the establishment of these bureaus and their increasing understanding of the financial advantages of attracting film production prompted a concerted effort towards regional film production.[9] According to Gary Edgerton, by 1983 about 30 per cent of all films produced in the US were shot "on American soil outside California,"[10] while by the mid-'80s critics had started talking about "regional cinema," focusing on the "cultural benefits" it could provide as well as the themes and aesthetics it might contain.[11]

With a few significant exceptions, Hollywood's shift to regional film production in the '80s did not necessarily mean an emphasis on stories that were interested in regional and local issues or in authentic representations of life outside the major metropolitan areas in the country. Despite an emphasis on "location authenticity" within debates about production in the US in the '70s,[12] a lot of the films shot outside Los Angeles at the time "hardly represent[ed] a flowering of regional cultures."[13] However, this is not the case for the films discussed within the dominant discourse of American independent cinema at the time. A significant number of such films in that period were funded by grants from national institutions supporting regional filmmaking and therefore demonstrated a very strong interest in regional themes, especially life in rural areas and its faithful representation on screen.

Not surprisingly, such depictions invited often-distinct uses of narrative tropes and visual style to the extent that such films became emblematic of the American independent cinema movement, at least in the first half of the '80s. Such characteristics include an emphasis on the minutiae of human life, the frequent absence of happy endings, and even a strong degree of "restraint," a stylistic and narrative sobriety that, among other things, also opposes the excesses of the breakneck narratives in synergy-driven, high-concept Hollywood studio films.[14] With the body of such films increasing throughout the decade and into the '90s, it was clear that "regional cinema" was becoming a significant subcategory of independent cinema. Writing with the benefit of hindsight in 1999, Emanuel Levy saw all these developments as part of a "Regional Cinema," through which a number of filmmakers "explored indigenous subcultures, drawing on their firsthand familiarity with their regions' distinctive look and feel. Several regions were put on the national cinematic map through the work of their local directors."[15]

In these developments, Illinois and its largest city, Chicago, played a significant part. Writing in 1986, Gary Edgerton located Illinois as part of a cluster of "high profile states . . . boasting their own production centers,"[16] while in a survey of the industrial conditions surrounding US independent films conducted in the early '80s, Betsy McLane named Chicago as one of the key major cities where independent films have historically been centered.[17] The Hollywood majors, on the other hand, rarely used Chicago and other Illinois locations until the mid-'70s, with Edgerton citing only five major films and television shows shot in Illinois in the 1956–75 period.[18] However, in the next few years and until 1983, approximately 95 films were shot in the state, in the process creating 48,000 temporary jobs.[19] Despite sounding impressive, this figure also includes Hollywood-based productions only partially shot in the state (shooting Chicago exteriors with all interior scenes shot in a backlot in California). This was because even as late as 1979, the region had only sufficient infrastructure in place to support up to two film productions at one time.[20] However, by the end of the '80s, the Illinois Film Office, together with other organizations and filmmakers like John Hughes who decided to locate their productions in the state, increased the level of resources substantially.[21]

As is clear from this brief discussion, regional film production, both as a key contributor to an emerging American independent cinema and as an increasingly sustainable supplement to Hollywood production, was becoming important in the period when Hughes entered the film industry and quickly established himself as a screenwriter. By the mid-'80s, when he was branching out to producing and directing, Hughes had the potential to locate film production wholly in regional Illinois under the aegis of an independent production outfit with a first-look deal with a Hollywood major (category a] in Wyatt's article). This took place under the umbrella of Ned Tanen's Channel Productions and its deal with Universal, the studio with which Tanen had a long-established relationship at the highest level for the previous 13 years (1969–82).

JOHN HUGHES AS WRITER-DIRECTOR AND PRODUCER: EMBRACING INDEPENDENCE IN HOLLYWOOD VIA REGIONAL PRODUCTION

John Hughes broke into Hollywood through the screenwriting route. As Elissa Nelson states, Hughes's history provides no indication that he wanted to be a filmmaker.[22] Instead, focus tends to be placed on his writing skills that were pronounced from a young age and that reached the media industries in various ways, including through submitting jokes to comedians such as Rodney Dangerfield and Joan Rivers.[23] However, because Hughes had been married as early as 1970 (at the age of 20) and had a family to support after the mid-'70s, he settled into jobs with advertising companies in Chicago, while pursuing freelance writing assignments for magazines like *Playboy*.[24] Having risen quickly through the ranks as a strong copywriter, Hughes continued to pursue his comedic writing, and in 1977 he contacted *National Lampoon*, expressing his interest to write for the magazine. Launched in 1970, *National Lampoon* was enjoying tremendous popularity in the late '70s, and was branching out to other media industries via the production of *Animal House* (1978), a very commercially successful film that was based on stories published in the magazine.[25] Hughes had initially contributed to *National Lampoon*'s August 1978 issue with a parody of a teen magazine and a "then and now" visual narrative about how the concept of "cool" was being redefined,[26] before having two of his own stories published ("My Penis" in November 1978 and "My Vagina" in April 1979[27]). However, it was the publication of his short story "Vacation '58" in the September 1979 issue that proved a pivotal moment as Hughes made the decision to give up his job in advertising and work full time for the magazine, becoming one of its editors.[28] That particular story would become the basis for a *National Lampoon* film a few years later, which Hughes would also write.

His success with *National Lampoon*'s particular type of humor brought Hughes screenwriting assignments, including writing four teleplays for the *Delta House* television series (ABC, 1979) and the poorly executed and received sequel to *Animal House*, *Class Reunion* (1982). However, a year later, two of Hughes's screenplays turned into high-grossing Hollywood films: *Mr. Mom* (1983) and *National Lampoon's Vacation* (1983), his adaptation of "Vacation '58," which earned $64.8 million and $61.4 million at the North American theatrical box office, for Fox and Warner Bros. respectively. And even though that same year Hughes also had a big commercial failure with his screenplay for the swashbuckling adventure *Savage Islands* (1983), the remarkable success of the first two films (which landed respectively in the 9th and 11th places on the list of box office champions that year) was sufficient to announce the arrival of a major new voice in American cinema. Indeed, such was Hughes's emerging reputation that he was offered an opportunity to write and direct his own films before *Mr. Mom* and *National Lampoon's Vacation* were released and proved commercially successful.[29] An independent film production company called Channel Productions was successful in recruiting him, having been established by Ned Tanen following his departure from Universal after a ten-year period as head of production (1972–76) and president (1976–82); prior to that he had been an executive with a remit to produce films for young audiences for the same studio (1969–72).

Given his high-profile role at Universal in the previous 13 years (and before that for Universal's then-parent company MCA and its music subsidiary Uni Records), it was clear that Tanen's company was "independent" in that it was not owned by a major studio (category a] in Wyatt's taxonomy) and therefore it was free to develop and finance whatever kinds of films it wanted. However, if it wanted to have its films optioned and released by a global distributor of Universal's caliber, it was obvious that Channel Productions would have to develop, finance, and produce commercial films with clear selling points that would enable a distributor of Universal's size to invest in the increasingly substantial marketing and advertising costs for a national and international release. Indeed, by 1983, the year of the establishment of Channel Productions and the release of the two successful Hughes-scripted films, the average budget for a Hollywood film was $11.8 million, while the print and advertising costs in the US alone had reached $5.2 million.[30] In this respect, Channel Productions would have to secure substantial financing for its films (much more than the average Hollywood film budget at the time if it wanted to make blockbuster or star-driven films). To do this, Channel Productions would need to convince its backers that its films could return profits on their investment via Universal's global distribution, as well as convince Universal that its films could be competitive in the global marketplace.

The alternative would be to engage in production of low-budget genre films such as comedy, horror, or teen films. These types of films are marketed on their genre expectations and are often budgeted very modestly as they tend to use up-and-coming or even unknown actors, making the films a relatively low-risk investment bet. Given the size of salaries that major Hollywood stars started to command from the mid-'80s onwards, pushed by the excesses of an industry under the spell of conglomeration and its increasing focus on synergy-driven blockbusters and high-concept films, films in these genres represented the best option for a company such as Channel Productions that did not have a track record in film production. Furthermore, with youth audiences (12–24 years old) making up more than a third of all annual admissions (in 1984) and teen audiences (12–17 years old) revealed to be the most frequent moviegoers of all demographics,[31] it was clear that Channel had much more potential for success if it operated in that particular market. Staying with a *National Lampoon* example, *Animal House*, a film that depicted life in a college fraternity, was budgeted at $3 million and recorded $121 million at the American theatrical box office alone, which put it in third place for the year above expensive sequels such as *Jaws 2* (1978), and star-driven, high-concept titles such as *Every Which Way But Loose* (1978), and very close to high-budgeted blockbuster films such as *Superman* (1978), which was in second place that year.

Perhaps more importantly, the advent of the next decade saw this trend intensifying with a number of films explicitly targeting the teen audience that achieved often great box office success while costing very little to produce. Table 3.1 contains the five biggest commercial successes of "youth" films (targeting specifically children, teens, and young adults), with their place in the annual charts in parenthesis.

Besides not having a track record, Channel Productions also did not have any talent involved in making its films because it was led by a former executive and not a filmmaker. With most major talent affiliated through production pacts with the major studios, it was clear that Channel would need to identify new talent and bring it into the company fold with an attractive production

Table 3.1 Top five films targeting explicitly youth (children, teen and young adult) audiences, 1980–83 with their place in the annual charts in parenthesis.

1980	1981	1982	1983
The Blue Lagoon (9)	*Taps* (16)	*Porky's* (5)	*Flashdance* (3)
Friday the 13th (18)	*The Great Muppet Caper* (21)	*Annie* (10)	*WarGames* (5)
Little Darlings (20)	*Endless Love* (22)	*The Dark Crystal* (16)	*Risky Business* (10)
Fame (32)	*An American Werewolf in London* (23)	*Friday the 13th II* (21)	*National Lampoon's Vacation* (11)
Herbie Goes Bananas (40)	*Private Lessons* (28)	*Fast Times at Ridgemont High* (29)	*Porky's II* (21)

deal. This was an area in which Ned Tanen had immense experience since he was known in Hollywood for his ability to work with young filmmakers and to give opportunities to talent who had often been untested in major Hollywood productions.[32] Such a reputation goes back to Tanen's first position at Universal as the head of a unit created in 1969 to make low-budget films in the mold of *The Graduate* (1967) and *Easy Rider* (1969), the critical and commercial successes of which had taken the industry by surprise. These films were intended to cost under $1 million each and would involve young filmmakers who would have the creative freedom to make their films the ways they wanted.

True to these principles, Tanen's unit at Universal became responsible for such films as *Diary of a Mad Housewife* (1970), *Taking Off* (1971), *The Last Movie* (1971), *The Hired Hand* (1971), *Two-Lane Blacktop* (1971), *Minnie and Moskowitz* (1971), and *Silent Running* (1972).[33] With filmmakers such as Miloš Forman, Dennis Hopper, Peter Fonda, and Monte Hellman getting their first opportunity to direct for a major studio, it was clear that the credit Tanen received was well deserved. And even if none of these films became the breakthrough hit Universal was hoping for, Tanen was vindicated when, as Universal's production chief in 1973, he agreed to a $750,000 investment in George Lucas's second film, *American Graffiti*, which returned $55.3 million in domestic rentals.[34] Besides demonstrating that sticking with young talent could have enormous financial benefits, *American Graffiti* confirmed Tanen's belief that films focused squarely on teenagers and their experiences could become runaway hits for little investment. Tanen continued to support such films even after he became president of Universal in 1976. Despite concentrating primarily on the development of star-driven, blockbuster films, both *Animal House* and Amy Heckerling's lucrative debut *Fast Times at Ridgemont High* (1982) were greenlit during his tenure.

As soon as Tanen hired development executive/producer Michelle Manning to bring projects to Channel Productions, the latter suggested that they approach Hughes, whose screenwriting jobs for *Mr. Mom* and *National Lampoon's Vacation* were bringing him increased industry attention.[35] However, following reported clashes between Hughes and the *Vacation* director (Harold Ramis) and star (Chevy Chase),[36] Hughes decided to pitch his next screenplay with the stipulation that he would be attached as director in order to maintain control of his project, a proposition that major studios were not ready to accept.[37] At that time (late 1982–early 1983) Hughes was developing a film with A&M, an independent record label that was branching out to film production. Under the working title *Detention*, this was an early effort to produce what became *The Breakfast Club*.[38] However, once he was approached by Channel, the script Hughes submitted was for *Sixteen Candles*, which he had written after *Detention*, and on the strength of which Channel made a deal with Hughes.[39] Furthermore, understanding the potential of *Detention*, Tanen approached A&M (the executives of which he knew from his tenure in Uni Records) with a view to partner on the production of the film, which he suggested they do after *Sixteen Candles*, a more formulaic and commercially promising property. That way, Hughes would be more established after *Candles*, and should it be successful at the box office, it would be easier for Tanen to pitch *Detention* to a studio than if Hughes was a first-time director.[40]

With the main ingredients of the package in place, including Hughes as writer-director, Tanen approached Universal for a distribution deal for *Sixteen Candles*. Having budgeted the film at $8 million (though other sources bring this figure to a substantially lower $6.5 million),[41] and with an easily marketable storyline about a girl whose family forgets her sixteenth birthday because they are occupied with her older sister's wedding, Universal did not have a problem with a first-time film director. This was especially due to Tanen himself assuming the role of executive producer, with Michelle Manning also getting an associate producer credit, along with Hilton A. Green, a long-time producer, assistant director, and production manager who took on the main producer credit. To this key above-the-line personnel, Tanen added several other extremely experienced practitioners, including a director of cinematography (Bobby Byrne) with credits in such successful films as *Smokey and the Bandit* (1977) and *Blue Collar* (1978), an editor (Edward Warschilka) who apprenticed under Hal Ashby and had over a dozen credits before Hughes's film, and a similarly experienced production designer (John W. Corso). Tanen also secured the services of Jimmy Iovine, a major music producer who at the same time was also overseeing the soundtrack of Universal's key 1984 high-concept film *Streets of Fire*.

What becomes clear then is that the novice Hughes embarked on his first film as a writer-director surrounded by very experienced craftspeople who were able to support his filmmaking approach and materialize his vision on screen. Importantly, these craftspeople were also steeped in Hollywood filmmaking tradition and therefore were able to ensure that the final product would be sufficiently commercial so as not to jeopardize the film's box office potential. For instance, reports suggest that right from his very early films as a director in the mid-'80s, Hughes shot double the amount of film from the industry standard, which would allow him "to experiment with different ideas and improvisations . . . in the editing room."[42] While such a practice is acceptable for established auteurs, at that time it was "unheard of for a low-budget teen picture."[43] It also explains why Tanen insisted on securing experienced editors, with legendary editor Dede Allen working with Hughes on *The Breakfast Club*. Furthermore, Molly Ringwald was quoted saying that for *The Breakfast Club*, Hughes would "let the camera roll for 20 minutes," asking actors to improvise in order to get the essence of a scene.[44] As Susannah Gora suggests, Hughes wanted to "try different versions of scenes" while benefiting from the input of the young actors who performed them.[45] All these practices do not easily reconcile with efficient genre film production, which rarely shows evidence of artistic ambitions.

To these practices, one should also add Hughes's branching out from writing to directing (and producing in *The Breakfast Club*) that also are unusual in studio financed low-budget films. Besides additional remuneration, more often than not hyphenate filmmaking has its origins in individuals' efforts to maintain creative control, especially in situations where financing and distribution are provided by a major studio. But while Hollywood in the '80s was willing to accept hyphenates when they were established players who wanted control to produce strongly commercial high-concept films (such as Sylvester Stallone's writer-director-actor credit in *Rocky IV* [1985]), hyphenate filmmaking became the trademark of filmmakers associated with the dominant independent discourse. This is because such filmmakers as John Sayles, Jim Jarmusch, and Wayne Wang often assumed several major production roles to cut costs, and because they were responsible for most aspects of their films. In this respect, Hughes's branching out to directing and then producing in the low-budget teen film genre was unusual and showed that he was more akin to an independent filmmaker rather than a studio player. This is especially true since Hughes famously accepted payment at scale (a minimum fee as contractually negotiated between Hollywood studios and the various Guilds) in order to have complete creative control over *The Breakfast Club*, including casting, for a film that was a hard sell given its limited action and emphasis on character.[46]

One could argue then that Hughes used his hyphenate status to expand gradually his control over his projects, which would also enable him to use practices not condoned by the industry for the types of films he was working on, and in the process reworked a genre and created an authorial style. Following his triple credit in *The Breakfast Club*, Hughes was ready to bring this practice to its logical conclusion through establishing Hughes Entertainment, his own independent production company based in Chicago, in 1987. In doing so, he first left behind a $30 million three-picture deal that Channel had negotiated with Universal,[47] and later stopped producing films directly for Paramount when Tanen surprisingly left Channel to become that studio's president in 1985. At that time, Tanen immediately recruited Hughes Entertainment to make films for the studio.

As this account suggests, the "independence" that Channel Productions was able to provide Hughes with was of a very particular kind: so long as Hughes was able to direct his screenplays for the low budgets agreed, he would have the freedom to use his own practices, no matter how uncommon for the type of production he worked on, and he would have the support to make his films according to his own vision. This vision entailed experimentation with the genre's conventions and the inclusion of particular stylistic and narrative choices that would be seen as part of Hughes's authorial signature. Such an articulation of independence would also provide Channel's product with a distinct brand identity and give the distributor (Universal) product differentiation in an increasingly congested marketplace for youth films. This is because the trend of relatively low-budget teen films succeeding at the box office was by that time in full force, with 1984 becoming a banner year for the genre as seven films explicitly targeting the youth demographic ended up among the top 20 domestic box office champions for the year: *Gremlins* (4th), *The Karate Kid* (5th), *Footloose* (7th), *Purple Rain* (11th), *Revenge of the Nerds* (16th), *Breakin'* (18th), and *Red Dawn* (20th). With Paramount leading the way with its high-concept *Karate Kid* and *Footloose*, Warner Bros. catering to both horror and music fans with *Gremlins* and *Purple Rain*, Fox covering the frat house/gross-out comedy niche with *Revenge of the Nerds*, Cannon exploiting the breakdancing phenomenon with *Breakin'*, and MGM/UA hybridizing the teen film in the action/adventure genre under John Milius's authorship of *Red Dawn*, Universal did not seem to have too many alternatives.

However, a look at its 1984 releases reveals that Universal actually invested in a number of films targeting the youth demographic: *The Last Starfighter*, a teen film hybridized with science fiction (Universal's 4th most successful release, 31st in annual domestic box office total); *Firestarter*, a horror film based on a Stephen King story about a young girl (6th and 61st); *Hard to Hold*, a music drama starring teen pop star Rick Springfield (9th and 75th); *The Wild Life*, a film in the spirit of *Fast Times at Ridgemont High* (10th and 76th); and of course *Streets of Fire*, the company's major high-concept film that nonetheless proved a huge financial and critical failure (13th and 90th). Hughes's female teen-oriented *Sixteen Candles*, then, completed a very comprehensive package of youth films for Universal's release slate. And given the increasing visibility and success of the genre and its subgenres at the box office, the conditions were ripe for a filmmaker like Hughes to experiment with its rules and conventions under the aegis of an independent production company.

It is at this point that Hughes's relocation to Illinois for the production of *Sixteen Candles* becomes important as a number of stylistic choices he made during the production remove the film from pillars of the genre as well as from Hollywood's emphasis on high-concept, style-led, synergy-driven approaches to filmmaking. As I demonstrate below, Hughes's stylistic choices do not exactly make the film a niche proposition in the way dominant discourses defined independence at that time, nor imbue it with a strong regional authenticity that was also associated with dominant discourses of independence. They do, however, give *Sixteen Candles* a sensibility that make it stand out from other similar films at the time. Critics agreed, pointing to the film's idiosyncrasies and its ability to represent teens better than other films, despite its perceived lack of realism. For instance, David Denby called the film "an odd mixture of brutality and tenderness" that "understands kids better than most movies,"[48] while Owen Gleiberman saw it as "a youth movie hybrid" that combines the "black humor of *National Lampoon*" with "jittery adolescent anxieties."[49]

Hughes's experimentation with generic conventions do not involve a deconstruction or even a questioning of their key expectations, but rather a playful mixture of tropes, tones, and registers that result in a novel "syntax" for a genre whose semantic blocks remain familiar and stable.[50] This can be seen clearly in a number of scenes, such as when Samantha (Molly Ringwald) accepts her father's apology for forgetting her birthday, which oscillates between the awkward and the sentimental, or more so in the wide gamut of music choices across scenes. We hear Brahms' *Hungarian Dance No. 5* when Samantha and her friends enter the school bus for the first time; Nino Rota's theme from *The Godfather* (1972) accompanies her sister's Italian-American in-laws' visit; Frank Sinatra's "New York, New York" plays when Jake (Michael Schoeffling) and Ted (Anthony Michael Hall) improbably drink martinis together at the end of the party; plus there are popular hits of the era by David Bowie, Spandau Ballet, Wham! and Billy Idol. This playfulness can also be found in scenes where narrative direction gives way almost completely to a gag (as in the scene where two boys talk while doing pull-ups on a high bar only for the camera to reveal that their feet are firmly on the ground and therefore they are not really exercising) or in scenes not integrated in the narrative and played for laughs (all the scenes with Joan Cusack's character whose neck brace prevents her from doing the simplest things like drinking water from a fountain).

Figure 3.1 Generic playfulness and visual gags: not exercising.

Hughes's playful approach to the genre is also reinforced by the ways in which he shifts tone (and genre expectations) through narrational choices that privilege different perspectives. As Holly Chard argues, the film mixes a variety of generic elements as well as different tones and styles via changes in focalization as part of its narrative strategy.[51] For instance, the narrative is led firmly by Samantha's effort to get to grips with her family forgetting her birthday while also navigating life at school, which involves the sexual advances of geeky Ted and a potential romance with school hunk Jake. However, at points the film changes perspectives, often unexpectedly, giving the spectator the viewpoints of Ted and Jake as well as using optical point-of-view shifts, including a radical one that legitimates a female nudity scene, which becomes motivated by a female gaze.[52] For Chard, this technique manages to keep intact the film's main identity as a female teen-oriented narrative but without "purging [it] completely of elements of the sex comedies that had been popular with a sizeable teenage audience" at the time.[53] On the other hand, this interesting mixture of conventions, perspectives, and tonal approaches from the wide variety of teen cinema makes *Sixteen Candles* come across as a fresh take on a genre that thrives on convention, a point also supported by Timothy Shary, who considers in particular the mixture of perspectives from teen life a key distinction of Hughes's teen movies.[54]

Finally, Hughes's distinct approach to generic expectations is also emphasized by his choices with casting and characterization, which, as I noted above, were extremely important in his effort to maintain control of his work. For the three leading roles, Hughes opted for two actors (Michael Schoeffling and Anthony Michael Hall) with few credits before this film and the more experienced child-actor Molly Ringwald, so he was able to dispense with expectations that come part and parcel with established teen stars and their personas. A very interesting outcome of this practice is the ensuing characterization that often breaks with established genre conventions of the time and gives Hughes and his films another key distinction. For instance, Chard highlights the blandness and lack of personality in the representation of Jake, the romantic lead and point of desire for the heroine and female audiences alike. Despite his good looks and the fact that he is established from the start as Samantha's romantic match, Jake spends the entire narrative "being the embodiment of physical and emotional restraint."[55] His clothes are dull and conservative and his interactions with everyone in the film are underwhelming for such an archetypal teen film character. Hughes admitted that this was a conscious choice and that he "had to fight pretty hard for [such a representation]" as the producers and distributor did not think "he had enough life to him."[56] On the other hand, such a characterization made Jake the exact opposite of hyperkinetic geek Ted, which helped to distinguish clearly between archetypal teen characters and to make their drinking scene together even more improbable

Figure 3.2 A humanized geek! John Hughes gives a much-maligned teen archetype full characterization.

and unexpected. However, since this representation made it into the film, it is evident that Hughes (with Tanen's support) prevailed, which suggests that his hyphenate role had given him enough clout to fend off interference and avoid compromise.

Equally surprising was the characterization of Ted, who in another archetypal teen film role (the geek), emerges as a full-fledged character, breaking the mold of caricature from which he starts his narrative trajectory. In one of the film's celebrated scenes, Ted and Samantha bond in the remains of an old car in the school garage, which allows him to be represented in a humanized manner. As a matter of fact, Ted receives such strong attention as a rounded character that he is even allowed narrational agency beyond the diegesis when on one occasion he breaks the fourth wall and addresses the spectator in a self-congratulatory mode. Add to the mix the casting of a red-haired, freckle-faced teenager for the female lead (Ringwald was 16 during the film's shooting), a girl substantially removed from the image of the ideal teen beauty that had been reinforced by teen films over the previous years (with Brooke Shields, Phoebe Cates, and Lori Singer coming much closer to the ideal of—White—teen beauty), and it is evident that *Sixteen Candles* was a teen film that was doing things differently. In this sense, one could argue that Hughes's location of the film's production away from Hollywood and the direct purview of Universal's executives enabled him to make these choices (or to prevail in battles about their acceptance), especially as he also felt empowered by his hyphenate status under the protective shield of Channel Productions and Ned Tanen.

Figure 3.3 Opposite teen archetypes in harmony: the restrained hunk and the hyperkinetic geek.

Equally important, the production location in Illinois allowed Hughes to make some decisions at a more local level that contributed to the freshness of the film. For instance, he selected a number of students from his former Glenbrook North high school as extras.[57] Although these young Illinois natives do not provide the film with any sense of regional authenticity, they nonetheless contribute to the film's "visual" and "cultural" accuracy, which, according to Lev, are key indicators of regional cinema.[58] From the clothes, hair, and make-up styles they wear to the ways they become part of the film's setting, they provide authenticity in a film that borrows eclectically from a variety of styles and genres, while also counter-balancing the less realistic (and some downright derogatory) representations. Similarly, the Illinois locations that feature prominently throughout the film do not so much telegraph a particular region as they represent affluent suburban America, which (White) young people around the country could identify with and aspire to, an aspect that Hollywood studio productions often try to recreate with broad strokes and little attention to detail. In this respect, regionalism and its required visual and cultural accuracy are placed here at the service of representing the cultures and subcultures of teenagers of the time. It is not surprising then that *Sixteen Candles* was appreciated by a sizable audience that made the film a modest financial success. Grossing $23.6 million, the film placed 44th for the year's domestic box office and 5th among all Universal releases that year. It confirmed that there was space for innovative teen genre filmmaking in an increasingly corporate American cinema in the 1980s.

CONCLUSION

John Hughes had a very particular place in American cinema defined by a love-hate relationship with the Hollywood studios, the only distributing companies he worked with throughout his career. Driven by a strong impulse to control his work, Hughes set out to be as independent a filmmaker in Hollywood as he could. At a time when independence was becoming increasingly institutionalized and practiced within an abundance of industrial and institutional arrangements, Hughes was able to exploit particular developments in the film industry and achieve his objective almost from the start of his career. This was especially true after signing with independent production company Channel Productions, when he succeeded in branching out to directing and producing while also continuing to write his own screenplays. Hyphenate filmmaking gave Hughes increasing control over his productions, while also enabling him to produce his films through practices that were rarely associated with the then disreputable genre of the low-budget teen film. Casting against the grain (including giving the roles of teenagers to actual teenagers), encouraging improvisation in performance, testing different versions of scripted scenes, experimenting with editing—all became practices that came to underpin his work in the teen film genre.

These practices produced teen films that mixed visual styles, narrative tropes, tonal approaches, and genre conventions in eclectic and creative ways. They also came to constitute the backbone for the articulation of a style that signaled a distinct authorial signature in a genre not known for authorship, visual style, or for any artistic pretensions. The development of this style was greatly assisted by an early decision to shoot his films in his native Illinois, away from Hollywood. In doing this, Hughes exploited other important developments in the American film industry at the time that revolved around the increasing significance and visibility of regional film production. Being away from Hollywood under the aegis of an independent production outfit enabled Hughes to put his filmmaking practices to work with less interference while also using local services and resources to make his films according to his very particular vision. Although this vision did not provide his films with any sort of regional authenticity and accuracy, it did give his films a particular sensibility that made them stand out from other teen films of the time.

The success of *Sixteen Candles,* and especially of *The Breakfast Club* that followed a year later, proved that in the increasingly corporatized Hollywood of the 1980s it was still possible for certain filmmakers to make personal, idiosyncratic films in genres that rarely allowed it. Industrial and institutional factors aligned in particular ways to create conditions that certain talented individuals managed to exploit. Striking a delicate balance between mainstream and independent cinema, regional production and the demands of an industry run by Hollywood, genre conventions and the establishment of an authorial signature, these filmmakers proved that they could not only break into the industry but also that they could become major players in it. John Hughes is arguably one of the best such examples, and deserves fully both the title of "king of teen comedy"[59] and "most prolific independent filmmaker."

NOTES

1. Unless stated otherwise, all box office figures are for the North American theatrical box office and were obtained from BoxOfficeMojo.com. The figures for 1986 are available at https://www.boxofficemojo.com/yearly/chart/?yr=1986&p=.htm. Of course, the domestic theatrical box office figures are only just one indicator to gauge Hughes's films' success or failure. Given their popularity with youth audiences and the boom years of home video in the 1980s, his films may have very well been more commercially successful if one adds revenues from ancillary markets. But as such figures are often impossible to obtain, this chapter will use domestic (North American) box office figures as its guide.
2. Elissa Nelson, *The Breakfast Club: John Hughes, Hollywood and the Golden Age of the Teen Film* (London: Routledge, 2019), 96.
3. Justin Wyatt, "Independents, Packaging and Inflationary Pressure in 1980s Hollywood," in *A New Pot of Gold: Hollywood Under the Electronic Rainbow 1980–1989* by Stephen Prince (Berkeley: University of California Press, 2002), 142–59.
4. Wyatt, 142–3.
5. Yannis Tzioumakis, "From Independent to Indie: The Independent Feature Project and the Complex Relationship between American Independent Cinema and Hollywood in the 1980s," in *A Companion to American Indie Film*, ed. Geoff King (Oxford: Wiley Blackwell, 2017), 242, 243, 250.
6. Yannis Tzioumakis, "'Indie Doc': Documentary Film and American 'Independent', 'Indie' and 'Indiewood' Filmmaking," *Studies in Documentary Film*, 10, no. 2, 1–21.
7. Bill Carter, "Him Alone," *New York Times*, August 4, 1991, https://www.nytimes.com/1991/08/04/magazine/him-alone.html; Ryan Gilbey, "John Hughes: Director, Screenwriter and Producer Who Was One of the Most Prolific Independent Film Makers in Hollywood History," *The Guardian*, August 7, 2009, https://www.theguardian.com/film/2009/aug/07/john-hughes-film-director-dies1.
8. Gary Edgerton, "The Film Bureau Phenomenon in America and Its Relationship to Independent Filmmaking," *Journal of Film and Video*, 38, no. 1 (1986), 40–7.
9. Camille Johnson-Yale, *Runaway Production: A History of Hollywood's Outsourcing Debate* (Lanham, KY: Lexington Books, 2017), 92.
10. Edgerton, 41.
11. Peter Lev, "Regional Cinema and the Films of Texas," *Journal of Film and Video*, 38, no. 1 (1986), 60.
12. Johnson-Yale, 91.
13. Lev, 60.
14. Tzioumakis, 7.
15. Emanuel Levy, *Cinema of Outsiders: The Rise of American Independent Film* (New York: New York University Press, 1999), 154.
16. Edgerton, 41.
17. Betsy McLane, "Domestic Theatrical & Semi-Theatrical Distribution and Exhibition of American Independent Feature Films: A Survey in 1983," *Journal of University Film and Video Association*, 35, no. 2 (1983), 21.

18. Edgerton, 44.
19. Edgerton, 44.
20. Dennis Rodkin, "John Hughes: A True Friend of Chicago," *The Hollywood Reporter ShoWest Producer of the Year Special Report* (1991), S20.
21. Rodkin, S20.
22. Nelson, 23.
23. Nelson, 23.
24. Ellie Stein, "John Hughes: How National Lampoon led to 'The Breakfast Club' and 'Ferris Bueller'," *Salon*, June 24, 2013, https://www.salon.com/2013/06/24/john_hughes_how_national_lampoon_led_to_the_breakfast_club_and_ferris_bueller/.
25. This had been preceded by the less successful *National Lampoon Radio Hour* in 1973–74.
26. A copy of the magazine with details of Hughes's contribution is available at: http://www.luckyfrogfarms.com/cook/NL/1970's/1978/1978_08.pdf.
27. http://www.tgfa.org/fiction/MyPenis.htm and http://www.tgfa.org/fiction/MyVagina.htm.
28. Stein.
29. Susannah Gora, *You Couldn't Ignore Me If You Tried: The Brat Pack, John Hughes and Their Impact on a Generation* (New York: Crown Publishers, 2010), 24.
30. Velvet Light Trap, "The 1980s: A Reference Guide to Motion Pictures, Television, VCR, and Cable," *Velvet Light Trap*, no. 27 (1991), 79, 80.
31. Nelson, 18.
32. Dennis McLellan, "Ned Tanen dies at 77; Former President of Universal, Paramount," *Los Angeles Times*, January 8, 2009, http://articles.latimes.com/2009/jan/08/local/me-tanen8.
33. Peter Biskind, *Easy Riders, Raging Bulls: How the Sex-Drugs-and-Rock-'N'-Roll Generation Saved Hollywood* (New York: Bloomsbury, 1998), 126.
34. David A. Cook, *Lost Illusions: American Cinema in the Shadow of Watergate and Vietnam, 1970–1979* (Berkeley: University of California Press, 2002), 499.
35. Kirk Honeycutt, *John Hughes: A Life in the Film* (New York: Race Point 2015), 3.
36. Stein.
37. Honeycutt, 3.
38. Nelson, 26.
39. Honeycutt, 2.
40. Nelson, 26–7.
41. Spence, for instance, cites $8 million (Sharon Lloyd Spence, "Chicago Screenwriter Makes His Directorial Debut," *Back Stage*, August 12, 1983, 54), while Barth suggests it was $6.5 million (Jack Barth, "John Hughes: On Geeks Bearing Gifts," *Film Comment* [June 1984], https://www.facebook.com/notes/john-hughes/film-comment-june-1984-john-hughes-on-geeks-bearing-gifts/109931123952/).
42. Andrea King, "John Hughes: An Exclusive on the Ordinary," *The Hollywood Reporter ShoWest Producer of the Year Special Report* (1991), S16.
43. David Kamp, "Sweet Bard of Youth," *Vanity Fair* (March 2010), https://www.vanityfair.com/news/2010/03/john-hughes-201003.
44. Ringwald as quoted in King, S38.
45. Gora, 35.
46. Nelson, 24.
47. Joshua Greenberg, "Universal Signs Hughes to 3-Year Pact," *Variety*, May 2, 1984, 19.
48. David Denby, "Happy Birthday, Sweet Sixteen," *New York*, May 1984, 96.
49. Owen Gleiberman, "Bittersweet Sixteen: Burning the Candles at Both Ends," *Boston Phoenix*, May 8, 1984, C4.

50. This is a point that Betty Kaklamanidou also makes with reference to the teen film *Easy A* as, following Rick Altman's work, she accounts for the playful and knowing way it borrows from key texts in the genre: Betty Kaklamanidou, *Easy A* (London: Routledge, 2018), 18.
51. Holly Chard, "Mainstream Maverick? John Hughes and New Hollywood Cinema," unpublished PhD dissertation, University of Sussex, 2014, 194.
52. Chard, 195.
53. Chard, 193.
54. Timothy Shary, *Teen Movies: American Youth on Screen* (New York: Wallflower, 2005), 67.
55. Chard, 197.
56. Chard, 198.
57. Rodkin, S54.
58. Lev, 61.
59. Kamp.

CHAPTER 4

Ferris Bueller vs. *Parker Lewis*: "Adapting" *Ferris Bueller's Day Off* for Television

Stephen Tropiano

There is an unexpected moment in the first scene of the pilot episode of *Ferris Bueller*, the 1990 NBC television situation comedy based on writer-director John Hughes's 1986 hit film *Ferris Bueller's Day Off* starring Matthew Broderick.[1] The episode opens on Ferris, played by Charlie Schlatter, waking up in his bedroom on the first day of school. Breaking the fourth wall, Ferris looks into the camera and introduces himself to the audience: "'Life is one damn thing after another,' Mark Twain said that after he changed his name. I'm Ferris Bueller and I've never changed mine. Once they put me up on the big screen it was out of the question. But come on—"

He goes into his closet and takes out a life-sized, stand-up cardboard cutout of Matthew Broderick as Ferris Bueller.

"Matthew Broderick as *me*?" Ferris asks, "No way. He's too white bread. Too two-dimensional."

He then pulls out a chainsaw and proceeds to decapitate Broderick.

"This is television," Ferris explains, "*This is real*."

This self-referential, postmodern opening is unexpected because it involves Ferris Bueller, a fictional television character, informing viewers that *Ferris Bueller's Day Off*, a fictional film, is based on *his* life, and that Matthew Broderick, the actor who played him in the film, was miscast. He then makes the startling claim that television, unlike cinema, is real.

The same point is made at the start of the second episode ("Behind Every Dirtbag") as a testament to the cult status the film had achieved four years after its release. The scene begins with footage of First Lady Barbara Bush delivering the 1990 commencement address at Wellesley College. In her speech, she dispenses some advice to the graduating class that includes *Ferris Bueller's Day Off*'s most often quoted line: "Find the joy in life, because as Ferris Bueller said on his day off, 'Life moves pretty fast. If you don't stop and look around once in a while, you're gonna miss it.'"[2]

The camera then pulls out to reveal Ferris Bueller watching the First Lady on television. He turns to the camera and says, "I don't remember saying that. But if it's on TV, it must be true."

In addition to a television character breaking the fourth wall, it's highly unusual for a television series to openly acknowledge the film on which it is based. As series creator and executive producer John Masius explains, the opening scene of the pilot was designed to send an immediate message to the fans of the film who were presumably tuning in: "People have the expectation of getting the movie on the small screen. We're telling them that we're going to give them something different."[3] Masius believed the problem with television series based on films is "they don't try to distance themselves, or they can't because there isn't a lot of opportunity."[4] Fortunately, he felt this was not the case with *Ferris Bueller's Day Off*: "John Hughes left a lot of room for a television series, because what he did was to leave all those 'days on.' He never sent Ferris to school, which is where he operates best."[5]

It is highly unlikely John Hughes was thinking about television when he wrote and directed *Ferris Bueller's Day Off*. Throughout his career the prolific filmmaker distanced himself from television projects based on his work. Hughes was not involved in the creation and production of TV's *Ferris Bueller*, nor did he participate in the making of other television series based on his screenplays (an animated version of *Beethoven* [1994–95] and a failed pilot for *Mr. Mom* [1983]) and films he wrote and directed (*Uncle Buck* [1990–91] and *Weird Science* [1994–98]).[6] Ironically, Hughes's writing career began in television as a staff writer on a series based on a film: *Delta House* (1979), the short-lived ABC comedy based on the hit film *National Lampoon's Animal House* (1978). In addition, Hughes created and wrote the original pilot for a military sitcom entitled *At Ease* (1983). The show's premise—a pair of pranksters wreak havoc in the US Army—is strikingly similar to the plot of the 1981 box office hit *Stripes*, starring Bill Murray and Harold Ramis as a pair of unsuitable army recruits.

Fans of *Ferris Bueller's Day Off* undoubtedly tuned in to the pilot episode, which NBC aired one week before the official start of the 1990–91 television season in a coveted time slot on the network's Thursday night schedule: 8:30 p.m., between reruns of NBC's highest rated comedies, *The Cosby Show* (1984–92) and *Cheers* (1982–93). The pilot of *Ferris Bueller* was watched by an estimated 13.2 million households and ranked 6th in the Nielsen weekly ratings, which was good news for both the series and the network.[7] Unfortunately, when *Ferris Bueller* moved to its permanent day and time (Mondays at 8:30 p.m.), the audience did not follow. The comedy was scheduled after another new youth-oriented NBC situation comedy, *The Fresh Prince of Bel-Air* (1990–96), starring Will Smith as a teenager from the streets of Philadelphia sent to live with his aunt and uncle in upscale Bel-Air, California. *Ferris Bueller*, *The Fresh Prince of Bel-Air*, and a third series, *Hull High* (1990), a high school drama/musical hybrid that capitalized on the hip-hop music craze, were all part of the network's narrowcasting strategy to attract the "MTV generation" with "light-hearted" shows about high school that didn't preach or condescend to their young audience.[8]

The Fresh Prince of Bel-Air, which would run for six seasons, initially struggled a bit in the ratings, though by the fifth episode (October 8, 1990), *Fresh Prince* ranked 29th while *Ferris Bueller* ranked 45th in the weekly ratings.[9] *Bueller*'s ratings did not improve, and by late October it ranked 50th out of the 90 prime-time series on the four networks (ABC, CBS, NBC, and Fox) in the Nielsen season averages.[10] By mid-December, *Ferris Bueller* was cancelled.[11] *Hull High* fared even worse—it was the first casualty of NBC's 1990–91 season.[12] If it was any consolation, *Ferris Bueller* was the third most-watched show for viewers aged 12–17 for the 1990–91 season (*Fresh Prince* ranked 1st).[13]

Meanwhile, over at the Fox Network, another new half-hour situation comedy, *Parker Lewis Can't Lose* (1990–93), was added to the network's Sunday night comedy lineup. Like Ferris Bueller, Parker Lewis (Corin Nemec) is an affable high school student whose mission in life is to maintain his cool demeanor as he gets himself in and out of trouble. In addition to serving as the show's narrator, many of the characters in Parker Lewis's universe—his clueless parents, annoying little sister, devoted best friend, pretty girlfriend, and scheming high school principal—bear a close resemblance to the characters in *Ferris Bueller*. The obvious similarities between *Ferris Bueller* and *Parker Lewis Can't Lose* sparked a high school rivalry between the two situation comedies fueled by the television critics, who generally deemed *Parker Lewis*, to quote one critic, "the comedy *Ferris Bueller* wants to be—and isn't."[14]

To what can we attribute the success of an imitation of *Ferris Bueller's Day Off* over a generally faithful television adaptation of the original? Four years after the film's success at the box office, why was *Parker Lewis* more appealing to critics and culturally relevant to teenagers than a small-screen version of *Ferris Bueller*? The answers lie in a three-way critical comparative analysis of John Hughes's *Ferris Bueller's Day Off*, the television series *Ferris Bueller*, and *Parker Lewis Can't Lose* in terms of their respective title characters, visual style, and treatment of a recurring theme in John Hughes's oeuvre: teenage rebellion against adult authority.

FERRIS BUELLER'S DAY OFF (1986) VS. *FERRIS BUELLER* (1990–91)

While most television series based on a popular film have been critical and ratings failures, some motion pictures have survived the transition from the big screen to the small screen: *Buffy the Vampire Slayer* (1992/TV, 1997–03), *Fargo* (1996/TV, 2014–present), *Friday Night Lights* (2004/TV, 2006–11); *M*A*S*H* (1970/TV, 1972–83), and most recently, *Westworld* (1972/TV, 2016–present). The critical and ratings success of these and other titles did not necessarily depend on the shows' producers remaining faithful to the films. In fact, the series' creators understood changes needed to be made—both major and minor—to the shows' premises, characters, settings, and attitudes in order to adapt a two-hour feature film into an hour or half-hour weekly television series that could potentially run for five or more seasons.

Unfortunately, in most instances, the creative energy, time, and money poured into adapting a feature film for the small screen doesn't pay off. This was the case during the 1990–91 season when four new comedies based on recent box office hits debuted and were cancelled after a relatively short run due to low ratings: ABC's *Baby Talk*, based on *Look Who's Talking* (1989); *Parenthood*, a one-hour comedy/drama based on the 1989 comedy directed by Ron Howard; *Uncle Buck*, based on John Hughes's 1989 comedy of the same title; and *Ferris Bueller*. In addition, the recent list of causalities also included two series based on films that debuted the spring of 1990: *Bagdad Café* (1990) and *Working Girl* (1990), starring newcomer Sandra Bullock.

In most instances, the films' "above the line" talent—directors, producers, writers, and actors—were not directly involved in the television series, though screenwriters Babaloo Mandel and Lowell Ganz wrote the pilot to *Parenthood* and director Ron Howard's production company, Imagine Television, produced the series. At the time, CBS reportedly also had a television version of the 1988 comedy *Big* in the works, and ABC was developing two series, one based on the Blaxploitation parody *I'm Gonna Git You Sucka* (1988), and the other derived from the 1989 courtroom drama *True Believer* (1989) starring James Woods. *Big* and *I'm Gonna Git You Sucka* never found a home on their respective networks' prime-time schedules, though six episodes of *True Believer*, under the title *Eddie Dodd*, aired in the spring of 1991.

The creative advantage of turning a hit film into a television series can also be a major liability. As with adapting bestsellers into films or adding another title to a movie franchise, a television series based on a film has a built-in audience. At the same time, the audience has high expectations, particularly in regards to casting, as there is naturally some resistance to recasting another actor in an iconic role like Ferris Bueller. Peter Tortorici, former senior vice president of programming for CBS, contends television series based on films are a "high-risk venture" and a "double-edged sword" because audiences have expectations "about a look and a production quality, done on an incredibly high budget . . . [and] about a certain actor in a role. It's hard for a weekly series to measure up to all that."[5]

The failure of the television versions of *Ferris Bueller* and *Uncle Buck* may have surprised some television executives. On paper, the films on which they are based may have seemed television-ready without fully considering that they were star vehicles for the actors in the title roles. The film *Uncle Buck* is a fish-out-of-water comedy about an uncle (John Candy) whose bad habits and boorish behavior make him a less-than-suitable babysitter for his brother's three children when their parents are away from home.[16] In the CBS series, Uncle Buck, as played by stand-up comedian Kevin Meaney, becomes the legal guardian of his two nieces and nephew when their parents are killed in a car accident. When asked about the show's failure, Tortorici admitted, "Kevin Meaney did a great job, but John Candy and John Hughes are a tough act to follow."[17]

Hughes, who rarely gave interviews, remained relatively quiet about the numerous television series based on his films. His disapproval of *Uncle Buck* was revealed posthumously in a statement released in October of 2014, six years after his death, signed by the families of Hughes and *Uncle Buck* star John Candy in response to Universal Television's announcement that a second series based on *Uncle Buck* was in the works: "Recalling that the director was displeased with the first *Uncle Buck* TV show effort which failed on CBS in 1990, it is well expected that he would not be supportive of this current attempt."[18] Universal Television moved forward with a second version of *Uncle Buck* featuring an all-Black cast, though instead of Uncle Buck (Mike Epps) becoming the kids' legal guardian, he becomes their "manny." The series aired on ABC in the summer of 2016 and was cancelled due to low ratings.

The film *Ferris Bueller's Day Off* follows a day-in-the-life of a popular high school senior. Ferris is charming, a bit cocky, and willing to take risks. He wakes up one morning and outsmarts his parents (Cindy Pickett and Lyman Ward), convincing them he is sick and needs to stay home from school. His resentful younger sister, Jeanie (Jennifer Grey), and his nemesis, Principal Rooney (Jeffrey Jones), know he is faking. After convincing his neurotic best friend Cameron (Alan Ruck) to join him on his day off, Ferris schemes to get a suspicious Principal Rooney to let Ferris's devoted girlfriend, Sloane (Mia Sara), out of school. Together the trio drives into Chicago, where they visit the Art Institute, the Sears Tower, and Wrigley Field to watch the Cubs play, having lunch at an upscale restaurant along the way. In one of the film's most memorable scenes, Ferris jumps on a float during the Von Steuben Day Parade and wows the crowd with a lip-synched version of The Beatles' "Twist and Shout." Meanwhile, Principal Rooney, determined to catch Ferris skipping school, finally comes face-to-face with his truant student, who is saved at the last minute by Jeanie.

The NBC press release for the series highlights the show's high school setting, describing Ferris as the "B.M.O.C. (Best Manipulator on Campus)" at Ocean Park High School: "Need a course changed? No problem for Ferris's mini-computer. Want a new cafeteria menu? Break out the portable phone. Don't have a parking pass? They're stashed in F.B.'s locker."[19] Masius elaborates on what makes Ferris's character so special: "We were all victims and powerless in high school. Ferris has adult sensibilities. He's a guy you'd want to hang out with who's always a couple of steps ahead. You'd want him as your friend."[20]

In adapting *Ferris* for television, Masius made a few significant changes yet retained most of the film's core elements. One major change, most likely dictated by the budget, is the show's setting. Like most of Hughes's films, *Ferris Bueller's Day Off* was shot on location in and around Chicago, but for the television series the setting was relocated to Santa Monica, California. Ferris still serves as the show's narrator, breaking the fourth wall at the start of each episode to set up the week's plot and conclude with some additional commentary at the end. Ferris's clueless parents still believe their son can do no wrong and Jeannie (played by pre-*Friends* Jennifer Aniston), now one year older than Ferris, still resents her brother and the fact that he gets away with everything. Compared to her film counterpart, Jeannie is spoiled, snobbish, and just plain unlikable. On the rare occasion that Ferris and Jeannie form an alliance, their motives are not entirely altruistic. In "Sloan Again, Naturally," Ferris enlists Jeannie's help when his girlfriend Sloan (Ami Dolenz) drops him for an Italian exchange student with whom Jeannie is smitten.[21] In "A Night in the Life," Ferris, Cameron (Brandon Douglas), and Jeannie get stranded downtown late at night. Jeannie pays to get Cameron's car out of a tow yard so he and Ferris can get to school the next morning. When their mom finds out that Jeannie, who was grounded, had snuck out of the house, Ferris covers for his sister. She sheds a tear and mouths "thank you" to him, suggesting there may be a truce in the future. Unfortunately, it was to be the show's final episode.

The one obvious difference between the film and the television series is that the title character of the film never sets foot in school. Principal Rooney's relentless, obsessive pursuit of Ferris happens off school grounds and the characters only come face-to-face in the climax of the film outside the side door of Ferris's house. In contrast, the battle between Principal Rooney (Richard Riehle) and Ferris in the series is ongoing, repetitive, and follows a basic pattern: Rooney is out to get Ferris expelled, but whenever Ferris does something wrong, he always manages to come out on top. When Principal Rooney changes the school's bylaws so Ferris can't run for student president because he's a junior, Ferris transforms a juvenile delinquent into a popular candidate, who defeats Rooney's preferred choice ("Behind Every Dirtbag"). In another episode ("A Dog and His Boy"), Rooney is in hot water with the school board because of a student protest led by Ferris and Sloan against dissecting frogs in biology class. In the end, Ferris manages to save Rooney, and in exchange, Rooney agrees to start a dance program to prevent Sloan from transferring to a performing arts high school. Even when Principal Rooney catches Ferris doing the worst thing imaginable—throwing Cameron an out-of-control surprise

Figure 4.1 Television's Ferris Bueller (Charlie Schlatter, left) and his nemesis, Principal Ed Rooney (Richard Riehle).

party at his principal's house while he's away ("Between a Rock and Rooney's Place")—Ferris dodges another bullet when he discovers Principal Rooney and a teacher, Miss Connelly (Myra Turley), are having an affair. Meanwhile, in the same episode, the vengeful Jeannie, who prevented Ferris from having the party at their house, endures a series of physical mishaps trying to get to Principal Rooney's house that is reminiscent of what Rooney endures in the film in his quest to find Ferris.

The initial reviews of the pilot episode of *Ferris Bueller* were mixed, though some critics felt the series looked promising. *Los Angeles Times* critic Howard Rosenberg felt that Schlatter is not as convincing as the "angelic phony" played by Broderick, but found him to be "nevertheless an appealing Ferris" and described Masius's writing as a "clever high school-spoofing script."[22] Similarly, the *Hollywood Reporter* praised Schlatter's "outstanding" performance and Masius's script for its "fine comic flair."[23] *Variety* criticized the pilot for its "flat jokes, silly situations and, worst of all, an overbearingly smug title character." But the same reviewer thought the series was "salvageable" because Masius, who won two Emmys for the darkly comedic medical drama, *St. Elsewhere* (1982–88), is a "terrific writer" and "star Charlie Schlatter's got charm; he just needs a chance to show it."[24]

The negative reviews were not simply harsh—they were downright nasty. The *Washington Post*'s Tom Shales, who one can only guess is not a fan of the film, considered "The *Ferris Bueller* brand of scamper . . . particularly hard to stomach . . . *Ferris Bueller* is a proverbial lead balloon." Matt Roush, television critic for *USA Today*, quipped that "TV's Ferris is more like a ferret . . . mean-spirited, self-obsessed, a teen demon with no apparent desire than to get the goods on everyone who gets in his way . . . He's also just not very funny. Smug monologues to the camera . . . and his misadventures . . . are awfully predictable."[25] The final lines of John O'Connor's review for the *New York Times* best summarized how he felt about TV's Bueller and the series: "But if Ferris were to suddenly disappear from prime time, most viewers might agree with the dreadful Mr. Rooney. 'I'll miss you, Bueller,' he tells him, 'like a 20-pound boil.'"[26]

Midway through the show's run, Masius responded to the negative criticism by defending the series and its title character as "a teenage fantasy with adult sensibilities . . . The show is not mean-spirited; Ferris cares about his friends, his family . . . He is a good person and he's honest—he doesn't take life that seriously."[27] It's important to remember that reviews are typically based on one or sometimes two episodes, so the negative criticism launched by television reviewers may not all necessarily apply by the fourth of fifth episode. This was the case with the later episodes of *Ferris Bueller* in which Ferris devotes his time and energy into helping his friend Cameron become his own person ("Without You I'm Nothing"), enjoy his birthday ("Between a Rock and Rooney's Place"), and date the girl of his dreams ("Stand-in Deliver"). Whatever complications occurred along the way, Ferris and Cameron remained the best of friends.

FERRIS BUELLER VS. PARKER LEWIS

John O'Connor's review of *Ferris Bueller*, entitled "When Boys Will, of Course, Be Boys," also includes a review of *Parker Lewis Can't Lose*, which the critic describes as a "Ferris Bueller clone" that "takes to television better than Ferris" because it "is so exaggerated that there's not much danger of anyone taking it seriously."[28] O'Connor pinpoints how, despite their similarities, the one major difference between the two series is their respective comedic tones. While *Ferris* is also exaggerated and there is little chance that anyone can take the characters and plotlines too seriously, *Parker Lewis* is shot in a highly stylized manner, employing visual tricks and exaggerated sound effects. Parker's "best buds" are Mikey Randall (Billy Jayne), a rebel who is into rock 'n' roll, and Jerry (Troy Slaten), a smart, nerdy freshman who calls Parker and Mikey "Sir" and adds a touch of magical realism by donning a trench coat, out of which he is able to pull any object his two buds might need to get Parker out of trouble.

Figure 4.2 Parker Lewis (Corin Nemec) and his nemesis, Principal Grace Musso (Melanie Chartoff). © 1990 Fox Broadcasting Company. Photo credit: E. J. Camp.

Parker also has a bratty little sister, Shelly (Maia Brewton), who enjoys interfering with her brother's life at school. Like Mr. and Mrs. Bueller, Parker's parents are good but clueless people. His main nemesis is Principal Grace Musso (Melanie Chartoff), who rules the school with help from her lackey, an odd, evil student named Frank Lemmer (Taj Johnson), who is politically conservative, always wears black, and, in another example of magical realism, can communicate telepathically with Miss Musso. Like Principal Rooney, Principal Musso is on a power trip, though she also has a naughty streak when it comes to men, which Parker is usually able to exploit to get himself out of trouble. One running joke is that every time Principal Musso slams her office door, the glass breaks. The one time it doesn't, she only needs to look back at the door, causing it to shatter into pieces.

In an interview with the *Hollywood Reporter* conducted 25 years after the debut of *Parker Lewis Can't Lose*, the show's creators, Lon Diamond and Clyde Phillips, revealed the series was originally commissioned by CBS, but it was considered "too out-there for the even-then 'older-skewing' network."[29] CBS was not known for their youth-oriented programming (*Square Pegs* [1982–83], a high school single-camera comedy from the early 1980s, lasted only one season). It was the "out-there" visual style that made *Parker Lewis* unique and *Ferris Bueller* seem more 1980s than 1990s. When *Washington Post* staff writer Todd Allan Yasui asked Phillips in 1991 about the similarities between *Parker Lewis* and *Ferris Bueller*, Phillips was honest (and, as Yasui noted, "slightly irritated"): "I'm aware *Ferris Bueller* exists. I saw the movie. I liked the movie a lot. But when you're putting together a high school show, there's a natural order of things and ours fall into it."[30] Likewise, the producers of *Ferris* were also aware of *Parker Lewis*. Michael DiGaetano, writer and supervising producer of *Ferris Bueller*, said having *Parker Lewis* on a competing network didn't help because "it was looked upon as the hipper show, especially since the Fox Network was only a few years old at the time."[31] Ironically, the failure of *Ferris Bueller* helped *Parker Lewis* because the Fox show received more critical attention after the comparisons critics made between the two shows.

DiGaetano and his writing partner tried to interject some hipness into *Ferris Bueller* with a gay-themed episode entitled "The Father, the Son, and the Wholly Estranged," in which a gay British boy is interested in Ferris. DiGaetano said the episode had the best table read of the season, but NBC decided not to shoot it. "These days, a gay episode might save a show and make it look daring," DiGaetano explains, "but in 1990, it was the opposite."[32] At the time, gay, lesbian, bisexual, and transgender teen characters were still a rarity on television, though the situation would change later in the decade with shows like *Buffy the Vampire Slayer*, *Dawson's Creek* (1998–2003), and *Degrassi: The Next Generation* (2002–09).[33]

In addition to the differences between their respective characters, *Parker Lewis*'s appeal can be attributed to the show's experimental visual style. There is nothing distinct about the world inhabited by Ferris Bueller; the series looks and sounds like most single-camera situation comedies. By comparison, Parker Lewis's world is distinctly his own because the show's creative team used ultra-bright colors, unusual camera movements and angles, fast editing, and digitized sound effects that at times make the live-action series look and sound like a cartoon or a video game. From the point of view of Parker Lewis, high school is skewed, manic, and totally bizarre.

Visually, one of the sources of inspiration for Diamond and Phillips was *Three O'Clock High*, a 1987 teen comedy directed by Phil Joanou about a high school student who is challenged by a bully to fight after school. Joanou and cinematographer (and future director) Barry Sonnenfeld created tension with stylized camera movements and zooms, and unusual camera angles; similarly, the first shot of the *Parker Lewis* pilot is from inside the Lewis family's refrigerator. Diamond and Phillips encouraged the writers and the show's directors, many of whom were just starting out, to not hold back. "If you can think of it," Diamond and Phillips told them, "we can shoot it."[34] Diamond describes the show's style as "stylized reality": "It's sort of rooted in reality, but we twist up the jokes and the situations. It's not like we're in a regular proscenium sitcom show where you have the character and the joke. We have the character, the joke, and the style, too. It's like one extra weapon we have to go crazy with."[35]

The result was some wild, innovative experimentation with sounds and visuals. For example, the footsteps of Santo Domingo High School's six-foot, seven-inch superhuman bully, Larry Kubiac, aka Kube (Abraham Benrubi), shake the hallways and sound like an earthquake tremor. In another episode ("Close But No Guitar"), a camera is attached to Mikey's guitar to add dramatic effect during a dream sequence in which he throws it off the school roof and into the screaming crowd.[36] Television director Bryan Spicer, who directed 21 episodes early in his career, credits the show for giving directors the opportunity to experiment: "A lot of shows, they want you to shoot what's on the page and not be creative and not transcend it. And *Parker Lewis* was all about transcending and bringing it to life on the screen and making it three-dimensional and creating a world."[37]

The visual style of *Parker Lewis* suits the show's cheeky, self-referential sense of humor, which appealed to its young, media-savvy online fanbase. Characters also occasionally mention commercial breaks ("Where's a commercial break when you need one?" Parker asks). In one episode, Parker wakes up to a fake radio commercial for another Fox show, *Married . . . with Children* (1986–97). A promo for *Parker Lewis* parodies Fox's other teen show, *Beverly Hills, 90210* (1990–2000), which includes a cameo by the show's star, Jason Priestley (the other *90210* cast members also made cameos). In addition to the long list of pop culture references inserted into the dialogue (including John Hughes), there are guest appearances by cultural icons like Elvira, Sonny Bono, Ozzy Osbourne, and *Leave It to Beaver* cast members Barbara Billingsley (Mrs. Cleaver), Jerry Mathers (Theodore Beaver), and Ken Osmond (Eddie Haskell). The episode titles are also derived from actual film titles ("Father Knows Less"/*Father Knows Best*; "Raging Kube"/*Raging Bull*; "Goodbye, Mr. Rips"/*Goodbye, Mr. Chips*; "Full Mental Jacket"/*Full Metal Jacket*).

The comparative reviews of *Ferris Bueller* and *Parker Lewis Can't Lose* focused on the difference between the shows' title characters. *Entertainment*

Weekly's Mark Harris contended that Parker Lewis and Ferris Bueller are "leading parallel lives . . . But, perhaps because the movie doesn't offer much to steal in the way of wit, *Parker Lewis* transcends its source. It's loose and goofy where *Ferris* and its television counterpart are smug and smarmy."[38] In his review of both shows, Michael Hill of the *Baltimore Evening Post* noted that the correct title for *Ferris Bueller* should be *Ferris Bueller Can't Lose* because he never does: "Robbed of that possibility, his smart-alecky manner quickly becomes insufferable."[39] Ferris seems to have a solution for every problem or situation he faces, but that is not the case with Parker Lewis, who does occasionally lose and go too far. The show even takes a more serious turn when Parker pulls one prank too many ("I went a goof too far") on his beloved poetry teacher (in the episode "Teacher, Teacher"), who decides to resign. Feeling genuinely sorry for what he has done, he apologizes and she returns to school. He even regrets getting Principal Musso demoted (in "Saving Grace") after her replacement turns out to be an unstable control freak (he forces Parker to serve his detention in a dungeon). With some help from the student body, Parker succeeds in driving the new principal crazy and Musso is reinstated.

When the show was becoming too repetitive during the first season, Fox told Phillips and Diamond "to mix it up and make it even crazier," which they did. Toward the end of its run, there was pressure from the network to tone down the wacky visuals and broaden the show's audience appeal so it would fit better with other Fox shows, particularly *Beverly Hills, 90210*. Parker Lewis does mature (a little), gets a girlfriend, and starts to deal with more serious subjects like drinking and sex.[40] There are even serious moments that seem like they are right out of *Beverly Hills, 90210*, such as when Parker has a heart-to-heart talk with Mikey, whose anger and irresponsibility costs him his job and a potential girlfriend (in "Money Talks"). Mikey says, "I don't deserve a best friend like you," and the best buds share a hug.

Parker Lewis also liked to poke fun at its competition with references to *60 Minutes* (CBS) and *Eerie, Indiana* (NBC, 1991–92), a short-lived horror/mystery/sci-fi show. Another easy target is the cancelled *Ferris Bueller*. In the final episode of season one ("Parker Lewis Can't Win"), the camera pulls out in the final shot to reveal a soundstage. Sitting in the back, their faces hidden in the shadows, are two teenagers. One guy, presumably Ferris, says to the other, "So that's how they do it." His friend responds, "C'mon Ferris, let's get out of here!"

FERRIS BUELLER'S AFTERLIFE ON THE SMALL SCREEN

Twenty-two years after the failure of *Ferris Bueller*, television has continued to contribute to keeping the legacy of *Ferris Bueller's Day Off* alive in more creative ways, beginning with a Super Bowl commercial for the 2012 Honda CR-V. Directed by Todd Phillips (*The Hangover* [2009], *Old School* [2003]), the commercial, entitled "Matthew's Day Off," is a two-minute-and-thirty-second version of *Ferris Bueller's Day Off*. Like the film, the commercial opens with Matthew Broderick pretending he's too sick to go to work today, presumably on a movie shooting in Los Angeles. He talks to his agent, who tells him to stay in bed, which is Broderick's cue to begin his day off in his Honda CR-V. The montage that follows is a series of scenes based on key moments from the film (minus Cameron and Sloane). Ferris rides a roller coaster, goes to the racetrack, dances on a float in Chinatown singing in Mandarin, and dines at a fancy restaurant. As a gift to the film's die-hard fans, there are dozens of "Easter eggs" scattered throughout the commercial that refer to specific props, costumes, names, and lines from the film.[41]

More evidence that *Ferris Bueller's Day Off* is still very much part of the American cultural zeitgeist is a season two episode of the ABC situation comedy, *The Goldbergs* (2013–present). Set in the 1980s, the "tribute episode" ("Barry Goldberg's Day Off") focuses on teenager Barry Goldberg (Troy Gentile), who is inspired by the film to take a day off from school and have an adventure, but due to a series of mishaps (e.g., his grandfather's car gets stolen), his day doesn't go as planned. He manages to salvage his day and impress his girlfriend by making a surprise appearance on a float at his school's homecoming, where he leads the crowd in "Twist and Shout." But the episode's biggest surprise is a cameo appearance by Charlie Sheen, who re-enacts the scene in the police station with Jeanie Bueller and tells Barry's sister to stop worrying about her brother and start worrying more about herself.

More recently, in the summer of 2020, Josh Gad devoted an episode of his YouTube series, *Reunited Apart*, to *Ferris Bueller's Day Off*, virtually reuniting Broderick, Ruck, Sara, Ward, Pickett, Ferris's economics teacher (Ben Stein), and Kenny Ortega, who choreographed the "Twist and Shout" parade sequence. The actors reminisce about making the film and working with Hughes and re-enact some of the film's iconic moments. They also try to answer trivia questions about the film posed by *Ferris Bueller* super-fan, actor Jake Gyllenhaal.[42]

Ferris Bueller's Day Off is not the only popular 1980s teen film that failed to duplicate its success on the small screen (who can remember *Fast Times* [1986], the short-lived sitcom based on *Fast Times at Ridgemont High* [1982], or the 1992 television version of the slacker comedy *Bill and Ted's Excellent Adventure* [1989]?). So why did the television adaptation of a popular teen film comedy about a day in the life of a beloved, iconic high school student also get a failing grade from viewers and critics? The answer lies with Ferris Bueller's creator, John Hughes, and the differences between his original conception of the Bueller character and his television counterpart.

Hughes's Ferris Bueller is a mid-1980s version of a Hollywood teen rebel. He defies authority and liberates himself from the confines of the oppressive world of the suburban high school that is at the center of Hughes's previous teen comedies, *Sixteen Candles* (1984) and *The Breakfast Club* (1985). *Ferris Bueller's Day Off* takes place over a single day, during which Ferris takes major risks and dodges a series of bullets until he finally comes face-to-face with his nemesis, Principal Rooney. His adventures in Chicago with his two best friends are grand and cinematic, culminating with his performance of "Twist and Shout" on the top of a parade float. After empowering his best friend Cameron to stand up to his father, he even manages, with his sister's help, to escape Rooney's clutches one more time.

Whether it was contractual or by choice, the absence of John Hughes's name from the credits of the series seems fair considering how little the two characters with the same name have in common. Ferris Bueller was imported from the big screen to the small, where he was transformed into a one-dimensional sitcom character confined to the very place from which Hughes's Ferris was liberated—high school. In true situation-comedy fashion, in episode after episode, Ferris repeatedly outsmarts Principal Rooney. There may be a grain of truth in the critics' negative reactions to the show's casting, performances and writing, yet compared to its hipper, edgier rival, *Parker Lewis Can't Lose*, *Ferris Bueller* seems terribly dated—a 1980s sitcom based on a 1980s film.

Television should have simply let Ferris have his day. End of story.

NOTES

1. The series aired in the fall of 1990. After its cancellation, the final episode ("A Night in the Life") was shown on August 11, 1991.
2. Barbara Bush, "Commencement Address," Wellesley College, June 1, 1990, https://www.wellesley.edu/events/commencement/archives/1990commencement/commencementaddress.
3. "NBC's Early Fall Previews Score Big in Nielsens," *Los Angeles Times*, August 28, 1990, P10.
4. Jay Bobbin, "Once is Not Enough," *Santa Ana Orange County Register*, August 26, 1990, TV Section, 6.
5. Bobbin, 6.
6. Hughes did not receive on-screen credit for the *Ferris Bueller*, *Uncle Buck*, *Weird Science*, and *Beethoven* television programs.
7. "NBC's Early Fall Previews Score Big in Nielsens," *Los Angeles Times*, August 28, 1990, 10.
8. Rick Sherwood, "TV's Blackboard Bungle," *Los Angeles Times*, October 27, 1990, F1, F7.
9. "TV Ratings," *Los Angeles Times*, October 17, 1990, F9.
10. "TV Ratings," F9.
11. Claudia Puig, "TV & Video," *Los Angeles Times*, December 13, 1990, F2.
12. Rick Sherwood, "TV's Blackboard Bungle," *Los Angeles Times*, October 27, 1990, F1.
13. Drew Jubera, "In front of TV 12 Hours a Day: Is Marathon Television Viewing as Dangerous as Some Claim?" *San Francisco Chronicle*, August 9, 1991, F7.
14. Ray Richmond, "Check Out 'Parker Lewis' and You Can't Lose," *Orange County Register*, August 31, 1990, P46.

15. Bill Carter, "Hear About a Film That Became a Hit TV Series? You're Not Alone," *New York Times*, December 17, 1990, C11.
16. See Holly Chard's chapter in this volume for further analysis of John Candy's star persona in *Uncle Buck*, and elsewhere in Hughes's oeuvre.
17. Carter, C11.
18. Nellie Andreeva, "'Uncle Buck' Series: John Hughes & John Candy Families Displeased," Deadline Hollywood, October 10, 2014, https://deadline.com/2014/10/uncle-buck-series-john-hughes-john-candy-disapprove-849424/.
19. *Ferris Bueller* press release, Media Relations, National Broadcasting Company, August 1, 1990, author's collection.
20. *Ferris Bueller* press release.
21. The "e" at the end of Sloane's name was dropped for television.
22. Howard Rosenberg, "NBC's *Ferris Bueller* Premieres Tonight," *Los Angeles Times*, August 23, 1990, F11.
23. Review of *Ferris Bueller*, *The Hollywood Reporter*, August 23, 1990.
24. Review of *Ferris Bueller*, *Variety*, August 23, 1990, 22.
25. Matt Roush, "This *Ferris* Should Be in Detention," *USA Today*, August 23, 1991, 3D.
26. John O'Connor, "When Boys Will, of Course, Be Boys," *New York Times*, October 8, 1990, 43.
27. Rick Sherwood, "TV's Blackboard Bungle," *Los Angeles Times*, October 27, 1990, F7.
28. O'Connor, 43.
29. Pete Keeley, "*Parker Lewis Can't Lose* at 25: Co-Creators Clyde Phillips and Lon Diamond on Creating a Cult Classic," *The Hollywood Reporter*, June 13, 2018, https://www.hollywoodreporter.com/live-feed/parker-lewis-cant-lose-are-they-now-creators-interview-1119715.
30. Todd Allan Yasui, "Corin Nemec; Trying Anything in *Parker Lewis*," *Washington Post*, January 27, 1991, Y8.
31. Michael DiGaetano, email message to author, September 16, 2018. Special thanks to Mr. DiGaetano for sharing his experiences working on *Ferris Bueller*.
32. DiGaetano, email message.
33. Stephen Tropiano, *The Prime Time Closet: A History of Gays and Lesbians on TV* (New York: Applause Books, 2002), 168–84.
34. Tropiano, 168–84.
35. Daniel Cerone, "Stylized Reality? Not a Problem. Fox's *Parker Lewis* Combines Imaginative Dubb, Creative Sound Effects," *Los Angeles Times*, *TV Times*, March 17, 1991, 3.
36. Keeley.
37. Keeley.
38. Mark Harris, "Parker Lewis Can't Lose!" *Entertainment Weekly*, August 31, 1990, https://ew.com/article/1990/08/31/parker-lewis-cant-lose/.
39. Michael Hill, "Fox's *Parker Lewis* Gets It Right," *Hutchinson News*, September 9, 1990.
40. Keeley.
41. Benjamin Svetkey, "*Ferris Bueller* Super Bowl Ad: All the Easter Eggs in One Basket," *Entertainment Weekly*, February 6, 2012, https://ew.com/movies/2012/02/06/ferris-bueller-super-bowl-ad-easter-eggs/.
42. Josh Gad, "Ferris Bueller's Day Off," *Reunited Apart with Josh Gad*, June 29, 2020, https://www.youtube.com/watch?v=dOaa3Znh75w.

PART II

Reconsidering Youth

Over the span of three years from 1984 to 1987, John Hughes wrote (and in most cases directed) six films about teenagers that would become their own trend, aligning him with and yet positioning him in difference to the teen genre that had seen a resurgence earlier in the decade. The early '80s teen slasher films and sex romps that turned low-budget products into potentially profitable franchises (particularly within horror after *Halloween* [1978] and *Friday the 13th* [1980]), were critically reviled, even if their modest incomes justified their enduring cheap thrills. By 1984, when the nation was supposedly waking up to "Morning in America," as Ronald Reagan's infamous re-election campaign assured the citizens, Hollywood had all but exhausted the titillation wrought by teen sex and violence, and the softer, sensitive side of adolescence was welcomed by young viewers seeking a little solace. Acclaimed teen dramas had started gaining considerable attention the year before (*Bad Boys*, *The Outsiders*, *WarGames*), depicting teenagers affected by social conditions. While Hughes's first film for teens, *Sixteen Candles* (1984), was certainly not intended as serious drama, its sensitivity in handling family dynamics and its female protagonist's romantic anguish had rarely been seen previously in the genre.

Further, the few other sympathetic films about teens in the early '80s that had begun to explore their psychological states—akin to the depths probed by serious teen films of past generations, e.g., *Rebel Without a Cause* (1955), *Splendor in the Grass* (1961), *The Learning Tree* (1969), *Carrie* (1976)—rarely provided their characters with the opportunity to explicitly express their feelings, not only to parents and adults, but to teach other. Examples such as *Fame* (1980), *Endless Love* (1981), *Class of 1984* (1982), and *Valley Girl* (1983) showed a certain appreciation for struggling and tormented teens, yet tended to dwell on the sensational aspects of their experiences. Hughes was able to maintain some level of that sensationalism through parties, dances, chases, and fights, while still providing his characters with meaningful dialogue that explored their motivations. His films delved into the reasons behind teens' actions in ways that most other filmmakers were simply too timid or detached to explore, resulting in the lengthy dialogues we see among young characters (most remarkably in *The Breakfast Club* [1985]), even when his stories were too fantastic for reality (*Weird Science* [1985]) or relied on a certain suspension of disbelief (*Ferris Bueller's Day Off* [1986]).

Along with that sense of "taking teens seriously" for which Hughes became known, his stories specifically addressed certain political and social concerns, which the chapters in this section each address. In "'Life moves pretty fast': Mobility, Class, and Power in John Hughes's Teen Films," Christina Petersen considers how Hughes's films explore youth as a socially constructed identity like that of social class, a liminal state between dependence and self-reliance that can apply to an individual of any age. She traces how the formal aesthetics of Hughes's teen films suggest that chronological age is no ultimate guarantee of power, because adult authority figures are depicted, like upper-class bullies, initially able to command the film frame but ultimately condemned to passivity as they lose their control over others. In *The Breakfast Club*, static framings of teenagers in close shots emphasize their class differences while camera movements are reserved for the adult characters that supervise them. The teenagers become empowered when they begin to see beyond these external differences and the frame transforms from a device of containment into an accelerated space of community and belonging. *Ferris Bueller's Day Off* extends this motif to a trio of teenagers who discover that the upper-class status of adulthood is defined by the ability to move beyond one's immediate situation. The chapter thus seeks to reframe the canonical status of Hughes's teen films as meditations on youth into an experience of social mobility.

Barbara Brickman focuses on *Ferris Bueller* in "'When Cameron was in Egypt's land': The Queer Child of Neglect in John Hughes's Films," taking up the best friend of the film's title character, Cameron, as an exemplar for the "fantasy of neglect" that Pamela Wojcik has recently explored in her work. As Brickman elaborates, Cameron seems to be always awaiting furious castigation from his unseen father, who hangs over his son (and even his son's friends) as a specter of parental authority. Brickman carries this beyond mere family politics though, and analyzes how the implicit mistreatment of Cameron works to bring him, like other wayward youth, back into societal (hetero)normalization. Cameron's potential queerness is thus restrained and contained, devoid of the teen genre's enclosing nuclear family unit and happy heterosexual coupling that we see his friends enjoy. His development goes astray along a different narrative path from his friends, one that defers instead of matures and remains queerly incomplete, one that is, at last, not "normal" maturation at all.

The third chapter here, "We Need to Talk About Kevin McCallister: John Hughes's Careless Parents and Abandoned Children," by Melissa Oliver-Powell, takes its title from Lionel Shriver's *We Need to Talk About Kevin*, later adapted to the screen by Lynne Ramsay (2011), in which a sociopathic teenage boy slowly escalates his violence against family and friends while his exasperated mother tries to avert the inevitable catastrophe he enacts. Hughes's films featured minimal violence by comparison, though the torments of family in his films certainly engender ample tensions between youth and adults. Oliver-Powell examines how Hughes's characters' maturing identities are set against the backdrop of parental figures who represent the oppressive, dangerous, or tedious capacities of the "adult world," which is generally characterized by joylessness and misrecognition. Hughes's child characters by the '90s—in *Home Alone* (1990), *Home Alone 2: Lost in New York* (1992), *Beethoven* (1992), *Dennis the Menace* (1993), *Baby's Day Out* (1994), and *Miracle on 34th Street*

(1994)—are often forgotten or overlooked (whether literally or emotionally) by their parents, who are distracted by the various ephemera of adult responsibilities. Hughes's family cinema foregrounds comings-of-age and characters' increasing capabilities in confronting the challenges of adulthood; however, the conventional adult world is presented as a false model. In order to achieve successful mature identities, both children and parents must negotiate growing competency and responsibility while maintaining the irreverence and creativity of childhood.

In considering the evolution of Hughes's stories from the mid-'80s to the mid-'90s, we witness not only his shifting attention away from teens to younger children and away from adolescent angst to family disruption, but also the changing interests of the movie industry and the national culture. Hughes seemed to suggest with his films of the '90s that he was not following the trend toward tackling the traumas of history and social life that were carrying the culture away from the escapism of the '80s (e.g., *Dances with Wolves* and *GoodFellas* [1990], *Boyz N the Hood* and *Silence of the Lambs* [1991], *Unforgiven* and *Malcolm X* [1992]), but rather he regressed into childhood daydreams of liberation from parental tyranny. In many ways, Hughes apparently needed to abandon the strained humor of adolescent anguish so that he could find more secure comic relief in the lighter gravity of children's laughter.

CHAPTER 5

"Life moves pretty fast": Mobility, Power, and Aesthetics in John Hughes's Teen Films

Christina G. Petersen

At the beginning of *Ferris Bueller's Day Off* (1986), after successfully faking illness to stay home from school, young Ferris (Matthew Broderick) sits up, turns directly to the camera, and announces triumphantly: "They bought it." More than a fly in the face of the conventional closed diegesis of classical Hollywood narrative, Ferris's rupture of the fourth wall offers the film's first significant instance of camera movement. During the three-minute opening, composed of forty shots, the camera alternates between largely stationary shots of Ferris in bed, his parents hovering over him, and his sister Jeanie (Jennifer Grey) expressing her disapproval. Yet when Ferris rises, the camera sits up with him, reinforcing this moment as a break from the usual power dynamics between parent and child, spectator and character. In another moment similarly punctuated by subtle camera movement as Ferris moves from his bedroom to hallway to bathroom, he again addresses the camera, this time with the famous pronouncement: "Life moves pretty fast. If you don't stop and look around once in a while, you could miss it." At this moment the camera reframes to stay with Ferris when his quick, confident movement threatens to leave the spectator behind. From the first, *Ferris Bueller's Day Off* sets up the motif that power derives from the ability to direct the film frame.

The link between movement and power is not confined to Hughes's final teen film as writer, director, and producer. Like *Ferris Bueller's Day Off*, *Sixteen Candles* (1984), *Weird Science* (1985), *The Breakfast Club* (1985), *Pretty in Pink* (1986), and *Some Kind of Wonderful* (1987) all employ mobile framing to emphasize distinctions between privilege and disenfranchisement. In Hughes's teen films, adult authority figures are often depicted in a similar manner to upper-class bullies, initially able to command the frame but ultimately condemned to passivity as they lose their control over others and themselves. In contrast, youthful protagonists often begin these films isolated by static framing but become mobile once they connect to a larger community of their peers and define themselves on their own terms. In this sense, while Hughes's teen films have been considered canonical entries in the genre for their high school settings, teenage characters, and focus on the development of individual identity,[1] these films also offer examples of the genre's tendency to explore youth as more than chronology. As Adrian Martin argues, the "teen in teen movie is itself a very elastic, bill-of-fare word; it refers not to a biological age, but a type, a mode of behavior, a way of being." Youth in these films is a "liminal experience: that intense, suspended moment between yesterday and tomorrow, between childhood and adulthood, between being a nobody and a somebody."[2] In line with Martin's assertion that teen films correlate distinctions between child and adult with other markers of social status, Hughes's films are more concerned with exploring youth as a socially constructed identity like that of gender or class, a liminal state between objectification and subjecthood as well as between dependence and self-reliance that can apply to an individual of any age. Yet rather than focus solely on narrative or ideological analysis, this chapter considers these aspects in relation to a long-neglected area of teen film scholarship: aesthetics.[3] As I will trace, the formal construction—*mise-en-scène*, cinematography, editing, and sound—of Hughes's teen films suggest that chronological age is no guarantee of power. This chapter rather considers Hughes's teen films as explorations of youth as a form of social mobility between child and adult, nobody and somebody, yesterday and tomorrow, predicated on moving past socially constructed frames of identity.

FROM NOBODY TO SOMEBODY: *SIXTEEN CANDLES* AND *WEIRD SCIENCE*

Written and directed by Hughes, *Sixteen Candles* marked his first foray into the teen genre but not his first film to represent adolescence as a form of stasis. Hughes's initial screenwriting credit, *National Lampoon's Class Reunion* (1982), depicts a ten-year high school reunion as a site of arrested development where one alum, unable to move past a sadistic senior-year prank, returns to take his murderous revenge. *Mr. Mom* (1983) and *National Lampoon's Vacation* (1983) similarly explore male mid-life identity crises as the inability to get ahead in the context of the changing economic and social dynamics of 1980s America. These early efforts would introduce the dialectic of automobile and suburban house in Hughes's films as symbols of new gender and class dynamics in the United States in the wake of second-wave feminism and globalization. *Sixteen Candles* would transfer these concerns to the contemporary suburban high school and the adolescent body. Like its younger sibling *Weird Science*, *Sixteen Candles* explores how the possession of a mature body transforms nobodies into somebodies in adolescent society, able to move through the high school hallways with ease.

With a beginning that fuses the sound design of *American Graffiti* (1973) with the chaotic suburban house on the eve of a big event from *Home Alone* (1990), *Sixteen Candles* opens with a stationary long shot of a car slowly delivering newspapers, the arrival of which sets off the alarm of a conventional suburban brick colonial house complete with station wagon parked in the driveway. The opening interior shot is populated with frames-within-the-frame as the Baker parents move swiftly from one door to the other, the camera panning to follow their movement. By contrast, the film's newly minted sixteen-year-old Samantha "Sam" Baker (Molly Ringwald) is introduced in a pan and tilt that emphasizes her unchanged status as she stares at herself in a framed mirror with Paul Young's "Love of the Common People" (1982) playing over her actions. The soundtrack's engagement with poverty and unemployment at first seems at odds with Sam's obvious middle-class lifestyle until she remarks to herself: "Chronologically you're sixteen today. Physically you're still fifteen. Hopeless." Sam's perception of such disadvantage is reinforced by the fact that no one in her family remembers her birthday, since they've all been made frantic by the impending wedding of her older sister Ginny (Blanche Baker). Without the womanly "four inches of bod" she hoped to have by now, Sam occupies a lower step on the family hierarchy than even her little brother. But Sam's not alone in her plight. In an opening school montage sequence doubled in *The Breakfast Club*, Sam's fellow school bus riders are equally trapped, introduced pressed up against the bus window before exiting onto campus en masse in a stationary medium shot. As the montage unfolds, it reinforces the motif set up in the opening: when the camera moves out of synchronization with the body on-screen (or vice versa), it indicates that that body belongs to someone on the lower rung of the high school hierarchy. By contrast, camera movement in sync with the on-screen body indicates elevated status.

In *Sixteen Candles*, heterosexual couplehood is the primary means to achieve upper-class status. The opening montage reserves matching camera movement for two-shots of male-female pairs walking together, pinkies linked or hands plunged into each other's back pockets. Sam's single status is clear from her initial position in this peer-oriented space, pressed up against the lockers like a wallflower until she outlines her dreams for what her sixteenth birthday was supposed to look like. The camera tracks along with Sam and her best friend as Sam describes her fantasy in similar terms to a wedding—"big party, band, tons of people," "pink TransAm," an "incredibly gorgeous guy"—in an indication that expressing desire for couplehood is enough to get a taste of mobility. This camera movement returns after class when Sam discusses her desire for one specific "gorgeous guy": senior Jake Ryan (Michael Schoeffling). In Sam's words, Jake is her "ideal," and he is immediately depicted as her match in the next sequence when he discusses Sam with his muscle-bound friend Rock (Tony Longo) while doing pull-ups in the gym. The camera remains stationary as the two draw themselves up and down, in and out of frame, effecting a version of a shot/reverse-shot conversation without cuts, until the camera pulls away to reveal their full bodies just as Rock tries to dissuade Jake from getting involved with Sam. For Rock, who, like Jake, possesses an adult male body, Sam is not worth romantic consideration because she's a "child"—a "void"—a literal no-body. Instead he advocates strongly in favor of Jake's current girlfriend, Caroline (Haviland Morris), who is a "*woman*." The film's *mise-en-scène* further reinforces Rock's conflation of mature bodies with power when a full-grown man, who has been engaged throughout this conversation in the background in a wrestling match with a much smaller boy, finally catches his pint-sized quarry and lifts him over his head. Again, high school represents a space where mature and immature bodies meet and mingle but the childlike have no control over their own movement.

The balance of the film works to overturn this hierarchy for Sam and freshman geek "Farmer" Ted (Anthony Michael Hall). Introduced as a budding lothario who makes Sam the object of his unwanted attentions, Ted subjects her to his uncontrolled, uncoordinated dancing in a tight close-up at the school dance. Later though, Sam and Ted find common ground in the immobilized chassis of a convertible in the school auto shop, confessing in a series of stationary shot/reverse-shots how they find themselves stuck in relation to cultural and personal rites of passage. For Sam, it is her family's failure to remember her birthday, while Ted confesses that he has not yet lost his virginity.[4] This interchange then sets both on the path toward achieving greater social status not through the development of their own bodies but by acquiring access to more mature ones. For Ted, this begins with borrowing Sam's underwear as evidence of physical intimacy with an older woman, and culminates in a man-to-man talk with Jake during which Jake proposes that Ted give him Sam's panties in exchange for custody of Jake's unconscious girlfriend. Although previously introduced as the ideal womanly body, Caroline is reduced to a piece of cargo after Jake's rejection, an object that Ted deposits in the Rolls Royce that he borrows from Jake to take her home. As Jake and Ted make their way to the car with Caroline slung over Ted's shoulder, the camera pans and tracks to follow Ted for the first time, underscoring his transformation from geek to man through the linked acquisition of a mature female body and a vehicular symbol of upper-class mobility. Ted's initial stop-and-start attempt at driving reads like a metaphor for a loss of virginity, particularly when his ultimate transition to maturity takes place when he loses control of the car and drives onto the sidewalk, prompting Caroline to fall drunkenly into his lap after he admonishes her like a parent to stop her "childish antics." As she strokes his head and declares her love for him just out of frame, with third base just on

Figure 5.1 Ted (Anthony Michael Hall) takes control of the frame in *Sixteen Candles*.

the horizon, Ted turns to the camera and pronounces, "This is getting good," before driving off, the camera panning to follow his ride into the night. In Ted's case, his control over the frame is in direct proportion with his influence over more a mature female body.

For Sam, the female path to being somebody provides more fraught examples as both Caroline and Ginny achieve social mobility by losing control over their bodies (Caroline gets drunk, Ginny takes muscle relaxers), forcing men to take care of them. When Sam and Jake finally get together at the end of the film, the camera pans to follow them to Jake's car, seemingly signifying her independent transition to female adulthood. Yet the editing constructs this shot from her father's point of view, suturing the spectator into a male gaze in which Sam becomes another object exchanged between men, transformed into cargo like Caroline and Ginny.[5] Sam's successful transition to womanly object culminates in the film's final shot in which she and Jake are shown in a medium long shot perched over a cake lit with the titular sixteen candles. Sam thanks Jake for getting her "undies back" and he thanks her for coming over, the frame freezing their movement at the moment of their kiss over the cake. The film thus ends with Jake, in the place of Sam's family, recognizing her new status as a woman. Yet while Sam may provide Jake with a romantic interest that is more (or less) a body than Caroline, he forfeits his own mobility in the process, reduced to another figure contained within the frame.

The science fiction animal comedy *Weird Science*, also written and directed by Hughes, even more clearly links possession of mature bodies to adolescent social mobility and control over the frame. Nerdy Wyatt (Ilan Mitchell-Smith) and Gary (Anthony Michael Hall, back again) are on the lowest rung of the Shermer High School social hierarchy. They are introduced in an opening crane shot accompanied by nondiegetic music in the style of Richard Strauss's *Also Sprach Zarathustra* (evoking *2001: A Space Odyssey*'s "Dawn of Man" sequence and indicating Wyatt and Gary's pre-evolved state) that travels up their scrawny physical frames as they gaze unnoticed at a girls' gym class, with a poster for "future homemakers" framed in the background reinforcing their association with femininity. In stationary close-ups, Wyatt and Gary announce their desires for what they would do with these female bodies if they could, including adolescent sexual aspirations ("shower with them") to more adult social activities ("hit the city" for drinks, nightlife, dancing, and a "huge party"). Like Sam in *Sixteen Candles*, the spectator is privileged to the protagonists' fantasies, but in the male version their expression is not represented as a means of mobility, but instead as part of their fixed position as passive nobodies. The opening completes this characterization when two jock bullies overhear the boys' conversation and pull down their shorts while shouting for the girls' attention. Unmanned by their tormentors, the boys stand clad only in their underwear and gym shirts, subjected to a disapproving female gaze through a series of reaction shots from the girls' point of view. *Weird Science* thus constructs a different status modality: for teenage boys, becoming the object of another's gaze is the lowest of the low, the social equivalent of a pair of sweaty gym shorts on the locker room floor.[6]

Like *Sixteen Candles*, the rest of the film plays out in a more extended fashion in which the boys' ability to realize their fantasies of female objectification are directly correlated with their rise in social status. As in *Sixteen Candles*, horizontal camera movement indicates social mobility but *Weird Science* punctuates this with vertical movements as well. While watching *Frankenstein* (1931) on television, Gary pushes Wyatt to sit down as he suggests they produce their own woman using Wyatt's computer. In this moment the camera mirrors their movement for the first time, much like the opening of *Ferris Bueller's Day Off*, when they suggest using a new means—technology—to obtain a girl of their own by making her from scratch. In the subsequent creation sequence, the camera alternates between static shots of Gary and Wyatt as they stare at the computer screen, simulated horizontal tracking shots into the *mise-en-abîme* of the computer world, and close-up shots of the various models (*Playboy* bunny, Einstein, MTV veejay) they feed into a scanner to create their simulation. Along the way, the sequence is punctuated by vertical camera movements (crane shots, tilts) at moments when they reach a breakthrough in their experiment, culminating in an overhead shot out of *Frankenstein* that apprehensively approaches the two, bras capped on their heads in a final embrace of femininity, as they finish the experiment. And after this first reality-breaking moment, the film descends (or ascends) into a world ruled by the carnivalesque.

According to Mikhail Bakhtin's categorization, the carnivalesque world is one turned topsy-turvy, mingling the high and the low in ways previously kept separate, a site of resistance to traditional authority often represented through bodily "acts of defecation and copulation, conception, pregnancy, and birth."[7] In three shots, the film depicts the consequences of Gary and Wyatt's reproductive crime against nature as suburban Shermer, Illinois is turned on its head, cutting from the sudden conflagration of a "Welcome to Shermer" sign to a shot of a dog barking while sitting upside down on a kitchen ceiling to an explosion in front of the local power and water plant. The final sign that Newtonian physics and existing frames of power no longer apply comes when the door to Wyatt's bathroom (with the telling homonym signage "I brake for women") begins to bulge and pulse like a rubberized entry into a David Cronenberg film, finally exploding outward to reveal their creation. In the film's iconic liminal moment, Gary and Wyatt's perfect woman, Lisa (Kelly LeBrock), is introduced in a shot that hearkens back to our introduction to the two boys, a crane shot up and over her body clad only in an athletic shirt and briefs. In this moment, the tables have definitively turned: the objects have become subjects who now gaze on the mature female body that they have made for themselves.

Now armed with the ultimate marker of male adolescent status, the rest of the film moves away from the boys' original plans for Lisa as a sex slave to their growing empowerment over male bullies at school and home. Like the high school bullies who humiliate Gary and Wyatt throughout the first act of the film, Wyatt's boorish older brother Chet (Bill Paxton) is introduced in a low-angle medium close-up that, along with his tight white tank top, muscular arms,

Figure 5.2 Older brother Chet (Bill Paxton) controls the frame in *Weird Science*.

and 1950s-style flattop haircut, emphasizes his elevated status as the owner of a mature male body. Unlike Wyatt, who is pinned to a low-angle stationary frame during their conversation, the camera follows Chet in a track out and crane downward as he descends the steps to confront Wyatt. However, the film does not associate this intrinsic superiority with humanity, and instead reveals Chet to be the true monster in this *Frankenstein* tale.[8] Like Lisa, the bullies, and the grotesque punks that Lisa summons at the film's climax, the camera obeys Chet's command, becoming mobile only when he is in the frame. The worm turns though when Lisa transforms Chet into a grotesque Jabba the Hutt pile of excrement, finally matching his exterior appearance with his loutish disposition. In this case, the adult male body may be recognized as of superior status, but if the owner's personality does not meet the body's level of maturity, one can become the lowest of the low, a grotesque body confined in the frame.[9]

In *Sixteen Candles* and *Weird Science*, adult status is associated with control over the frame as well as the bodies contained within it. For a teenage girl like Sam, one achieves womanhood and social mobility by becoming an object transported by men, although without a womanly body, she can trap her partner in the frame along with her. For the male adolescent such as Ted, Wyatt, or Gary, social mobility derives from control over the mature female body, which is correlated with increased control over the frame. Yet there is a tipping point, as in the case of the bullies, the punks, and Chet in *Weird Science*, who possess mature male bodies but immature personalities, and this hybridity transforms them into monsters who ultimately lose their mobility and control over the frame when revealed for their true selves. In each case, stasis and lower-class status stem from remaining suspended between childhood and adulthood rather than successfully moving from one into the other.

FROM YESTERDAY TO TOMORROW: *THE BREAKFAST CLUB* AND *FERRIS BUELLER'S DAY OFF*

In between *Sixteen Candles* and *Weird Science*, Hughes wrote, directed, produced, and appeared in the first of two teen films that would explore adolescent liminality in temporal rather than corporeal terms. In *The Breakfast Club* and *Ferris Bueller's Day Off*, youth is a state of suspension between yesterday and tomorrow where the freedom to move is afforded to those who can envision a world not predicated on external frames of identity. Yet social mobility is not correlated to leaving childhood in one's rearview. In *The Breakfast Club*, surveillance and anxiety mark the present of five teenagers from all walks of the high school hierarchy confined to Saturday detention. However, when they learn to see that their shared experience of powerlessness as teenagers outweighs their gender and class differences, they are transformed from anxious stereotypes into a community of playful individuals. In *Ferris Bueller's Day Off*, learning to play allows the film's three teenagers to escape their present as high school students and experience a taste of freedom to come. In these films, the youthful, liminal state between past and future is not confined to the chronologically young but available to anyone who knows how to play.

The Breakfast Club's emphasis on moving past existing frames of identity begins with an opening quote from David Bowie's "Changes" (1971)—". . . And these children that you spit on as they try to change their worlds are immune to your consultations. They're quite aware of what they're going through . . ."—accompanied by the Simple Minds song "Don't You Forget About Me" (1985). After a moment, the frame containing the quote appears to crack and shatter, glass bursting toward the spectator to reveal the dull grey edifice of Shermer High School,[10] exploding the first of many frames through which we initially view "these children" from the inside out. The static frame retakes the film in an opening montage of close shots of high school detritus—ticking clock, school newspaper, graffiti, trophies, Rorschach tests—intercut with shots of empty hallways, a classroom, a locker room, a cafeteria, and lockers. The essay that "brain" Brian (Anthony Michael Hall) will write for all five Saturday morning detainees is read over these images, telling the spectator that it does not matter what identities these young people choose for themselves, instead outsiders will "see us as you want to see us." The link between outward markers of adolescent identity and the frame is thus established. When one's persona is determined by others, the frame is stationary; it gives a snapshot of selfhood, a partial indicator of the most obvious characteristics. In these opening moments, the frame contains the individual.

Figure 5.3 The high school class system in *The Breakfast Club*.

The static frame continues when we are introduced to the five students as peers. After each is dropped off or appears outside of the school, they silently enter the cavernous library in high-angle extreme long shots that reinforce the school as a space of surveillance and immediately arrange themselves in an ersatz version of the school class system. Princess Claire (Molly Ringwald) and athlete Andrew (Emilio Estevez) sit in the front row closest to the door, as social equals, while nerdy Brian initially sits right behind them, an aspiring social climber. Working-class Bender (Judd Nelson) quickly and silently rousts Brian from his seat and the nerd moves laterally to the other side of the room where "basket case" Allison (Ally Sheedy) sits behind him, furthest from the door. By the time detention supervisor Richard Vernon (Paul Gleason) arrives, the students have already disciplined themselves through surveillance; the other four stare at misfit Allison with incredulity and rejection, their gaze as well as her placement in the frame emphasizing her untouchable status.[11]

The power of the gaze is quickly linked to the mobile frame. Early in the film, camera movement is reserved for Vernon, who is able to move through the disciplinary space of surveillance with ease, the camera tracking to follow his movements. We first meet Vernon when he struts into the library, the camera reframing slightly to the left to follow him. As he introduces their assignment to write an essay detailing "who you think you are," the camera reframes and then tracks left to follow his movements. As the one administering this detention and demanding that these teenagers define themselves, Vernon has the power to move the frame. Yet after Vernon leaves, the gaze and control of the frame as forms of power transfer to Bender, who takes on a similar menacing role to his peers. After Bender asserts his authority over Brian, the camera follows Bender's movement as he turns his gaze toward Claire; it tilts, pans, and tracks as Bender sits across from Claire and Andrew, suggesting that they close the door to the library, thereby interrupting Vernon's surveillance and reclaiming this space as their own. The mobile frame thus becomes an indicator of class mobility (Bender is now equal to school celebrities Claire and Andrew) but also the power to reframe one's social status.

Bender's initial act of rebellion is just the film's opening feint in representing adolescence as a state of anxiety. In relation to film form more generally, Eugenie Brinkema defines anxiety as that which "disturbs the continuity and completion of activity," an interruption or "absolute breach" in a system, a cessation of forward progress.[12] Andrew ascribes to this definition when he states that he has a wrestling meet the next week and doesn't want to miss it by bucking the system today. For Andrew and the others, this day is simply a detention, an interruption in his forward movement toward his future. Their angst stems from the pressure caused by "squeezing time and choking the possibility for forward progress that nevertheless persists," from "the *failure* or inability to interrupt a system."[13] However, in the second act of the film, just as these teenagers begin to realize that this detention offers just such a respite from the pressures of the everyday high school class system, the camera becomes unmoored to follow them as they discover their own individuality and deal with the anxiety of straying outside of their predetermined identities. Instead of expressing adult power, the mobile frame in this segment itself becomes anxious, presenting "a new form of carved-up, iterable movement" in the repetitive and constricted shots during the group's escape from the library that render the school a labyrinth from which they cannot escape.[14]

The transition from adolescent anxiety to youthful play begins when the film breaks free from these abstracted moments of camera movement. While the tracking shots in the second act contain the group through their repetition, there is a shift toward circular and vertiginous movement in the last act of the film. The beating heart of *The Breakfast Club* is a group confession that details how these five teenagers received detention and what will happen after this interval in their daily lives is over. Andrew, who has continually proven to be the most other-directed in his identity, finally explains what he has done to land in detention. As he describes bullying another young man in order to gain his father's approval, the frame takes on a new orientation. As opposed to tracking figure movement, the camera tracks and pans around the periphery of the group as Andrew recounts his story. While Andrew remains the focus, the frame moves behind the adolescents listening in the foreground, first showing Allison, then Bender, and finally Claire as fuzzy, out-of-focus silhouettes before resting just next to Brian's position in the semicircle. Less an experience of seeing from these teenagers' respective positions, this shot represents their acknowledgement of each other as equals for the first time, finding commonalities in their experience as individuals at a similar point in their lives rather than divided by perceived differences according to economic class and social hierarchies.

This shot thus marks the beginning of *The Breakfast Club*'s transition from representing adolescence as an experience of anxiety to presenting youth as a feeling of play. Immediately after the group expresses their wish to extend the twin intervals of detention and adolescence, as Allison notes that "when you grow up, your heart dies," the film cuts to a cathartic dance sequence set to Karla DeVito's "We Are Not Alone" (1985), which Brian cues on a record player. In this sequence, the circular movement of the frame during Andrew's confession is transferred to the bodies of the teenagers themselves as Allison, Claire, Brian, and Bender twirl frenetically as the camera reframes to capture their movements. In his analysis of play, Roger Caillois notes that the ludic experience of *ilinx* is "an attempt to momentarily destroy the stability of perception" through feelings of great height or rapid twirling.[15] Following his discussion, it is striking that this sequence offers shots of whirling teenagers intercut with those dancing and sitting at new heights, such as the second floor of the library, on top of a statue, or on top of the library railing. What was previously a space of anxiety has been transformed into one of play as those who were earlier antagonists share the frame as equals for the first time when dancing together in low-angle shots that directly contradict the earlier high-angle surveillance shots.

In a similar fashion, *Ferris Bueller's Day Off* argues for a fundamental irony with regards to youth. While adolescence is often romanticized as a time of leisure that predates adult responsibility, Hughes's film suggests the opposite. Here, teenagers serve as proletarian inmates sentenced to hard labor in the colorless classrooms of a middle-American high school. By contrast, adults represent the leisured upper class (except for the dreary and vindictive middle class of educators and maître d's) whose jobs allow them the freedom to escape to communal spaces of connection. Yet the slippage between age and class allows for some mobility. By posing as an adult, Ferris Bueller, along with his best friend Cameron Frye (Alan Ruck) and love interest, Sloane Peterson (Mia Sara), is able to slip away to the pleasures of urban Chicago. During visits to, among others, the Sears (now Willis) Tower, the Chicago Board of Trade, an exclusive downtown restaurant, a Chicago Cubs game, and the Von Steuben Day Parade, the three teenagers ruminate on how they will soon enter the ranks of adulthood and win their liberty. According to the film, Ferris Bueller's "day off" is a symbol of things to come rather than an aspect of youth left behind. In fact, the film suggests that leisure and play are not restricted to the young. Instead play is the exclusive province of youthful adults.

In its way, *Ferris Bueller's Day Off* repeatedly asserts that in order to escape from the prison of adolescence, one must learn to enjoy the present. While Ferris is primed for the adult world, negotiating the high school bureaucracy with ease, Cameron begins his day off drained of life, wasting away in bed, openly wishing that he were dead because his parents have provided him with a flawed model of adulthood. Over the course of the film though, Cameron learns to play, becomes revitalized, and ends the film with the declaration that he will become his own man. Cultural historian Johan Huizinga defined play as "a free activity standing quite consciously outside 'ordinary' life as being 'not serious,' but at the same time absorbing the player intensely and utterly."[16] This definition fits well with Ferris, Cameron, and Sloane's entire day, as a series of liberating activities presented in stark contrast to their compulsory high school classes. However, it would seem difficult to argue that several sightseeing stops and a lunch constitute activities that absorb the player "intensely and utterly."

Each of the teens' activities nonetheless falls within one of the four types of games—*ilinx*, *alea*, *mimicry*, and *agôn*—that Caillois located on the spectrum between childlike and adult play. *Ilinx* is most apparent in activities that engender the feelings of dizziness, disorder, and vertigo (such as a trip to the world's tallest building); games of chance over whose outcome the player has no control

Figure 5.4 Glass as a barrier in *Ferris Bueller's Day Off*.

fall under the category of *alea* (for example, playing the stock market); the act of simulation in playacting serves as an example of *mimicry* (as when Ferris imitates an absent adult in order to poach his reservation); competitions such as baseball or football function as *agôn* (found at the Cubs game).[17] As the trio engages in each of these forms of play in turn, Cameron becomes increasingly able to deal with the prospect of his future and to take responsibility for the consequences of his actions rather than following the dictates of Ferris or his parents.

In this manner, *Ferris Bueller's Day Off* presents the process of maturation as something of a paradox: in order to become an adult, you must know how to play. Further, the act of play allows one to feel young while enjoying the freedom of adulthood. Cameron's development throughout this series of sequences bears this out. Although Ferris convinces him to play like an adult by borrowing his father's coveted 1961 GT Ferrari California, Cameron quickly relapses into adolescent anxiety about the car (which boasts the telling license plate "NRVOUS") once they arrive in Chicago. In response, Ferris suggests that they climb onto the railing at the Sears Tower observation deck and lean their heads against the window in order to look down at the tiny world below. The film then offers three low-angle close-ups of Sloane, Ferris, and Cameron pressed against the glass, staring down at the spectator, and then cuts to a high-angle point-of-view shot from Cameron's perspective. This sequence presents an early example of the film's motif of distinguishing between playful adults and imprisoned adolescents by framing each on either side of a glass partition, similar to the shots of bus riders from *Sixteen Candles*. In this instance, we are identified with Cameron's vertiginous point of view as he begins to push against this class divide through *ilinx*, stating that he thinks he can see his father down below. Glass barriers play a further significant role in the film's representation of *alea* at the Chicago Board of Trade. As Ferris leans against an observation window with the exchange floor in the background, he asks

Sloane to marry him, which prompts a discussion of the merits of marriage and Cameron's denunciation of the practice based on his parents' example. The deep staging for this discussion underscores Cameron's greater distance from adulthood as Ferris, the most grown-up of the three, is positioned closest to the exchange floor, while Cameron, the most childish, sits furthest away.

In addition to the representation of *ilinx* and *alea*, the group engages in *mimicry* at several points during the day, most notably when they crash the reservation list at the swanky downtown restaurant, Chez Quis. In this sequence, Ferris first attempts to bribe the snooty maître d' only to be rebuffed. He then poses as reservation-holder Abe Froman, "the sausage king of Chicago," through a ruse that exploits Ferris's knowledge of call-waiting technology. As Caillois discusses, *mimicry* serves as a form of imitation in which the player passes for another, acting out a part.[18] The child imitates the adult, as Ferris does Froman, and Cameron reluctantly gets into the act by reprising a deep "adult" voice to emulate a policeman over the phone. Later that afternoon, when the three friends attend the Cubs game and watch the players engage in *agôn*, Cameron softens toward the adult world of ludic independence and he and Ferris are presented as equals in a medium two-shot. Ferris even comments, "You know, if we played by the rules right now, we'd be in gym." At this, Cameron laughs for the first time, acknowledging that their experience of leisure stems from the fact that they have broken the rules of the larger game of adolescence, a game that they can only win by aging out or becoming more like adults through play.

While Cameron's maturation takes place after he breaks through the transparent boundary between childhood and adulthood when he crashes his father's car through a glass garage window, his school's dean of students Ed Rooney (Jeffrey Jones) undergoes a parallel reversion to powerless childishness over the course of the film as he engages Ferris in a game of cat-and-mouse. Rooney's return to a more childish state grows as he is outsmarted by Ferris at every turn, first by Ferris's superior understanding of technology (computers, call waiting, and answering machines) and then by Rooney's inability to see beyond his own immediate situation. In the unfamiliar arena outside of school, Rooney first runs into trouble in a suburban pizza joint. As Rooney surveys the busy lunch scene, we take on his point of view briefly, panning across the tables full of lunching adults to light on a dark-haired teenager in a familiar jacket. In a rare moment of access to the subjectivity of an adult, we hear Rooney's thoughts as his voice intones "Bueller" triumphantly and smiles. We then walk toward the youth along with Rooney, in a Steadicam point-of-view shot that doubles that of Cameron at the garage, until Rooney approaches and announces to the teenager: "Les jeux sont faits. Translation: the game is up. Your ass is mine." Rooney finds himself sorely mistaken though as the youth turns to reveal that "Ferris" is in fact a teenage girl wearing a similar jacket, who then sprays soda on Rooney in retaliation. As a doused Rooney stands nonplussed, a *Pac-Man* sound effect plays, denoting that a player has lost a life. The comparison is clear: rather than an adult doing his job, Rooney has become a poor player who has lost this round because he has failed to imagine that the playing field for this contest extends beyond the suburbs.

Imprisoned by his own limited point of view, Rooney only regresses further. After the soda soaking, Rooney proceeds to lose other outward markers of his adult independence, including a shoe, his clean suit, and his car. During the closing credits, after Ferris has returned safely home with his parents none the wiser as to his urban exploits, the camera follows a defeated Rooney limping along the sidewalk in his torn and muddy suit, face bloodied (after Jeanie has kicked him) as a school bus pulls up beside him. The driver offers him a lift, which Rooney reluctantly accepts, and he ends up riding the bus along with his students. In this ending, Rooney represents the negative side of the regression offered by play. While Cameron becomes more of an adult through successful play, Rooney becomes more childish and vindictive because he takes the game too seriously, relegated to just one of the crowd of adolescents confined to the school bus.

In this sense, *The Breakfast Club* and *Ferris Bueller's Day Off* share an aesthetic engagement with adolescence as a form of imprisonment while depicting youthfulness as an experience of mobility. In both films the frame remains ambivalent, a space of anxiety as well as play. *The Breakfast Club*'s iconic final freeze frame, in which Bender walks past the goal posts on the football field, bleachers in the background, his fist raised in the air, exemplifies this tendency. In this shot, time stills, an interruption and an interval located within a field of play. In *Ferris Bueller's Day Off*, the film ends with a similarly contradictory, post-credits, deep focus shot of the hallway in Ferris's house, initially empty except for several framed photos on the wall and three doorframes. Ferris appears in one of them, clad again in his bathrobe, and walks toward the spectator, the camera racking focus to keep him in frame but remaining stationary as he informs us that the film has concluded and we should leave. He then disappears back into the frame from whence he came and the film cuts to black. While Ferris has the power to end the film, it occurs at the moment that he must face the film's tomorrow as a senior who may have played hooky one too many times. In these films, youth's liminal position between yesterday and tomorrow is a two-way street that allows the young to experience the freedom of adulthood while stripping childish adults of their power.

FROM DEPENDENCE TO SELF-RELIANCE: *PRETTY IN PINK* AND *SOME KIND OF WONDERFUL*

Hughes wrote and produced two more prominent teen films in the '80s, *Pretty in Pink* and *Some Kind of Wonderful* (both directed by his associate Howard

Deutch). Despite Hughes's reduced credits on these films, they offer the most explicit correlation between economic class and the high school social hierarchy of his oeuvre, suggesting the crystallization of a recognizable Hughes youth aesthetic by 1986. Reviews of these films further identify them as Hughes productions with Deutch serving as a member of Hughes's "team."[19] The cross-class romantic comedy *Pretty in Pink* depicts a vast economic and social divide between "richie" Blane (Andrew McCarthy) and lower-middle-class Andie (Molly Ringwald) although both exhibit, along with their peers, remarkable independence from the world of adults, who are rarely glimpsed except for Andie's depressed father (Harry Dean Stanton), whom she takes care of like a child. In this film, camera movement is employed when characters don't recognize or acknowledge inequality, suggesting that social mobility is a form of willful blindness to social structures. By contrast, shot/reverse-shot editing predominates when characters see through social frames of identity such as class, gender, and age to acknowledge commonalities. Attraction (as with Blane and Andie), hostility (as with Andie and the school's resident "richie" mean girls), or love (Andie and her father) allow opportunities for social transcendence. In these shot constructions, close-ups and medium close-ups of objects of desire, enemies, and family instantaneously replace each other on the screen, taking up equal space in the frame, suggesting an equality in their similar experiences caught between independence and self-reliance.

Some Kind of Wonderful continues this motif by suggesting that a character's isolation in the frame is a desirable form of individuality. *Some Kind of Wonderful* opens with a montage that suggests commonalities between its three protagonists—tomboy Watts (Mary Stuart Masterson), blue-collar Keith (Eric Stolz), and middle-class popular girl Amanda (Lea Thompson)—despite their discrete locations and activities (practicing drums, fixing cars, and having sex, respectively). Each commands the frame as the camera tilts, tracks, and pans to follow their movements yet only the two social outcasts (Watts and Keith) are shown in their own frames while Amanda is introduced in the same frame as her boyfriend, Hardy (Craig Sheffer). An independent frame thus serves as a marker of autonomy from what others think. The film tracks Amanda's journey from Hardy's possession to Keith's acquisition to her final repudiation of defining herself in relation to others and standing on her own, shown alone in the frame as she exits the film.[20] In a telling shot during their first (and last) date, the camera follows Keith and Amanda as they walk through the halls of the local art museum (doubling Ferris, Cameron, and Sloane's trip to the Art Institute of Chicago during their day off), passing framed representations of other places and times. Right before the film cuts to a point-of-view shot of a framed painting of a baptism, Keith tells Amanda that the museum is his "church. I can come here and what anybody says about me doesn't matter." In this space filled with frames, he can see beyond those of the outside world.

Yet the film still suggests that such transcendence relies on the continued existence of frames. When Keith reveals the painting he has done of Amanda, he demonstrates that his desire for her relies on his perception of her in a frame.

As we have seen, through their formal construction, particularly the use of the film frame, Hughes's teen films offer a sustained consideration of the ways in which youth can be understood as a socially constructed identity like that of gender and class. In *Sixteen Candles* and *Weird Science*, social status stems from possession and control over mature bodies, but not necessarily your own, as even those with adult bodies can be rendered powerless. *The Breakfast Club* and *Ferris Bueller's Day Off* similarly explore youth as a state of suspension between past and future that can trap the chronologically young and old alike if they cannot see past their own immediate frames of reference. Although not directed by Hughes, *Pretty in Pink* and *Some Kind of Wonderful* offer the most explicit spin on this theme as isolation in the frame points to a character's individuality and self-reliance in rejecting social conceptions of who they should be. In all of these films, control over the film frame is an indication of status not just in the diegesis but over the spectator as well. Just like Ferris's advice, in those moments when the frame calls attention to itself, we are invited to stop and look around for a while to consider the construction of John Hughes's representation of youth.

NOTES

1. See Steve Bailey and James Hay, "Cinema and the Premises of Youth: 'Teen Films' and Their Sites in the 1980s and 1990s," in *Genre and Contemporary Hollywood*, ed. Steve Neale (London: British Film Institute, 2002), 218–35; Timothy Shary, *Generation Multiplex: The Image of Youth in American Cinema since 1980*, rev. edn (Austin: University of Texas Press, 2014), 29–39, 40, 60–3, 74–6, 102–3, 223, 245–6; Catherine Driscoll, *Teen Film: A Critical Introduction* (Oxford and New York: Berg, 2011), 45–56; and Roz Kaveney, *Teen Dreams: Reading Teen Film and Television from Heathers to Veronica Mars* (New York: I. B. Tauris, 2006), 11–45.
2. Adrian Martin, "Teen Movies: The Forgetting of Wisdom," in *Phantasms: The Dreams and Desires at the Heart of our Popular Culture* (Ringwood, Vic: McPhee Gribble; Penguin, 1994), 66, 68.
3. For a recent entry into this area, see Frances Smith, *Rethinking the Hollywood Teen Movie: Gender, Genre and Identity* (Edinburgh: Edinburgh University Press, 2017).
4. For more on cultural and personal rites of passage in the youth film, see Catherine Driscoll, 66.
5. For more on the male gaze and female objectification conveyed through shot structures, see Laura Mulvey, "Visual Pleasure and Narrative Cinema," in *Feminism and Film*, ed. E. Ann Kaplan (New York: Oxford University Press, 2000), 34–47.
6. For an excellent reading of *Weird Science* in relation to issues of masculinity, particularly the opening, see Andrew Scahill, "Bizarre Love Triangle: Frankensteinian Masculinities in *Weird Science*" in this volume.

7. Mikhail Bakhtin, *Rabelais and His World*, trans. Hélène Iswolsky (Bloomington: Indiana University Press, 2009), 21.
8. For more on the concept of the monster as a liminal "contradictory, incomplete, or formless" figure (not unlike the adolescent), see Noel Carroll, *Philosophy of Horror: Or, Paradoxes of the Heart* (New York: Routledge, 1990), 31–2.
9. For more on the grotesque body as overturning hierarchies in Hollywood cinema, see William Paul, *Laughing Screaming: Modern Hollywood Horror and Comedy* (New York: Columbia University Press, 1994), 45–8.
10. As evidenced by its reuse from *Weird Science*, Hughes set nine of his films in the fictional suburb of Shermer, Illinois where characters from these films existed in the same universe of American suburbia, if not the same classes. David Kamp, "Sweet Bard of Youth," *Vanity Fair*, February 10, 2010, https://www.vanityfair.com/news/2010/03/john-hughes-201003.
11. For more on discipline as an "uninterrupted play of calculated gazes," see Michel Foucault, *Discipline and Punish: The Birth of the Prison* (New York: Vintage Books, 1995), 177.
12. Eugenie Brinkema, *The Forms of the Affects* (Durham, NC: Duke University Press, 2014), 196.
13. Brinkema, 194.
14. Brinkema, 196.
15. Roger Caillois, *Man, Play and Games*, trans. Meyer Barash (Chicago: University of Illinois Press, 2001), 23–4.
16. Johan Huizinga, *Homo Ludens: A Study of the Play-Element in Culture* (Boston: Routledge, 1949), 13.
17. Caillois, 12–23.
18. Caillois, 21.
19. See Roger Ebert, "Some Kind of Wonderful," RogerEbert.com, February 27, 1987, https://www.rogerebert.com/reviews/some-kind-of-wonderful-1987; Janet Maslin, "Film: John Hughes's 'Pretty in Pink,'" *New York Times*, February 28, 1986; Gene Siskel, "The John Hughes Magic Missing in 'Pretty in Pink,'" *Chicago Tribune*, February 28, 1986; Dave Kehr, "'Some Kind of Wonderful,'" *Chicago Tribune*, February 27, 1987; and Janet Maslin, "'Some Kind of Wonderful,'" *New York Times*, February 27, 1987.
20. For more on autonomy in *Some Kind of Wonderful*, see Kaveney, 35–40.

CHAPTER 6

"When Cameron was in Egypt's land": The Queer Child of Neglect in John Hughes's Films

Barbara Jane Brickman

At the dramatic climax of the second episode of the popular Netflix original series *Stranger Things* ("The Weirdo of Maple Street," [2016]), the series creators offer viewers a haunting, almost iconic, tableau: an awkward, tall, redheaded teenage girl with glasses, who has been abandoned poolside as a pitiable third wheel, sits, lonely and chastened, at the end of the diving board, her feet dangling through the mist and into the pool. Hanging her head, she seems caught between leaving now that the couples have paired off or waiting alone for her best friend, but in an instant, achieved by shot/reverse shot, she is gone—the misty pool deck eerily emptied of her presence. This climactic moment when Barb (Shannon Purser) is snatched into the "Upside Down" of *Stranger Things*' first season not only gives us our initial glimpse of its supernatural creature but also signals the season's preoccupation with the struggle for survival of a host of "weirdos" like the mysterious, gender-ambiguous foundling Eleven (Millie Bobby Brown) and the missing boy Will Beyers (Noah Schnapp), who is singled out by his own mother as different and "sensitive," teased by other kids, and called "queer" by his own father. In her own way, I would argue, Barb has likewise been marked as queer, appearing from the beginning as an easy stereotype—the less-attractive, nerdy, prudish best friend of the prized Nancy (Natalia Dyer), who tries to steer her friend away from (hetero)sexual experience and then is painfully excluded from the normative coupling scenario; Barb stands too close in the school hallway and is overly concerned with Nancy's love life—even noticing that her friend has worn a new bra to her date—and in the end, of course, she is abandoned by Nancy and thus neglected in her traumatic moment of need.

As if to establish their contrasting positions and the queer's tragic vulnerability, the next episode in the series begins pointedly by crosscutting between

Nancy's "first time" with Steve (Joe Keery) and the mysterious monster's brutal attack on Barb. In other words, the queer friend's destruction takes place in the Upside Down of adolescent heterosexual congress, and a question presses itself: is Barb lost, along with Will, because she *belongs* in the Upside Down—a terrifying, atavistic, primal queer limbo? And can she never escape because her queerness is irredeemable, or, one might argue, because queerness is irreconcilable with the normative story of growing up, the central narrative paradigm of the series? Indeed, teens like Barb so rarely survive to see the end of this narrative told. As a genre, teen film has seldom imagined a future for queer kids (when it imagines queer kids at all), typically either reconciling them to heteronormativity and the reproductive futurity represented in the nuclear family or excising them through the most tragic of ends. Yet in the landmark teen films of John Hughes such as *Ferris Bueller's Day Off* (1986), particularly with the remarkable example of the title character's best friend Cameron Frye (Alan Ruck), a queer adolescence, often under siege, is allowed to trouble the normative maturation plot without the violent erasure so typical of the genre, then and since. Cameron's queer survival, perhaps even triumph, I would argue, offers another path for growth—one perhaps not straight up but, at least, very clearly out.

JOHN HUGHES: AUTEUR OF NEGLECT

Fans and critics of the Duffer Brothers' *Stranger Things* have long noted how the series pays homage to or directly cites numerous cinematic maturation stories from the 1980s, so it should hardly be surprising that Barb's isolation and poolside vulnerability encourages this redolent connection to that earlier third wheel in distress at the end of a diving board, Cameron Frye, whose traumatized catatonic pose and mock suicide off the board, of course, ends quite differently from Barb's violent abduction.[1] Truly, one would be surprised if there was *not* such an allusion or correspondence to the Hughes teen films of the 1980s considering the long shadow the writer-director-producer's work has cast over the history of teen media since that period. Despite helming other extremely successful films, from *National Lampoon's Vacation* (1983) to *Home Alone* (1990), Hughes's name has become nearly synonymous with the teen film genre and its phenomenal ascendance in the 1980s, and his distinct style, adolescent narrative concerns, and brand of humor have thereby become easily recognizable. The Hughesian teenage world typically combines a love of farce and broad, even offensive, humor with an unabashed commitment to taking "teenagers seriously," as Roz Kaveney asserts, delving into adolescent fears, conflicts, and problems with rich and, at moments, complex depth.[2] Often acknowledged for his remarkable sympathy for adolescent experience as it is

Figure 6.1 Cameron's (Alan Ruck) traumatized isolation on the diving board represents an iconic moment in Hughes's oeuvre of neglect.

realized in teenage characters (and muse-like actors like Molly Ringwald) with "such depth and dimension," Hughes particularly honed in on the painful divide and dysfunction between parents and teens in this era.[3] Hughes's teen films, in short, create a veritable pantheon of parental neglect, abuse, or shameful indifference.[4]

Although Hughes's *Home Alone* represents perhaps the most obvious and renowned installment in what one might call an "oeuvre of neglect," Kevin McCallister (Macaulay Culkin) comes at the end of a long line of forgotten, mistreated, and abandoned Hughesian youth—from Samantha Baker (Molly Ringwald) in his directorial debut *Sixteen Candles* (1984) to, of course, the members of *The Breakfast Club* (1985) and, most centrally for my argument, Cameron Frye. As Jonathan Bernstein dramatically concludes in his popular history of teen film, Hughes reserves possibly his greatest enmity for parental figures in his films who neglect or mistreat his favored youths: "Parents were tyrannical in their expectations. They were criminal in their neglect. They were simpleminded. They were devious. They were archaic in their remove from modern times."[5] While Samantha's parents (and grandparents) forgetting her birthday comically sets the action of *Sixteen Candles* in motion, *The Breakfast Club* takes much more serious aim by offering a grim procession of parental failure and abuse—from John Bender's (Judd Nelson) abusive cigar-wielding father to Allison Reynolds' (Ally Sheedy) achingly lonely neglect—and almost all of Hughes's penned or directed teen films follow suit: absent parents and a tyrannical brother-guardian in *Weird Science* (1985), a pitiable but childishly dependent father (and completely absent mother) in *Pretty in Pink* (1986), and, lastly, the clueless parents, vindictive dean of students, and Cameron's terrorizing, unloving father in *Ferris Bueller's Day Off.* While some of his young protagonists turn their forsaken condition to their own advantage, most remarkably Culkin's forgotten but fiercely resourceful Kevin and the parade-float-riding, unofficial "king" of Chicago, Ferris Bueller, Hughes more often dwells on the painful victimization and suffering of his otherwise privileged teenagers at the hands of their parents' abuse, mistreatment, and/or negligence—a tendency singled out by reviewers critical of his seemingly shameless "pandering" to the films' teenage audiences.[6]

But rather than focus on these adult figures of abuse and abandonment, who are, in any case, often nameless, faceless, or even left outside the frame in Hughes's films, this chapter considers his children of neglect and the queerness enacted by them. In *Fantasies of Neglect: Imagining the Urban Child in American Film and Fiction* (2016), Pamela Wojcik identifies a powerful set of competing popular fantasies that have been paramount in constructing the very concept of the child in twentieth-century American culture. Focused particularly on the urban child, the prototypical stories that she explores offer two opposing representations of children and youth outside of—or distressingly deprived of—adult supervision and care: in one fantasy, a victimized and even abused child's lack of supervision is presented as a sign of social, political, and/or familial dysfunction in the urban milieu, while in the other, the joyfully unaccompanied child embraces the thrills, risks, and freedoms of independent movement and creative way-finding on city streets. While Kevin McCallister and Ferris Bueller certainly fit the mold of the latter masters of neglect examined by Wojcik, more often than not Hughes's tormented youth resemble the "melodramatic," even "Dickensian," suffering of popular texts in the former vein—from the environmental dysfunction of social problems films of the 1930s to the emotional abuse of psychological studies of the 1970s—although, of course, reconfigured for the suburban context.[7] Time and again we are drawn into the high emotions and wrenching accusations of Hughes's confessional young protagonists, weaving various fantasies of parental failure, but now from the prosperous confines of 1980s suburban Chicago.

Significantly, though, Wojcik argues for a specific function served by these popular melodramatic imaginings of parental neglect, in that they are often used to achieve a final containment of the wayward or abandoned youth being represented. In other words, if the urban child is suffering or shamelessly victimized, then she or he is clearly in need of rescue, protection, and restraint. Most pointedly, for example, in the post-Second World War narratives focused on African American youths, their parental (often, maternal) neglect and exposure to criminality and urban dereliction necessitates "some kind of rescue for the child from his family and, in some cases, from the city itself."[8] Indeed, Wojcik contends, following Kathryn Stockton's formulation of the queer child, that the urban children in these works are seemingly imbued with abuse in order to rationalize their non-normative state, i.e., their lack of innocence, and to instigate fantasies of neglect where the child is necessarily "rendered innocent" by the abuse and, thereby, "in need of protection" and containment.[9] While I agree with her that the urban child is more typically figured as non-normative, experienced, and victimized by abuse than suburban youths, this intertwined mechanism of dramatized neglect as the catalyst for adult fantasies of rescue and as a justification for the normalizing of othered youth certainly can function on leafy, more affluent streets, especially for queer children who are so often violently excised from the "ideals of family and home" that Wojcik finds there.[10] In Hughes's films, for example in the story of Cameron, the interdependence between the non-normative youth and the filmmaker's fantasies of parental neglect and abuse cannot be understated. Yet, while I recognize that Hughes characteristically employs this mechanism for containment and conservative resolution like others before him, the queer child in Cameron suggests another possibility.[11]

To be sure, identifying Cameron as a "queer child" does require some close reading. He is not immediately distinguishable within Stockton's major classifications of the queer child, such as the "Grown Homosexual" looking back on his youth, or the "Child Queered by Freud," or, as alluded to above, the "Child Queered by Color" (or class), nor is he marked by obvious signifiers of the closeted gay teen who rarely appeared in the teen film genre before more recent twenty-first-century examples (in the male version, signaled by "suspect" sartorial choices, hairstyle, musical taste, and, of course, effeminacy).[12] While Cameron is surely "endow[ed]" with abuse, to use Stockton's phrasing, it is *not* because his race or class denies him the "privilege of both weakness and innocence" and, therefore, requires suffering and non-consensual abuse to trigger rescue and fabricate innocence.[13] One might argue, rather, that his abuse helps both to identify him as queer and simultaneously mask his queerness as innocent. As an affluent White male, Cameron should be bestowed with all the privileges of normative childhood/youth, but queerness brings with it the inevitable taint of sexual experience that haunts the queer child (and adult), and so his queerness must be disguised through the abuse.[14] Indeed, the abuse has the potential to be a kind of alibi for his queer sexuality, but, significantly, I would argue, his rejection of abuse at the film's end potentially announces a queer future for Cameron, although one, of course, never pictured by Hughes.

Cameron presents an example, then, of what Stockton calls the "sideways growth" of the queer child—delaying, deferring, and swerving away from the kind of growing up that leads inexorably to heterosexual maturation—and thereby he gestures towards a queer future. However, this particular plotting—this queer narrative trajectory—has seemed almost an impossibility within the teen film genre and certainly would not be considered characteristic of Hughes's 1980s teen oeuvre, where, as his own actress-muse Molly Ringwald has noted, homophobic slurs like "'fag' and 'faggot' are tossed around with abandon."[15]

Indeed, historians of the genre, such as David Considine and Timothy Shary, have long lamented either the dearth of queer representations in teen film or the cautionary and punitive treatment of those few gay (usually male) teens on screen, even through the end of the twentieth century.[16] Shary notes that despite Considine's optimistic hope for better representation, queer youth were still "rare in American cinema" of the 1980s, and those on screen in the 1990s "were almost always troubled and trying to deny their non-heterosexual impulses, lest they face the consequence of ridicule, condemnation, or even death."[17] In other words, according to the heteronormative path of maturation demanded by the genre's typically conservative (adult) values, a queer youth in these media texts has two options: deny your non-normative gender and/or sexuality and conform to heteronormalization, or suffer a traumatic or tragic end. Characters of the genre like Allison Reynolds, Duckie (Jon Cryer), and Watts (Mary Stuart Masterson) must be magically made over and paired off (like the exemplary Tom Lee [John Kerr] of *Tea and Sympathy* [1956]), or they must suffer the fate of characters like Plato (Sal Mineo), Billy Joe (Robby Benson), and the hustlers of *My Own Private Idaho* (1991).[18] Cameron Frye, however, follows neither of these paths. He finds no expectant female suitor on the other side of the prom and he does not end up looking down the barrel of tragically isolated, loveless future or no future at all. He does not find himself in the "Upside Down" of queer tragedy. He's "gonna be good," and so, perhaps unwittingly, a John Hughes film imagines for the queer child a possible (or even bright) future.

PLEASE, PLEASE, PLEASE LET ME GET WHAT I WANT: CAMERON FRYE AND QUEER POSSIBILITY

When we first meet Cameron in *Ferris Bueller's Day Off*, shortly after Ferris's first direct-address charm offensive, he resembles nothing so much as a rarified invalid or sanctified corpse, almost already a ghost. After his disembodied hand emerges from the sick bed to answer the phone, we initially see Cameron from a distance, in profile, at the center of a dimly lit room, with his head just visible from under the covers of his raised bed, positioned as if on a dais or perhaps a funeral bier. Ferris's cheery voice cuts through the somber synthesized score, demanding, "Cameron, babe, what's happening?" from (we find out shortly) his poolside, one-man luau. The camera brings us closer to Cameron as the scene progresses to establish his apparent illness, signified by close-ups on his host of medicines and repeated views of his weary, beleaguered face. Then, ironically, there is a sudden cut to Ferris seated in a rattan chair by the pool, all sunny arrogance and kitsch Polynesian-inspired leisure. Ferris, famously, ignores his best friend's insistence that he is truly "sick" or, melodramatically, "dying," and he demands Cameron come over to pick him up. According to Ferris, his tightly wound friend "has a lot of things to sort out" before college, which seems confirmed by the climax of the scene when Cameron self-pityingly revises the renowned Negro spiritual "Go Down Moses," closing his eyes and singing alone to the elevated score, "When Cameron was in Egypt's land," before the denouement, "Let my Cameron go," when he is phantasmatically joined by a background chorus in the style of the Fisk Jubilee Singers who first popularized the spiritual.

In an uncritical moment regrettably foreshadowing the insulting, unaccountable use of a group of African American background dancers for Ferris's parade antics, Cameron here is not only likening his situation to that of the Israelites in bondage to Pharaoh (the original lyrics read "When Israel was in Egypt land / Let my people go"), but of course also to the African slaves who used this biblical reference in the spiritual to symbolize their violent oppression. Yet, for Cameron, and presumably for the intended audience, his suffering feels significant and authentic, even though we also recognize a melodramatic, adolescent self-pity. The scene may be, at times, gently mocking his maudlin self-absorption, but we are also encouraged to sympathize with the fact that there is genuinely something troubling Cameron. Throughout the film, he appears sick and miserable, anxious and depressed, under intense pressure from his father *and* Ferris, and eventually traumatized into a semi-catatonic state. Furthermore, from this brief introductory scene, Cameron's otherness and painful dysfunction are clearly signified as queer: this melancholic scene from his sickbed concludes not with Cameron's pathetic plea for freedom from suffering but instead with Ferris's glib, manifestly homoerotic assessment that his despondent friend is "so tight that if you stuck a lump of coal up his ass, in two weeks you'd have a diamond"—this from a shirtless best friend and harasser, who calls him "babe" and is camping it up with kitsch ceramic Tiki tumblers by the side of his parents' pool.

Cameron's queer miserabilism and conflicted anxiety mark his character from our very first introduction, but perhaps more importantly, his close relationship with his best friend both serves as a central catalyst for the narrative (i.e., Ferris just wanting to "give him a good day") and provides the audience with the film's one genuine relationship, the only one with a measure of depth and complexity.[19] This film is, fundamentally, about their relationship and how Ferris's mastery of parental neglect and institutional cruelty enables Cameron to overcome his own paternal abuse and crippling fears. Moreover, as the film's action progresses, Cameron's subjectivity and concerns become the emotional center of the film, as Ferris's supernatural actions and fantastic plotting transform him, at times, into mere archetype—the "trickster" let loose on Chicago's streets.[20] Although one might argue that Cameron plays a subordinate role to the traditional heterosexual plot, as a classic "third wheel" merely used for his father's car in order to spring the female love interest Sloane (Mia Sara) from school, I would contend that Ferris remains consistently focused on his male friend's well-being while Sloane is less developed as a character than even his sister Jeanie (Jennifer Grey); we get only a glimpse of her being pulled out of class in the first third of the film before she joins the male buddy exploits.

Meanwhile, the first act is predominantly driven by scenes of the two male friends coming closer, both physically and emotionally: we begin with Ferris pouting on the phone about Cameron making him "wait around the house" for him, then watch an ill Cameron passionately wrestle with the decision to leave his home in the face of his mate's unrelenting harassment ("he'll just keep calling me"), and then finally join in the fun at Ferris's house as a wooed Cameron excitedly collaborates in deceiving Mr. Rooney, only to be abused and then seduced once more after threatening to leave. All the while, Ferris has employed the tactics of a mercurial but controlling lover, from demanding and relentless pressure to flirtatious exhibition and insinuating persuasion, contritely apologizing for losing his temper while simultaneously working toward the "small favor" of using Cameron's father's beloved Ferrari.

This quasi-romantic companionship between Ferris and Cameron has not gone unnoticed by critics and commentators. Although Andrew Sarris's scathing review only makes a passing swipe at the "very fey Ferris Bueller," other commentators like Bernstein zero in on Cameron in order to press gay-baiting questions about why the unhappy young man never ends up with a girl, even through the short-lived television spin-off.[21] With his distinctive style and apparently "fey" mannerisms, not to mention his moments of camp best exhibited in the "Danke Schoen" performance, Ferris (and, to be fair, Broderick) surely lends a queer tenor to the film, but it is Cameron's character, denied a heterosexual partner, who as the "sexually ambiguous" best friend sustains a possible romance plot between him and Ferris.[22] Kaveney, in fact, posits their companionship as the only "truly romantic relationship in the film," noting not only Cameron's apparent "self-hatred" but also his catatonic dive into the pool as proof that perhaps his "problem is that he is in love with his oblivious best friend."[23] While one might be hard pressed to find a great deal of cinematic evidence of Cameron clearly besotted with his best friend (in distinction from, say, Plato's longing looks at Jim (James Dean) in *Rebel Without a Cause* [1955]), Kaveney's recognition of a "free-floating eroticism" in this Hughes film as well as others makes a compelling argument for locating queerness throughout them.[24] What she describes as the "sexual unease of the mid-1980s" and Hughes's "sexually conservative" values do seem to collide in his films and produce not only this "free-floating eroticism" (a phrase itself nearly synonymous with queerness) but also the accompanying and inevitable disruptions, contradictions, and subtexts it brings. Accordingly, rather than subscribing to Jeffery Dennis's categorical finding that conservative youth films of the 1980s remained always "vigilant about rejecting the homoerotic other," I posit that

Cameron, and a few other examples, show a more ambivalent and undecided fate for a repressed but emerging queer subject in the period.²⁵

Moreover, as the film progresses through its second act, it becomes clearer and clearer that *Ferris Bueller's Day Off* could easily be named "Cameron Frye's Day Off," since it is his subjectivity we are drawn into and his happiness that appears to be Ferris's main concern, just as he dedicates his command performance at the Von Steuben Parade to a "young man who doesn't think he's seen anything good today." Yet, I would argue, the stunning stillness and emotional depth of the scene immediately preceding the parade climax actually forces us to recognize the centrality of the *queer* subject's experience. In a film largely driven by broad farce and outsized adolescent wish fulfillment, the scene in the Art Institute of Chicago almost beggars belief. Set to the Dream Academy's ephemeral instrumental cover of The Smiths' "Please, Please, Please Let Me Get What I Want," the electronic, symphonic notes lead the viewer through a dreamscape of childish play: the three friends run up the stairs of the imposing Art Institute building and gently join a line of school children holding hands through a museum tour; they playfully mock the grandiose position of an Auguste Rodin statue and silently stand in awe, with their backs to us, spellbound by some of Pablo Picasso's women. Nevertheless, it is Cameron's deep, searching, and affective engagement with Georges Seurat's pointillist masterpiece *A Sunday Afternoon on the Island of La Grande Jatte* that comes to define and elevate this striking scene and, perhaps, even redefine teen film itself.²⁶

Figure 6.2 Cameron, alone, initially dwarfed by Seurat's pointillist masterpiece.

As he stands before the large pointillist study of a teeming social world, we are drawn into Cameron's interiority just as the camera forces us closer and closer to the painting's kaleidoscopic surface and to the face of the young girl near its center. Cameron, at long distance, initially stands with his back to the viewer, isolated and dwarfed by the painting, which dominates its own large wall space. After cutting away to Ferris and Sloane, the scene comes back to Cameron, over whose shoulder we see the object of his intense concern: a young girl and (presumably) her mother emerge from the central surface of the painting as the girl's brightly lit white dress and direct stare out at the viewer foreground her. Of all the bourgeois figures enjoying their Sunday afternoon along the river Seine, only this young girl looks directly out from the painting, confronting our (and Cameron's) gaze. As the Dream Academy's symphonic notes reach crescendo, the scene cuts back to a shot of Ferris and Sloane only once more before moving into a mesmerizing shot/reverse shot exchange of increasingly closer and revelatory shots of the two faces and subjects—Cameron and the girl—who seem to plead for our understanding. In close-up and then extreme close-up, Cameron's face appears almost aghast or stunned at first, mouth open and eyes wet, and then as the camera brings us closer in to just his eyes, his distress, bewilderment, and anxiety are conveyed by small twitches and broken blood vessels. Simultaneously, through the abstraction of bringing the viewer progressively closer to the pointillist technique, director Hughes signifies both the complexity and unknowability of the human subject: like a myriad of colored dots on an enormous canvas's surface, the ground of any existential quest is fragmented and confusing. In this incredibly evocative and moving moment, Cameron's imploring eyes seem to ask, "Who am I? What do I want? How can I be?" and the response comes back as abstraction, undecidability, and profusion. Yet in his noble quest and through our being sutured into it, Cameron becomes the controlling (and only significant) subjectivity of the film.

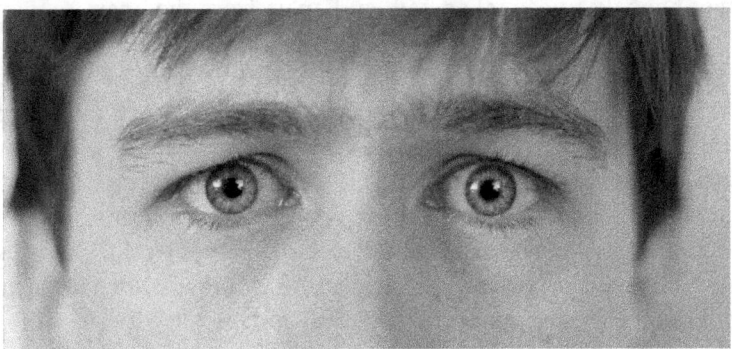

Figure 6.3 Cameron's imploring eyes.

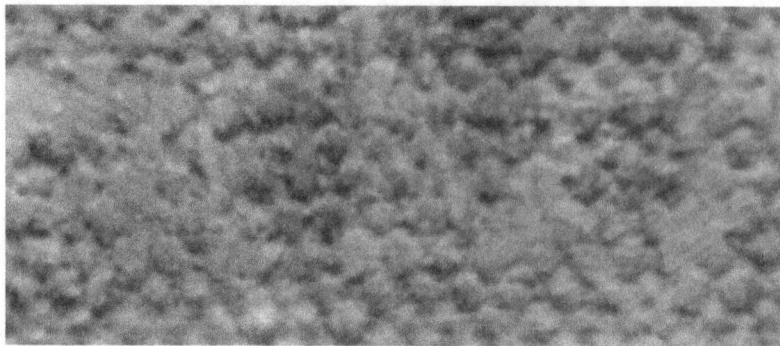

Figure 6.4 The abstraction of the extreme close-up brings us into the existential quest.

Cameron here defines for us the affective experience not just for any adolescent subject, but rather, specifically, for a queer one. Alone with his questions of selfhood and desire, he is explicitly counterposed to and separated from blissful heterosexual union, i.e., a figure of young lovers silhouetted in the blue glow of Marc Chagall's stained glass "American Windows," to whom he is contrasted through parallel editing. As the scene cuts back (twice) from lingering holds on Ferris and Sloane's kiss in front of the Chagall, the juxtaposed Cameron falls into the "Upside Down" of their heteronormative pairing, seemingly submerged into the melancholy, bewildering, and isolating queer experience of his search for identity. In the background of his troubling passage into confusion, yearning, and fear, one can almost hear Smiths front man Morrissey's pleas below the instrumental score: "See the life I've had / Can make a good man bad / So, for once in my life / Let me get what I want / Lord knows, it would be the first time."[27] The imploring queer subject remains outside of or barred from heterosexual normalcy, forlorn and dwarfed by the controlling institutions around him. Like the girl in Seurat's painting, he is distanced, alienated, and apart from the unaware, normative social world. And perhaps to belabor the obvious, his queer existential journey is sparked by and reflected in the face of a young *girl*. This gangly teenage male, with his Gordie Howe jersey and his hands crammed into the pockets of his khakis, apparently enters into a profound moment of self-exploration and questioning only when he finds his own subjectivity represented by the startling otherness of this challenging young girl in Seurat's masterpiece—not by Rodin's grandiose masculine figure or Jackson Pollock's virile action painting. His search and his desires place him outside of both sexual and gender conformity and normalcy, thereby undeniably queering this central male figure of 1980s teen film.

CONCLUSION: WHO DO YOU LOVE?

It must be said, nevertheless, that recognizing Cameron's queerness within the frameworks, generic motifs, and paradigmatic narratives of teen cinema proves difficult and most likely is not a conscious undertaking, even for a master of the form like Hughes. Instead, the film presents this queerness obliquely, refracted through the prism of parental/paternal neglect and abuse. Cameron's otherness, desires, dissatisfactions, and emotional distress signal his queerness, but the film disguises it, I would argue, through the figure of the abusive father and his victimized son. In other words, his alienation from heteronormativity becomes tied up with, or even interchangeable with, his neglect and abuse by his father, and the controlling emotion binding them, of course, is fear.[28]

Yet, as the film proceeds to its denouement, the Ferrari's ruin, this connection between parental neglect and Cameron's queerness becomes more pronounced and pressing until his post-catatonic awakening exposes their dependency through one of the most powerful, if strangely realized, coming-out scenes in teen film. Deconstructing the use of paternal neglect as a mask for Cameron's queerness, the violently cathartic scene of his destruction of the Ferrari not only works as a dramatization of coming out but also proposes a queer future—a way to grow "sideways," to use Stockton's term. While Ferris speculates that Cameron's catatonic state, triggered by seeing the increased mileage on his father's car, is partly explained by his lack of heterosexual experience, having "never been in love," Cameron's own behavior and declarations point to a decidedly queer cause. Set to the backdrop of a ridiculous attempt to avoid punishment by turning the odometer back, an awakened Cameron is finally able to confront his own fears in a deeply emotional monologue where the queer subject emerges from the abused child, realizing "it's ridiculous being afraid, worrying about everything, wishing I was dead."

The Ferrari scene, in short, performs a kind of defiant queer self-actualization. Cameron declares that his father is "not the problem"—"*I'm* the problem"—and when he decides to "take a stand," his father and the car clearly stand in for his "problem," the fear and pain of unrealized desires. The scene, again, signals his queer otherness through juxtaposition with the heterosexual couple, cutting back and forth between a two-shot of an increasingly concerned Ferris and Sloane and shots of Cameron's solitary outpouring of emotion. All at once, the tearful, nearly suicidal, unhappy queer transforms into a figure of incandescent rage, twice demanding angrily, "Who do you love?" and then smashing the hood and grill of his father's perversely cherished car. Finally, just so "tired of being afraid," Cameron refuses to kill himself, and, instead, he "kills" the car—the symbolic object of his neglect which *is* able to secure his father's love and engender happiness. So evocative of the "queer child" imagined by Sara Ahmed, whose unhappiness is formed in the "failure" of making the family happy, Cameron, however, does not follow the narrative trajectory of that child "inevitably" toward an unhappy life, but instead uses this moment to violently, if accidentally, declare himself—to come out.[29] He casually leans on the hood of the teetering car and sends it sailing through the plate glass window, forcing his own hand—jettisoning himself into the outside where "I can't hide this." With a final shot of the mangled car, Cameron moves away from fear, silence, and unhappiness, and this action appears to set him free—to let my Cameron go.[30]

Unlike the few queer kids in teen films before or after, Cameron is not paired off with a heterosexual mate or sacrificed to the exigencies of normative order, violently excised by a tragic end. He is left smiling, refusing to hide anymore. Moreover, Cameron's atypical version of enlightenment and maturation here *is* visible in a few other Hughes characters, such as the "nerd" Brian (Anthony Michael Hall) in *The Breakfast Club* or even Amanda Jones (Lea Thompson) in *Some Kind of Wonderful* (1987), who swerve away from normative heterosexual pairings and assert a different path.[31] Yet, it must be noted that these figures are the exception to the rule: Brian may speak for everyone, but his isolation from the preferred romantic pairings cannot be ignored. In theorizing her "fantasies of neglect," Wojcik proposes that certain non-normative children are imbued with abuse to render them "innocent" and to trigger a rescue narrative by adult (normative) order; thus, the victimized child is saved through parental "protection" and containment.[32] Significantly, most of Hughes's teen films (and the films influenced by him) reveal a different, but certainly related, mechanism for the containment or rehabilitation of the non-normative child typically enacted in the teen genre. In it, the fantasy of neglect is employed in order to engender a rescue and recuperation not by the parental but by the heterosexual couple. Think here of the classic example of *Rebel Without a Cause*: Jim *does* reconcile with his abusive and neglectful parents but only through the redemptive grace of his final pairing with Judy (Natalie Wood). But, of course, for this redemption to occur, Plato has to die. It would appear that the adolescent child of neglect may have outgrown the need for parental rescue, but only so long as he or she finds salvation in a heteronormative (reproductive) future.

Therefore, I argue, Cameron's survival and his elated achievement of maturity become that much more remarkable. Although the car, the house, and Cameron himself signal that this queer liberation is only available to certain privileged teens—predictably, affluent White males—we should not wholly dismiss this exceptional view of the queer teen as unafraid, and, stunningly, still alive at film's end.[33] He is not rescued by heterosexual romance, nor mourned as a ghostly queer child. He is allowed to take a stand, growing sideways towards a possible queer future, although one, sadly, still too rarely imagined in teen film and media.

NOTES

1. See, for example, Celia Wren's review in *Commonweal*, "A Bath of Déjà vu: 'Stranger Things'," 143, no. 15 (September 2016), 22; also, Neil Genzlinger, "A Nostalgia Fix of the Eerie Kind," *New York Times*, July 15, 2016, C4 (L); and Bill Keveney, "Strangest Thing: '80s Ardor Just Keeps Growing," *USA Today*, August 27, 2017, 2D.
2. Roz Kaveney, *Teen Dreams: Reading Teen Film from Heathers to Veronica Mars* (London: I. B. Tauris, 2006), 45.
3. Timothy Shary, *Teen Movies: American Youth on Screen* (New York: Wallflower, 2005), 71.
4. See Melissa Oliver-Powell's chapter in this collection for an expansion on the centrality of family dysfunction in his films of the 1990s and the role of the "ameliorative" child consumer in them.
5. Jonathan Bernstein, *Pretty in Pink: The Golden Age of Teenage Movies* (New York: St. Martin's Griffin, 1997), 52.
6. David Ansen, "Goofing Off in Grand Style," *Newsweek*, June 16, 1986, 75. Ansen cautions that too often Hughes's remarkable "rapport" with teens devolves into "pandering," showing the writer-director to be "more interested in flattering his suburban, middle-class audience than enlightening it." Similarly, in his excoriating review, Andrew Sarris finds *Ferris* and other "Hughes-Ringwald collaboration[s]" perfect gauges of "the bottomless self-pity of the '80s," concluding that if the film "weren't so hopelessly trivial, it would be thoroughly hateful in its pandering to the worst impulses of young people" ("Anodynes for Adolescents," *Village Voice*, June 17, 1986, 56).
7. Pamela Wojcik, *Fantasies of Neglect: Imagining the Urban Child in American Film and Fiction* (New Brunswick, NJ: Rutgers University Press, 2016), 117. While perhaps *The Breakfast Club*'s John Bender bears the closest resemblance to the children Wojcik examines who suffer "neglect and poverty at the hands of a drunken father," most of Hughes's tormented youth benefit from racial and socio-economic privilege inseparable from their suburban settings, and thereby his films portray more her notion of psychological neglect found in films after World War II. Contrastingly, Ferris's forays through the Chicago cityscape, enabled by his parents' unbelievable ignorance, exhibit the "spatial mobility" and "freedom" possible in the "positive" version of these fantasies of neglect (26).
8. Wojcik, 145.
9. Wojcik, 12.
10. Wojcik, 13.
11. One of the most notorious of Hughes's moments of conservative containment is the hasty resolution of Allison's aching neglect, otherness, and queer sadness in *The Breakfast Club*, when a quick, awkward makeover brings her to the attention of jock Andrew (Emilio Estevez), with whom she shares a completely unanticipated heteronormative embrace. While Bernstein singles out this moment as the film's "biggest blunder" (67), De Vaney views it as merely representative of Hughes's larger set of "neoconservative values" around class, race, and gender, where particularly White, middle-class girlhood is "reinscribe[d]" into a "domestic ideal" of "safe bedrooms" and the family. Ann De Vaney, "Pretty in Pink? John Hughes Reinscribes Daddy's Girl in Homes and Schools," in *Sugar, Spice, and Everything Nice: Cinemas of Girlhood*, eds Frances Gateward and Murray Pomerance (Detroit: Wayne State University Press, 2002), 204, 202. Roz Kaveney more bluntly refers to this aspect of the filmmaker's oeuvre as "Hughes' sometimes Neanderthal sexual politics" (21).
12. See Stockton's classificatory headings in her "Introduction" to *The Queer Child, or Growing Sideways in the Twentieth Century* (Durham, NC: Duke University Press, 2009), 1–57.

13. Ibid, 33.
14. Stockton begins her theorization of the queer child by citing the work of James Kincaid and Lee Edelman to deconstruct the "sexual titillation of innocence" around the child—an idea that clearly encircles the "ghostly gay child," who becomes unimaginable as a "child" (defined by innocence) due to the unavoidable sexuality that always-already defines him or her (12).
15. Molly Ringwald, "What About 'The Breakfast Club'? Revisiting the Movies of My Youth in the Age of #MeToo," *The New Yorker*, April 6, 2018, https://www.newyorker.com/culture/personal-history/what-about-the-breakfast-club-molly-ringwald-metoo-john-hughes-pretty-in-pink. For just one example, Andrew Clark uses the slur to defend himself, unsuccessfully, in response to John Bender's mockery about "guys that roll around on the floor with other guys."
16. See David Considine, *The Cinema of Adolescence* (Jefferson, NC: McFarland, 1985), 242.
17. Timothy Shary, *Generation Multiplex: The Image of Youth in Contemporary American Cinema* (Austin: University of Texas Press, 2002), 238–9.
18. Duckie in *Pretty in Pink* and Watts in *Some Kind of Wonderful* (1987) have been frequently described by commentators as at the very least gender queer, although Watts is called a "lesbian" within the film itself (see, for example, Kaveney). Possibly the archetypal queer kid in teen film, Plato does not disguise his troubled attraction to Jim (James Dean) in *Rebel Without a Cause* (1955) and seemingly must suffer the most tragic of ends (at the hands of normative authorities) in order for the heterosexual couple to complete their reunification with the patriarchal family. For a closer reading of the sympathetic but tragic queer kid "Billy Joe" in *Ode to Billy Joe* (1976), see Barbara Brickman, *New American Teenagers: The Lost Generation of Youth in 1970s Film* (New York: Bloomsbury, 2012).
19. Clearly, one can recognize in Cameron the classic figure of the tragic or "unhappy queer," who has been so deftly theorized by Sara Ahmed and other scholars of affect who delve into the "unhappy queer archive," as she calls it. Sara Ahmed, *The Promise of Happiness* (Durham, NC: Duke University Press, 2010), 89.
20. Kaveney proposes Ferris's antics as part and parcel of the "world of farce" Hughes so often creates, with him as its central "trickster" figure (42). See also Elizabeth G. Traube, *Dreaming Identities: Class, Gender, and Generation in 1980s Hollywood Movies* (Boulder, CO: Westview Press, 1992) for a reading of Ferris as a Reagan-era capitalist trickster (esp. 78–81).
21. Sarris, 56. While Bernstein singles out Cameron as the audience for Ferris's "Danke Schoen" serenade, he does not pursue the extent of their close relationship, preferring instead only to hint at what might be troubling Cameron in a film that refuses to let "the poor bastard meet a girl" (83).
22. In his personal account of coming to terms with her queer sexuality and gender non-conformity, T. Cooper adds Cameron to a list of influential "sexually ambiguous" best friends in Hughes's films such as Anthony Michael Hall's "nerd" character in *The Breakfast Club*, as well as Duckie and Watts, although Ferris served as the central model for his drag king performances. "You Look Good Wearing My Future, or The Sexually Ambiguous Best Friend," in *Don't You Forget About Me: Contemporary Writers on the Films of John Hughes*, ed. Jaime Clarke (New York: Simon Spotlight, 2007), 55–6.
23. Kaveney, 44, 43, 41.
24. Kaveney, 45.
25. Jeffery Dennis, *Queering Teen Culture: All-American Boys and Same-Sex Desire in Film and Television* (New York: Harrington Park Press, 2006), 151.
26. In her *Teen Film: A Critical Introduction*, Catherine Driscoll singles out this scene and Cameron's search for something "beneath the surface" of postmodern existence as evidence that he is able, in this moment, to "[transform] Ferris's day off into something

significant" (Oxford: Berg, 2011), 56. See also Steve Almond, "John Hughes Goes Deep: The Unexpected Heaviosity of *Ferris Bueller's Day Off*," in Clarke, 9–10.

27. The Smiths' 1984 original release of "Please, Please, Please Let Me Get What I Want" was as the B-side for the single "William It Was Really Nothing," which is commonly interpreted as depicting the strains of a love triangle where a woman comes between two men (https://www.rollingstone.com/music/music-lists/500-greatest-songs-of-all-time-151127/the-smiths-william-it-was-really-nothing-165655/).

28. For example, in the taxicab scene following Ferris's parade hijinks, the film again separates Cameron on the other side of the heterosexual couple, but this time he responds with anger and perhaps some jealousy, lashing out at Ferris with the self-pitying retort, "I know you don't care, but it does mean my ass," thereby aligning homoeroticism—caring for my ass—with his fear of his father's abuse—that his father will "have his ass" for taking the car.

29. Ahmed, 94–5.

30. As Grindon asserts, Cameron finds his own "worth in the car's destruction" and this act "liberates" him. "1986: Movies and Fissures in Reagan's America," in *American Cinema of the 1980s: Themes and Variations*, ed. Stephen Prince (New Brunswick, NJ: Rutgers University Press, 2007), 159.

31. An iconic moment in all of Hughes's films, the reading of the chapter at the end of *The Breakfast Club* is preceded by Brian's solitary appreciation of his work. He does not pair off with a girl, but instead happily kisses his own rhetorical achievement, the essay on "Who You Think You Are." Evocative of the Art Institute scene, Shary notes how Brian's kiss and the final couple's kisses are shot in "parallel sequences." *Teen Movies*, 70.

32. Wojcik, 11–12.

33. Although predictably White and affluent, one might hold up Veronica Sawyer (Winona Ryder) in Lehmann's teen masterpiece *Heathers* (1989) as the female counterpart to Cameron's queer male survivor. In a film that takes dominant culture's homophobia as one of its central satirical targets—even representing the ghostly queer child in a casket, wearing a football uniform—*Heathers* concludes with the self-immolation of the genre's male "J. D." (Christian Slater), with whom Veronica should pair off, and presents her as a queer survivor, aggressively kissing Heather Duke (Shannen Doherty) in the school hallway before propositioning Martha Dunnstock (Carrie Lynn), with whom she exits the film.

CHAPTER 7

We Need to Talk About Kevin McCallister: John Hughes's Careless Parents and Abandoned Children

Melissa Oliver-Powell

From the teen movies that helped define the American youth culture of the 1980s to the preteen escapism of the 1990s family films, the cinema of John Hughes is littered with forgotten children. One of the most consistent themes throughout his work is the presentation of the adult world as a problem to overcome, characterized by its comprehensive failure to "authentically" recognize youth identities. This misrecognition takes a number of literal and symbolic forms and it explains why, for instance, the disparate members of *The Breakfast Club* (1985) are able to find community in their shared frustration with a network of parenting and schooling that addresses them only as stock figures (a brain, an athlete, a basket-case, a princess, a criminal). It is also responsible for the parents in *Sixteen Candles* (1984) failing to recognize their daughter's passage to maturity by forgetting her sixteenth birthday.

That same failure to appreciate youth authenticity is inflicted on Kevin McCallister (Macaulay Culkin) in *Home Alone* (1990), whose identity is considered so arbitrary by his adult family members that he is substituted for another, unrelated child as part of an undifferentiated blur of youth in their family head count. This frustration of misrecognition, and the impulse it produces to resist and define oneself and one's world "authentically," animates Hughes's films. Though it is a source of deep resentment for Hughes's child protagonists, the adult world's failures of vision also provide them with distinct opportunities. His characters negotiate their passages to maturity by finding the blind spots in the homogenizing panopticon of hierarchical adult institutions, seeking spaces of escape in which they can creatively define autonomous and "authentic" identities.

It could be argued that Hughes's family films are anything but family-centered. After all, *Home Alone*, perhaps the most enduring titan of this genre, centers on a child who achieves self-realization precisely by rejecting (and being rejected by) the family. Parents, furthermore, are almost universally repressive and deeply flawed, often to the point of abusiveness were they not inflected with comic foibles. The original *Home Alone* trilogy[1] has in fact provided American "pro-family" conservatives with a resonant metonym for poor parenting. More than a decade after the release of the first film, Mary Eberstadt published a prominent book provocatively entitled *Home-Alone America: The Hidden Toll of Daycare, Behavioral Drugs, and Other Parent Substitutes*,[2] which placed "home-alone" parenting and maternal neglect at the center of a vast range of societal problems and moral decline.[3]

All considered, we may be forgiven for assuming that the middle-American family at the end of the twentieth century was a pretty bad place to grow up. Yet, Hughes's films do retain a deep-rooted attachment to the idea(lization) of the family. Invariably, his preteen-oriented comedies of the '90s resolve in a consolidation of the upper-middle-class nuclear family, but only after the children have successfully asserted—and adults have learnt to appreciate—their independent youth identities. The children are represented as materially independent (all of Hughes's preteen protagonists are or become highly resourceful and streetwise), yet they continue to demonstrate an emotional need for an affectionate and attentive family. The family is depicted as a positive and important force; the only problem, Hughes's films suggest, is that families are run by parents. Instead, the family must be reoriented toward its potential by adopting a child-centered existential model, which in many ways is child*ish* itself.

In this chapter I look at those narrative processes of parental re-education by children that are central to the representation of the American family in Hughes's early '90s family films, including *Home Alone*, *Home Alone 2: Lost in New York* (1992), *Beethoven* (1992), *Baby's Day Out* (1994), and *Miracle on 34th Street* (1994). I begin by observing how the adult world is characterized through child focalizers as flawed and dangerous, and I locate its dissatisfactions in either corporate or criminal greed. I then show how this relates to the state of the mythologized middle-class ideal of the American family and how self-serving pursuits of wealth and status are represented as causing adults to parent carelessly and attribute to themselves and (their) children "inauthentic" identities that undermine family stability. Finally, I argue that Hughes's films present an ameliorative model of childhood as offering solutions to the dysfunctional adult-run family. This model is, specifically, the *child* consumer. Whilst a particular "adult" type of corporate materialism that seeks wealth but defers gratification is demonized, consumerism plays a vital role in the children's self-definition. The child consumer is therefore constructed as a fantasized ideal citizen, equipped with the fiscal powers, mature values, and skilled competencies of adulthood along with the impulsive pleasure-seeking nature of childhood. This figure becomes instructive throughout Hughes's family cinema as part of a set of strategies to repair the dissolute American family in the necessary context of "moral capitalism."

Following his illustrious and genre-defining canon of teen films of the '80s, much of John Hughes's output throughout the '90s was characterized by his work in family cinema. Throughout this decade, Hughes wrote, produced, and/or directed multiple landmarks of the genre, which shaped images of American childhoods across the globe. As his teen films had previously struck a chord with a generation of disaffected high school students, the family films of the early '90s astutely identified a new youth demographic emerging in American society: the preteen. This preteen demographic, according to Filipa Antunes, had been "discovered" in the late '80s as a significant social, but primarily commercial, category.[4] Antunes describes how marketers at this time began to exploit the considerable power of "kidfluence," or the recognition that commercial decisions on a vast range of family products were increasingly led by children, whose desire for novelty and material stimulation was also potentially limitless.[5] It is therefore important to bear in mind that when preteens came into being on the cultural landscape, they did so as consumers.

From this perspective, the commercially savvy preteen is addressed as an empowered figure capable of defining a robust identity and controlling family practices. However, this was not the only cultural model of childhood prevalent in late-twentieth-century America; alongside the well-informed, confident "kid" was the vulnerable child. Joel Best has produced a thorough account of how images of child-victims rose to prominence and became politically rhetoricized during the '80s;[6] as moral victim *par excellence*, the child-victim became attached to a breadth of social panics including abortion, alcoholism and HIV.[7] The "missing children movement" also meant that the fragility of childhood was a consistent subtext of domestic life, brought daily to the breakfast table on the side of a milk carton.[8] This construction of child vulnerability also became deeply intertwined with anxious discourses on degradation and decline in the (perceived) moral fiber of the American family. This is demonstrable, for instance, in Eberstadt's consolidation of her diffuse account of social ruin around the single issue of child welfare or Joe Kincheloe's account of the *Home Alone* franchise as announcing a new, socially troubling kind of distracted parenting.[9] However, Hughes's family films do not focus only on the vulnerable child but rather adeptly draw on both competing popular models, presenting children who are certainly potentially vulnerable (to crime, violence, and neglect) and are also reassuringly able to overcome these anxieties through discovering their mature identities as consuming agents.

Precisely this attitude is played for laughs as the plot of *Baby's Day Out*, a slapstick comedy in which three bungling kidnappers chase an uncannily indestructible baby around New York, hoping to hold his parents to a multi-million-dollar ransom. From a parental standpoint, the film draws out the most axiomatic terrors of the "missing children movement": Baby Bink (Adam Robert Worton and Jacob Joseph Worton) is snatched from his wealthy family home in the apparently safe upper-middle-class suburbs, and plunged into the chaos and criminality of the metropolitan streets. However, the adults' hand-wringing over the child's helplessness is roundly mocked, as Bink quickly escapes his abductors and spends the day happily roaming the city, recreating images from his favorite picture book. The locations he visits all pose a multitude of threats (the roof of an apartment block, a gorilla cage at the zoo, a construction site staffed by remarkably careless workers), yet the child emerges from his adventures delighted and entirely unscathed. Instead, the adults demonstrate infantile incompetence and vulnerability: it is the criminals rather than the baby who fall from heights, cover themselves in messes, fall asleep reading a storybook, and call out for "mommy" when in danger. Even when the nanny (Cynthia Nixon) reflects that it would be time for Bink's nap, the cut is to a close-up of an adult construction worker asleep at his post. A wider shot reveals Bink sitting next to him, very much awake and purposeful. The comedic drive of the film is therefore based in mockery of the "child-victim" discourse, suggesting that even a baby is cannier and more resilient than adults. It is therefore not the child's imagined vulnerability that should terrify the mother, but her own failure as a parent.

We are constantly identified with a childish viewpoint in Hughes's family films, through which the adult world is presented in all of its ridiculousness and self-absorption. Using the childish perspective of apparent innocence and simple wisdom, Hughes's family films critique the idiosyncrasies of the adult world and the potential dangers it poses to children on the cusp of entering it. This disappointing, pretentious, or threatening adult world has two main faces: the corporate and the criminal. The differences between the two are largely defined along class(ist) axes, but present the same issue at their center: a world in which consumption is reified but in which material greed has become an end in itself, divorced from actual enjoyment. Corporate and criminal adulthoods are represented as both in their own ways disruptive to the nuclear family and the social values it represents. Ultimately, Hughes's family films seek not to challenge the centrality of consumption but to reorient its mature practices toward "authentic" child-centered values.

Corporate greed and immoral wealth hoarding are the upper-middle-class expressions of corrupt adulthood in Hughes's family films. At its most gratuitous and most threatening, this world is represented by wealthy, deceitful adults in hyper-capitalist occupations. The principal villains of *Miracle on 34th Street*, for instance, are the CEO of the rival department store and his two enforcers, and a similar corporate pair is depicted in the venture capitalists-cum-white collar fraudsters of *Beethoven*, along with the corrupt veterinarian who moonlights as a stooge for an arms dealer. Though several of these characters come in male-female couples, all are firmly coded as childless. Out of earshot of the parents they are attempting to con, the corporate couple in *Beethoven* are disgusted by the children and any suggestion of messy, childish irreverence. Similarly, in *Miracle on 34th Street* the visual construction of both the Shopper's Express boardroom and the store itself suggests sterility and lack of emotional warmth with austere color palettes, low lighting, and baldly angular lines. All of these characters realize their anti-child aggressions by engaging in subterfuge that seeks directly to undermine the nuclear family materially (as in the financial scam that would be ruinous to the family in *Beethoven*) and morally (the plot to frame Kris Kringle in *Miracle on 34th Street*).

Underscoring the capacity of parents for misrecognition, the mothers and fathers of Hughes's child protagonists are often easily seduced by these characters and the dangerous adult world they represent. These misguided parents are tricked into placing the false idols of abstract wealth and social status at the center of their interests, leading them to neglect the nobler values intelligible to their children. As Jyotsna Kapur puts it, *Home Alone* initiated a trend of family films in which children successfully raise themselves while their parents "feverishly pursue money and the things it can buy."[10] Unlike the childless CEOs, "corporate parents" are not represented as malicious but as foolish and blinkered, having approached the cynical game of adulthood with rather too much sincerity. Their lack of discernment means that they are at risk of becoming obliviously complicit in the corporate adults' destruction of the family. However, the egregiousness of the corporate villains means that corruption and antisocialism are always represented as only a chosen *style* of adult capitalism rather than inherent to its systems. As shall be shown below, Hughes's happiest resolutions of maturity are found in the "moral capitalism" that combines adult powers with childish values.

From one direction, therefore, Hughes's child protagonists are under threat from a sterile adult plutocracy that harbors undisguised hatred toward youth, which it sees as an undifferentiated mass of neediness. This subset of menacing adulthood is complemented by another: petty criminals and thieves. Both groups are identified with non-domestic space; while white-collar villains belong in boardrooms and dark, imposing offices, the small-time crooks represent the dangers of the urban streets. Often, these criminals are lackeys of the corporate villains; Tony (Jack McGee), the drunken Santa replaced by Kris Kringle (Richard Attenborough) in *Miracle on 34th Street*, and Harvey (Oliver Platt) and Vernon (Stanley Tucci), the dognappers from *Beethoven*, are depicted as unintelligent, delinquent, and immoral, willing to carry out the "dirty work" necessary to their employers' schemes.

In *Home Alone*, the burglars Harry (Joe Pesci) and Marv (Daniel Stern) share these negative personal qualities but are independent agents. As Kincheloe points out, they (along with Tony and Vernon and the three kidnappers in *Baby's Day Out*) are needlessly coded as working class and ethnic, in a racist and classist choice that draws on White, middle-class suburban anxieties over the "Other" as an imagined threat to romanticized middle-American familial domesticity.[11] This presence of roughly sketched urban deviance as a constant threat to the wholesome family is an enduring theme of mainstream American cinema, signaling the "traditional" family's potential to collapse into dystopia should it not observe the structures and values of nuclear patriarchy.[12] Sarah Harwood describes how the fear of urban threat became particularly prominent in late-twentieth-century commercial cinema, which asserted the separation of the urban and suburban as necessary to familial happiness:

> [Utopian suburban homes] are the insulated fortresses of middle Americans privileged to concentrate on their own affairs rather than those of others. Even when the urban milieu does intrude on the domestic scene, it is carefully regulated, maintained outside the front door by wealth and conspicuous security. In the dystopian films, however, the domestic fortress is unable to prevent the penetration of the urban environment, and even the suburbs, the perfect family space, are corrupted.[13]

In the cultural imagination of missing and vulnerable children to which *Home Alone* and *Baby's Day Out* respond, such self-indulgent and emotionally shallow criminals are a distinct part of the corrupt adult world threatening to destroy the family.

Hughes's films represent both corporate corruption and small-time criminality as uncomplex and motivated purely by the characters' pleasure in destructive greed. After abducting Beethoven from a pet store, Harvey excitedly congratulates himself on his "first felony." Harry and Marv, furthermore, seem only to choose those crimes that maximize moral outrage rather than profit, hence the restriction of their activity to Christmas time and the family home in *Home Alone*, and specifically to children's toys in *Home Alone 2*. No question of need or poverty is raised; they are simply shown as reveling in malice. Even in *Curly Sue* (1991), in which the father and daughter protagonists are small-time con artists, a distinction is drawn between the heroes and "real" criminals, as the film takes care to ensure that Bill (James Belushi) explains how they take only necessities (food, shelter, basic clothing). *Other* criminals, this suggests, are simply greedy and selfish. This outlook is further corroborated by the fact that Bill is able to find a decent job almost instantaneously once he has committed to a more traditional family lifestyle. Both corporate and criminal corruption, therefore, are lifestyles and existential modes that have been actively chosen by childless adults who stand outside the family and conspire against its integrity, respectively through financial ruin and physical invasion.

The careless parents of the child protagonists are, furthermore, largely oblivious to these dangers; much as they are seduced by the CEOs and corporate fraudsters, their flawed optical models lead them to misidentify the petty criminals. During the opening scene of *Home Alone*, only the children are able to "see" Harry, the criminal in the center of their home, until he is finally responded to by their mother, who misrecognizes him as a genuine police officer and discloses the family's vacation schedule. In *Beethoven*, the father's failure to recognize the murderous intentions of the veterinarian risks similarly disastrous consequences for the family. This adult failure to see risk and vulnerability is taken to a curious extreme in *Baby's Day Out*. Similarly to *Home Alone*, the film begins with the mother failing to perceive the danger within her own home represented by disguised criminals. The wealthy socialite mother is fixated on getting her baby's picture in the newspaper in order to compete with her peers, leading her to blindly trust the kidnappers masquerading as prestigious baby photographers whilst the nanny – at this point a more maternally attuned caregiver – regards them with suspicion. The kidnappers' pursuit of the runaway baby then takes place over crowded New York streets and attractions, and a busy construction site, yet both baby and criminals remain persistently unnoticed by vast multitudes of distracted adults.

Through close identification with children's perspectives, the family films present an adult world in disarray: one that is ridiculous, dangerous, and fundamentally dishonest. The worst elements of this world pose a threat to the family from the outside. Implicitly, therefore, the home should be a contrasting space of resistance and refuge against anti-family social disorder. However, the parental figures of Hughes's films have failed woefully to provide this nurturing domestic space. Enticed by the corporate and oblivious to the criminal, they are unable to constitute adequate identity models for their maturing children. Hughes's films therefore perform an operation of re-establishing the child at the center of the family, as his young protagonists become responsible for defining their own, more discerning narratives of adulthood and take up the parentally neglected mantle as defenders of familial ideology.

There has been interesting critical debate around the extent and nature of Hughes's family films' commitment to (however vague a notion of) "traditional family values." Kincheloe sees the *Home Alone* franchise as a thoroughly non-idealistic commentary on fracture and dysfunction in the modern American family, arguing that the chaotic McCallisters compare unfavorably with the nostalgic suburban community of Frank Capra's *It's a Wonderful Life* (1946), which plays in their Parisian hotel room.[14] Others have refuted Kincheloe's view of *Home Alone* as a harbinger of the dissolution of the middle-American family, pointing out that such an unflattering mirror of its target market would hardly have sold so well. Dismissing Kincheloe's portentous interpretation, Kapur argues that "Packaged for bourgeois consumption, [the family film] is the most conservative of genres"[15] and is therefore hardly likely to present untested moral statements and risk polarizing a lucrative audience.[16] Dysfunctional families are only presented in the context of their rescue, and the films always resolve in reassuring scenes of domestic stability, so audiences and critics have interpreted these presented values as sincere.[17] R. C. Allen points out that these films see family as above all else a market, arguing that they resist moralistic position-taking altogether. Instead, Allen claims the narrative strategies of family films highlight "ambivalence and indeterminacy"[18] and shows how *Home Alone* could be read equally as an affirmation of the nuclear family or of preteen independence.[19]

However, belonging to a family-oriented genre, the films absolutely maintain a surface commitment to "traditional" domestic values. Precisely what this means, however, is difficult to define. Mainstream Hollywood cinema has always relied on romanticized images of the nuclear family,[20] and, amidst rising social pressures of the late twentieth century, "individuals increasingly searched for a moral framework within the forms of popular culture. The family was at the heart of this quest and became the moral center for political and cultural rhetoric."[21] Yet, as Stephanie Coontz has discussed convincingly and at length, such a desired familial "moral framework," grounded as it is in nostalgia for an imagined golden era, is generic to the extreme, little more than a cherry-picked amalgam of various vague notions and images that correspond to no single lived experience of family.[22] This semantic fluidity and generalized appeal prove useful to Hughes's family films. Being "for the family" or "for the children" is a position that is more or less impossible to stand against; as demonstrated internally to the films, to oppose the family explicitly is to be cartoonishly villainous. It is therefore straightforward enough to establish the moral confidence of target audiences. However, the question of who interprets this ideology is up for grabs, and in Hughes's films, the champion of the "traditional" family becomes the figure of the modern preteen.

Allen's arguments on possible anti-nuclear-family tendencies of Hughes's and other popular family films are largely based on the fact that this genre heroizes streetwise preteens who mature only in relation to themselves to find that they do not need families or parents.[23] However, this theme of preteen maturing and independence is not necessarily in tension with the family, as whilst none of Hughes's protagonists *need* the support or affection of parents, they universally *desire* it. Otherwise put, the material caretaking and disciplining Hughes's parents provide are insufficient and irrelevant acts of parenting to modern youth; instead, the films insist, the substance of domestic harmony is found in parents' emotional attention and respect. This defines the ways in which Hughes's careless parents fail to uphold the integrity of the nuclear family. Inattentive and preoccupied, they misrecognize the true needs and rich personalities of their children. The domestic environments they have built are stifling and frustrating because they have been designed for adults and their self-serving goals rather than for children, and it is this positioning that Hughes's child-focused narratives ultimately seek to correct.

Beethoven is one of the few Hughes family films in which the father is primarily responsible for the moral precarity of the family. George (Charles Grodin) is also perhaps Hughes's clearest caricature of a suburban social climber, whose keeping-up-with-the-Joneses catalyzes the film's narrative jeopardy. He is a narcissistic adult, demanding the constant attention and admiration of his wife Alice (Bonnie Hunt) and their children, as is established clearly in a scene around the breakfast table. Accustomed to holding court in the family home and expecting recognition for his achievements from his children rather than appreciating theirs, George theatrically attempts to share an anecdote about his business success and becomes angry and envious when Alice's attention is on the children and the children's attention is on the eponymous dog. Regardless of the interests of the family, he expects all of its members to be subservient to his business ambitions and appetite for social prestige.

His self-absorbed, adult-focused perspective is presented as endangering the family in numerous ways. Aside from his disastrous inability to recognize the true intentions of the corporate scammers and corrupt veterinarian, his coercion of Alice into the workplace (disrupting the gendered logic of the "traditional" family) has near-fatal consequences. On Alice's first day of work, the children are left with an exaggeratedly inappropriate babysitter, an older woman represented as incompetent and threatening to the family through her apparent childlessness and self-indulgence. Distracted by her own hobbies and forcing the clearly unwilling children to sing her old-fashioned music-hall songs, the babysitter fails to notice the youngest child falling into the swimming pool (saved only by Beethoven's supernatural sense of safety). Were the ideological subtext of this scene not clear enough, the mother makes explicit the type of child-centered emotional parenting advocated in the family film, answering, in response to the babysitter's claim that the children need "a little discipline," that "what they need is their mother." The same logic is applied to the two older children who, while not physically endangered, lack emotional recognition of their maturing identities; whilst George fails to notice his daughter's burgeoning crush on a boy at school or his son's struggles with bullies, Beethoven – a portable transmitter of family values – is able to identify and resolve these problems, helping the children to achieve the confident development not facilitated by their disordered family.

Elsewhere, it is more directly the mother who bears the burden of blame for producing inadequate family environments. As indicated in *Beethoven*, it is particularly mothers who are at fault because they work, or are otherwise distracted from their children. This criticism touched rather directly on a widespread sense of guilt and anxiety over the increased entry of women and mothers into the workforce throughout the twentieth century.[24] Unapologetically "sort of hard on parents [as he] grew up in a family where kids came first,"[25] Hughes suggests in his films that working mothers were right to be concerned when they worried that they were damaging their children and failing to live up to the fantasy of the middle-American domestic mom.

Dorey (Elizabeth Perkins), the single, working mother of *Miracle on 34th Street*, is depicted as an archetypal example of this maternal failure. She holds a senior managerial position in a large department store, Coles, which absorbs most of her time and attention and, despite providing herself and her daughter Susan (Mara Wilson) with a materially comfortable apartment, she produces only a sad and inadequate home. She is held responsible for failing to establish for her daughter a "traditional" family, as she resists intimacy with Bryan (Dylan McDermott), the idealized paternal substitute. At the outset of the film, Dorey is characterized as joyless, stoic and embittered. Her "disordered" focus on her career is made explicit as she regularly leaves Susan alone or in the care of others and, catching her talking to Kris Kringle's Santa Claus, reminds her that "customers come first," indicating that the profitable happiness of other children is forefront. Her parenting is characterized by inauthenticity; at the iconographically crucial moment of Thanksgiving dinner, Susan reminds Dorey that "the vegetables were catered" and Bryan had secretly restuffed the turkey after she had prepared it incorrectly. Dorey's failure as a mother extends to her inability to recognize Susan's desire for a "traditional" family. Susan is an affectionate and, in many ways, extremely mature child, yet when prompted to ask Santa Claus for something she would never communicate to her mother, her only desires are for a house, father and brother. The adult-centered family is, therefore, represented as a tragedy for children.

Home Alone is another openly mother-blaming film, in which Kate McCallister (Catherine O'Hara) is held more or less solely responsible for abandoning Kevin. The establishing shots of the McCallister household show a large, well-kept house in a suburban neighborhood, cosmetically typical of nostalgic "golden age" middle-American clichés. The cutting in of the soundtrack, however, marks a subversion of this romanticized trope, as we hear a cacophony of screaming children, arguments and chaos. The "traditional" American family, it suggests, is in disarray. And at the heart of this disarray is the overworked, inattentive mother. Despite the father's callousness toward his son, he emerges relatively unscathed from the film's moralizing narrative. Though it is not made explicit whether Kate works outside the home, she, like Dorey, is characterized as careless and distracted. In the opening scenes of the film, much of Kevin's frustrating family situation derives from Kate's inability to "authentically" recognize her children; this is to the advantage of Kevin's older brother, Buzz (Devin Ratray), who has learnt to capitalize on parental blind spots to appear more innocent, but to the detriment of Kevin, who is mistakenly interpreted as a disruptive, incompetent, and needy obstruction to adult enjoyment. This failure of discerning vision leads Kate to both over-parent Kevin with discipline, and under-parent in individual emotional nourishment.

There is little question that the McCallisters, despite their abundance of children, are an adult-focused family. For their family Christmas holiday – usually a time emotionally devoted to family unity and commercially focused on children – they have chosen Paris, a location strongly associated with adult interests in culture and romance, but of less interest to children. The parents secure seats in first class for themselves whilst the children sit, distant and anonymized, in coach. The McCallister family is therefore represented as one that revolves around the material desires of parents. By contrast, Kevin is shown consistently to have a keen sense of the "traditional family values" his parents have neglected. Although the narrative centralizes Kevin's passage to maturity, as Kapur argues, the competent child is made less threatening by the fact that his desires are entirely commensurate with the social fantasies of middle-class audiences, "retain[ing] the old image of the child in spite of having played out the new by retaining the notion that the bourgeois family is the ideal place to raise a child."[26] When Kevin wishes away his family, therefore, he is not acting against family per se, but expressing frustration with the disordered *type* of adult family he is experiencing. Like Susan, he demonstrates profound desire for an "old-fashioned", child-focused family and possesses unique expert knowledge in how to orchestrate it, demonstrated in his continuous insistence that Christmas should be spent in the family home, his attachment to Christmas trees and generous gift-giving, and his ability to reunite the splintered families of the various alienated adults he meets in *Home Alone* and its sequel.

The child protagonists are burdened with the limitations of childhood without experiencing its joys. Distracted by selfish pursuits and greedy social ambition, and caught unknowingly between the dangers of the corporate and the criminal, Hughes's parents are universally unable to discern the values, competencies, and "authentic" personalities of modern preteen children, on whom they continue to place emotional and physical limitations as anonymous non-adults. Against their parents' expectations, however, these children are quite capable of "parenting" themselves (Kevin produces a responsible shopping list of "eggs, milk and fabric softener," and Susan puts herself to bed and restricts her own sugar intake), but they want to repair the fabric of the idealized middle-class American family to fulfill an emotional need. Key to their processes of maturity, therefore, is the operation of reinducting their parents into the meaning, morality, and organization of (child-centered) family through engaging with "authentic" youthful modes of vision and understanding.

Hughes's family films all have as their object what Harwood terms a "final romance," or the narrative coda to the unification of the heterosexual couple that establishes the utopian family as a coherent generative unit.[27] This "romance," the teleology of all heterosexual exchange, achieves ideal fruitfulness when it shifts its center from adult protagonists to the child. Fundamental to this shift in Hughes's films is the replacement of disordered and insufficient adult models of vision with clearer and more "authentic" childlike counterparts. Growth therefore occurs for all family members in spaces outside the strictures of the negative "adult world" and its dysfunctional family. Capitalizing on the moral clarity offered by these spaces, characters are able to return to the family wiser and with renewed purpose.

In *Home Alone*, Kevin and Kate, the mother-and-child dyad at the heart of the family romance, embark on symmetrical "arcs"[28] that take them literally and symbolically back to the family. Both figures achieve a mature and "authentic" recognition of the utopian, child-centered family but it is essential that they enter spaces outside the adult word and family to do so. For this reason, at the conclusion of the first two *Home Alone* films, Kate and Kevin are uniquely able to share a mutual, knowing gaze (in the utopian settings of the quiet family home and the Rockefeller Center plaza with its enormous Christmas tree) expressing their now profound understanding of each other and the moral meaning of family before the re-entry of the other characters only moments later. Meanwhile, the siblings and father, who spend the film in the dysfunctional "adult" family, remain unchanged. The objects of Kate and Kevin's respective arcs are highly symbolic: whilst it falls to the child to literally defend the family home and its urgent discourses, the mother's objective is the reclamation of her "traditional" position in the orbit of the child, thereby confirming primary feminine purpose as child-centered mothering. Establishing this "correct" directionality of vision amongst key family terms, the film thereby affirms a conservative ideal in which anything less than absolute child-centeredness within a middle-class, White, and heterosexist context is equated with tragedy, dysfunction, and the imminent material jeopardy of the nostalgic middle-American family.

A very similar narrative is at work in *Baby's Day Out*. Whilst the father leaves for work at the beginning of the film and reappears only once Bink has been found, the mother Laraine Cotwell (Lara Flynn Boyle) is required to undertake an emotional journey that will re-educate her in family values and what it "really" means to be a mother. Her initial disordered subordination of her child's interests to her own desire for arbitrary social prestige is presented in no uncertain terms as largely responsible for the jeopardy of the family: she leaves the baby alone with the kidnappers whilst she changes into another chic outfit for the supposed photo portrait. Though Bink turns out to be more than capable of triumphing over his ordeal, Laraine is nevertheless punished for this failure, and is left reflecting on her poor parenting and selfishness throughout the police investigation. Her penitence is also shaped through instructive encounters with "real" maternal love. The nanny is a significant figure here; equally distraught over

Bink's disappearance, Laraine comes to realize that she has been Bink's de facto mother. It is the nanny's – rather than Laraine's – dedication to and knowledge of the baby's routine and interests that allow him to be located in a veteran's home resembling the last images in his beloved book. Elsewhere, in a scene awkwardly inserted into the narrative, Laraine also comes face-to-face with a "real" mother. Apparently living in near-Dickensian poverty with her many poorly dressed but happily playing children, this woman sympathizes with Laraine and offers her prayers that Bink comes back, adding "these kids are all I've got." Through these humbling encounters, Laraine is urged to take stock of her mothering and reorient it to revolve around the child. By the end of the film, her priorities have been "corrected" and her maternal sensibilities supersede those of the nanny, as she is able to interpret Bink's babbling and gestures to discover the location of the criminals. As in *Home Alone*, the space of "natural" mothering, family and clear, child-oriented vision is re-established.

Through their focal identification with children's perspectives, Hughes's films suggest that childish or child-centered models of vision are uniquely able to identify and resist the dangers to the family posed by the (childless) corporate and criminal adult worlds. Within all of the family films, whenever a "truth" is revealed that is essential to the narrative unfolding of the film and linked to the precarity of the family, we are generally invited into psychological and aesthetic complicity with a child, through identificatory devices including low-angle, point-of-view, and shot/reverse shots. For example, a point-of-view shot is used in *Beethoven* when the true intentions of the corrupt veterinarian are recognized by the youngest child. The first scene in *Miracle on 34th Street* similarly uses a low-angle shot to identify our perspective with that of the child who is able to "authentically" recognize Kris Kringle as Santa Claus, setting the tone for the film's thematization of the inability of jaded or corporate adults to appreciate childlike hope. In *Home Alone*, Kevin is the only McCallister able to recognize the sinister intentions of Harry and Marv. Even the preverbal Baby Bink demonstrates an immediate and perceptive mistrust of the criminal ringleader, Eddie (Joe Mantegna), in *Baby's Day Out*, kicking and setting fire to his crotch at various points during the film as a bizarrely explicit punishment for his disdain for the reproductive family. Childish optical coding is consistently associated with "authenticity" and directly opposed to the flawed and easily mistaken viewpoints of parental characters in Hughes's films. This is a viewpoint that must be reaffirmed by children and rediscovered by adults.

This ideal hybrid of adult responsibility and childish authenticity is modeled in a small number of Hughes's adult characters; a direct counterbalance to the corporate and the criminal, these are the childlike adults who construct the mature world in a positive way. These characters are always male and, though fatherly, rarely biological parents, standing as positive spaces outside of dysfunctional parenting and, potentially, maintaining a connection with childlike sexual purity, ensuring that their driving object of emotional attention is always the child's well-being. These characters include the "good stepfathers," Bryan in *Miracle on 34th Street* and Bill in *Curly Sue*, and the grandfatherly sprites, Kris Kringle and the kindly toy shop owner in *Home Alone 2*. This category could also reasonably include Beethoven who, like Santa Claus, becomes a semi-supernatural figure representing romanticized nostalgia for a personal or social lost childhood. Represented as very special figures and rare models of positive maturity, they are in imminent danger of destruction at the hands of the corporate or criminal adult worlds, symbolized most thoroughly in the central trial in *Miracle on 34th Street* as the corporate villains of Shopper's Express attempt to have Kris Kringle committed to a mental institution. The "bad" adult worlds, in other words, seek to pathologize "authentic" childlike values.

Fundamental to Hughes's family films is the critique of parental understanding of the world, with a redemptive shift to models of competent childlikeness, which are promoted as uniquely in touch with "authentic family values." It is now, finally, necessary to examine more closely what these values are. The films take a moral structure that is shaped around something we are firmly assured is the solid, traditional, all-American family. Yet Hughes's films commit to "family values" in only the most generic sense. Allen pertinently describes how Hollywood's new marketization of the family (essential to profitable VHS sell-through) coincided with a rapid demographic diversification of family types, precipitating high political stakes in ownership of the family and its considerable rhetorical and imaginative properties:

> [P]oliticians of every stripe desperately grasp for some purchase on "family values," while their constituents turn to the popular media for models of family life [. . .] In short, since the 1980s, family has become the "black hole" of contemporary American social discourse and popular culture: impossible to identify in its exact characteristics yet exerting inescapable gravitational force.[29]

This vagueness is imported into Hughes's family films, which are careful not to alienate any particular type of family by producing an inarguable but ambiguous discourse of happy family relations that plausibly affirms multiple preconceptions. The large, suburban McCallister household in which parents can be both radically superfluous and absolutely necessary, therefore, begins to suggest Coontz's one-size-fits-all familial nostalgia[30] that leaves us with a feeling that it is something good, whilst carefully avoiding taking any actual positions. After all, the films are commercial products rather than political vehicles, heroizing the preteen, itself a creation of popular markets; it is finally commercial persuasiveness rather than moral advocacy that constitutes the most consistent opinion in Hughes's family films.

If we were to consider what the films position as clearly bad (the adult corporate and criminal worlds), then we might expect to find what is clearly good at its opposite point. Yet, while the childlike is certainly positioned as superior to the adult, there is no wholesale resistance to materialism or mass consumption. What unites the corporate and the criminal is, essentially, their motivation by adult greed. From Harry and Marv to the Shopper's Express CEO, the adult antagonists are depicted as devious individuals breaking the rules of games they are not skilled enough to win and taking wealth that does not belong to them. However, these characters are never positioned as representative of social systems of commerciality; as mass-market commodities, the films have no interest in this kind of critique. As John Belton describes, "Within mainstream American thought, capitalism works, but it just sometimes goes a bit crazy."[31] Certainly, Hughes's films are at their most didactic in their assertion of capitalism as fundamentally the best of all systems, once its few bad eggs have been removed.

It is not material desire and mass-consumption per se that the films critique in the adult world, it is simply a deviant *style* of doing things. The films ultimately advocate a diluted "moral capitalism" distinguished by two factors: merit and immediacy. The criminal world has the immediacy of material pleasure (Harry and Marv are connected to unmoderated childish enjoyment as we see them unwrapping and playing with toys in the first house they burgle), but no merit. After all, they emanate from and embody disordered urban spaces, whereas "moral capitalism" was distinctly associated with the private (middle-class, White, heterosexual) family. As Coontz describes, "the 'normal' families moved to the suburbs during the 1950s. Popular culture turned such suburban families into capitalism's answer to the Communist threat."[32] Therefore, even whilst their self-absorption and dysfunctional organization of family articulates their failure, it is never suggested that Hughes's misguided upper-middle-class parents do not deserve their wealth. Kincheloe rightly highlights that as Kevin's father "drinks from crystal in first class on the plane to Paris, he alludes to his hard work and humble origins. The message is clear – the American dream is attainable for those willing to put in the effort. The McAlisters [sic] deserve their good fortune."[33] The father in *Beethoven* and mother in *Miracle on 34th Street*, similarly, are consistently depicted as talented and hardworking, despite the misdirection of their energies.

The frustration that children experience with the parental world derives principally from its deferral of enjoyment: it is merit without immediacy. The parents humorlessly pursue wealth itself, but their object is the abstract status it confers on them rather than the opportunities it can offer for parents and children to enjoy themselves together. This is why Susan is prohibited from indulging in the childish material indulgences of Christmas, and Kevin is, on the night before the holiday, confined to the family's attic, with its iconography of childhood poverty and neglect. It is at this point that the figure of the preteen returns as the ideal (consuming) subject, and redemptive model against this type of careless and distracted parenting. In films like *Beethoven* and *Curly Sue*, misguided and myopic "corporate parents" are consistently educated by children in how their hard-earned wealth is to be better enjoyed by committing it to the irreverence, immediacy, and, ultimately "family values" of which the preteen has unique understanding. Maturity, for these children, is to become a discerning consumer, adult enough to appreciate the material comforts of "moral capitalism," but childlike enough to direct them toward messy, irreverent, and immediate enjoyment in the family.

However, it is the Christmas films in which the "ethics" of family commercialism are clearest. After all, Christmas annually provides the most abundant confluence of morality and materialism, an opportunity Hughes certainly capitalized on, working "with Tiger Electronics to develop two toys that could be used by Macauley [sic] Culkin's character in [*Home Alone 2*] and then sold commercially."[34] Further, in *Miracle on 34th Street*, though a corporate department store is responsible for Kris Kringle's near-downfall, it is a "good" department store that saves him (after, moreover, their new child-first business model has spectacularly redeemed the brand). When the court case appears hopeless, Brian brandishes a dollar bill at the judge, an undisguised analogy for consumer-capitalism, insisting on its responsibility for Kris's destruction – yet it is precisely the same bill that ultimately saves him after Bryan recognizes the definitive entwining of profit and morality in the printing of "In God We Trust" onto American currency. The instructive power of money is questioned by no one, as the judge and the entire courtroom naturally accept the dollar as an existential representative of their society. The duality of capital is therefore confirmed: it is a powerful tool, but its moral status is defined by whether its wielder acts in self-interest or for the child.

At the film's outset, Susan is shown to be living an "inauthentic" life. As discerned by Kris Kringle, who has been established as having an innate affinity with children, and able to bridge language and disability in his communication with them, Susan desires childish faith and beliefs but is inhibited by her mother's joyless commitment to work and the cynical, adult expectations of her. The family's collective journey toward "authenticity" is also one toward "moral" consumption. After all, in the triumphant final scene, the now complete heterosexual nuclear family – secured by Dorey and Bryan's marriage – literally comes to inhabit a consumer image. The house that Kris Kringle obtains for them is in fact a model used for the store's Christmas catalogue. The problem at the start of the film, this suggests, was not that the moral integrity of Christmas and the family has been diluted by consumer-capitalist forces and the commercial packaging of "traditional values," but that these images were being sold and advertised without "authentic" realization. The family is returned to the broad-stroke picture of the suburban American ideal home, replete with presents and festive ephemera, in which Susan can now flourish and live commensurately with her desired, childlike self-image. Naturally, the child-centered Christmas film is one such product that we can feel morally good about because its purpose, like toys and presents, is to unite the "good" family.

In *Home Alone*, toys, mass culture and other commodities take on explicitly heroic characteristics; these are exactly the tools that allow Kevin to succeed in his defense of the family home. The Tiger Electronics "'Talk Boy' voice-altering cassette recorder and Monster Sap soap"[35] are only two examples of the various (often purchasable) toys that Kevin uses to construct elaborate traps for the burglars, exemplifying the virtues of distinctly childlike creativity and its facilitation through abundant commercial products. The film also seeks to assuage any anxiety or conservative axioms about the dangers to the family posed by popular film and television by allowing Kevin (in the first two *Home Alone* movies) to comically use a film noir to pose as his father and avert the stifling gazes of the adult world. In *Home Alone 2*, furthermore, the ideal familial dyad of mother and child are finally, intuitively, reunited in the moral-commercial space of the Rockefeller Center Christmas tree, exploiting connotations of familial harmony expressed through abundant wealth and presents. Fulfilling this promise, in the final shot inside the hotel, we see that the family has been rewarded with an excessive stack of presents provided by Mr. Duncan (Eddie Bracken), the kind and generous toy store owner, who is successful and wealthy, but apparently motivated only by a fatherly love for children, and therefore an ideal model of "moral capitalism."

John Hughes's family films both exhibit and are complicit in a mass consumer culture that reifies childhood. As marketers discovered in the late twentieth century, middle-American preteens provided the ideal model for consuming agents of late capitalism: enriched, impulsive, and highly literate in mass culture. This sophisticated and abundant use of the market is exactly the type of subjectivity that becomes aspirational not only for children but also for their parents through Hughes's films. Of course, stating the conviction plainly could only appear grotesque; the voracious consumer who is (however sophisticated) ultimately a prop of consumer-capitalism is hardly a reflection likely to appeal broadly. Commercial purposes are therefore packaged attractively in an eminently agreeable moral discourse of the "traditional family." Though their trajectory is profoundly commercial, the films and their heroes are set apart from the boogeyman of immoral greed through the depiction of caricatured, childless corporate and criminal villains, allowing the films to reassure us that, whatever they are, they are definitely *not that*. Having established their audience (the family) as nominally on the side of the good, however, the films enter into social cultures of child-victims and the dissolution of the traditional

American family by exploiting parental fear of failure. Parental modes of visualizing and understanding the world, they confirm, are inadequate to the complexity of modern society. It is the commercially savvy preteen, however, the childlike adult or mature child, who has the panoramic wisdom both to navigate modern capitalism and to vitalize "traditional" values. And thankfully, the expressions of the happy family can be bought: through toys, commodities, treats, and family films.

NOTES

1. Hughes wrote the scripts for the first three *Home Alone* films, released in 1990, 1992, and 1997. The franchise continued with two television movies, *Home Alone 4: Taking Back the House* (2002) and *Home Alone: The Holiday Heist* (2012), although Hughes had no involvement with these projects.
2. Mary Eberstadt, *Home-Alone America: The Hidden Toll of Daycare, Behavioural Drugs, and Other Parent Substitutes* (New York and London: Sentinel, 2004).
3. This trend is also discussed in Joe Kincheloe, "The New Childhood: Home Alone as a Way of Life," in *The Children's Culture Reader*, ed. Henry Jenkins (New York University Press, 1998), 159–76, and Jyotsna Kapur, *Coining for Capital: Movies, Marketing and the Transformation of Childhood* (Piscataway, NJ: Rutgers University Press, 2005), 120.
4. Filipa Antunes, "Attachment Anxiety: Parenting Culture, Adolescence and the Family Film in the US," *Journal of Children and Media*, 11, no. 2 (2017), 214–28.
5. Antunes, 217.
6. Joel Best, *Threatened Children: Rhetoric and Concern about Child-Victims* (University of Chicago Press, 1990).
7. Best, 6.
8. Emma Wilson, *Cinema's Missing Children* (London: Wallflower, 2003), 2–4.
9. Kincheloe, 159.
10. Kapur, 2.
11. Kincheloe, 168–9.
12. Sylvia Harvey, "Woman's Place: The Absent Family of Film Noir," in *Movies and Mass Culture*, ed. John Belton (London: Athlone, 1996).
13. Sarah Harwood, *Family Fictions: Representations of the Family in 1980s Hollywood Cinema* (Basingstoke: Macmillan, 1997), 68.
14. Kincheloe, 160.
15. Kapur, 3.
16. Kapur, 3–4.
17. Antunes, 218–19.
18. R. C. Allen, "Home Alone Together: Hollywood and the 'Family Film'," in *Identifying Hollywood's Audiences: Cultural Identity and the Movies*, eds M. Stokes and R. Maltby (London: British Film Institute, 1999), 125.
19. Allen, 125–7.
20. Claire Jenkins, *Home Movies: The American Family in Contemporary Hollywood Cinema* (London: I. B. Tauris, 2015).
21. Harwood, 3.
22. Stephanie Coontz, *The Way We Never Were: American Families and the Nostalgia Trap* (New York: Basic Books, 1992).

23. Allen, 126.
24. Coontz, 149–79.
25. John Hughes quoted in Bill Carter, "Him Alone," *New York Times*, August 4, 1991, http://www.nytimes.com/1991/08/04/magazine/him-alone.html.
26. Kapur, 124.
27. Harwood, 61–4.
28. Antunes, 221.
29. Allen, 115.
30. Coontz, 9–14.
31. John Belton, "Introduction," in *Movies and Mass Culture*, ed. John Belton (London: Athlone, 1996), 7.
32. Coontz, 28.
33. Kincheloe, 169.
34. Allen, 119.
35. Allen, 119.

PART III

Family and Fatherhood

John Hughes exhibits an enduring fascination with the family, and with the pleasures, problems and complexities of fatherhood within that structure. It was family life to which Hughes first turned his attentions in the early 1980s; his scripts for *Mr. Mom* (1983) and *National Lampoon's Vacation* (1983) offer key examples of male characters' desire for a "normal" family life that is never quite fulfilled. In this, Hughes's work in this era found itself caught up in the aftermath of second-wave feminism, in which women increasingly questioned the desirability of the family unit that finds them shouldering a disproportionate amount of childcare and domestic duties, while neoconservative discourses called for a "return" to family values, and the reification of fatherhood as the head of the household. As the contributors to this section make clear, though, competent and responsible fatherhood always remains tantalizingly out of reach for Hughes's patriarchs, rendered either sympathetic, though comically ineffective, or pathologically abusive.

Hughes's films about the family have perhaps been overshadowed in the popular imagination by his more celebrated mid-1980s teen fare. Nonetheless, it was these family films, in the form of the *Home Alone* and *Beethoven* series in the 1990s, which were to prove his greatest commercial successes. This is not to say that these films present a departure from Hughes's earlier material. As was discussed in the introduction to this volume, Hughes began his career with an interest in the mechanics of family life, and his family films continued his work with prominent comedians like Chevy Chase, Steve Martin, and John Candy, the latter, like Molly Ringwald, serving as something of a muse for the writer-director. What is distinct from Hughes's early scripts, and which evidences his continued preoccupations with youth from the previous decade, is his focus on teenage or child characters, who frequently form the center of these narratives. Indeed, as the chapters in this section demonstrate, it is often the children that provide the moral authority of their respective family units.

A further element of these family films, which marks a continuity from Hughes's earlier career, is the attention to brand name props. These are the focus of Leah Shafer's chapter, and which, as she points out, continued Hughes's work in the grammar of advertising and television with which he began his career as an advertising copywriter. Notably though, as Shafer ably observes, Hughes satirizes and undercuts the utopian promise of consumer products throughout his oeuvre, noting that they are no substitute for functioning family life. Thus, Hughes is able to have it both ways; he can take advantage of lucrative product tie-ins, as he doubtless did with Mattel in using the Talkboy within *Home Alone 2*, which allows Kevin (Macaulay Culkin) to record and distort his voice, enabling him to pass for his own father over the phone. And yet the toy is no match for recuperating Kevin's place in the family, which the film resolves at its conclusion. What seems to be at issue, then, in both the positioning of fatherhood and of consumer goods alike in Hughes's films, is a rumination on the promise of normalcy, or of the "good life" as Sara Ahmed would put it.[1]

That patriarchs are not to be taken entirely seriously is apparent in Hughes's decision to cast a number of well-known comic players as fathers in his films. Holly Chard investigates the effect of these comedians' presence in Hughes's family films. Examining the role of the comedian in general, Chard argues that such comic figures are at a remove from societal norms. Indeed, it is the clash between the comedians' comic presence and those norms that often drives their narratives' humor. The disruptive presence of the comedian is illustrated in the physical form of John Candy, whom Chard aligns with Bakhtinian forms of the carnival and the grotesque. Candy's physical size is central to this, since his outsized body ill fits the domestic environments in which he appears in *Uncle Buck* (1987). There is, then, a productive tension in the comedian's disruptive presence, and the script's desire for normal family life. For Chard, this is resolved through a strategic containment of the comedian figure's troublesome potential. Buck, for instance, begins the film as a carefree bachelor reluctantly taking on childcare responsibilities. By the end of the narrative, however, he begins to lament that he does not have a family of his own. It appears, then, that Hughes's films, while sending up conventional family life, ultimately work to shore up this patriarchal institution.

In turn, Alice Leppert's chapter charts the numerous failed patriarchs that populate Hughes's worlds. From the hapless Clark Griswold (Chevy Chase) of the *Vacation* series through to the obnoxious strains of Mr. Vernon (Paul Gleason) in *The Breakfast Club* (1985) and indigent though sympathetic Jack (Harry Dean Stanton) in *Pretty in Pink* (1986), Leppert identifies the many and varied ways in which fathers and father figures are shown to fail throughout Hughes's work. In his family films in particular, Leppert observes that Hughes is especially critical of the traditional disciplinarian figure, and locates the undercurrent of bullying in such a position. What is more, in the *Home Alone* films, she argues that Kevin's father, Peter (John Heard), is a nonentity: he does not feel the same sense of guilt for having abandoned Kevin in either film, nor does he apparently see it as his responsibility to recuperate the family unit. These elements are left to the mother (Catherine O'Hara), who feels her son's absence instinctively, and whose appeals for help are framed by her position "as a mother." The father retains his position as the financial head of the household, while the mother shoulders the emotional burden of childcare.

In the place of the failed father, Leppert argues that children and teenagers emerge as more able potential patriarchs. As she observes, in *Home Alone*, Kevin refers to himself as "the man of the house," with the result that it falls to him to protect the family home from the two burglars who have been eyeing the property for some days. Kevin's command of the domestic space, and his use of direct address, connect him with an earlier child patriarch, Ferris Bueller (Matthew Broderick), who easily outsmarts his teachers and family in *Ferris Bueller's Day Off* (1986). Ferris's charm and quick wit allow him to secure a day off in Chicago with his friends, while gaining access to high-end restaurants and, ultimately, taking part in a parade running through the city. Hughes seems therefore to suggest that, if family life is to continue in its present structure, then it is best to look to its junior members as its future custodians.

NOTE

1. Sara Ahmed, "The Happiness Turn," *New Formations*, 63 (2007), 7–14.

CHAPTER 8

Brand Name Vision: Props in the Films of John Hughes

Leah R. Shafer

Advertising Age's special report on advertising in the 1980s claims that "no discussion of advertising in the 1980s would be complete without noting the high priority placed on TV advertising by the [1984] re-election campaign of President Ronald Reagan."[1] Though his campaign relied on a bespoke "Tuesday Team" of ad men headed by Hal Riney, the article attributes to Reagan himself, "an unprecedented understanding of the power of visual media."[2] Riney created the campaign's "Morning in America" TV commercial: a minute-long TV spot that features clichéd images of an ascendant country of happy White people prospering in their everyday lives. The ad depicts America as a space of forward momentum, a place of vehicles moving across the American landscape toward a singular image of "home." The forward motion promised by the voiceover is reinforced through a montage sequence that resolves in a marriage of a White, heterosexual couple. At the start of the commercial, Riney sonorously intones, "It's morning again in America. Today more men and women will go to work than ever before in our country's history." While Riney speaks, we see a montage made up of: a fishing boat sailing through a harbor; a crowd of commuters crossing a street in front of a taxi; a farmer plowing a field; a paper boy slinging a paper from his bicycle; a carpooling businessman striding towards a Jeep; and, a wood-paneled station wagon pulling up in front of a suburban center hall colonial house with a white picket fence.[3]

Anyone with a passing acquaintance with the films of John Hughes will recognize the iconic status of the image of the wood-paneled station wagon and the center hall colonial house—they've seen a version of them in *Mr. Mom* (1983), *National Lampoon's Vacation* (1983), *Sixteen Candles* (1984), *Ferris Bueller's Day Off* (1986), *Planes, Trains and Automobiles* (1987), *She's Having a Baby* (1988), *Uncle Buck* (1989), *Home Alone* (1990), *Dennis the Menace* (1993), and *Beethoven* (1992) as well as *Beethoven's 2nd* (1993), *3rd* (2000), *4th* (2001), and *5th* (2003). The "unprecedented understanding of the power of visual media" attributed to Reagan (though invented by his campaign advertising staff) may just as easily be read as an assessment of the films of John Hughes (and his team of art directors, location scouts, and prop masters).[4] The man Vincent Canby calls "the first real *auteur* of television style entertainment" created a body of work that evokes the very same promise of velocity, resolution, and home as Riney's iconic advertisement for the face of American late capitalism, Ronald Reagan.[5] The centrality and polysemy of the image of the wood-paneled station wagon pulling up in front of a suburban upper-middle-class lawn to the popular cinema of the American 1980s and, by extension, to cinema as a cultural practice, cannot be overstated.

Writing about imagery in twentieth-century cinema, John David Rhodes says, "The image in cinema is often an image of the house; thus cinema's spectacle often constitutes what I call the "spectacle of property."[6] Rhodes's emphasis on property as a central spectacle for cinema speaks directly to the work of John Hughes as a writer and director of American cinema. The center hall colonial house and wood-paneled station wagon of Hughes's imaginary Shermer, Illinois function as potent, polysemous cultural metonymies—allegories for the relationship between spectators and the complex of cinematic materiality invoked by Rhodes in his reading of the "experience of cinema."

> The experience of cinema . . . does not merely refer to the image onscreen; it also encompasses the material (whether industrial or artisanal) practices of its production; as well as the means of its distribution and exhibition, and includes, moreover, the lived, embodied experience of its reception by human spectators. In all of these areas of the cinematic experience, property reigns.[7]

In this chapter, I take up Rhodes's definition of the "experience of cinema" with its emphasis on "the lived, embodied experience of its reception" and shift the focus from houses to what is in them. I extend Rhodes' definition of property to include properties: film props. I argue that Hughes's sensibility, his brand identity, can be located in the particular way he uses props as vehicles for humor, affective connection, and narrative resolution. I begin to unpack this argument by contextualizing the use of props for the creation of a Hughes brand within the industrial structure of "television style entertainment."[8] I discuss the work of John Hughes as an example of the kind of "television style entertainment" that circulated in the American 1980s. Where Canby uses the term to suggest that Hughes's work does not fit within the canon of directors properly referred to as *auteurs* (and denigrates television while enshrining the notion of film as something created by a singular artistic vision) I use it here to suggest that Hughes can be read as having an authorial signature that functions like a brand. Unlike Canby, I do not invoke "television style" as an aesthetic judgment, but, rather, as reference to a specific style that relies on a particular economic engine: the advertisement.

Of course, most American feature film is commercial in nature, and, as such, contains both formal and aesthetic elements that are, in essence, advertisements, but what I mean to point out here is the way that the structure of "television style," or the televisual, is (or at least was in the twentieth century) organized around interruptions for commercial breaks. Hughes famously began his writing career crafting copy for television commercials and his film work resonates with the television advertising style with its focus on brands, interruption, repetition, witty clichés, and affective lures. The moments when props appear and/or are used temporarily interrupt the narrative and/or visual flow of the film, and, as such, function like commercial breaks. As on television, these commercial breaks are moments of desire-producing velocity, of affective repetition that fuels attention to brand identity and ignites brand loyalty. This dynamic functions in Hughes's work on several levels. We can see it in the visual fields of Hughes's works, which are riotously populated with the banal consumer goods of suburban 1980s America. We can feel it in the comic narrative structure of Hughes's screenplays, which are studded with moments of reversal and interruption. We can locate it in Hughes's industrial practices, particularly his stated intention to create films that grow a market. And, we can find it in the historical context of the American 1980s: in both the substantial changes to film culture seen in the growth of the blockbuster with its attendant reliance on product placement and merchandising as a prominent revenue stream, and in the larger socio-political changes brought about by the nascent neoliberalism of the Reagan era.[9]

This "television style," this embrace of the commercial break, I argue, appears in the way that properties function as markers of the John Hughes brand. To make this argument, this chapter offers select close readings of properties in the films of John Hughes. It unpacks representative examples of props—cars, lawnmowers, underpants, vacuum cleaners, Christmas ornaments, intercontinental ballistic missiles—as a way to locate Hughes's place within cinema of the 1980s. John Hughes's work as a writer and director provides an axiomatic example of the products coming out of the radically diversified film industry of the 1980s.

The chapter focuses primarily on Hughes's films that dramatize and satirize family life—*Mr. Mom*, *National Lampoon's Vacation*, *She's Having a Baby*, and *Home Alone*—while including references to iconic prop moments in his teen films—*Sixteen Candles* and *Weird Science* (1985)—and the teen/family film hybrid *Career Opportunities* (1991). In all of these films, the anarchic surrealism of domestic objects drives narrative progress and functions as a challenge to, and cynical affirmation of, the status quo. Scenes built around props address cultural anxieties about consumerism by featuring comical examples of automatism and mass production in revolt; they also lay bare the ways that the mass culture of the 1980s propped up a status quo that normalized casual racism and misogyny.[10] John Hughes's films, with their second and third lives in video release (whether in material or digital form), are exemplars of the cultural and historical moment of commodity culture and the new multi-platform entertainment industry out of which they were created. In these films, the push and pull, the visual and narrative velocity of things on screen, maps an oscillation between a rejection and an embrace of commodity fetishism that is constitutive of the era that sees the birth of neoliberalism. The films function as an advertisement for the Hughes brand, and the moments when characters encounter properties within the films become a model for the audience to desire further consumption of Hughes's films. Props literally set a stage that powerfully and paradoxically invites viewers to identify with and form relationships with consumer goods in general, and Hughes's brand in particular.

WHO, ME? YEAH, YOU!

As objects of analysis, props are ripe for critical reading. Props "help to amplify a mood, give further definition to a setting, or call attention to detail within the larger scene."[11] Props possess properties of both representational and mimetic forms: they stand for something *and* they call attention to themselves as standing for something. Props are ontologically metatextual and polysemous. They amplify and define setting while also moving the story forward. In Hughes's films, most of the props are commonplace, everyday items—Coke cans, boxes of laundry detergent, dog bones—and as such they are indexical representations of things found in the off-screen world: objects with industrial histories, and, for many spectators, correlative personal histories.[12]

Because the prop plays a role in dramatic action on the screen, it operates as a symbolically potent metonymy—a fragmented point of condensation—for the action and the milieu of the film. I suggest that this point of condensation functions like the interruptions in television narrative effected by television commercials. The point of condensation that functions as an interruption also functions as a crucial device for the creation of slapstick comic moments: a particular hallmark of the Hughes style. This functions much like the gag that Donald Crafton describes in his essay on slapstick and gag comedy in cinema, where he argues that the gag is a non-narrational element in narrative film:

> ... it was never the aim of comic filmmakers to "integrate" the gag elements of their movies, or to subjugate them to narrative. In fact, it can

be seen that the separation between the vertical, paradigmatic domain of slapstick —the arena of spectacle I will represent by the metaphor of the thrown pie —and the horizontal, syntagmatic domain of the story —the arena of the chase —was a calculated rupture, designed to keep the two elements antagonistically apart.[13]

While Crafton is invoking the pie and the throwing of the pie in his description of the calculated rupture, I am suggesting that the pie, itself, particularly "pies" that evoke the affective lures of consumer capitalism, evince a similar antagonistic separation, one that takes place both narratively and visually, or, to extend the allusion, in televisual style's horizontal and vertical flows. Of particular note is the way that the presence of this rupture typically functions as a location for pleasure and affective connection (whether around thrilling moments of desire or violence, or a combination of the two). Whether this connection is effected by what Andrew Sofer refers to as the "uncanny pleasure" of the prop's "intertextual resonance" or by the prop's laugh-inducing function as spectacle, the prop in Hughes's films functions as a location for spectator engagement with the Hughes brand.[14] Further, I suggest that in the films of John Hughes we see this antagonistic separation articulating a relationship to material objects that reflects a socio-historical moment invested in encouraging affective connection to branded items.

John Hughes films teach viewers how to be viewers of John Hughes films by modeling for them how to consume the properties of a John Hughes film. They stage scenes of spectatorship as models for how to respond with desire to things on display. One of the most instructive examples of this dynamic comes in the scene in *Sixteen Candles* when Jake (Michael Schoeffling) and his red Porsche appear across the street from Samantha (Molly Ringwald) in the doorway of the church where her sister has just gotten married. The iconic scene appears to be resolving the film's primary narrative conflict by delivering Jake to Samantha's sight, but a close reading of the scene reveals that the cars and buses part to reveal Jake in all his sweater-vested, Porsche-owning glory when Samantha's head is bowed.[15] Samantha, dejected at having again been forgotten by her family, stands at the door to the church—across the street from Jake and the red Porsche, with her head hung low. She eventually sees Jake, but she misses his miraculous unveiling. His appearance there, across the street from what appears to be Samantha's eyeline, is in fact an eyeline match with the spectator.

The spectacle of the reveal of Jake and the red Porsche is staged for the audience. Jake and his red Porsche pop out from behind the vehicles on the street across from the space where the spectatorial gaze is located with the fixed affective visual and narrative power of a brand logo. It's no mistake that Jake's red Porsche and Jake's Whiteness shine with the ubiquitous, brand-specific shimmer of a can of Coca-Cola. The reveal of Jake and his Porsche, staged for a thirsty audience primed by the film's relentless narrative drive toward this moment of narrative resolution, function as a signifier for the Hughes brand writ large.[16] It's a scene of affectively satisfying narrative resolution served with a splash of misdirection, staged with sightlines that cross a suburban lawnscape. The scene locates the viewer more precisely than it locates the characters and things populating the scene itself.[17] The moment locates the viewer of the John Hughes movie in an explicit relationship to the spectacle of an on-screen object that exceeds the film's diegesis.[18]

The Wagon Queen Family Truckster—the wood-paneled, metallic pea-colored station wagon that is, essentially, the star of *National Lampoon's Vacation*, is another paradigmatic example of this phenomenon. Where Jake's appearance is a scene of desire, the introduction of the Wagon Queen is a scene of violence. At the car dealer, Clark Griswold (Chevy Chase) discovers that he has fallen victim to a bait-and-switch, and the car he ordered is not available. In the moment after we hear the earnest, goofy Clark (dressed in an "Antarctic Blue" suit) insist that he has ordered the "Antarctic Blue Super Sports Wagon with the optional Rally Fun Pack," we hear the smashing of glass and see his butter-colored Vista Cruiser being pierced by giant steel pincers. The juxtaposition of violence being done to the car with Clark's foolish, fetishizing repetition of the phrase "Antarctic Blue Super Sports Wagon" illustrates the film's raw sensibilities and its simultaneous investment in and satirization of the incantatory power of the language of branding.[19] The comic effect of the juxtaposition, perfect in its timing, is startling. This moment vividly lays bare the violence and destruction invoked by Clark's desires. Clark says, "Where's my old car?" and then the spectators see and hear exactly where his old car is: crushed by a massive vice. The comical crosscut functions as a narrative designation shot explicitly for the audience. Clark does not see or hear the destruction of his car, which sets up the visual joke of Clark and his son attempting to drive off in their crushed wagon. In the films he writes and directs after *Vacation*, Hughes will use this type of prop-based set-up, rupture, and resolution, as well as direct extranarrative address of the audience, repeatedly. The comedy of this moment works, in part, because it acknowledges the spectator's complicity with the filmmakers and, in that moment of connection, asserts and engenders a kind of familiarity that breeds brand loyalty.

The *frisson* of complicity and familiarity engendered by these moments is complicated. The engine that runs the scene which introduces the Wagon Queen is not just the alignment of the spectator's delight at the "ordinary everyday fool" being bested; it is also fueled by racial Othering. The comedy in this scene relies, in part, on the way that Eugene Levy's shifty car salesman performs a coded anti-Semitism, while the scene's fall guy is a cigar-chomping, jumpsuit-wearing Black man called, simply, Davenport (Gerry Black). Not only is it absolutely clear that the comedy of the scene relies on a Jew openly shifting the blame for the missing Sport Wagon onto a Black man, but the Black man is named after a piece of furniture.[20] Moments of rupture linked to prop comedy often set the stage for status quo-reinforcing moments of Othering, such as in the moment when Clark misses his exit in St. Louis and ends up in a "bad neighborhood" (i.e., a neighborhood of Black people).

> Ellen: This is so dangerous! We have no business being in an area like *this*.
> Clark: Well, look at it this way, honey, this is a part of America we never get to see.
> Ellen: That's good!
> Clark: No, that's bad! I mean, uh, we can't close our eyes to the plight of the cities. Kids, you noticing all this plight? This will just, uh, make us appreciate what we have! [gun shot, scream] Roll 'em up![21]

Props, as things with correlative positions in the extranarrative world, carry with them the social status quo of that world. This sequence illustrates the ways that racial difference functions as a site of humor for the privileged. Clark's idea that he can roll up his car windows to protect his family from gunfire also suggests the idiotic fragility of the White nuclear family model.

Figure 8.1 Clark (Chevy Chase) asleep at the wheel.

BRAND NAME VISION 149

Soon after this scene, the Wagon Queen becomes sentient. As the kids sleep in the back seat, Clark and Ellen (Beverly D'Angelo) discuss a road trip they took in college and Clark encourages Ellen to give him oral sex while he is driving. She declines, but then agrees to rest her head in Clark's lap. At this point, her head becomes stuck beneath the steering wheel. The comic structure suggests that the Wagon Queen, itself, is trying to force Ellen to submit to Clark. This uncanny scene of the prop achieving its own consciousness is heightened when, soon after this moment, we see that the entire family has fallen asleep, including Clark, who is driving the car. In a scene marked by dramatic velocity, the car crosses lanes, exits the highway, and drives with abandon through the streets, wreaking havoc before depositing the Griswolds directly into a motel parking lot. It's not a giant stretch to read this as a scene of hegemonic, misogynistic ideation and as an allegory for Reagan's America, where the White middle-class family (under the power of a sexually rapacious father figure) cedes control to consumer goods and finds itself asleep at the wheel.

STRUNG OUT ON BEDSPREADS

If the culturally cathected image of Jake and his Porsche is emblematic of the way that Hughes's films teach spectators to locate themselves in relationship to their desire for things, and the Wagon Queen Family Truckster is emblematic of the way that consumer goods supplant and orient socio-political drives in the age of consumer capitalism, then the chaos of banal household objects that populate the bulk of his films represent the way that Hughes conditions spectators to consume more Hughes films. Hughes's family films—the *National Lampoon's Vacation* franchise, *Mr. Mom*, *She's Having a Baby*, *Planes, Trains and Automobiles*, the *Home Alone* franchise, the *Beethoven* franchise, *Curly Sue*, *Baby's Day Out*—are virtual storehouses of everyday goods. The visual and narrative fields of these films embody the "trenches of consumerism," the phrase that Ron (Martin Mull), Caroline's (Terry Garr) boss at the advertising firm in *Mr. Mom*, uses to describe being a housewife.[22] The characters in Hughes's films tend to perform the era's ambivalence about the traditional role of the housewife. We see this in the plot of *Mr. Mom*; in the resistance of Kristy (Elizabeth McGovern) in *She's Having a Baby*, to being just about "gold bands and bath towels"; in the absurd kitchen antics of *Uncle Buck*; and in Kevin's (Macaulay Culkin) inventive use of household objects to protect his house in *Home Alone*. The Hughes family films are, in many ways, a working through of the observations in Betty Friedan's 1963 classic essay "The Sexual Sell," which identifies in advertising literature the foundational argument that:

> The family is not always the psychological pot of gold at the end of the rainbow of promise of modern life as it has sometimes been represented.

> In fact, psychological demands are being made upon the family today which it cannot fulfill. Fortunately for the producers and advertisers of America (and also for the family and the psychological well-being of our citizens) much of this gap may be filled, and is being filled, by the acquisition of consumer goods.[23]

While the characters in Hughes's films seem to be drawing this idea into question, the ruckus of brands visible in the homes of Hughes's characters, and the function of those branded objects in the films' plots, is much less ambivalent. The films appear to lure the viewer by offering characters who are openly questioning the status quo of consumer society as models for identification, while functioning as resolute endorsements of the antiquated vision offered by the advertising professionals that Friedan critiques in her essay.[24]

Mr. Mom, for example, tells the ostensibly progressively gender-bending story of a family rethinking the role of the housewife by featuring a male character learning how to run a household and a female character achieving success in the workplace. But, the film's affective pleasures come almost entirely from Jack Butler's (Michael Keaton) slapstick encounters with basic housewifery. The encounters are mapped by Jack's relationship to things. A scene early in the film, when Jack faces the supermarket, is emblematic of this dynamic. In the supermarket, we first see the rattling front wheel of a grocery cart and Jack's shoes.[25] After the camera pans up, we see a wall of cans of Coke (a moment that evokes the imagery of Andy Warhol's 1962 painting *One Hundred Cans*). Banal things like pop (as it is called in the American Midwest) are ubiquitous features of the visual landscapes of all these films, suggesting that Hughes, like other Pop artists of the late American twentieth century, follows "the long tradition of interest in the banal and the popular" that is characteristic of American art.[26] The visual field has already been established as one that is full of objects, and this is the second time we see a scene against a backdrop that functions as a barrage of product names. During the supermarket scene, the following brand names are prominently displayed: Honey Maid, Sprite, Tide, Pepsi, Chex, Van Camps, Boss, Wonder Bread, Hobart, Kotex Maxi Pads, Stayfree, 7 Up, Quaker Oats, Wheat Thins, Coke, Scope, Band Aid, Scott Towels, Bacardi, Diet Pepsi, Schlitz, Smuckers, Hunts, and Ritz. The film's entire gestalt is an uncanny iteration in narrative space/time of the Pop aesthetic played for the spectator-oriented pleasures of narrative and visual rupture.

Jack Butler, with his attendant visual milieus, is characteristic of this particular historical moment. Though the film's narrative suggests to us that his ability to tell "tuna fish from a Cheerio" is crucial to his ability to function in the new economy, he makes his best moves when he makes explosive combinations of his resources. As Jack was fired from his auto-industry job, a job that relied on the rapidly disappearing Fordist economies of scale, he is attempting to learn how to function in the emerging neoliberal marketplace. Alison Pearlman identifies this phenomenon as being covered by David Harvey in *The Condition of Postmodernity*, when she cites his observation that "Fordist-style businesses were thus being replaced by new business practices he calls 'economies of scope,' which involve target-marketed and often briefly produced cycles of goods and services."[27] The economy of scope in *Mr. Mom* is literally mapped across the film's interiors. We see Jack buy Scope. As such, if we take our lessons from the pleasures of the film's riotous *mise-en-scène* (its insistent pop environment) rather than its narrative, we see that the accelerated diversification of mass culture still maintains, as its backbone, the ubiquitous presence of undifferentiated mass-produced commodities.

The dramatic backdrop of the film's role reversal is saturated with visual material, and the implication of the story is that being savvy about consumer knowledge is the best way to deal with being beset by a cultural crisis, whether it be across gender or class lines. Why would this lesson be here? A scene in Jack's house may hold one suggestion, in which a revolt is staged by the washing machine, the stove, the vacuum cleaner, and the television set. Jack mixes an entire table's worth of fabric softener (Downy), stain remover (Spray and Wash), and laundry detergents (Tide and Biz) in one large cup, which he stirs together with a screwdriver to add to his hilariously overstuffed washing machine. Jack's active rejection of the pragmatic differences between various brands of laundry soap leads to disaster. And while the washing machine responds to his rejection of brand awareness by becoming sentient and exploding, Jack battles the vacuum cleaner for his son's "woobie" (a colloquial term that refers to his son's beloved baby blanket). The "woobie" functions as the film's explicit acknowledgement of the role of the fetish object in individuation.[28] In a plainly satirical moment, Jack appears to acknowledge the relationship between desire and violence, between introjection and projection, that is evinced by fetish objects in consumer culture when he lectures his son about his "woobie," saying:

> I understand that you little guys start out with your woobies and you think they're great . . . and they are, they're terrific. But pretty soon, a woobie isn't enough. You're out on the street trying to score an electric blanket, or maybe a quilt. And the next thing you know, you're strung out on bedspreads, Ken. That's serious.[29]

Hughes's investment in rejecting the market forces that work against his brand empire is evident throughout his family films. His cynical embrace of the brand undercuts critiques of his work. In his discussion of the "New Breed" of comedy directors in the 1980s, Jack Barth contends that these directors, among whom he counts Hughes, "have synthesized nothing; they are like Pepsi to Coke, indistinguishable except to connoisseurs of junk."[30] Anyone who lived in America in the 1980s, however, can tell you that Pepsi does not taste like Coke: it was proven in taste tests.[31] Hughes knows this and uses his knowledge of "television style entertainment" to promote his brand. One compelling example of this dynamic appears in the block party scene of *She's Having a Baby*, when we see Hughes play out ambivalence around brand identity while reinforcing brand presence. The party appears to be a critique of the "suburban conformity" of Jake Briggs's (Kevin Bacon) life, but it does not entirely function as such, which we see when Jake talks with two neighbors:[32]

> Ken [John Ashton]: You know what two things I like about you most, Brigsy?
> Jake: I can't imagine.
> Ken: Your wife and your lawnmower.
> Hank [Larry Hankin]: I've seen your wife—what kinda mower 'ya got, Brigsy?
> Jake: Uh, it's the, you know, the kind you don't have to push, but you do it standing up . . . A power mower.
> Hank: What *brand*?
> [. . .]
> Ken: Wait a minute, wait a minute. You don't know what kind of mower you got? I mean when you . . . when you . . . got it didn't it have any specs that came with it? I mean, how can you not know what kind of mower you got? You got a Big Yard King 410. Remember that.[33]

Jake is more involved with the function than the commercial value of his lawnmower. One might see Jake here as a version of the child at play who "sides with use-value against exchange value," i.e., Adorno's figure for the one place where the advance of capital may not have substantially destroyed the qualitative and material character of things as things.[34] And in that case, Jake's lack of understanding might say something about his rejection of one of commodity culture's most important marks of identity—branding. The props in the scene, however, suggest otherwise: throughout his line about it being "the kind you don't have to push," we see Jake's hand repeatedly flashing the brand name and logo on a can of Pepsi.

"I'M GROWING A MARKET"

Perhaps the best example of the way that brand identity functions in a polysemous manner that ultimately props up the importance of brands, and of Hughes's own use of brand moments to evince affective connection to his own brand, lies in the film *Career Opportunities*.³⁵ The "O" in the word *Opportunities* in the film's title is literally a Target logo. The premise of the film, that there are almost limitless delights to being locked inside a Target store, is, in typical Hughes fashion, borne primarily in the overnight romance that develops between Jim Dodge (Frank Whaley) and Josie McClellan (Jennifer Connelly), but the film's visual field is littered with an abundance of branded goods, and the film's principal affective pleasures lie in the fantasy of unlimited access to consumer goods. The opening shots of the film, which introduce the secondary plot about the burglars who Jim and Josie will eventually encounter in the Target, are still images of a convenience store robbery that feature upended store aisles covered in things out of place. This framing device sets up the burglary narrative, but it also models, with the tableaux-setting style of its WeeGee aesthetic, the structural function of the branded items in the rest of the film.³⁶

The Target symbol is itself a very conscious articulation of what it means to be a consumer locked in the particular relationship with branded images that Hughes is capitalizing on in his films: what it's like to be, that is, the *target* of a marketing campaign. The creation and cultivation of a target audience for his films is, of course, central to Hughes's philosophy of filmmaking:

> I'm growing a market: "Sixteen Candles" will come out on videocassette as "The Breakfast Club" is opening. "Breakfast Club" will be on cassette as "Pretty in Pink" is coming. It created this wave. It took three years to get through it. And it worked. Those pictures are worth a lot of money. They're going to be worth a lot in the future because they play endlessly and they're a valuable part of somebody's catalogue. They rent consistently. A girl turns 16, she rents "Sixteen Candles." It's the No. 1 pajama party movie. And every four years there's a new crop of teenagers. And then again in 20 years it's going to be their nostalgia. And their kids are going to watch. It's going to be like Andy Hardy.³⁷

When Hughes outlines his plan for target audience domination, he explicitly invokes the viewing of his films on television, when people rent them after their initial viewing. As such, we can imagine Hughes anticipating his films' eventual televisual life during their initial conception and in his overarching aesthetic vision for the films.

One of the most memorable sequences in *Career Opportunities* is the montage that precedes Jim's discovery of Josie's presence in the store after closing time. The montage sequence is an uncanny pastiche of Reagan's "Morning in America" commercial: in it, Jim travels through the store, creating multiple distorted tableaux of domestic life. Most of the tableaux, like the image of Jim watching television with a mannequin, feature visible logos and visible price tags, and, as such, function as explicit advertisements. Right before Jim discovers Josie, he

Figure 8.2 Jim Dodge (Frank Whaley) and mannequin watch TV.

strips to his underwear, dons a bridal veil, and roller skates in circles around the Target. Like in Reagan's commercial, heterosexual union is a central image that propels the velocity of the larger narrative, promising an American success story. Here that image is amusingly distorted to focus on the power of consumer goods to secure romance.

The appearance of Josie, of the romance plot, results in the sudden stoppage of Jim's forward movement: as soon as he realizes he is not alone in the Target, he flies into a display of L'eggs pantyhose and falls to the ground, scattering the hose eggs across the floor.[38] Like the station wagon and the center hall colonial house, the sudden descent into a visual field littered with scattered objects is a Hughes signature. As *Career Opportunities* is, in most ways, a product-placement heavy revision of *Home Alone*, this moment is deeply reminiscent of the scenes of mayhem in Hughes's most financially successful film. *Home Alone*'s Kevin McCallister explicitly models for the audience a world in which the banal objects that you have acquired for your home are the things that give you protection, particularly if you carefully map how to use those things to create sudden, antagonistic, slapsticky descents into chaos.

We see Hughes delight in chaotic messes in films from *Mr. Mom* to *Home Alone*, especially in in the many bacchanalian party scenes in his teen films. Scenes of inventive, prop-laden destruction used as a narrative *mise-en-scène* are nowhere more spectacular than in *Weird Science*. We might consider the character of Lisa (Kelly LeBrock), herself, to be the most compelling prop object of the Hughes oeuvre, because she is literally created as a fantasy object out of a series of advertisements and a Barbie doll, and made by two young men from the target demographic of Hughes's films. I argue, however, that the teen party destruction of the house montage leads to an even more disturbing revelation in the form of a prop. When Gary (Anthony Michael Hall)

BRAND NAME VISION 155

Figure 8.3 Kevin's battle plan.

and Wyatt (Ilan Mitchell-Smith) are forced by Lisa to throw a party so they can solidify their social standing with their peers, they meet with the bullies who humiliated them earlier in the day at the mall. The bullies offer to *trade their girlfriends* for Lisa, and while Gary and Wyatt are unwilling to give Lisa to the young men, they do not, apparently, see any problem with creating a new Frankenstein's monster that they can offer in trade. As they work to do so, a dramatic montage sequence shows the party becoming intensely chaotic and infused with the absurd, hyper-stylized, brand-aware magic that marked Lisa's creation. The scene displays all the hallmarks of the Hughes brand: of particular note is the appearance of not one but two nonconsensual teenage girl upskirt images (both gained through abject violence being done to the young women); repeated images that literalize the transportation of target-market teenagers into a television; and, the auditory presence, throughout the sequence of the title song by Oingo Boingo which repeats the phrase "weird science" and, as such, functions as an aural brand logo for the film, itself.

This montage sequence features an escalating destruction of Wyatt's house in greater intensity than the destruction we see wrought by the party-goers at Jake's in *Sixteen Candles*; the partygoers at Steff's (James Spader) in *Pretty in Pink*; Jack's ham-fisted housewifery in *Mr. Mom*; the loose squirrel in *National Lampoon's Vacation*; *Home Alone*'s Kevin and the Wet Bandits; or by the canine antics of the *Beethoven* films and their many muddy puppies. The sequence ultimately builds up to the most compelling and, I would argue, distressing, illustration of the historical and cultural endgame of commodity culture expressed through a film prop. Because Wyatt and Gary have neglected to attach the computer to the Barbie doll, due to their excitement to show off to their bullies, they end up piercing the house with a medium-range ballistic nuclear missile, the Pershing II.[39] The appearance of this oversized prop, thrusting its way through the suburban home as a result of an explosive,

Figure 8.4 Pershing missile.

collective, juvenile assembly of advertising imagery and consumer electronics, is an overburdened emblem of the Hughes brand and its propensity for using pinpoint accuracy to target its audience with uncanny prop comedy. The omnipresent threat of nuclear annihilation that was characteristic of the American 1980s is being played here for a laugh. In an era that saw the establishment of the product-placement industry as a significant engine for industrial profit, this representative example of what we might call the brand identity of Reagan's America is chilling in its open visibility.[40]

CONCLUSION

Where the Classical Hollywood style is centered on a narrative style that strives to "avoid excess," Hughes created films that celebrate excess.[41] The films rely on the visual, literal excess of images and props so completely that one can read them as privileging the excessive milieu over the typical form of the character-centered narrative. The films' central interest lies in their evocation of milieu, and the relationship between the things on the screen and that milieu. Hughes's cynical, self-reflexive style is visible in his massively popular, mass-produced burlesques that rely heavily on prop comedy for their affective power. Hughes's films are exemplars of the cultural and historical moment of commodity culture and the multi-platform entertainment industry.

Props play a crucial role in the development of the John Hughes brand. Reading props in Hughes's films allows us to study the ways that props function in comic scenarios and in the ways that these scenarios reveal information about social and cinematic conventions in the blockbuster era. Close readings of comic sequences that rely on prop use or prop jokes open space for discussing the links between commercialism, branding, popular culture, and the John Hughes brand. It's difficult to read these films' staging of encounters with props and not pathologize Hughes's relationship to property: from Jaws seeking and eating our "woobie" in a chaotic house full of plumbers, painters, toddlers, and diapers, to the artfully sadistic marshaling of the home's most mundane resources in the service of protecting our abandonment. But, reading the Hughes body of work through the narrative applications of the prop diminishes the affective presence of the props' location within the visual world of the films. It also fails to entirely address the frisson of the real affected by product placement and the props' simultaneous presence in the spectators' filmic and everyday worlds. Ultimately, what we see in Hughes's work is a canny understanding of the way that props effect extranarrative reversals whose ultimate orientation is not toward the resolution of the narrative, but toward the spectator directly. Hughes's brand materially addresses the spectator: the films' paratexts targeted a variety of markets. Children could purchase toys, such as the Talkboy, a technologically "advanced" recording device that was designed by Hughes for *Home Alone 2* and released by Mattel; teenagers could purchase soundtracks and posters; adults could purchase VHS tapes, so they could watch the films and share them with their families.[42] The extranarrative orientation of the object in Hughes's oeuvre functions like an advertisement for things people can actually buy.

Hughes's works can be read as both critique of and collusion with the extratextual power of the branded thing. If we consider the span of his career, we see that Hughes's investment in these moments begins with playful, richly metatextual amusements and eventually becomes broader and angrier. In Hughes's films, props function as potent, polysemous cultural metonymies staged in scenarios that evoke repetitively affective connections between spectators and the films' visual and narrative landscapes, which are meant to fuel brand identity and brand loyalty. The ruptures and reversals effected by these designatory moments function like commercial breaks in extended advertisements for the consumption of more John Hughes films.

NOTES

1. "History: 1980s," *AdAge*, September 15, 2003, https://adage.com/article/adage-encyclopedia/history-1980s/98704/.
2. Ibid. Hal Riney is also the creator of the iconic '80s Bartles & Jaymes wine cooler ad campaign.
3. ElectionWallDotOrg, "Ronald Reagan Morning in America 1984," YouTube, video, 0:59, accessed January 4, 2020, https://youtu.be/1fyI671ePfE.
4. Hughes tended to work with a consistent group of folks for the creation of his films' visual landscapes. As Holly Chard notes, "In order to maintain continuity between his movies and to produce them as efficiently as possible, Hughes collaborated repeatedly with the same personnel during the late 1980s . . . John W. Corso and Marilyn Vance, in particular, made significant contributions to the visual style of Hughes' films." Holly Chard,

"Mainstream Maverick? John Hughes and New Hollywood Cinema" (PhD dissertation, University of Sussex, 2014), 104.
5. Quoted in Bill Carter, "Him Alone," *New York Times*, August 4, 1991.
6. John David Rhodes, *Spectacle of Property: The House in American Film* (University of Minnesota Press, 2017), 13.
7. Ibid.
8. Hughes developed his brand as a "creative producer" by "exploiting opportunities presented by expanding ancillary markets and changing production agendas." Chard, 3.
9. For an incisive analysis of the neoliberal style in Hughes's work, see Danielle B. Schwartz, "'You Look Good Wearing My Future': Resisting Neoliberalism in John Hughes's *Pretty in Pink* and *Some Kind of Wonderful*," *The Journal of Popular Culture*, 51, no. 2, 2018.
10. It is instructive that the most emblematic prop in Hughes's films is "underpants, girls' underpants." His films casually rely on the idea that actual young women can be traded as commodities for major narrative points of resolution. For the most part, Hughes's films invite confusion between character and commodity, particularly when the character is an attractive young woman. There is discussion of "trading" girls in both *Sixteen Candles* and *Weird Science*, and there are distressingly fetishized images of underage girls' underpants in both *Sixteen Candles* and *The Breakfast Club*.
11. Amy Villarejo, *Film Studies: The Basics* (New York: Routledge, 2013), 30.
12. How many of us have not held a can of Coke in our hand or eaten a birthday cake?
13. Donald Crafton, "Pie and Chase: Gag, Spectacle and Narrative in Slapstick Comedy," in *Cinema of Attractions Reloaded*, ed. Wanda Strauven, (Amsterdam: Amsterdam University Press, 2006), 356.
14. Andrew Sofer, *The Stage Life of Props* (Ann Arbor: University of Michigan, 2003), vii.
15. Of course, one might ask whether it is Jake or the Porsche that Samantha truly desires. Though it is less narratively explicit than in *Pretty in Pink*, the film clearly identifies class difference and dreams of economic mobility as the primary vehicle for desire.
16. The idea of what the John Hughes brand is circulates freely in American culture. For years I have had a Google News search for the phrase "John Hughes movie." The phrase appears in mass media to refer to a generic, yet oddly specific, idea about high school cliques and teenage romance: I have had the search for about ten years and during that time the phrase has appeared about once every other day. This *idée fixe* about the definition of a "John Hughes movie" is also evident in the robust market of popular cultural essays and documentaries such as *Don't You Forget About Me* (Matt Austin, 2009), and books like Jason Diamond's *Searching for John Hughes: Or, Everything I Thought I Needed to Know About Life I Learned from Watching '80s Movies* (New York: William Morrow Paperbacks, 2016) and Susannah Gora's *You Couldn't Ignore Me if You Tried: The Brat Pack, John Hughes, and Their Impact on a Generation* (New York: Three Rivers Press, 2011). While this idea of what a "John Hughes movie" is circulates in culture, it seems important to note that if one were using the typical metric of what distinguishes American film directors—box office success—a "John Hughes movie" would not be a teen film, but would be something more akin to *Home Alone* or *Beethoven*.
17. The phrasing here is adapted from Caren Deming's comment that "the televisual locates viewers more precisely than it locates the people and objects it presents for viewing" in her chapter about *The Goldbergs*, "Locating the Televisual in Golden Age Television" in *A Companion to Television*, ed. Janet Wasko (New York: Wiley-Blackwell, 2009), 131.
18. Hughes employs a similar red car device throughout his oeuvre. In *National Lampoon's Vacation*, Christie Brinkley in the red convertible clearly signifies the free-floating nature of desire as she repeatedly distracts Clark Griswold from the road. Another example

would be the extra-diegetic "oh yeah" that we hear when we see the red 1961 Ferrari 250 GT California in *Ferris Bueller's Day Off*.
19. Hughes, who began his writing career as an advertising copywriter, is particularly talented at writing this kind of dialogue.
20. Davenport, it should be noted, is a word like Kleenex or Frigidaire: a brand name used as the proper name for an object.
21. Harold Ramis, *National Lampoon's Vacation* (1983, Warner Brothers), Film. Transcription of dialogue is my own.
22. He says this the first time we see the boardroom at Caroline's new job, which is populated by a long table filled with: Dunkin' Donuts, Domino's Pizza, Kentucky Fried Chicken, McDonalds, Pepsi Free, and Marks-a-lot.
23. Betty Friedan, "The Sexual Sell," in *The Consumer Society Reader*, eds Juliet B. Schor and Douglas B. Holt (New York: The New Press, 2000), 40.
24. The polysemous nature of the films' possible interpretations reflects their historical context, "the New Hollywood's tightly diversified media conglomerates, which (favor) texts strategically "open" to multiple readings and multimedia reiteration." Thomas Schatz, "The New Hollywood" in *Film Theory Goes to the Movies*, eds Jim Collins, Hillary Radner, and Ava Preacher Collins (New York: Routledge, 1993), 34.
25. Many of the shots in this film begin at the bottom of the frame and move up, like a child looking up to its parent. This visual cue recalls one of the film's marketing tag lines: "Caroline's a rising executive. Jack just lost his job. Jack's going to have to start from the bottom up." Posters for the film feature Jack trying to dry his baby's bottom with a bathroom hand dryer, turning the "bottom up" line into a crude visual pun.
26. Tracy Atkinson, "Pop Art and the American Tradition," in Carol Anne Mahsun, *Pop Art: The Critical Dialogue* (Ann Arbor, MI: UMI Research Press, 1989), 164.
27. Alison Pearlman, *Unpackaging Art of the 1980s* (Chicago: University of Chicago Press, 2003), 149.
28. A Lacanian might suggest that Jack's house could be called "Fort Da," as the film is deeply invested in the role of the fetish object in individuation.
29. Stan Dragoti, *Mr. Mom* (1983, Twentieth Century Fox), Film. Transcription of dialogue is my own.
30. Jack Barth, "Kinks of Comedy," *Film Comment*, 20, no. 2 (May/June 1984), 45.
31. Commercials that asked random mall shoppers to distinguish between Pepsi and Coke were ubiquitous on American television in the 1980s. Barth may be suggesting that Hughes's work is as junky as soda pop, but this era's television provides compelling evidence that connoisseurs of junk were seen as cultural tastemakers.
32. Roger Ebert, "Gimmicks Distract in 'Having a Baby,'" *Chicago Sun-Times*, February 5, 1988, 25.
33. John Hughes, *She's Having a Baby* (1988, Paramount Pictures). Film. Transcription of dialogue is my own.
34. Bill Brown, "How to Do Things with Things (A Toy Story)," *Critical Inquiry*, 24, no. 4 (1998), 953.
35. If one were inclined to read the film within a larger assessment of Hughes's career, one might identify this film, which was a major box office flop, as his own *Mr. Mom* moment: when he mixes together elements from all of his previous films and then it ends up attacking him.
36. WeeGee is a photographer known for his fine art images of banal urban events.
37. Hughes quoted in Bill Carter, "Him Alone," *New York Times Magazine*, August 4, 1991, 36.
38. L'eggs pantyhose were sold in egg shaped containers designed by Roger Ferriter. The iconic homonym-evoking design, wherein eggs of hose are displayed on a carousel called

the "L'eggs Boutique," is included in the collection of the Museum of Modern Art. Julius Duscha, "The Problem of Living Up to L'eggs," *New York Times*, March 5, 1978, F5.
39. The Pershing II was noted for its ability to be directed toward targets at a great distance with "pinpoint accuracy." For more information, see the Federation of American Scientists section on weapons of mass destruction: https://fas.org/nuke/guide/usa/theater/pershing2.htm.
40. Ronald Reagan, himself, joked openly about nuclear annihilation. During a sound check for his weekly radio address, he was recorded saying, "My fellow Americans. I'm pleased to tell you today that I've signed legislation that will outlaw Russia forever. We begin bombing in five minutes." Associated Press, "President's Joke About Bombing Leaves Press in Europe Unamused," *New York Times*, August 14, 1984: https://www.nytimes.com/1984/08/14/world/president-s-joke-about-bombing-leaves-press-in-europe-unamused.html.
41. John Belton, *American Cinema/American Culture* (New York: McGraw, 1993), 22.
42. Reyes, Sonia. "Talkboy: 'Home Alone 2' Toy Is Hot, Hot, Hot," *New York Daily News*, December 16, 1993, https://archive.seattletimes.com/archive/?date=19931216&slug=1737234.

CHAPTER 9

Domesticating the Comedian: Comic Performance, Narrative, and the Family in John Hughes's 1980s Comedian Films

Holly Chard

During the 1980s, John Hughes participated in several movie projects starring high-profile comedy performers. *National Lampoon's Vacation* (1983), *National Lampoon's Christmas Vacation* (1989), *Planes, Trains and Automobiles* (1987), and *Uncle Buck* (1989) are among Hughes's most commercially successful movies and rely heavily on the established comic personas of Chevy Chase, Steve Martin, and John Candy. One of Hughes's major creative contributions to these films was the development of narrative frameworks that could accommodate the comedians' on-screen personas and, at the same time, tell a coherent story with a satisfying conclusion. In a departure from the conventions of earlier comedian comedies, such as the films of the Marx Brothers, Bob Hope, and Jerry Lewis, Hughes's movies prioritize narrative coherence over displays of the comedians' talents. The performances of Chevy Chase in *Vacation* and *Christmas Vacation*, Steve Martin and John Candy in *Planes, Trains and Automobiles*, and Candy in *Uncle Buck* reflect Hughes's development of a more "domesticated" form of Hollywood comedian comedy. Through his screenplays and, in the case of *Planes, Trains and Automobiles* and *Uncle Buck*, direction, Hughes sought to contain the disruptive, anti-establishment energy of the comedian figure by integrating him within the White, middle-class nuclear family.

To meet audience expectations, Hughes's movies deploy the performers' personas, but they do so in selective ways and at regulated moments in order to reduce narrative disruption. Gags involving the comedians typically perform a specific function within the narrative, rather than serving as standalone comic vignettes. Significantly, as the films progress, the comedians are increasingly integrated both within the narrative and within the White middle-class family. The comedians' performances and Hughes's narrative strategies in these movies also have wider ideological implications. In many pre-1980s comedies, the comedian is presented as an eccentric, potentially disruptive figure.[1] In contrast, by combining the elements of comedian comedy with a narrative that attempts to reinforce a stable social order anchored by the nuclear family, Hughes's films attempt to domesticate the comedian and try to contain the potential ideological disruptions that he represents. This more conservative message is further reinforced by the movies' othering of marginal groups, which asserts the superiority of the affluent, White protagonists and the importance of the suburban nuclear family.

COMEDIAN COMEDY IN THE 1980S

From the late 1920s through to the early 1950s, comedians typically built their reputations in vaudeville or live stand-up comedy before making the transition into movies. Hollywood cinema developed a range of narrative and stylistic strategies for accommodating the comedian's reputation as "an already recognizable performer with a clearly defined extrafictional personality," which responded to the styles of comic performance common in this period.[2] Many comedy performers who built their careers during the 1970s and 1980s did not acquire reputations for traditional, gag-based stand-up acts, however. Chevy Chase and John Candy both built their careers in improvisation and television sketch comedy, gaining notoriety via *Saturday Night Live* (starting in 1975) and *SCTV* (1976–84) respectively. Steve Martin gained fame as a highly unconventional stand-up comedian and further built his image through television appearances. While comedian vehicles in the post-studio era follow a less codified set of conventions, they retain aspects of the model of "comedian comedy," originally outlined by Steve Seidman and Frank Krutnik.[3] The comedian's on-screen presence heightens the tension produced in most star vehicles, whereby the performer's extratextual image has potential to exceed their "character" and thus to disrupt the fiction.[4] In the studio era, this disruption tended to be overt, as comedians often looked directly at and spoke to the camera in an explicit acknowledgement of the audience.[5] Although this device was occasionally used in later movies, such as Woody Allen's *Annie Hall* (1977), many comedians of the 1970s and 1980s adopted the subtler strategy of distancing themselves from the film's action through their performance style.

Chevy Chase is a prime example of the ironic, almost anti-professional stance towards entertaining people adopted by several comedians in the 1970s and 1980s. Rather than "inhabiting" characters with any considerable psychological depth, he deliberately exhibited shallowness and a lack of sincerity in many of his performances, signaling the narrative's artifice to the audience. During his time on *Saturday Night Live*, Chase capitalized on opportunities to establish a consistent on-screen persona. "As a performer," suggests Jim Whalley, "Chase benefited from a limited but highly developed range of skills, combining leading-man good looks and charm with expert physical slapstick . . ."[6] Compared to the other Not Ready For Prime-Time Players, he was allowed to perform a consistent set of traits on-screen and rarely wore heavy make-up or costumes that hid his facial features. Crucially, Chase secured himself a prominent slot in every show through his role as the news anchorman on "Weekend Update," which gave rise to his most famous catchphrases. Chase's deadpan delivery of variations on the oft-repeated line "Generalissimo Francisco Franco is still dead" served to emphasize his "ironic detachment to the absurdity of it all."[7] By distancing himself from the subject matter of this and other sketches, Chase assumed a superior and knowing position. His major catchphrase, "I'm Chevy Chase and you're not," reinforced his on-screen persona's heightened sense of self-satisfaction. With an athletic but lanky six-foot, four-inch frame, Chase's physique was particularly suited to physical comedy, and he was accomplished at spectacular, highly choreographed pratfalls. Thus, while many of his peers were focusing on relatively complex or absurdist humor, Chase was willing to exploit more accessible modes of comedy.

National Lampoon's Vacation was clearly built around Chase's *SNL* persona. Although he experienced mixed success both with critics and at the box office, Chase managed to cement his on-screen persona and performance style through his roles in movies including *Foul Play* (1978), *Caddyshack* (1980), and *Modern Problems* (1981). As the actor noted in January 1983, "My personality seems to have set in with people, and they like that. They enjoy knowing what to expect."[8] In *Vacation*, Chase plays Clark W. Griswold, a man who takes his family on a road trip to Walley World theme park for their summer vacation. Like "Vacation '58," Hughes's short story on which the movie was based, his screenplay probed the comic potential of the "disappointment" that characterized "middle-class, middle-American, suburban life."[9] Primarily addressing an audience of middle-class baby boomers, *Vacation* focuses on Clark's determination to compensate for 18 years of summer vacations where his family "never had fun" and to connect with a tradition rooted in America's past. Similarly, 1989's *Christmas Vacation* centers on Clark's desire to have a "fun, old-fashioned family Christmas." *Vacation* and *Christmas Vacation* therefore hinge on Chase's performance and on his character's role as a father.

Like Chase, Steve Martin adopted a highly ironic attitude towards the established conventions of comedy. Martin's mode of performance was "anti-comedy" which, as Lesley Harbidge describes, was "a comedy of disconnection and disavowal that would seem to challenge perceptions about the roles of the comedian and his audience in stand-up . . ."[10] By combining silliness with ironic disavowal, Martin distanced himself from the more politically committed stand-up comedians of the late 1960s and early 1970s. Although some of his material was derived from older performance traditions, such as the vaudeville staple of juggling, his act was also a reaction to the joke-driven comedy of the 1950s. As he would later observe, "I decided that to deny the audience the punch line was the secret of modern comedy."[11] His early stand-up performances thus discouraged audience identification with his onstage persona. His comedy also played on the fact that he looked like an "average insurance salesman," as he undermined the expectations created by his conventional appearance through the style and content of his performance.[12] Martin's extreme style of delivery and deviations into absurd pieces of "business" emphasized the separation between performer and persona. As audiences became more familiar with the comedian's absurdist form of humor, notes Harbidge, Martin's performances played with their awareness of the separation between Martin and "Steve," his stage persona.[13]

Planes, Trains and Automobiles confirmed Martin's move into less anarchic, more domestic comedy. Rather than attempting to replicate the success of his first starring role as Navin in *The Jerk* (1979), which drew heavily on his stand-up persona, Martin took on a variety of roles in the 1980s, including Arthur Parker in *Pennies from Heaven* (1981), C. D. Bales in *Roxanne* (1987), and Gil Buckman in *Parenthood* (1989). Press coverage of the comedian's personal life also revealed his muted personality and interests off-stage, including modern art, which contrasted starkly with his anarchic stand-up persona. His on-screen performances could therefore be seen as attempts to reconcile his rebellious style of comedy with his more bourgeois lifestyle. In *Planes, Trains and Automobiles*, Martin plays Neal Page, a tightly wound, yuppie marketing executive who embarks on a cross-country odyssey to get home to Chicago in time for Thanksgiving. At various points in his journey, Neal crosses paths with Del Griffith (John Candy), a well-intentioned but irritating and somewhat boorish travelling salesman. Hughes generates a great deal of humor through the clash between the two comedians and their contrasting personas, as is typical of many earlier comedian comedies.

John Candy's background was in improvisational comedy. After working in Second City's Toronto stage show, he was part of the cast of *SCTV* from 1976 until 1984. The show's move to NBC in 1981 brought its stars, including Candy, to the attention of a much broader audience. As part of Hollywood's attempts to cash in on the popularity of sketch comedy performers, Candy and his *SCTV* peers, including Eugene Levy and Rick Moranis, were offered roles in various movies during the 1980s. Candy's early film career consisted of supporting roles, often as part of an all-male group (*1941* [1979], *Stripes* [1981], and *Going Berserk* [1983]) or alongside another male comedy performer. In these movies, he typically played characters with excessive appetites for food, drink, tobacco, and/or women. After his breakthrough role as Freddie Bauer in *Splash* (1984), Candy starred in his first solo vehicle, *Summer Rental* (1985), which drew much more on his highly likeable "everyman" off-screen image at the core of his popularity with audiences. Interviews published in the mid- to late 1980s offer a consistent portrayal of Candy as "a warm and likeable human being" who "is simply incapable of projecting mean-spiritedness."[14] In his television appearances, such as on *Late Night With David Letterman* (1982–93), Candy came across as friendly but self-deprecating. Hughes sought to cultivate this funny but warm and modest persona in *Planes, Trains and Automobiles*, while drawing on the exaggerated traits that he had played on *SCTV* and in his earlier movies.

Building on the success of Hughes and Candy's collaboration on *Planes, Trains and Automobiles*, *Uncle Buck* managed to synthesize the appeal of John Candy's comic persona with scenarios from situation comedy. Candy starred as Buck Russell, a loveable but lazy bum who has to babysit his nephew and two nieces in suburban Chicago. The movie also included a subplot concerning Buck's adolescent niece, Tia (Jean Louisa Kelly), and her relationship with Bug (Jay Underwood), a pretentious and lust-driven high school senior. As Chris Willman observed in the *Los Angeles Times*, Hughes "devised a plot with which to fuse his two genres of choice: the clashing-family-members comedy and the tortured-teen pic."[15] While many of the comic incidents in the film are loosely linked, the conflict between Buck and Tia provides much of the narrative drive. It is through the escalating battle between uncle and niece that the film most overtly celebrates the importance of patriarchal authority and the protection of innocence. By integrating the comedian into the family, *Uncle Buck* harnesses Candy's traits to insist on the importance of the family and traditional values.

USING THE COMEDIANS' PERSONAS

Making extensive use of Chase's aloof persona, much of the comedy in the *Vacation* films is derived from Clark's inappropriate responses to emotionally trying or tragic events. In the first *Vacation*, when he accidentally kills a dog by dragging it behind the car for several miles, he attempts to convey the sincerity of his apology to a state trooper. However, Chase's exaggerated facial expressions suggest Clark's lack of genuine emotion. In a later scene, upon discovering that Aunt Edna (Imogene Coca) has died, Clark decides to strap her to the roof of the car. When they dump her at a relative's house, Clark delivers an improvised eulogy, as they huddle around Edna's tarpaulin-wrapped corpse in a lawn chair:

> Clark: Oh God, ease our suffering in this, our moment of great despair. Yea, admit this good and decent woman into thine arms and the flock of thine heavenly area, up there. And Moab, he laid us down by the band of the Canaanites, and yea, though the Hindus speak of karma . . .

Ellen [Clark's wife]: Clark . . .
Clark: I implore you . . . give her a break.
Ellen : Clark!
Clark: Baruuuuuuch Ataaaaaaah Aluuuuuuuyah . . .
Ellen: Clark, this is a serious matter, I'll do it myself!
Clark: Honey, I'm not an ordained minister; I'm doing my best, okay?

Hughes's dialogue heightens the absurdity of the situation, by following Clark's increasingly ridiculous quasi-religious speech with Ellen's reminder of the gravity of the situation. Chase's deadpan delivery, which creates ironic distance between the comedian and the scenario, clearly references his indifferent "Weekend Update" character on *SNL*. Given that the narrative of *Vacation* is focalized through Clark, this performance strategy legitimizes the audience's laughter at this scene and during other moments of dark humor in the movie.

In the first half of *Vacation*, Hughes's script creates numerous situations that undermine Clark's self-assured attitude. As William Paul observes, "A lot of the comedy in Chase's performances comes from his own conception of himself as suave and debonair while events around him conspire to puncture holes in that image."[16] His attempts to seduce a young woman in a Ferrari (played by supermodel Christie Brinkley) cause him to almost crash the family's car and to eat a sandwich covered with dog urine. Rather than showing how Clark's "pleasure-driven mentality pits [him] against a succession of killjoys, dupes, and other representatives of the social order, who work to contain and constrain [his] impulsiveness," Hughes uses coincidence to suppress Clark's sexual urges.[17] This strategy avoids addressing the moral and social implications of Clark's actions. In a later scene, he goes skinny-dipping with a woman, only to be publicly humiliated when he wakes up the whole hotel. *Vacation* also manages to negotiate the "demands of integration and responsibility for the male," signified by his wife.[18] Played by Beverly D'Angelo, Ellen Griswold is an attractive and sexually available spouse, rather than a traditional maternal figure. Scenes of showering and skinny-dipping allow for the display of D'Angelo's body. Ellen's presence nonetheless limits Clark's sexual behavior to within the Griswolds' marriage, as well providing a reminder of his responsibilities as a husband and father.

Although the final section of *Vacation* is closest in tone and content to earlier comedian comedies, Hughes uses a psychological breakdown to justify Clark's erratic and impulsive actions. In a scene that permits the kind of extreme comedic performance expected of Chevy Chase, Clark finally snaps at his family and launches into an expletive-filled rant, in which he tells his family, "I think you're all fucked in the head. We're ten hours from the fucking fun park and you want to bail out." Chase's manic delivery of the speech reveals a suppressed neurotic side to his character, previously masked by his muted reactions to events. "Generally cast as an outsider or misfit in some way," observes Frank Krutnik, "the comedian presents a spectacle of otherness by serving as a conduit for energies that are marginal, non-normative or anti-social."[19] In the scenes that follow, Clark punches a man dressed as a moose, torments security guards with a gun, and rides on theme park attractions. John Candy's appearance in these scenes as Lasky, a security guard, briefly creates a double act, allowing Chase to further exaggerate his manic performance. The pair's childlike bickering, which culminates with Clark shooting Lasky in the buttock with a BB gun, highlights how Clark has regressed to a childlike state and abandoned any pretensions of middle-class decorum. Through *Vacation*'s ending, Hughes seeks to contain the anarchic energy that accompanies Clark's temporary descent into insanity, however. Clark convinces theme park owner Roy Walley (Eddie Bracken) that his insanity was temporary and merely a heightened reaction to the pressure of taking the family on vacation. Chase's chaotic performance and Clark's antisocial impulses are therefore contained and the Griswold family is happily reunited.

Despite receiving a screenwriting credit, Hughes's involvement in the first *Vacation* sequel, *European Vacation* (1985), was extremely limited.[20] The film was a much less refined, loosely structured version of the original movie's road-trip narrative and relied heavily on crude humor, but lacked the satirical edge of *Vacation*. In contrast, when Hughes wrote and produced the second sequel to *Vacation* in 1989, he played an active role in the film's development and aimed to create a comedy with much broader appeal by including numerous moments of broad slapstick featuring Chase and setting the action in the Griswold's suburban neighborhood. Whereas *Vacation* relied on a gradual escalation of events, in *Christmas Vacation* Clark demonstrates a lack of physical and emotional control from the very start of the film. This is clearly signaled by Chase's facial expressions and his body movements, which are much more exaggerated and less constrained than in the original *Vacation*. From the outset, Clark's behavior is erratic and his attitude toward other people and adverse situations is much less subdued. In a scene that introduces the neighborhood, he responds to his yuppie neighbors who ask, "Where do you think you're gonna put a tree that big?" by wielding a chainsaw and retorting, "Bend over and I'll show you." Abandoning the more challenging satire of the original *Vacation*, *Christmas Vacation* uses Chase's skills as a comic performer to offer a more conventional, albeit highly comical, representation of American family life.

Hughes uses the conventions of the screwball road movie to give *Planes, Trains and Automobiles* its structural logic, "using the energy of the couple's friction and mutual frustration to drive the narrative forward."[21] He generates much of the film's comedy from the stark contrasts between its two protagonists, Del (John Candy) and Neal (Steve Martin). Most noticeably, the two men embody differing attitudes to the body and its relation to space, reflecting not only their different personalities, but also their social backgrounds. Del's unrestrained and public display of his consumption of unhealthy food, alcohol, and cigarettes suggests his *joie de vivre* and worldliness. Bakhtin states that, "Eating and drinking are one of the most significant manifestations of the grotesque body. The distinctive character of this body is its open unfinished nature, its interaction with the world."[22] Conversely, for the majority of the film, Neal demonstrates bodily discipline and tries to regulate his bodily functions, including his intake of food. "The grotesque body is opposed to the classical body," argues Mary Russo, "which is monumental, static, closed and sleek, corresponding to the aspirations of bourgeois individualism; the grotesque body is connected with the rest of the world."[23] Throughout *Planes, Trains and Automobiles*, Hughes signals that Neal is too neurotic and disconnected from his social and natural environment. When Del offers to buy him a hotdog at the airport, he states, "I'm kind of picky about what I eat." Martin's facial expressions throughout the film also signal his character's distaste towards Del's lack of restraint and his personal habits. Martin's performance therefore reinforces Neal's social status by emphasizing his attempts to resist the openness that Del represents. Neal's meticulously controlled lifestyle may be aspirational, but Hughes encourages the audience to view Del as a more authentic, likeable character.

Through Hughes's screenplay and direction, and Candy's performance, Del is presented as a carnivalesque figure who is clearly at ease with his body. Compared to Martin's twitchy mannerisms, Candy's uninhibited and fluid movements reinforce Del's rejection of bodily restraint. The scene in which Candy bops and sings along to Ray Charles's "Mess Around" embodies Del's ability to embrace pleasure and express his enjoyment through his body. Although he sits behind a steering wheel, Candy gives a highly animated and expressive performance. This scene contrasts with many dance performances in Hollywood musicals, which demonstrate bodily discipline and work to allay "the cultural anxiety that the grotesque body will erupt (unexpectedly) from the classical body."[24] Dragging on a cigarette, Candy goes through a series of gestures and movements that increase in size and intensity. Apparently unaware of the car swerving dangerously close to an icy verge, Del plays an invisible piano with his eyes closed. After playing air saxophone, he dances and almost loses control of the car. Because Neal is asleep, the focalization of the narrative shifts to Del and thus Hughes encourages the audience to share in Del's delight and sense of physical liberation. Candy's physical size, unrestrained appetites, and "exaggerated physicality" position Del as a liberatory force, via the display of his Bakhtinian grotesque body, which "resist[s] cultural discipline" and instead promotes "spontaneity, creative renewal, and egalitarianism."[25]

Uncle Buck builds on the persona Candy developed through *Planes, Trains and Automobiles*, through Hughes's screenplay and direction combined with

Candy's performance. Much of the film's humor concerns Buck's bodily excess and disorderly behavior, which offend middle-class sensibilities. His relationship with food characterizes his lack of restraint, and his nephew and nieces first encounter him in the kitchen, assembling breakfast while singing to the radio. Hughes uses this scene to establish Buck's haphazard but fun-loving approach to life. In another sequence, Buck flips enormous pancakes for his nephew's birthday breakfast using a snow shovel. Buck is also shown lying on the couch eating sugary cereal out of the box, while watching a workout show, and using a handheld vacuum cleaner to suck the crumbs off his sweater.

In *Uncle Buck*, Hughes also makes various jokes about the emissions that appear to emanate from Buck. A prominent running gag concerns the trail of smoke that follows Buck's battered, old car. His cigar smoking also prompts various pieces of comic business, as well as signaling his slovenly habits. When he visits the school of his younger niece Maizy (Gaby Hoffman), Buck suddenly realizes that he is not supposed to be smoking and has to hold the smoke in before dashing into a nearby toilet. He then decides that he needs to urinate and, because the stalls are all occupied, decides to use a urinal designed for children. The visual gag that follows relies on the absurdity of Candy, a heavy-set, six-foot, two-inch tall man, attempting to square up to a tiny urinal that is just a few inches off the ground.

Buck also seems unable to control his speech. During his first conversation with his sister-in-law, he jabbers, "I've been bound up lately. It's driving me crazy. I've been eating a lot of cheese for some reason . . ." Later, in a meeting with the vice principal of Maizy's school, Buck is unable to distract himself from the prominent blemish on the teacher's face and accidentally introduces himself as, "Buck Melanoma, Moley Russell's wart." When Maizy's vice principal then criticizes the six-year-old for being a "dreamer," he growls, "You so much as scowl at my niece or any other kid in this school and I hear about it, I'm coming looking for you." As he leaves, he flicks a quarter at her and, referring to her wart, tells her to "go downtown have a rat gnaw that thing off your face." This scene illustrates how Buck is, to some extent, a version of the carnivalesque figure that Candy played in *Planes, Trains and Automobiles*, but Hughes uses Buck's impulsiveness to tackle "threats" to childhood and the family.

UPHOLDING FAMILY VALUES

An unusual intervention within the road movie genre, *Vacation* is one of only a handful of American movies that show a nuclear family on the road together. Despite the opportunity for more subversive humor that the liminal spaces of the road offer, the movie focuses primarily on how Clark's nostalgic vision of the family road trip is at odds with reality. Even though its R-rating permitted the inclusion of distasteful jokes, profanity, and nudity, limits were still placed on the kinds of humor in the film. Several of the jokes in Hughes's screenplay, which were omitted from the movie, concern the incest taboo. The screenplay describes Clark accidentally lifting the shirt of his daughter Audrey (Dana Barron) to reveal her training bra, and includes a piece of dialogue where her brother asks her if he can have her breasts, while eating fried chicken.[26] These jokes do not imply any incestuous activity but, rather, are based on anxieties that circulate around inter-familial relationships and the possibility that interactions between family members can be misconstrued. By limiting the kinds of comedy *within* the Griswolds' nuclear family to everyday, observational humor, director Harold Ramis not only makes the characters more relatable, he also avoids subjecting the nuclear family to a sustained critique. As it would turn out, *Vacation* was Hughes's most satirical screenplay. The films that Hughes subsequently wrote in the latter half of the 1980s work even harder to promote the family ideal and to contain the comedian figure's subversive potential as part of his attempt to cater to a wider audience.

By situating the action in the suburban home, Hughes makes the family dynamics in *Christmas Vacation* much more sitcom-like than in the original *Vacation*. Clark's children are generally sympathetic towards their father and, while still conventionally attractive, Beverly D'Angelo's character has become much less sexualized and her clothing more conservative. Unlike the first *Vacation*, the movie does not refer to the Griswolds' sex life. When they are shown together in bed, they are reading magazines and the joke is that Clark is unable to flick the pages because he has tree sap on his hands. When Audrey complains about having to share a bed with her brother, Ellen comments, "Well, I have to share with your father." Given that the Griswold children are still the same age as in the original *Vacation*, the absence of sexuality in *Christmas Vacation* seems to be less a result of the parents' advancing years and more a reflection of Hughes's attempts to appeal to a family audience. Admittedly, Clark's inability to control his lust is briefly referenced in a scene at a department store, when he tells an attractive female store clerk that "it's a bit *nipply* out." In a later scene, he fantasizes about the woman and she strips for him, although strategic camera angles and editing mean that more is left to the imagination. At no point, however, does a woman pose a genuine threat to the Griswolds' marriage.

In *Christmas Vacation*, Hughes also offsets much of the film's broad (sometimes crude) humor with a substantial dose of sentimentality. When Clark attempts to access the attic to hide Christmas presents, the attic steps immediately hit him in the face. The following sequence proceeds to mix slapstick and broad visual humor with more sentimental elements. He is struck several times in the face by planks of wood and falls partway through the ceiling of one of the rooms below. Then, finding himself trapped in the attic, he puts on a woman's fur coat, gloves, and hat, in order to keep warm. A syrupy strings score accompanies shots of him crying and laughing at a film of "Xmas 1955."[27] An unexpected slapstick gag then undercuts the heartfelt moment, as Clark falls through the attic hatch.

Hughes shifts the movie to a more nostalgic tone when Clark has a heart-to-heart with his father and recites Clement Clarke Moore's "A Visit from St. Nicholas." In these scenes, the notion of family is tied to an imagined past that cannot be recaptured, in spite of Clark's best efforts. The ending of *Christmas Vacation* is not dissimilar to that of the first *Vacation* movie. The film's conclusion combines a large number of visual gags and slapstick moments, including a visit from the local SWAT team, with a substantial dose of sentiment. At the film's conclusion, the family unites outside the Griswold house and joins together singing "The Star-Spangled Banner" and Christmas carols. Although it seems sudden, this ending is consistent with the conventions of Christmas films, albeit taken to an absurd extreme. Hughes's silly but heart-warming conclusion of *Christmas Vacation* thus meets audience expectations of the genre, through its evocation of family togetherness, while retaining a certain degree of satirical intent.

In *Planes, Trains and Automobiles*, cutaway scenes of Neal's wife and children, and Neal and Del's conversations about their wives, assert the link between masculinity and heterosexual marriage. Although the liminal spaces associated with the road have the potential to destabilize masculine identities, Hughes's screenplay and direction ensure that Neal and Del's heterosexual masculinity remains firmly intact. Hughes does, however, highlight anxieties that men feel when interacting with other men outside of clearly codified social situations, most obviously when Neal and Del wake up spooning. In a bizarre burlesque of heterosexual marriage, the two men wake up embracing like husband and wife. Hughes's use of "Back in Baby's Arms" as the soundtrack reinforces the parodic, and the scene does not imply sexual attraction between the two men. As in other comic representations of men sharing beds, the "point of these connotations is not to affirm or proclaim homosexuality but to raise the specter of it so that it can be dismissed."[28] The men's reactions to the situation indicate that they are anxious not to be perceived as gay. They leap from the bed and then proceed to briefly mutter some comments about the Chicago Bears in mock-macho voices. Ina Rae Hark argues that 1980s yuppie road movies are open to "queer readings" and experience "difficulty in bringing closure to their buddies' relationships."[29] However, *Planes, Trains and Automobiles* echoes the screwball genre's affirmation of the individual and societal benefits of marriage. Hughes presents a narrative resolution that reintegrates Del into middle-class society, following the revelation that his wife has died, and reunites Neal with his seemingly perfect suburban family. The significant difference, however, is that screwball movies had to argue in favor of matrimony, but *Planes, Trains and Automobiles* positions marriage as a universal and natural state.

Hughes's structuring of the narrative for *Uncle Buck*, which leads Buck to adopt a patriarchal role, means that deployment of Candy's comic persona takes on a different significance. In her analysis of *Uncle Buck*, Elizabeth G. Traube argues that, "What the plot identifies as Buck's adversary is neither bourgeois respectability nor adult authority in any form but rather the sexual promiscuity of over-privileged, under-regulated teenagers."[30] In his interactions with the teenagers, Buck often asserts his patriarchal authority through "jokes" that are thinly veiled threats towards Tia's boyfriend, Bug. When the boy mockingly asks him, "You ever hear of a tune up?" Buck mimics his laughter and says, "You ever hear of a ritual killing? [. . .] You gnaw on her face like that in public again and you'll be one." On finding Bug trying to have sex with another teenage girl, Buck binds the boy's body using duct tape and locks him in the trunk of his car. Buck and Tia then torment Bug into making an apology. Buck's robust response to Bug's actions is one of a number of scenes that show Buck's policing of the boundaries of childhood. Earlier in the film, Buck punches a clown that turns up for his nephew's birthday party drunk. In *Uncle Buck*, Hughes clearly encourages the audience to accept Buck's direct approach to protecting the children's innocence by using Candy's likeability to temper the character's aggression. Hughes also relies on a wider cultural valorization of the (White, middle-class) family and childhood to help validate this potentially conservative viewpoint.

WHITE, MIDDLE-CLASS SUPERIORITY

While the comedian figure has often been associated with society's outsiders, in Hughes's films the comedian is a more conformist figure who is integrated into, or aspires to be integrated into, middle-class family life. Socially marginalized groups and individuals are often the objects of scorn, serving to highlight the characters' apparent ordinariness. *Vacation* asserts the White, middle-class superiority of the Griswold family through the introduction of Cousin Eddie (Randy Quaid) and his family. The jokes in this part of the film center on Eddie's lack of sophistication and the family's conformity to "white trash" stereotypes. Eddie is introduced wearing a stained undershirt and a pair of trousers held up by rope. He almost always has a can of beer in his hand. He also has five children and his wife is pregnant with a sixth. Throughout these scenes, Chase and D'Angelo's facial expressions suggest their characters' distaste toward their "white trash" relatives. Hughes displaces anxieties about the dynamics of the American family onto Cousin Eddie's family, in order that they can be alluded to and then dismissed. Eddie's treatment of his wife, for instance, is presented as the product of his flawed character and a lack of education. One joke even suggests that Eddie might engage in incestuous activities with his daughter, Vicki (Jane Krakowski). She tells her cousin, "I'm going steady and I French kiss." To which Audrey replies, "So, everybody does that." Vicki responds, "Yeah, but Daddy says I'm the best at it." Cousin Eddie's dysfunctional family therefore creates a counterpoint to Clark's affluent, suburban family and confirms that, for all their quirks, the Griswolds are relatively "normal."

Vacation's evocation of affluent White superiority is most overt in the movie's controversial presentation of race. On their journey, the family makes an accidental diversion into the "ghetto." African Americans linger on the darkened streets, talking and dancing, while jazz plays, cars are resting on bricks, police sirens blare, and the sound of gunshots and a woman's screams are heard. Presumably, director Harold Ramis chose to represent the inner city, and its inhabitants, in this stereotypical manner, although Hughes's screenplay does provide some cues for how he envisaged the scene. In its efforts to parody White middle-class attitudes to the deprivation of the inner city, Hughes's screenplay is, at best, somewhat ambivalent in its engagement with racial politics. Much of the comedy relies the audience's familiarity with negative racial stereotypes. When Clark politely asks a pimp for directions, the pimp, flanked by two prostitutes, shouts, "Fuck yo' mama." In response, Clark smiles and says, "Thank you very much." The next time he asks another neighborhood denizen for directions, Clark says: "Say, uh, excuse me, homes. Ha, ha. What it is bro'. We're from out of town." The Griswold family's reactions and Clark's attempt to mimic the "vernacular" speech of the ghetto are humorous, but these interactions nevertheless reference, and perpetuate, negative stereotypes of African Americans and, consistent with much of Hughes's work, assert the "normalcy" of the White, middle-class identity.

Compared to his somewhat controversial portrayal in first *Vacation* movie, Cousin Eddie is an almost loveable caricature in *Christmas Vacation*. Most of the jokes relating to Eddie are still derived from "white trash" stereotypes, such as his dubious fashion sense and his rusting trailer, prompting Rita Kempley of the *Washington Post* to describe him as "hillbilly burlesque."[31] Indeed, one of the most memorable visual gags in the film involves Eddie drinking a beer and emptying his RV's chemical toilet into a storm drain, whilst clad in a bathrobe and trapper hat. When Clark spots him, he proclaims, "Shitter was full." Compared to the scenes involving Eddie in the first *Vacation* movie, there is less of an attempt to make the audience feel uncomfortable, and the characters' attitudes towards him are less hostile. Instead, the majority of aggression in the movie is directed at the Griswolds' yuppie neighbors, Todd (Nicholas Guest) and Margot (Julia Louis-Dreyfus). The movie uses comedy to work through the suppressed anxieties that these childless, ostentatious characters provoke. Through the numerous misfortunes that befall Todd and Margot during *Christmas Vacation*, Hughes reinforces the "correctness" of Clark's focus on his family and the film's promotion of fatherhood.

Planes, Trains and Automobiles, much like *National Lampoon's Vacation*, ridicules characters of a lower social status. This strategy is most explicit when Hughes introduces Owen (Dylan Baker), a "roughneck" who pulls up in a battered pick-up truck outside Neal and Del's motel. Reaction shots document the men's disgust as Owen snorts and swills his saliva. In the middle of the scene, Del shakes his hand and then Neal follows suit, although this time Owen's hand is covered with spit. The two men look aghast when Owen comments that his wife's "first baby come out sideways and she didn't scream or nuthin'." The link between "white trash" bodies and abjection is thus confirmed by Owen's ejection of body fluids and references to the female body and childbirth.[32] Whereas the movie's representation of Del's body articulates the utopianism and communality of Bakhtin's grotesque body, Owen's body and conduct transgress the bounds of acceptability.[33] In this way, Hughes creates boundaries between less affluent working men, like Del, and "white trash" like Owen. This is aided by Baker's lack of fame, because the audience lacked any connection with the performer.

As their journey proceeds, Neal and Del are reduced to using less sophisticated forms of transportation (a plane, a taxi, a train, the bus, and hitchhiking). In a scene that references the bus passengers' rendition of "The Man on the Flying Trapeze" in *It Happened One Night* (1934), Neal, Del, and their fellow travelers engage in a sing-along on the bus to Chicago. Neal's choice of song, the middlebrow hit "Three Coins in the Fountain" from the 1950s, is met with silence. In contrast, when Del breaks into the theme song from *The Flintstones*, he is joined by a rousing chorus. Although Neal is a marketing executive, he only understands people's tastes and behavior in the abstract. In contrast, Del is able to relate to his customers, a point emphasized in a montage sequence in which he uses his friendly face-to-face patter to sell shower curtain rings. Through *Planes, Trains and Automobiles*' depiction of a wealthy character forced to interact with ordinary working-class Americans, Hughes references Depression Era screwball comedies, which "set up the road as a liminal space," offering the potential for social transformation.[34] Consistent with its celebration of the nuclear family, Hughes's movie shies away from a broader social message. Although Neal learns from his experiences and grows to accept Del, he remains distanced from ordinary people and ultimately retreats to the comfort of his large suburban house.

CONCLUSION

John Hughes's comedian movies were, in many respects, examples of the commercial opportunism that shaped the filmmaker's career in the 1980s and early 1990s. They were also part of a wider production trend, which saw the Hollywood studios attempt to capitalize on the popularity of *Saturday Night Live*, *SCTV*, and other comedy oriented towards baby-boomer audiences. On a textual level, Hughes's films show a marked tendency toward containing the rebellious impulses that comedians' excessive and erratic behavior often implies. Perhaps the closest to more archetypal "comedian comedies," *National Lampoon's Vacation* features more anarchic and absurd humor than Hughes's later films. It also includes cruder and potentially controversial jokes. *Vacation* plays off Chase's privileged White man persona and allows the comedian to display his talent for slapstick and physical performance. However, Hughes's screenplay features various narrative devices that restrict Clark Griswold's antisocial urges, and the film's conclusion, in which he regains his sanity and narrowly avoids arrest, contains the comedian's lawless and hysterical actions.

In all of his comedian films, Hughes represents the White middle-class American family with affection, even reverence. In *Vacation* and *Christmas Vacation*, although Clark is a ridiculous father figure, the Griswold family is rarely the butt of the joke. Similarly, *Planes, Trains and Automobiles* constantly asserts the importance of the affluent nuclear family. Moreover, the film's critique is "not yuppie workaholism or acquisitiveness but yuppie self-enclosure in a sense of entitlement, refinement and obsession with style, connoisseurship and fitness."[35] Although Del's carnivalesque tendencies help Neal to undergo a process of personal development, the social system that supports his yuppie lifestyle and entrenches class divisions is not questioned. Hughes further reinforces this celebration of the "traditional" family though various scenarios that use othering to assert the main characters' normalcy. *Vacation* displaces anxieties about the family onto Cousin Eddie and his family, who are stereotypical "white trash" hicks. The film's "ghetto" sequence ridicules aspects of Clark's middle-class Whiteness but ultimately asserts his superiority via crude stereotypes of African Americans. Similarly, representations of Owen and other "white trash" characters in *Planes, Trains and Automobiles* reinforce the desirability of Neal and Del's middle-class and solidly working-class backgrounds. Thus, in Hughes's comedian films, as in many of his other movies, the sanctity of the nuclear family and White middle-class privilege are not challenged.

In his later comedian films, Hughes places further constraints on the comedians and uses narrative structures to harness the characters' energies, deploying them selectively to serve a more conformist agenda. Although *Planes, Trains and Automobiles* exploits and develops Martin and Candy's personas, it situates their performances within a structured and bounded narrative. The conventions of screwball comedy give the film a logical structure and provide a happy ending, which counterbalances the social issues the film alludes to. While

Uncle Buck has a slightly looser structure than *Planes, Trains and Automobiles*, it deploys a framing narrative that seeks to reassert patriarchal authority. Much of the film's humor derives from pieces of comic business that display Candy's body and physicality as a performer but, as the film progresses, these gags are often co-opted to serve a broadly conservative agenda. More than any of Hughes's other comedian films, *Uncle Buck* demonstrates that comedians' performances are not necessarily anarchic or liberatory.

Hughes's comedian films reflect his career trajectory across the 1980s, from an industry newcomer with a background writing adult humor pieces for *National Lampoon* to one of Hollywood's leading filmmakers. Alongside *Uncle Buck*, *Christmas Vacation* marked a turning point in Hughes's career, as he set his sights on high-profile projects with major cross-generational appeal. Lacking much of the satirical edge of Hughes's earlier work, it relies instead on sitcom-like situations, restricting the film's scope to the Griswold family and their suburban neighborhood. Although the movie foregrounds Chevy Chase's manic performance, the film is ultimately a celebration of a buffoonish, well-intentioned patriarch's efforts to bring his family together for a traditional holiday celebration. *Christmas Vacation* showed that Hughes had successfully reoriented his brand at the end of the 1980s, and its box office gross of $71 million confirmed that his movies could appeal to a more mainstream family audience.[36] The festive comedy's combination of broad slapstick humor, sentimental moments, and focus on the family would become defining characteristics of Hughes's films in the following decade.

NOTES

1. Frank Krutnik, "The Clown-Prints of Comedy," *Screen*, 25, no. 4/5 (July–October 1984), 53.
2. Steve Seidman, *Comedian Comedy: A Tradition in Hollywood Film* (Ann Arbor, MI: UMI Research Press, 1981), 3.
3. See: Seidman; Krutnik, "The Clown-Prints of Comedy", 50–9; Frank Krutnik, "A Spanner in the Works? Genre, Narrative and the Hollywood Comedian," in *Classical Hollywood Comedy*, eds Kristine Brunovska Karnick and Henry Jenkins (New York: Routledge, 1995), 17–38.
4. Krutnik, "The Clown-Prints of Comedy", 51; Krutnik, "A Spanner in the Works?", 24.
5. Seidman, 19–25.
6. Jim Whalley, *Saturday Night Live, Hollywood Comedy, and American Culture* (London: Palgrave, 2010), 34
7. William Paul, *Laughing Screaming: Modern Hollywood Horror and Comedy* (New York: Columbia University Press, 1994), 158.
8. Bob Thomas, "He's Still Chevy Chase and You're Not," *Associated Press*, January 4, 1983.
9. John Hughes, "Vacation '58 / Foreword '08," *All-Story*, 12, no. 2 (2008), https://web.archive.org/web/20080731165748/http://www.all-story.com/issues.cgi?action=show_story&story_id=389.

10. Lesley Harbidge, "Audienceship and (Non)Laughter in the Stand-up Comedy of Steve Martin," *Participations: Journal of Audience and Reception Studies*, 8, no. 2 (2011), 133.
11. Richard Zoglin, *Comedy at the Edge: How Stand-up in the 1970s Changed America* (New York: Bloomsbury, 2009), 133.
12. John J. O'Connor, "TV: Incongruities of Steve Martin," *New York Times*, February 14, 1980, C27.
13. Harbidge, 10–14.
14. Phil Dellio, "Some Candy Talking!" *Graffiti*, January 1986, 45.
15. Chris Willman, "*Uncle Buck*: John Hughes' Valentine to Teenhood," *Los Angeles Times*, August 16, 1989, http://articles.latimes.com/1989-08-16/entertainment/ca-376_1_uncle-buck.
16. Paul, 156.
17. Jenkins and Karnick, "Introduction: Funny Stories," in *Classical Hollywood Comedy*, 76
18. Krutnik, "A Spanner in the Works?", 37
19. Frank Krutnik, "General Introduction," in *Hollywood Comedians: The Film Reader* (London: Routledge, 2003), 3.
20. Matty Simmons, *If You Don't Buy This Book, We'll Kill This Dog: Life, Laughs, Love and Death at National Lampoon* (New York: Barricade Books, 1994), 248–9.
21. Tamar Jeffers McDonald, *Romantic Comedy: Boy Meets Girl Meets Genre* (London: Wallflower, 2007), 45.
22. Mikhail Bakhtin, *Rebelais and His World*, trans. Hélène Iswolsky (Bloomington: Indiana University Press, 1984), 281.
23. Mary Russo, "Female Grotesques: Carnival and Theory," in *Feminist Studies/Critical Studies*, ed. Teresa de Lauretis (Basingstoke: Macmillan, 1988), 219.
24. Ann Cooper Albright, "Strategic Abilities: Negotiating the Disabled Body in Dance," in *Moving History/Dancing Cultures: A Dance History Reader*, eds Ann Dillis and Ann Cooper Albright (Middletown, CT: Wesleyan University Press, 2001), 62.
25. Frank Krutnik, "Mutinies Wednesdays and Saturdays: Carnivalesque Comedy and the Marx Brothers," in *A Companion to Film Comedy*, eds Andrew Horton and Joanna Rapf (Malden, MA: Wiley-Blackwell, 2012), 91.
26. John Hughes, *National Lampoon's Vacation*, script, fourth draft, April 20, 1982, 7, 72.
27. Although the title card says "Xmas 1955", the film case is labeled "Xmas '59", which is the title of Hughes's *National Lampoon* piece on which the screenplay is based.
28. Mark Simpson, "The Straight Men of Comedy," in *Because I Tell A Joke Or Two: Comedy, Politics and Social Difference*, ed. Stephen Wagg (London: Routledge, 1998), 139.
29. Ina Rae Hark, "Fear of Flying: Yuppie Critique and the Buddy-Road Movie in the 1980s," in *The Road Movie Book*, eds Steven Cohan and Ina Rae Hark (London: Routledge, 1997), 224.
30. Elizabeth G. Traube, *Dreaming Identities: Class, Gender, and Generation in 1980s Hollywood Movies* (Boulder, CO: Westview Press, 1992), 149.
31. Rita Kempley, "*National Lampoon's Christmas Vacation*," *Washington Post*, December 1, 1989, http://www.washingtonpost.com/wp-srv/style/longterm/movies/videos/nationallampoonschristmasvacation.htm.
32. Julia Kristeva, *Powers of Horror: An Essay on Abjection*, trans. Leon S. Roudiez (New York: Columbia University Press, 1982), 32–55.
33. Although a number of analyses conflate the grotesque with the abject, they are not the same. Whereas Bakhtin's grotesque body is a potentially positive force, Kristeva's abject body is more ambivalent. Sue Vice offers a succinct discussion of the connections and distinctions between the two concepts. Sue Vice, "Bakhtin and Kristeva: Grotesque

Body, Abject Self," in *Face to Face: Bakhtin and Russia in the West*, eds Carol Adlam et al. (Sheffield: Sheffield Academic Press, 1997), 160–74.
34. Kathleen Moran and Michael Rogin, "'What's the Matter with Capra?': *Sullivan's Travels and the Popular Front*," *Representations*, 71 (2000), 118.
35. Hark, 216.
36. BoxOfficeMojo, "*Christmas Vacation*: Box Office Summary," https://www.boxofficemojo.com/movies/?id=christmasvacation.htm.

CHAPTER 10

Fatherhood and the Failures of Paternal Authority in the Films of John Hughes

Alice Leppert

Film scholar Alan Nadel has observed that in John Hughes's films, "the patriarch is tantamount to dead."[1] Indeed, critics have long noted the curious absence of parents in teen film writ large.[2] Yet Hughes's work was consistently preoccupied with the family unit, especially fathers and father figures, in his early comedy screenplays for *Mr. Mom* (1983) and *National Lampoon's Vacation* (1983) through to the wildly popular *Home Alone* films of the 1990s. In his teen films, Hughes makes the parental absence so typical of teen films *present*, deeply felt by his teen characters. Though parents only appear on-screen as bookends in *The Breakfast Club* (1985), the teens all reveal by the end of the film that their own individual neuroses and social identities have been shaped, in one way or another, by their parents, and they delight in acting out their aggression on a high school teacher, a substitute pathetic patriarch on a power trip. Although the father of Cameron (Alan Ruck) never appears in *Ferris Bueller's Day Off* (1986), Cameron's ultimate willingness to stand up to the fearsome man provides as much of a narrative climax as the titular hero's evasion of his high school principal.

I argue that Hughes's films (by which I mean films that he wrote as much as those he directed) participate in a broader cultural narrative running throughout the 1980s and early 1990s that sought to renegotiate paternal masculinity amidst political jockeying over "family values," and perceived gains in women's rights. As an early example, *Mr. Mom* undoubtedly inspired many gender role-reversal comedies across film and television screens in the 1980s, and Mary Vavrus has noted that many stay-at-home fathers treated the film as a how-to guide.[3] More commonly, however, Hughes's films include a range of fathers and father figures, all vying for influence on, or power over, teens and children. Many of Hughes's paternal authority figures are, at best, compassionate failures in one way or another, such as Clark Griswold (Chevy Chase) in *Vacation* and the title character (John Candy) in *Uncle Buck* (1989); at worst, they are pathologically abusive, such as Mr. Vernon (Paul Gleason) in *The Breakfast Club* and Principal Rooney (Jeffrey Jones) in *Ferris Bueller*, or the numerous dads who are described but left unseen in these films. These ritualistic failures of paternal authority both large and small allow for the complex, emotionally sensitive representations of White suburban teens that made Hughes famous—in effect, the teens appear more mature and introspective than their parents, as Stephen Tropiano has observed.[4] By considering Hughes's family comedies alongside his teen films, I analyze how fatherhood and paternal authority shaped his narratives and ultimately enabled his teen and child protagonists to define themselves against the patriarchal foibles that attempt to limit them at a time when the US was caught between a conservative insistence on a return to "family values," and feminist calls to redefine the family.

A focus on fatherhood was central across these cultural debates. As more and more women sought full-time employment outside the home, liberal feminists called upon men to perform a more equitable amount of care work. At the same time, "family values" conservatives, while often aiming much of their ire at working mothers, kept fatherhood at the center of their agenda, especially in the creation of a moral panic over "fatherlessness." In the 1980s, social conservatives and liberal feminists made strange bedfellows, with both demanding more involved fathers. As Lynne Segal cautions, "The contemporary reinforcement of fatherhood is problematic insofar as it can be used to strengthen men's control over women and children."[5] Pointing toward the eventual founding, in 1990, of the US evangelical male group, the Promise Keepers, Yvonne Tasker notes that a focus on "transformative male parenting" could be found in "conservative, mainstream, and liberal manifestations. Across diverse formulations, fatherhood movements emphasise the joys and responsibilities of male parenting."[6] Indeed, Hannah Hamad shows that "emotionally articulate, domestically competent" fathers have become the norm in Hollywood film.[7] With an influx of films and television series that depicted men as nurturing and domestically inclined, many critics observed that mothers had been at best displaced and at worst demonized. As Segal puts it, "in films like *Kramer vs. Kramer* [1979] and *Ordinary People* [1980], Hollywood was creating men whose tamed domesticity produced fathers who were *more* sensitive, and *more* nurturing, than their self-centered, ambitious wives."[8] In Hughes's films, mothers are often absent or vilified, at best taking a back seat to their husbands' attempts at nurturance.

Susan Jeffords, in her seminal analysis of the "hard body" in 1980s film, notes that the "sensitive family man" was a complementary image central to both Ronald Reagan's and George H. W. Bush's rhetoric. She suggests that the Reagan and Bush years (1981–89 and 1989–93) saw a "rearticulation of masculine strength and power through internal, personal, and family-oriented values."[9] Many of Hughes's films enact a similar rearticulation through rejecting, mocking, or disempowering traditional patriarchs while empowering a younger generation to appropriate a more flexible patriarchal power that comes from emotional sensitivity and quick wit rather than brute strength. Hughes's films from the early 1980s through the early 1990s engage with contemporaneous debates about family and fatherhood, critiquing the traditionally strict, disciplinarian image of the father and ultimately positioning the children or teen characters as uniquely capable of taking on adult responsibilities so as to create a kinder, gentler patriarchy. To this end, Hughes's adult male heroes (Jack [Michael Keaton] in *Mr. Mom*, Clark in *Vacation*, and Buck in *Uncle Buck*) are lovably immature but well-meaning, and Hughes regularly puts the viewer in the position of a child, teen, or childish adult character, all of whom ultimately learn how to take responsibility for themselves—a key component of the neoliberal political milieu that was beginning to take hold across liberal and conservative discourse at that time.

HUGHES'S FAMILY COMEDIES

Marsha Kinder identifies a trend in the 1980s and 1990s wherein films adopted a "transgenerational address": adult viewers are treated as juveniles while "young spectators are encouraged to adopt adult tastes, creating subject positions for a dual audience of infantilised adults and precocious children."[10] While Kinder's primary case study is *Home Alone* (1990), Hughes places the viewer in an adolescent position starting with early 1980s family comedies *Mr. Mom* and *Vacation*, poking fun at the various inadequacies of fathers and patriarchal authority figures. In *Mr. Mom*, following his failure to maintain employment, protagonist Jack struggles to complete basic household tasks as his wife goes back to work. *Vacation* thwarts Clark Griswold's every attempt to provide his family with an enjoyable road trip. *Uncle Buck* follows its manchild title character as he struggles to perform the basic tasks of adulthood. All three characters are the primary source of comedy in the films, with the viewer largely led to laugh at their pathetic antics while simultaneously rooting for them to succeed.

Though Jack's children in *Mr. Mom* are very young, the film supplies him with a number of comic foils that relate to him in a similar way that a teenager would. In one early scene, Jack, an auto engineer, tries to deliver an inspirational speech to some assembly-line workers who are worried about layoffs. The scene presents the assembly-line workers as working class and more authentically masculine than Jack, who wears a lab coat and tries to impress them with his knowledge of football. Jack attempts to be "hip" by referencing *Rocky* (1976), but the scene revolves around his progressive loss of credibility as the men ask him a series of questions that expose his ignorance of the popular film series. When Jack is paged over the intercom and walks away, one of the men chuckles and predicts that Jack is the next to be fired, in part because "he didn't see *Rocky*." Indeed, Jack is fired, which sets the film's gender role-reversal plot in motion. Already sensitive about being perceived as a failure, Jack insists that he was not fired or laid off, but rather "furloughed," and laughs off the suggestion of his wife Caroline (Teri Garr) that she get a job by challenging her to a competition to see who can get hired first. Just as the scene at the auto plant mocks Jack's inspirational speech by cutting to him being fired, the film mocks his overconfidence here with a cut to Caroline preparing for her first day of work, suggesting that Jack presented very little in the way of competition for the role of breadwinner.

On the face of it, *Mr. Mom* suggests that Jack's position as homemaker is, in itself, emasculating, and thus contributes to his sense of failure. He struggles to complete the basic tasks Caroline performed (the deli counter at the grocery store befuddles him; he puts a comically large amount of soap in the washing machine resulting in disaster), while Caroline excels at her new job. At the same time, these scenes foreshadow the film's ending, implying that women are more naturally suited to perform these chores, despite Jack's eventual mastery of them. To the tune of the *Rocky* theme, Jack adapts to homemaking in a montage that demonstrates his newfound aptitude for domestic labor. Tellingly, however, the montage masculinizes Jack's position in the home and family—he climbs a tall ladder to wash windows, paints the fence, and uses his engineering skills to remote control the vacuum cleaner. He also takes on a more assertive role in the family and community, directing traffic during school drop-off and waking his children as a drill sergeant would with a trumpet. The sequence concludes with Jack burning the shirt he's been wearing for weeks (which has become symbolic for his failure), while his son Kenny clutches his security blanket and looks up at him with a proud smile. The child looks at his blanket for a moment, as if pondering whether or not to toss it on the fire, but then runs off with it. Jack follows Kenny to his room, which is decorated with a *Rocky III* (1982) poster, and tells him that they need to have a "man-to-man" conversation that ends with Kenny giving up his blanket. The extended allusion to *Rocky*, alongside Jack's struggle to appropriate the film's message early on, suggests that Jack has finally succeeded, not only as a man, but also as a father.

In *Vacation*, patriarch Clark Griswold's masculinity is continually undermined from the very beginning. In anticipation of an elaborately planned road trip from Chicago to Los Angeles's family theme park Walley World (a thinly veiled reference to Disneyland), Clark has purchased a new car—a "super sportswagon." However, following a mix-up at the car dealership, the only available car is a "Wagon Queen Family Truckster," a wood-paneled station wagon that horrifies both Clark and his teenage son Rusty (Anthony Michael Hall). Clark protests to the salesman that he's "not your ordinary, everyday fool," but he quickly undermines this claim, not only by consenting to purchase the family truckster, but also by parroting the salesman's ridiculous pitches to his wife Ellen (Beverly D'Angelo) when he brings the car home, telling her, "If you want to drive across the country, trust me, this is *your automobile*."

Throughout the film, Clark attempts to rally Ellen and their children—Ellen suggests that they fly to California before the trip even begins, and everyone except Clark makes numerous suggestions to abort the trip along the way. When the family finally makes it to Walley World, against all odds and after dropping off the corpse of Ellen's aunt along the way, they find an empty parking lot: Walley World is closed for repairs. Clark remains dedicated to family fun, however, purchasing a gun at a sporting goods store and forcing a security guard at the park to accompany them as the family enjoys the rides. Just as the film opened with the emasculating joke of the feminized station wagon, in the final act of the film, the security guard calls Clark's bluff, guessing that his gun is not real, but rather a BB gun that "couldn't break the skin." Flustered, Clark protests, "It could put a lodge under the skin and cause a very bad infection," and as the security guard attempts to escape, Clark shoots him in the buttocks, at once proving he can follow through on his threat and proving the security guard correct—he is holding up the theme park with a BB gun.

Despite the fact that *Vacation* is largely Clark's story—one man's obsessive quest for family fun—the film puts the viewer in the position of his teenage children. The film relentlessly pokes fun at him, making him look pathetic and ridiculous in a variety of situations. On the first day of the journey, as Clark and Ellen attempt to foster a family sing-along with classics like "Jimmy Crack Corn," the film sonically aligns the viewer with Rusty and his sister Audrey (Dana Barron), as they simultaneously roll their eyes and put on their headphones, cuing The Ramones' "Blitzkrieg Bop" on the soundtrack, and drowning out the sound of their parents' voices. When the family stops overnight at a hotel, Clark attempts to romance Ellen with wine and a vibrating bed. His efforts are first undermined by the bed going haywire, forcing the couple to move their sexual encounter to the floor, but are further interrupted when the kids walk in on them. Horrified by their witnessing of the primal scene, Rusty manages to unplug the vibrating bed while Audrey remarks, "weird-o-rama."

Vacation highlights Clark's position as failed patriarch when he crashes the car in the desert. Before setting off alone to find help, Clark takes Rusty aside for a "man-to-man" chat. In an attempt to carry on a familial masculine rite of passage, Clark suggests he and Rusty share a beer, which he once did with his father and thought was "the coolest thing in the world." Clark takes a single sip from the can and passes it to Rusty, who swiftly chugs the rest and belches while Clark distractedly muses about family togetherness. Feeling confident in Rusty's newly minted maturity, Clark imbues him with the patriarchal responsibility to look after the family while Clark sets off into the desert. Emphasizing the ridiculousness of this decision (after all, Rusty is charged with looking after his mother and great aunt in addition to his sister), the film follows this scene with a montage of Clark's descent into delirium as he stumbles, dehydrated and exhausted, through endless sand dunes. The next scene finds Ellen on a payphone giving Clark's description to the police, suggesting that she was more capable of taking care of the family than either Clark or his patriarchal substitute Rusty.

Vacation pokes fun at Clark's identity as a "lame dad" through the secondary plot line featuring the "Girl in the Red Ferrari" (as the credits label Christie Brinkley). Seemingly haunting Clark with the possibilities his paternal identity have foreclosed, Brinkley's character appears on the road, at rest stops, and finally at a motel, and Clark's interactions with her are always embarrassing. From awkwardly winking at her, to attempting a seductive dance with a urine-soaked sandwich, to expressing elaborate, ridiculous lies such as, "I could have been in the Olympics," his chances of wooing her end when he jumps naked into the unheated motel pool and wakes all the guests by screaming about the temperature. As a result, Ellen and the kids once again witness his humiliation, and Rusty attempts to talk to his father "man-to-man," in a reversal of the desert scene, counseling his father on how to make amends with Ellen. Still, *Vacation* is always sympathetic to Clark's plight, and ends with a freeze frame of the Griswold family's triumphant rollercoaster ride after Clark manages to convince Walley World's head honcho to call off a SWAT team.

Figure 10.1 Clark Griswold flirts with the Girl in the Red Ferrari in *Vacation*.

Similarly, *Uncle Buck* paints a sympathetic picture of its title character, a happy-go-lucky bachelor who delights in his lack of responsibilities until he is called upon to take care of his nieces and nephew during a family crisis. In a departure for Hughes, the film's teen character, Buck's niece Tia (Jean Louisa Kelly), functions as his remarkably unlikable nemesis, evident through a reliance on close-ups of Tia's face twisted in a menacing glare. At the same time, the film makes it clear that Buck suffers from arrested development, and as Tia softens and becomes more reasonable, so Buck matures and actively seeks the adult responsibilities of marriage and potential fatherhood that he had been avoiding. *Uncle Buck* combines themes from both *Mr. Mom* and *Vacation*—it is rife with slapstick gags about Buck's domestic ineptitude (especially his struggles with the laundry), yet Buck is also fiercely dedicated to family harmony, planning an elaborate birthday celebration for his nephew Miles (Macaulay Culkin) and playing overprotective patriarch to Tia. Nadel argues that childishness is endemic to Hughes's films in general, and that "Hughes's adult heroes, Uncle Buck, Clark Griswald, and Del Griffith (of *Planes, Trains, and Automobiles* [1987]), are most notable for their extreme immaturity."[11]

Uncle Buck opens with a predictable commentary on 1980s upper-middle-class family life—with both parents working, Tia and her younger siblings Miles and Maizy (Gaby Hoffmann) are latchkey kids, a state of affairs that the film critiques by depicting Maizy spreading Cheez-Whiz on cheese puffs while Tia angrily pushes Miles around. Tia gestures toward a critique of absentee fathers, telling Maizy that they need boys, so that "they can grow up, get married, and turn into shadows." Yet she heaps most of her abuse on her mother, whom she seems to blame for everything. To continue the critique of the latchkey kid diet, the next scene opens with a close-up of Chinese food takeout boxes. Tia glares at her mother and sarcastically snarls, "This is such a wonderful dinner, mother. Where *do* you find the time?"

While on the surface Tia's mother appears to be the source of her surly disposition, a conclusion the film alludes to with its opening scenes, the fact that Buck manages to turn around Tia's attitude, an accomplishment achieved through his absurdist dedication to protecting her chastity, suggests that her real lack is in paternal, rather than maternal, presence. He threatens her boyfriend, Bug (Jay Underwood), with physical violence at every opportunity by using a variety of phallic objects, assuring him that he carries a hatchet with him at all times. Buck and Tia begin to mend their relationship when he heads to a party armed with a comically oversized drill that he uses to enter the bedroom he suspects contains Tia and Bug. Instead, Buck finds Bug making unwanted sexual advances on another girl, and abducts him, binding and gagging him, and leaving him in the trunk of his car as he goes searching for Tia. Once Buck discovers Tia walking alone and crying, Tia reveals that Bug tried to take advantage of her, and admits that Buck was right. *Uncle Buck*'s climax finds Tia tearfully embracing her mother, but the film ends with a shot/reverse shot of Tia and Buck, smiling at each other in close-up as Buck prepares to leave the family, and again reinforcing that although Tia may have blamed her mother for her unhappiness, what she really needed was a father.[12]

Paradoxically, Buck's immaturity and refusal of adult responsibilities are precisely the characteristics that make him the ideal father, as he has unlimited time to devote to childcare. After Tia demands that Buck stay out of her personal life, he asks, "Do your parents stay out of your personal life?" to which she responds, "They don't know my personal life," suggesting that her parents are so uninterested that she need not concern herself with sneaking around. If Buck were balancing a career, a marriage, and fatherhood, as Tia's father does, he couldn't possibly provide the extreme oversight of Tia's relationship that seemingly marks him as a "good" father figure. Yet, throughout the film, other characters use Buck's lack of a job, wife, and kids as part of a diagnosis of things that are "wrong" with him—his sister-in-law believes this disqualifies him from being able to care for her kids; Miles accusatorily quizzes him as to why he's unmarried, childless, and unemployed; and he comes to this realization himself one night when he splits a beer with the family dog and muses that no one tells him he's "got it made" like they used to. That realization, along with his reconciliation with Tia, prompts Buck to seek the responsibilities of marriage and fatherhood. As he tells Tia before asking for her help in smoothing things over with his long-suffering girlfriend Chanice (Amy Madigan), "I've been riding your butt all week about how you live your life . . . I realized maybe somebody should've been riding mine." While Tia assures Chanice that Buck will excel at fatherhood, the film seems to suggest that the combination of adult responsibilities Chanice wants Buck to take on (including gainful employment) would preclude the intensive dedication to parental oversight that won over Tia and her siblings.

TEENS VS. PRINCIPALS

In Hughes's teen films, the teen characters usually appear more mature and more capable of taking on adult responsibilities than the actual adults. *The Breakfast Club* and *Ferris Bueller's Day Off* both depict their respective high school administrators as the ultimate villains, power-hungry patriarchs desperate to control their teenage charges, especially *The Breakfast Club*'s Mr. Vernon, a teacher seemingly put in charge for the day, left to play-act as a sadistic principal. The actual fathers in *The Breakfast Club* are largely invisible, appearing only briefly at the beginning and end of the film as they drop off and pick up their children from Saturday detention.[13] The film highlights father-son conflict through Andy's (Emilio Estevez) and Bender's (Judd Nelson) confessional narratives of patriarchal pressure and abuse. Bender's abusive father doesn't appear on-screen, however, his presence looms large through the cigar burn Bender displays on his arm, and especially through the relationship between Bender and Mr. Vernon, which acts as a corollary to the abuse Bender suffers at home. On the one hand, Vernon functions as the butt of jokes, and like many Hughes films, the viewer is asked to laugh at him much as the teenage characters do. On the other hand, Vernon's increasingly tense relationship with Bender pulls the character into darker territory, as the film aligns Vernon with Bender's father.

Hughes sets up Bender and Vernon as antagonists from the beginning, with an early scene where the two engage in a battle of wills as Bender continually insults Vernon and Vernon continually assigns more detention. Edited in a shot/reverse shot pattern, the camera positions move closer as the exchange goes on, capturing Bender's increasingly shaky performance of masculine bravado. When Bender later reveals the nature of the abuse he suffers from his father, he puts on a similar performance for his fellow students, acting out both his own role and that of his father, as he attempts to deflect his father's abuse with smart-aleck responses that only inspire more of his father's rage. The doubling of Vernon and Bender's father comes to a head when Vernon locks Bender in a closet as punishment for sneaking out of the library. Hughes shoots the scene again in shot/reverse shot, with Bender seated, looking vulnerable and avoiding Vernon's gaze as Vernon crouches menacingly over him:

> Vernon: That's the last time, Bender. That's the last time you ever make me look bad in front of those kids, do you hear me? I make $31,000 a year and I've got a home, and I'm not about to throw it away on some punk like you. But someday, someday when you're out of here and you've forgotten all about this place, and they've forgotten all about you, and you're wrapped up in your own pathetic life, I'm gonna be there. That's right, and I'm gonna kick the living shit out of you. I'm gonna knock your dick in the dirt.
> Bender: Are you threatening me?
> Vernon: What are you gonna do about it? You think anybody's gonna believe you? You think anybody is gonna take your word over mine? I'm a man of respect around here, they love me around here, I'm a swell guy. You're a lying sack of shit, and everybody knows it.

Here, Vernon makes clear that Bender's biggest mistake was undermining Vernon's authority—making him look bad in front of the other students. He likewise sees Bender as a threat to his salary and his property (and thus implicitly his breadwinner status), drawing a comparison to Bender's father, who burned him with a cigar as punishment for spilling paint in the garage. Following this exchange, Vernon tries to goad Bender into punching him in the face, in an attempt to call Bender's bluff, and thus to assert himself as more masculine. Bender looks terrified, and Vernon fakes a punch at him, making Bender flinch. Victorious, Vernon declares Bender a "gutless turd" and leaves, locking the door behind him. Though this is perhaps one of the most intense scenes of the film, Hughes follows it with levity, as he cuts to Vernon entering a bathroom stall, presumably to defecate, thus aligning himself with his own "turd" insult. Vernon's trip to the bathroom also allows Bender to have the last laugh, as Hughes cuts back to the closet, where Bender has already escaped into the ceiling to return to the library.

The students outsmart Vernon consistently throughout the film, and Hughes figures Vernon's failures through a series of visual gags: the single folding chair he attempts to use to prop open a heavy door, the toilet seat cover hanging from the back of his pants, the thermos of coffee that explodes all over his desk. By the end of the film, the janitor, Carl (John Kapelos), confronts Vernon and notes the unreasonable animosity Vernon harbors toward the students. Hughes crosscuts this scene, where Carl and Vernon drink beer and reminisce about their youth and their disappointment with their adult lives, while the students are smoking marijuana and bonding in the library. Both Brian (Anthony Michael Hall) and Andy reveal the reasons for their assigned detention, since both committed delinquent acts as a result of parental pressure. While the pressure Brian feels to excel academically seems to come from both parents, Andy reveals the pressure his father puts on him to perform masculinity—as Timothy Shary puts it, "Andy is the jock as conflicted masculinity, determined to maintain his physical power but desiring to explore his more emotional—if not intellectual—dimensions."[14] While Andy claims he "fucking hate[s]" his father, he also points to a wider culture of emotionally abusive fathers, sympathizing with his victim, and imagining how awful it must have been for him to tell his father what happened to him—here Andy clearly understands the stakes of confessing weakness to one's father.

Ferris Bueller's Day Off revels in Mr. Rooney's humiliating failure to apprehend Ferris (Matthew Broderick), leaving Ferris gleefully unscathed in contrast to Bender's relationship to Vernon. As Catherine Driscoll notes, "Rooney is a slapstick version of *The Breakfast Club*'s Vernon, spitefully determined to destroy the life of a student who defies him. In *Ferris Bueller's Day Off* this determination is comedic because it seems so improbable that he could succeed."[15] Yet Rooney's concerns are similar to Vernon's—as he explains to his assistant, Grace (Edie McClurg), his motivation for catching Ferris in his lie is to avoid having "fifteen-hundred Ferris Bueller disciples running around these halls. It jeopardizes my ability to effectively govern the student body." Grace aptly replies, "Well, he makes you look like an ass is what he does . . ." Rooney's quest is for control, to assert his authority over Ferris, and thus over the entire school.

In contrast to Rooney, Ferris's father Tom (Lyman Ward) is completely clueless and taken in by Ferris's act. Throughout the afternoon, Tom just narrowly misses catching his son playing hooky—they cross paths numerous times, once while Tom reads a newspaper with the headline "community rallies around sick youth," a reference to Ferris. He even spots the parade that Ferris performs in, twisting along to his son's performance of "Twist and Shout" from his office. Finally, as Ferris races to beat his parents home and keep them in the dark as to the day's activities, he ends up jogging alongside his father's car. Tom looks directly at him, but fails to recognize his own son.

Ferris deals Rooney one of his first major defeats by asserting himself as a patriarchal authority figure, first by orchestrating a phony phone call wherein his best friend Cameron pretends to be the father of his girlfriend Sloane (Mia Sara), then by dressing in a trench coat and fedora and literally posing as Sloane's father, astride Cameron's father's prized Ferrari. Nicole Matthews observes a broader trend in 1980s Hollywood film wherein the father and child are collapsed,[16] and Ferris's role lines up neatly with what Robin Wood describes as "the young heterosexual male, father of the future, whose eventual union with the 'good woman' has always formed the archetypal happy ending of the American film, guarantee of the perpetuation of the nuclear family and social stability."[17] Indeed, Ferris playacts as patriarch throughout his day off, first asking Sloane, "Do you have a kiss for daddy?" as they perform for Rooney, and later jokingly asking her to marry him. As Steve Bailey and James Hay point out, "Clever Ferris, though, is balanced by the neurotic Cameron . . . who is emotionally stunted by the bland, unloving materialism of his parents, represented, significantly, in the prohibition on his use of the father's automobiles."[18] Ferris consistently treats Cameron as though he were a child, making decisions for him and dragging him unwillingly from place to place. Despite Cameron's protestations, however, in the end he decides Ferris was right all along, and when Ferris offers to take the blame for the demise of Cameron's father's Ferrari, Cameron refuses, almost as if Ferris has mentored him into manhood.

Bailey and Hay suggest Cameron's maiming of his father's car "works symbolically as both a renunciation of parental authority . . . and a simultaneous marking of adulthood, of independence from the social and material resources of the parents."[19] At the same time, this act marks Cameron's embrace of Ferris's values—up to this point, Cameron has lacked confidence, while Ferris has confidence to spare. Cameron constantly worries about getting caught, while Ferris effortlessly talks and schemes his way through every situation. In the end, Cameron cathartically plans to "have a little chat" with his father. His choice of words boasts confidence and downplays the severity of potential consequences, in much the same way that Ferris has approached the day, and, seemingly, life in general. As Leger

Grindon puts it, Cameron's "concern and caution finally collapse when the car accidentally crashes down an embankment to its death. Facing disaster, Cam recovers his own worth in the car's destruction. He doesn't care and it liberates him."[20] Indeed, Cameron's newfound carefree and liberated attitude is exactly what Ferris has modeled throughout the film. Yet both Ferris and Cameron are ready to take responsibility for their actions (at least those against the Ferrari), and Cameron's calm willingness to be responsible marks his transition from child to man.

Ferris Bueller's Day Off contrasts Rooney, the pathological, discipline-obsessed father figure, with Tom, the well-meaning but dim pushover. Ferris appears as the ideal patriarch—smart and savvy, unlike his father, and able to persuade others to follow his lead without going to the extreme measures Rooney undertakes. Ferris effortlessly controls everything in the diegesis—from the perfectly orchestrated *mise-en-scène* that conceals his lie, to the characters' actions, both his own and others'; and, of course, he controls the narrative through repeated direct addresses to the camera, imparting his authoritative knowledge straight to the viewer. Elizabeth Traube suggests that Ferris's ultimate power in the film is the primary source of pleasure for the viewer, claiming, "the escalating demonstrations of Ferris's omnipotence" are more satisfying than narrative suspense, as Ferris's actions guarantee "that all interfering adults will be made fools of, at best, and utterly humiliated, at worst."[21] Even at the end, as the film revels in Rooney's humiliating school bus ride while the credits roll, Ferris gets the last word. The credits end and Hughes cuts to the exterior of the school bus, then to the hallway of Ferris's house, where Ferris enters and instructs the viewer to "get out of here."

KEVIN McCALLISTER, CHILD PATRIARCH

Home Alone and *Home Alone 2: Lost in New York* (1992) follow a similar structure to *Ferris Bueller's Day Off*, despite the fact that Kevin McCallister (Macaulay Culkin) is a good deal younger than Ferris. Still, much like Ferris, Kevin controls the narrative with remarkable precision, expertly anticipating every move of his antagonists, bumbling burglars Harry (Joe Pesci) and Marv (Daniel Stern), while taking care of himself and even providing emotional counseling to adults in his spare time. Observing a clear pattern in Hughes's work, Nadel notes, "The idea of empowering the child is taken to its logical limits in *Home Alone*."[22] Just as Ferris serves as ideal patriarch in *Ferris Bueller's Day Off*, Kevin is thrust into an adult masculine role by virtue of defending his home from Harry and Marv.

The film's opening establishes the McCallister house as particularly vulnerable, as Harry stands in the entryway trying to get the family's attention, seemingly having gained entry on his own accord. Both of Kevin's parents unwittingly aid the burglars by revealing the details of their trip—his mother, Kate (Catherine O'Hara), falls for Harry's police disguise in the opening scene, and his father, Peter (John Heard), leaves a message on a neighbor's answering machine while Harry and Marv are burgling their house. When the thieves first attempt to ransack the McCallister house, Kevin hides under the bed, then quickly comes to a revelation, telling himself and the viewer, "I can't be a wimp. I'm the man of the house." He subsequently arms himself with his brother Buzz's (Devin Ratray) BB gun and plans an elaborate course of action, declaring with a snarl, "This is my house. I have to defend it."

On the one hand, *Home Alone* clearly marks Kevin's mission to defend the home from intruders as a masculine pursuit: his assaults on Harry and Marv are violent and gory, intending to inflict bodily harm. Shortly after Kevin shoots Harry in the crotch with his BB gun, Harry threatens to "snap off [Kevin's] cojones." On the other hand, the film shows Kevin as just as empowered in care work. Despite his siblings labeling him as "helpless" in the opening scene, Kevin proves adept at taking care of himself, and his domestic skills are significantly more advanced than Jack in *Mr. Mom* or Buck in *Uncle Buck*. Unlike these adult characters, Kevin knows how to do laundry and easily navigates grocery shopping. Kevin further appropriates a role as head of household by sleeping in his parents' bed and eating dinner at the head of the dining-room table.

Joe Kincheloe rightly notes that Kevin's father Peter is of minor importance to the narrative:

> In the *Home Alone* movies child care is the mother's responsibility. John Heard's father character is virtually a nonentity. He is uninterested in, condescending toward, and hostile to Kevin. He knows (along with the audience) that he is not responsible for Kevin's abandonment even though he was present during the entire episode. He has no reason to gnash his teeth or rend his garment in displays of penitence—this is the domain of the mother.[23]

Home Alone details Kate's desperate quest to return home to her son, alone, while the rest of the family remains in Paris, and Kevin repeatedly wishes for his mother's return. Yet Kevin recognizes the symbolic power of the patriarch—when he sees Harry's face peering into his living room window, he calls out, "Dad, can you come here and help me?" in an effort to scare him away. As Kevin listens to the burglars laying out their plans to rob his house, he whispers to himself, "Mom, where are you?" Here, Kevin clearly longs for maternal care, yet understands the cultural power of the patriarch when it comes to property. Still, this scene cuts to Kevin seeking out and later encountering substitute paternal figures. He goes to see Santa Claus, the ultimate symbol of patriarchal plenitude, and asks him to bring his family back in lieu of presents. Kevin then goes to a church, where his neighbor, an elderly man, sits with him and asks him the standard Santa question, "Have you been a good boy this year?" In this scene, however, Kevin reverses the roles, as he gives the old man advice on how to reconcile with his estranged adult son. The conclusion of the film proves Kevin to have given solid fatherly advice, as he looks out the window of his home to see the old man hugging his son and grandchild, and Kevin and the old man exchange a smile and a wave, mirroring the ending of *Uncle Buck*. Not only does Kevin act as patriarch, securing the family home, but he restores patriarchal order to his neighbor's family as well.

While Kevin is largely concerned with securing property in *Home Alone*, *Home Alone 2* finds him away from his home turf, and his imperative shifts to protecting a benevolent patriarch's charitable support for children.[24] Rushing with his family to make a flight to Miami, Kevin gets distracted and mistakes another man for his father, resulting in him getting on a flight to New York. Fortuitously, Kevin has his father's carry-on bag, allowing him access to Peter's address book (which reveals that his uncle has a house in New York) and credit cards that enable Kevin to once again easily slip into the role of the father, this time as breadwinner/provider. When he calls the Plaza Hotel to make a reservation, he greets the receptionist by saying, "Howdy-do, this is Peter McCallister, the father. I'd like a hotel room please." He manages to trick hotel staff into letting him check into the room by himself by playing on the cultural expectations of paternal absence, telling the front desk staff that his father is busy in a business meeting. Kevin's initial misrecognition of another man as his father, along with his resourcefulness with technologies of misrecognition, further align him with Ferris Bueller. Though Ferris orchestrates his father's failure to recognize his own son and deceptively presents an ill version of himself, here Kevin takes it one step further, first misrecognizing his father, and then misrepresenting himself in his father's place.

Having recently escaped from prison, Harry and Marv arrive in New York and quickly plan to rob Duncan's Toy Chest on Christmas Eve. Kevin stops by the same store, and when Mr. Duncan (Eddie Bracken), the storeowner, asks Kevin if he's shopping by himself, Kevin praises his concern as "very responsible." Mr. Duncan further ingratiates himself to Kevin and aligns himself with Santa Claus by explaining that the store is donating money to the children's hospital. Mr. Duncan inspires Kevin to donate (his father's) money to the children's hospital, aligning Kevin with Mr. Duncan as a provider for children in need. Later in the film, Kevin walks by the children's hospital, waves to a boy sitting in a window, and Mr. Duncan's pledge to donate money echoes in voiceover, followed by Marv's voice detailing his and Harry's plans to rob the store. The camera moves from a medium shot to medium close-up to capture

Kevin's resolve as he declares, "You can mess with a lot of things. But you can't mess with kids on Christmas." Kevin then runs out of the frame, setting into motion a montage wherein he booby-traps his uncle's house in order to save Christmas for the kids at the children's hospital. To lure the burglars away from the toy store, Kevin throws a brick through the window, triggering the alarm. When the police talk to Mr. Duncan after the fact, they bring him a note Kevin had attached to the brick, wherein Kevin proves himself every bit as responsible as he praised Mr. Duncan for being: the note asks if Mr. Duncan has insurance to cover the window, and if not, promises to mail him the money to fix it.

In the end, Kevin proves to be the ultimate provider—the Plaza provides his entire family with a penthouse suite (in stark contrast to the cheap motel his father had booked in Miami) and Mr. Duncan sends over an enormous number of wrapped gifts. When Kevin's cousin Fuller (Kieran Culkin) wakes up, Kevin warns him not to get his hopes up for presents (because Santa doesn't visit hotels). Fuller replies, "Are you nuts? He's omnipresent. He goes everywhere!" Here the film makes a clear comparison between Kevin and Santa Claus, as much of the pleasure viewers derive from the *Home Alone* films comes from the fact that Kevin is always two steps ahead of the burglars, anticipating and thwarting their every move. Even Buzz has to admit that Kevin is essentially the Santa Claus of the family and the narrative, telling everyone, "If Kevin hadn't screwed up in the first place, again, then we wouldn't be in this most perfect, and huge hotel room with a truckload of all this free stuff." While *Home Alone* opens with nearly every family member resenting Kevin in some way, *Home Alone 2* concludes with the entire family grateful for all that his hijinks have provided. Kevin emerges as the ideal neoliberal subject—he manages to take care of his family, their house, and the sick children of New York City without any help from state institutions.

CONCLUSION

Hughes's patriarchs occupy an ambiguous, contradictory position in his films, reflecting the cultural and political debates over changing family dynamics in the 1980s. His family comedies both mock their father characters while ultimately celebrating them, and his teen films suggest at once that teens need their fathers and that their fathers have failed them, pointing to an anxiety about the role of the father and the stability of patriarchal authority writ large that animated both the neoconservative political landscape and the feminist resistance to it. The overwhelming popularity of the *Home Alone* films, with their plucky, self-sufficient child patriarch, points not only to the emerging neoliberal politics of the 1990s, but also to the shift from the Reagan/Bush era to the ascendancy of Bill Clinton.

As Hughes's heroes grew progressively younger (from fathers in the early 1980s to teens in the mid-1980s to children in the early 1990s), so did those of American presidential politics. Following twelve years of aging, traditional patriarchs occupying the White House, Democratic presidential nominee Bill Clinton's breakout moment came on late-night television in 1992, wherein he played the saxophone while donning sunglasses on *The Arsenio Hall Show*. Despite the fact that his policy positions were decidedly centrist, and later identified as the epitome of neoliberalism, Clinton embodied a youthful sense of hope not unlike Kevin McCallister's belief in the magic of Christmas.

From the bumbling father figures of his family comedies to the villainous principals of his teen films to the child patriarch of the *Home Alone* films, Hughes's films wrestle with the role of the father at a time when the family was being used as a ploy across the political spectrum. Ultimately, his films have it both ways, installing a new and improved patriarch, either in the figure of a childish man or a mature child. After all, when the teens in *The Breakfast Club* worry about whether or not they will grow up to be like their parents, Allison proclaims, "It's unavoidable."

NOTES

1. Alan Nadel, *Flatlining on the Field of Dreams: Cultural Narratives in the Films of President Reagan's America* (New Brunswick, NJ: Rutgers University Press, 1997), 147.
2. See, for example, Steve Bailey and James Hay, "Cinema and the Premises of Youth: 'Teen Films' and Their Sites in the 1980s and 1990s," in *Genre and Contemporary Hollywood*, ed. Steve Neale (London: British Film Institute, 2002), 221; Timothy Shary, *Generation Multiplex: The Image of Youth in Contemporary American Cinema* (Austin: University of Texas Press, 2002), 192; Robin Wood, *Hollywood from Vietnam to Reagan . . . and Beyond* (New York: Columbia University Press, 2003), 319.
3. Mary Vavrus, "Domesticating Patriarchy: Hegemonic Masculinity and Television's 'Mr. Mom'," *Critical Studies in Media Communication*, 19, no. 3 (2002), 352–75.
4. Stephen Tropiano, *Rebels & Chicks: A History of the Hollywood Teen Movie* (New York: Back Stage Books, 2006), 185.
5. Lynne Segal, *Slow Motion: Changing Masculinities, Changing Men* (New Brunswick, NJ: Rutgers University Press, 1990), 51.
6. Yvonne Tasker, "Perfectly Perfect People: Postfeminism, Masculinity and Male Parenting in Contemporary Cinema," in *A Family Affair: Cinema Calls Home*, ed. Murray Pomerance (London: Wallflower, 2008), 183.
7. Hannah Hamad, *Postfeminism and Paternity in Contemporary US Film: Framing Fatherhood* (London: Routledge, 2014), 2.
8. Segal, 29.
9. Susan Jeffords, *Hard Bodies: Hollywood Masculinity in the Reagan Era* (New Brunswick, NJ: Rutgers University Press, 1994), 13.
10. Marsha Kinder, "Home Alone in the 90s: Generational War and Transgenerational Address in American Movies, Television and Presidential Politics," in *In Front of the*

    Children: Screen Entertainment and Young Audiences, eds Cary Bazalgette and David Buckingham (London: British Film Institute, 1995), 77.
11. Nadel, 156.
12. *Uncle Buck* ends with a freeze frame, which, like many of Hughes's films, seems to capture a moment of family harmony and/or triumph.
13. Notably, Hughes appears in a cameo as Brian's father at the end of the film.
14. Shary, 73.
15. Catherine Driscoll, *Teen Film: A Critical Introduction* (Oxford: Berg, 2011), 52.
16. Nicole Matthews, *Comic Politics: Gender in Hollywood Comedy after the New Right* (Manchester: Manchester University Press, 2000), 108.
17. Wood, 152.
18. Bailey and Hay, 220.
19. Bailey and Hay, 230.
20. Leger Grindon, "Movies and Fissures in Reagan's America," in *American Cinema of the 1980s: Themes and Variations*, ed. Stephen Prince (New Brunswick, NJ: Rutgers University Press, 2007), 159.
21. Elizabeth G. Traube, *Dreaming Identities: Class, Gender, and Generation in 1980s Hollywood Movies* (Boulder, CO: Westview Press, 1992), 77.
22. Nadel, 157.
23. Joe L. Kincheloe, "*Home Alone* and Bad to the Bone: The Advent of a Postmodern Childhood," in *Kinderculture: The Corporate Construction of Childhood*, third edn, ed. Shirley R. Steinberg (Boulder, CO: Westview Press, 2011), 275.
24. All of the lead actors from *Home Alone* reprise their roles in the sequel.

PART IV
Contested Identities

Chapters in this section return to Hughes's celebrated teen films. Centered on White, middle-class adolescents in the North Shore suburbs of Chicago, Hughes's films also offer up a portrayal of liminality, a moment in which identities are temporarily in flux. It is these identities that are the focus of the chapters here, considering the construction of masculinities, of social class, and of racial and ethnic identity across Hughes's teen films. Given that more than 30 years have passed between the last teen film Hughes wrote and produced, *Some Kind of Wonderful* (1987), and the present day, these chapters offer the opportunity to reflect on the impact of Hughes's particular constructions of gender, racial identity, and social class in the 1980s, and their continued resonances today. These chapters rethink elements that have hitherto been taken for granted in scholarship on John Hughes, and see their authors looking again at Hughes's works from the position of hindsight. In this, they echo Molly Ringwald's reconsideration of her work with Hughes with which this book began.

Hughes's films all demonstrate that adolescence is a critical, and often undervalued, moment when an individual's life is in flux. Although the teenager's circumstances are not fixed, the teen film typically sees the teenager coming of age, and in so doing, moving towards a state of stability. It is within that indeterminate phase where identity is at its most unstable, and in which the ideological machinations mandating conformity along pre-established norms of gender and class may be made visible. *Weird Science* (1985), the film to which Andrew Scahill devotes a chapter, provides a significant example of this phenomenon. The film ostensibly portrays the science fiction wish-fulfillment fantasy of two teenage boys, Wyatt (Ilan Mitchell-Smith) and Gary (Anthony Michael Hall), creating their ideal woman, Lisa (Kelly LeBrock). However, as Scahill ably observes, the film is perhaps better thought of as an examination of the construction of masculinity, and Wyatt and Gary's inability to live up to those norms. John Hughes's teen films provide spaces in which the liminality of adolescence can find expression.

Weird Science is itself something of a liminal piece for Hughes's teen films. Bracketed between two of Hughes's best-loved works, *The Breakfast Club* (1985) and *Ferris Bueller's Day Off* (1986), Scahill observes that *Weird Science* is a crass, oddball outlier by comparison, which rarely commands the affection or critical attention of Hughes's other teen films. Taking up a well-worn science fiction premise, the film sees its protagonists create an ideal woman through their home computer. Examining the film's attention of masculinities, Scahill deploys close textual analysis and turns to the film's literary antecedents in the form of *Frankenstein*, *Pygmalion*, and, perhaps more surprisingly, *Mary Poppins*. In so doing, Scahill makes a compelling case that, while Lisa provides the film's eye-catching sideshow, it is the relationship between the two young men that is principally at issue in the film. Taking up approaches from masculinity studies, Scahill demonstrates Hughes's continued preoccupation with norms of masculinity, and, just as with the father figures examined in the previous section, the teenager's tentative, precarious grasp over those norms.

Robert Bulman's sociologically informed take on John Hughes's teen films continues the focus on identity, but here takes in Hughes's preoccupation with social class disparity. Hughes's teen films have been widely praised for their attention to differences in social class, even within the same high school.[1] These differences are frequently the source of conflict between students, and of conflicting feelings for those working-class students who are frequently the subject of class-based marginalization. As Bulman observes, Hughes's attention to differences in social class is all the more remarkable given that Americans, despite clear evidence to the contrary, do not see themselves as possessing a given social class identity. Rather, they work on the presumption of equality, and of equality of opportunity, that governs much of American discourse. With the exception of Hughes's films, this is often the basis of much American teen cinema, in which social class distinction is mediated through differences in clothing, or personal tastes, which have more individualistic bases.

For Bulman, social class is central to a number of teen films, and especially those made by John Hughes. He identifies the ways in which filmmakers portray youths of different class backgrounds in strikingly different ways, whether the teachers themselves become the focus of an assumed middle-class adult audience's identification, or if, as in Hughes's worlds, the individual differences between characters might take priority over their position in a broader social class hierarchy. Taking just one foundational example, in *The Breakfast Club* the characters refer to the class differences between one another, yet they seem to be resolved when wealthy Claire (Molly Ringwald) gives Bender (Judd Nelson) one of her diamond earrings. As Bulman makes clear, romance, and the motif of diamond earrings, recurs in Hughes's work to magically resolve the class disparities made clear in his narratives.

The individualist strain Bulman identifies also finds expression in the portrayal of romance in Hughes's teen films. A significant example of the tendency is observed in *Pretty in Pink* (1986), which was written and produced by Hughes. Here class differences are seen to be embodied by two distinct characters. While the film is at pains to demonstrate the injuries caused by class-based antagonism, ultimately these difficulties appear to be resolved through the romance between working-class Andie (Molly Ringwald) and upper-class "richie" Blane (Andrew McCarthy). The narrative thus sees her class ascension, while the structures that maintain the class divisions, made hitherto so visible, remain unquestioned.

Finally, Frances Smith turns her attention to the construction of racial identity, and the reification of Whiteness in John Hughes's teen films. Of course,

Hughes's equation of normalcy with Whiteness occurs elsewhere in his oeuvre. In *Vacation*, the Griswolds find themselves intimidated when they get lost and drive through an area predominantly inhabited by African Americans. Humor is attempted when Clark (Chevy Chase) mimics the speech patterns of the people he encounters, and the scene ultimately works to create the spectacle of African Americans as threatening and alien, and the Griswolds as hapless embodiments of the White, middle-class family. In a very similar vein, Scahill observes the moment when Gary and Wyatt attend the Kandy Club, which is likewise presented as a Black space. Scahill astutely observes the ways in which the pair find themselves feeling threatened in the space even as they continue to enjoy the considerable privileges incurred by presenting as White. What is more, as Smith observes, the presentation in Hughes's work of abject racial identities is often commensurate with abject gender and sexual identity as well. Throughout Hughes's body of work, whether in family or teen cinema, ethnic diversity is portrayed as a threat.

Some of the most damaging elements of Hughes's reification of Whiteness occurs not only in the form of racial stereotyping of the type witnessed above, but also in the appropriation of Black music by White characters. Smith notes a cringeworthy moment in *Pretty in Pink*, in which Duckie (Jon Cryer) unexpectedly takes to the shop floor of Trax to lip sync and dance to Otis Redding's "Try a Little Tenderness." The moment is jarring not only because the character's appearance is unexpected, but also because Duckie's demeanor and awkward dancing have little in common with Redding himself. A similar moment occurs at the conclusion of *Ferris Bueller's Day Off*, in which the lead character (Matthew Broderick) takes over a parade running through the city, and a group of African American dancers appear marginalized on the periphery of the scene. While Ferris is undoubtedly a highly privileged character, it is notable that Duckie is not presented in these terms. In Hughes's worlds, then, it appears that Whiteness trumps other marks of lesser social status. All three of these chapters work to reconsider elements of Hughes's teen films that have become apparent only in recent years.

NOTE

1. See for instance Jonathan Bernstein, *Pretty in Pink: The Golden Age of Teen Movies* (New York: St. Martin's Griffin, 1997); Timothy Shary, "Buying Me Love: '80s Class-Clash Teen Romances," *Journal of Popular Culture*, 44, no. 3 (2011), 563–82; Anthony C. Bleach, "Postfeminist Cliques? Class, Postfeminism and the Molly Ringwald-John Hughes Films," *Cinema Journal*, 49, no. 3 (2010), 24–44.

CHAPTER 11

Bizarre Love Triangle: Frankensteinian Masculinities in *Weird Science*

Andrew Scahill

John Hughes's 1985 film *Weird Science*, a teen sex comedy about the creation of a perfect woman by tech-savvy teens, was written by Hughes in only two days following the success of *The Breakfast Club* (1985). The two films share many similarities: both are set in the town of Shermer outside of Chicago, both explore the complex social hierarchies of high school, and both films feature Anthony Michael Hall as a high school nerd desperate for the approval of his more popular classmates. As Brian Johnson in *The Breakfast Club*, Hall is the most damaged member of the detention crew, and is considering suicide at the film's opening. But he ultimately becomes the moral center of the film, and the only member able to put his angst into words—a fitting cypher for filmmaker John Hughes within the text (Hughes would play Brian's dad in the film). During the production of *Weird Science*, Hughes would write his screenplay for his next film—the anarchic teenage fantasy *Ferris Bueller's Day Off* (1986).

Produced between two of his most well-regarded films, *Weird Science* is often discounted as a bizarre outlier in the filmography of John Hughes: "a vulgar, mindless, special-effects-cluttered wasteland,"[1] Gene Siskel called it in his 1985 review. But when examined as the middle panel of a triptych on male identity in the mid-1980s, *Weird Science* becomes all the more revealing for its muddled and contradictory views on masculinity. As part of John Hughes's Nerd Trilogy, the social outcasts of *Weird Science* vacillate between the paralyzing depression of Brian Johnson and narcissistic freedom of Ferris Bueller. *Weird Science* is an intermediary film in every way: excited to leave the past behind, but unsure what the future holds. It is adolescence writ large. It is a road movie because it cannot be a destination.

Weird Science is a loose adaptation of a story from the early 1950s EC Comics book of the same name, to which producer Joel Silver had acquired rights during the 1980s. In the story "Made of the Future," a lonely man orders a perfect android bride who leaves him once she reaches sentience. The story is a familiar retread of Ovid's telling of the story of Pygmalion from *Metamorphoses*, in which a sculptor who abhorred women calls upon the gods to bring his beautiful statue to life. *Weird Science* operates as progeny to both Pygmalion and *Frankenstein*, and also draws deeply from such wide-ranging intertextual sources as the *I Dream of Jeannie* TV show (1965–70), *Mary Poppins* (1964), and *Mad Max* (1979), as well as the screwball antics of the Dean Martin and Jerry Lewis road movies, becoming a Frankensteinian pastiche of Western mythologies and Hollywood cinema.

The plot of *Weird Science* goes a little like this: best friends Gary (Anthony Michael Hall) and Wyatt (Ilan Mitchell-Smith), high school nerds, create a beautiful woman through a mix of technology and occultism. Though intended as a sexual slave, their creation Lisa (Kelly LeBrock) evidences seemingly limitless powers. A hybrid genie/headmistress, Lisa pushes the boys into increasingly precarious situations in their journey towards manhood. The film culminates in a chaotic house party where the boys violently assert themselves against a biker gang, resulting in a newfound popularity among their schoolmates.

In what follows, I argue that the creation of a woman from bits and pieces is simply the pretense of the film. The true project of *Weird Science* is the attempt to create a modern man out of disparate and insufficient models of manhood. In doing so, the boys stand in for Hughes-as-director, using the cinematic tools of intertextual collage to draft his new American Adam in the shifting landscape of 1980s White masculinity.

SWEET DREAMS (ARE MADE OF THIS)

The film opens with a scene familiar to even the most casual consumer of 1980s teen pics: two teenage boys ogling the bodies of their nubile female classmates. The leering gaze of the boys is aligned with the camera's eye, which is in turn aligned with the gaze of the (presumed) teenage male spectator, providing a textbook Mulveyan formation of cinema's "male gaze." This places the film in familiar company with other teen pics of the era like *Porky's* (1981), *Fast Times at Ridgemont High* (1982), and *Revenge of the Nerds* (1984), which feature young men sharing voyeuristic pleasure, secretly spying on unknowing females from windows or peepholes or hidden cameras. Likewise, in *Weird Science*, best friends Gary and Wyatt stand on the sidelines of the school gymnasium, staring at girls' gymnastics practice as they exchange stories of what they'd like to do with the girls: showers, wild parties, naked bodies everywhere.

But something is different in *Weird Science*. The girls are presented in long shot, punctuated by short insert shots which emphasize their gymnastic

Figure 11.1 Their fantasies of voyeuristic male power come up short when Gary (Anthony Michael Hall) and Wyatt (Ilan Mitchell-Smith) become spectacles to the female gaze.

athleticism: running, leaping, vaulting. The boys, meanwhile, are introduced in a slow tilt up their bodies—like Phoebe Cates emerging from the pool in *Fast Times at Ridgemont High*—a shot later repeated to introduce sex goddess Lisa. In contrast with the shots of their female classmates in full-body leotards, the boys' smooth legs and lithe frames are exposed, with Wyatt's bare nipple on display through his tank top. Wyatt and Gary's exposed, passive bodies contrast sharply with the covered, active bodies of the young girls.

This is not to suggest that *Weird Science* is performing some feminist inversion of the male gaze. Rather, as the ironic strains of "Also Sprach Zarathustra" play on the soundtrack, the film stages a mock epic of male voyeuristic power. And behind the boys a sign looms large: "Future Homemakers, Every Wed., 3:00 – Rm 208," further emphasizing the chasm between their fantasies and their reality. For Wyatt, the fantasy of voyeuristic power feels incomplete. "They don't know my name," he bemoans. "Nobody likes us. Nobody." Gary responds, indignant: "Why are you messing with the fantasy? We know about the reality. Don't ruin the fantasy, okay?"

But this fantasy proves short-lived as school bullies Max (Robert Rusler) and Ian (a young Robert Downey Jr.) pull down the shorts of Gary and Wyatt in full display of their female classmates, and thus the boys are exposed and made the object of the female gaze. No longer the possessors of the active gaze, the young men are embarrassed and emasculated in their exposure to the judgment of their once-fantasy objects. So begins the narrative of *Weird Science*, the story of two boys who begin at the very bottom of a male dominance hierarchy, lower even than the young women who mock their inadequacies.

Their fragile fantasy of male voyeuristic power has given way to the reality of their masculine insufficiency. Throughout the course of the film, these "future homemakers" will strive to escape their homosocial effeminacy and enter into something more recognizable as gender normativity.

The film cuts to the title card, and the theme song by Oingo Boingo lays bare the contradictory elements of identity formation. Danny Elfman's lyrics foreground the combination of oppositions: magic and technology, fantasy and microchips. Articulating the formulation of self as "something like a recipe," the song catalogs masculine/scientific and feminine/domestic signifiers as containers waiting to be filled with meaning: "plastic tubes and pots and pans." But this seems to be creation without recipe, as the song articulates over and over the sheer unknowingness of "real" gender in a frenzy of contradictory signifiers: "not what teacher said to do," "something different we're making," "things I've never seen before." Such is the weird science of gender formation.

In the chorus, Elfman asks "My creation—Is it real?" And responds, twice repeating "I do not know, I do not know." As the middle film in Hughes's Nerd Trilogy, *Weird Science* allows unknowingness to be its engine, an adolescent boundary-testing phase of character maturity. In their episodic adventures with Lisa, Gary and Wyatt are revealed to be collages themselves, unsure what to make of the contradictory discourses about masculinity in the 1980s. But the film does know this: the boys (and all boys) must reject the queerness of homosocial bonding to enter into proper heterosexual maturity. In *Weird Science*, Hughes tentatively champions a new "yuppie" masculinity for White men based upon technological mastery, conspicuous consumption, and the display of status. But the film remains fearful that such masculinity is simply the accumulation of empty signifiers.

TAINTED LOVE

In 1995, sociologist Raewyn Connell presented a model of multiple masculinities, including *hegemonic masculinity*, *subordinated masculinity*, *marginal masculinity*, and *complicit masculinity*.[2] This pluralistic mode allowed scholars to discuss conflicts of power between men, indicating that not all men benefit from gender inequality in the same manner.

Hegemonic masculinity refers to those in a patriarchal system of power who benefit the most from gender inequality and the subjugation of women. Such formations are not ahistorical; as Connell notes, "[h]egemonic masculinity is not a fixed character type, always and everywhere at the same time. It is, rather, the masculinity that occupies the hegemonic position in a given pattern of gender relations, a position always contestable."[3] Indeed, masculinity in the hegemonic position must suppress both women and other competing forms of masculinity.

As Michael A. Messner notes, "hegemonic masculinity [is] the form of masculinity that, for the moment, codifies the collective project of men's domination of women—is defined in relation to emphasized femininity, but also in relation to marginalized and subordinated masculinities."[4] Don Sabo describes these performative acts against subjugated masculinities as part of "an intermale dominance hierarchy"[5] in which the struggle for superiority in group-based relations requires outward displays of intermale subjugation. In *Weird Science*, the school bullies and Wyatt's brother Chet (Bill Paxton) represent this most culturally exalted and hegemonic form of masculinity, as their combination of race, class, sexuality, and gender performance place them at the top of the gender hierarchy. Their ability to possess, display, and transfer their girlfriends as property speaks to their successful domination of women. Their dominance of Gary and Wyatt is predicated on their ability to make them "like woman," either by exposing their flesh to the gaze of others, or by pouring a cherry red Icee on their heads in a recreation of the prom scene from Brian DePalma's *Carrie* (1976).

Within the narrative world of *Weird Science*, Wyatt and Gary are presented as possessing *subordinated masculinities*, or those with less access to the benefits of patriarchy. Despite having significant race and class benefits, the film presents them as deeply deficient, by virtue of their age and gender performance, from reaping the full benefits of hegemonic masculinity. As "nerds," their proficiency in computer technology provides them none of the demonstrative markers of athleticism and competition that hegemonic masculinity demands. Further, the home computer contains them within the domestic sphere and not the more public domains of male power.

For Connell, it is queer men who most readily occupy this subordinated space in the stratification of male power. Says Connell, "Oppression positions homosexual masculinities at the bottom of a gender hierarchy among men. Gayness, in the patriarchal ideology, is the repository of whatever is symbolically expelled from hegemonic masculinity, the items ranging from fastidious taste to home decoration to receptive anal pleasure."[6] This notion of "expulsion" is useful, as it is suggestive of the necessary abject presence of homosexual Otherness to define and police the boundaries of heterosexual masculinity.

Though not denotatively queer, Wyatt and Gary are coded as a domesticated male couple, whose de facto queerness serves as an impediment to their mature heterosexuality. From the opening moments in the school gymnasium, the boys are presented as "Future Homemakers" who will be forever stuck in homosocial stasis if not properly rerouted. The next scene cuts to Wyatt's bedroom, where the wifely Wyatt reclines in bed as his husband Gary pretends to shave his nonexistent moustache in the bathroom while they discuss the day's affairs. To punctuate their queerness, the boys then settle in to watch James Whale's *Bride of Frankenstein* (1935), in which Dr. Frankenstein and his male companion labor to create life.

Mary Shelley's *Frankenstein* and its film adaptations are one of many intertexts that are stitched together to animate the narrative of *Weird Science*. The potential for queer readings abound in Shelley's novel, as Victor's intense emotional intercourse with men (such as Clerval and Walton), the evacuation of women from the narrative, and the Monster's final designation of Victor as his one true Mate ask us to reconsider the intense bonds that form between men. The film adaptation *Bride of Frankenstein* picks up on many of these suggestions, as queer director James Whale depicts a scientist lured away from his matrimonial bed to create life with the sissified scientist Dr. Septimus Pretorius. In her analysis of the homoerotics of *Bride of Frankenstein*, Elizabeth Young extends Eve Kosofsky Sedgwick's examination of the intense bonds of male rivalry to argue that the film repeatedly stages a triangulation of male homoerotic desire between Dr. Frankenstein and male companions through the creation and exchange of a female creation. "Women serve, then," says Young, "not merely as a medium of exchange in the homosocial system but also as a desperate cover-up, a means of channeling suspicion of homosexuality into heterosexual appearances."[7] Such a formulation of triangulated male desire becomes canon in nearly all adaptations of *Frankenstein*, either in the form of a disfigured assistant (Fritz or Igor) or a rival (Dr. Pretorius).

The inherent queerness of such triangulations do not go unnoticed by *Weird Science*, and in fact they serve as the subtext against which the boys' flight from homosocial relations must occur. The film's conclusion may be tempting to read as a progressive challenge to the jingoistic hypermasculinity of the Reagan era. For certain, the main avatars of this worldview (Chet and the bullies) are resoundingly rejected by the boys and punished by an anarchic female presence. This is the explicit conflict of *Weird Science*—but the true engine of this film is the implicit conflict, which is the panicked flight from homosocial queerness.

SHE BLINDED ME WITH SCIENCE

The film ameliorates the queerness of this bizarre love triangle by presenting the use of technology to create Lisa as an intensely heterosexual act—penetrating the digital gateways and inserting informational DNA into the awaiting womb of the internet. Their new creation will serve as female power writ large, a digital manic pixie dream goddess who will shape them into men. "Lisa" was named after Apple's Locally Integrated Software Architecture, an early Macintosh desktop computer released in 1983. Marketed simply as "The Lisa," early commercials for the technology promised businessmen the ability to free themselves from the office building and create a masculine "home office" in the domestic space. It also lauded the manner in which Lisa responded to the user's touch: "We control Lisa by pointing to these images on the screen with this unique item called a 'mouse'," says one commercial. Sleek and stylish, the powerful new domestic technology "Lisa" seemed to usher in a new era of feminized technology ready to be harnessed by the Pygmalion-esque male user.

Youth-driven cinema of the 1980s championed technology, particularly the home computer, as a means by which teenagers could carve out a separate and distinct youth culture and simultaneously craft a better future. Films like *WarGames* (1983), *My Science Project* (1985), and *Real Genius* (1985) mapped technological prowess onto a new and more ethical worldview.[8] Meanwhile, films like *Revenge of the Nerds* saw technology as a way that subjugated masculinities could compete in sports and other traditional arenas of male competition. "New information technology," claims Connell, "became a vehicle for redefining middle-class masculinities at a time when the meaning of labor for working-class men was in contention."[9] Similarly, *Weird Science* sees boys attempting to lay claim to this new techie manhood, but like any good Frankenstein tale, their hideous progeny proves too much for them to harness.

The creation of Lisa is marked by the boys plunging themselves into a seductive and dangerous feminine space and witnessing its power overtake them and wreak havoc on their small suburban town. Gary and Wyatt begin with a *WarGames*-like hack into the government's mainframe, which visualizes the act as a series of uterine-like tubes that the boys "penetrate" to access more computing power. This is hacking-as-seduction, and the virginal boys overestimate their mastery. "We gotta fill this thing with data," says Gary, suggestively. The boys then input their digital DNA into the computer's slot to make their perfect woman. Soon the boys lose control of their creation, and Gary attempts to destroy the computer with a baseball bat, only to find his replacement phallus shattered upon contact. Finally, the closet door breaks, leaving the buxom Lisa standing in the pinkish glow of the vaginal orifice.

Locking eyes with her two male creators, Lisa says coquettishly, "So . . . what would you little maniacs like to do first?"

I RAN (SO FAR AWAY)

But hold one moment: in addition to being a version of Mary Shelley's novel, *Weird Science* also serves as an update of the story of Pygmalion, an amalgamation that has served as the basis for such creation-as-love-object films like *The Rocky Horror Picture Show* (1975), *The Stepford Wives* (1975, 2004), *Deadly Friend* (1986), *Frankenhooker* (1990), and *The Skin I Live In* (2011). But how should we attend to this adaptation in terms of its gender politics? Pygmalion is, after all, a story of sexual slavery—the story of a man who so abhorred women that he implored the gods to deliver him a woman to own without the inconveniences of free will. How can a story with a baseline conceit of human trafficking be a comedy at all?

The Pygmalion myth has undergone its own transformation in popular culture, most notably in George Bernard Shaw's 1913 play *Pygmalion*, in which university professor Henry Higgins transforms a low-class woman named Eliza Doolittle into a respectable woman through educating her on the accent and mannerisms of proper British womanhood. In the end, Doolittle leaves Higgins and threatens to tutor others as she has been trained in the ways of respectability. This play, of course, becomes the basis for the film adaptation *My Fair Lady* (1964), which serves as a template for every makeover romantic comedy film afterwards, from *Pretty Woman* (1990) to teen pic standbys like *Can't Buy Me Love* (1987), *She's All That* (1999), and *The Princess Diaries* (2001).

The one way in which the film softens its sexual slavery narrative is through presenting Gary and Wyatt's sexuality as infantile, unthreatening, and problematically homosocial. The scene of Lisa's creation cuts directly to one of the boys' articulated fantasies: to take a shower with a sexy woman. Once there, however, the boys find themselves huddled in the corner, their clothes on, more comfortable with their homosocial bond than with heterosexual contact.

Further, Lisa emerges fully sentient and fully capable. Unlike previous Galateas, she is not limited by her silence, her ignorance, her class, or her resources. In the Shaw adaptation, Eliza Doolittle gains a tempered independence through the acquisition of her voice. In *Bride of Frankenstein*, the female monster again uses her voice to emit a scream, which effectively rejects her mate and the purpose of her creation. Lisa, on the other hand, seems to have limitless powers: she is able to materialize objects out of nothingness, stop and reverse time, and transmutate the bodies of living things. And though she grants the boys' wishes, she seems to do so on her own terms. Such an unruly figure seems less Galatea and more like the myth of the genie, a trickster god who grants three wishes but manipulates the seeker into unwanted situations. As a screwball figure, Lisa seems to evoke *I Dream of Jeannie*, but something more akin to Barbara Eden's evil twin sister genie during sweeps week. The British accent and schoolmarmish ways of actress Kelly LeBrock also suggest an intertextual indebtedness to the children's classic *Mary Poppins*, as Lisa arrives in a puff of smoke to nanny the boys into proper maturity before shuttling off to help others in need.[10] The very fact that Gary and Wyatt create a grown woman at all, and not the teenage objects of their lust from the start of the film, suggests that their fantasy creation delivers what they subconsciously desire all along—not a sexual conquest, but a mother/mentor. These intertextual references serve to temper and neuter the story of Pygmalion in a manner that better serves the needs of the teen pic and eliminates the specter of sexual coercion and rape.

YOU SPIN ME ROUND (LIKE A RECORD)

In fact, most of the sexuality of *Weird Science* is relegated to the realm of connotation: the "penetration" of the internet, the replacement phallus of the bat, and the vaginal orifice of the broken door. If Lisa's creation feels pointedly (even embarrassingly) sexual, it really serves to underscore the juvenile Freudianism of the fantasy creation sequences. Indeed, the film invites a psychosexual reading of Lisa as a kind of manifestation of abject female power, what Julia Kristeva identifies as that which does not "respect borders, positions, rules," that which "disturbs identity, system, order."[11] In Barbara Creed's essay "Horror and the Monstrous Feminine: An Imaginary Abjection," she extends Kristeva's analysis to figurations of horror in which the female body represents a terrible, consuming, and castrating power to patriarchy. Its forms, like the phallic mother, the vagina as Pandora's box, and the regenerative mother, speak to an archetypal fear of the power of women.[12]

In Hughes's hands, Lisa is a powerful archaic mother who invites chaos in the service of male maturity—and comedy. In her 1995 book *The Unruly Woman: Gender and the Genres of Laughter*, Kathleen Rowe takes another approach to female abjection, noting that in the screwball comedy, the abject woman is a venerable object who disturbs identity, system, and order in the form of "unruly women" like Mae West and Katherine Hepburn.[13] Lisa updates that tradition in skirting the conventions of respectability and passivity. A combination of Hepburn's "Swinging Door Susie" from *Bringing Up Baby* (1938) and the eponymous Mary Poppins, Lisa brings danger into the boys' lives in the interest of accelerating their maturity. She is bringing up babies and making them into properly aligned heterosexual men.

On the closet door in Wyatt's room rests a bumper sticker: "I BRAKE FOR WOMEN." It is one of many juvenile sight gags scattered throughout the film, like the "Future Homemakers" sign early on. But Lisa also "breaks" their homosociality—symbolized here by the closet door—in her dominating agency and power, rerouting them on the path to heterosexual masculinity. What Lisa provides for Wyatt and Gary is not masculinity per se, but rather a litany of replacement phalluses to compensate for their lack of demonstrative heterosexual masculinity. The film continually plays a kind of "fort/da" game[14] with masculinity—stripping the boys bare and allowing them a signifier of the dispossessed phallus—the cars, the clothes, the gun, the girlfriend. As Marianne H. Watley notes, the films of John Hughes tend to equate sexuality with power, in particular "possession, even temporarily, of symbols of adult men's power, such as an expensive car, and in the possession of a woman. Lack of power is represented by virginity, the 'feminized' man, and the lack of a high-status car. Part of this message is possession of a desirable woman enhances a man's status and power among other men."[15]

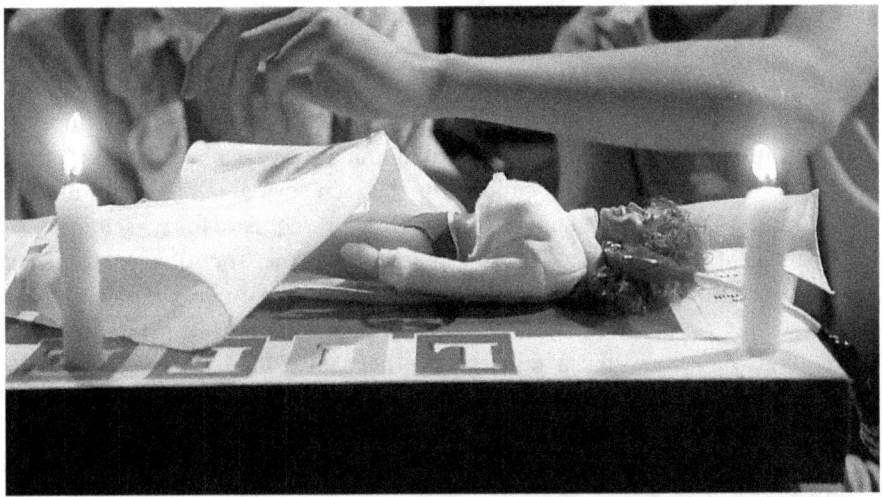

Figure 11.2 Lisa (Kelly LeBrock) is fittingly created on an altar of heteronormativity: Milton Bradley's Game of Life, in which players compete to accumulate the markers of heterosexual maturity.

Maybe this is why the boys create their fantasy woman on the altar of Milton Bradley's Game of Life. Promoted with the slogan, "You will learn about life when you play The Game of Life," the board moves players along a successful path to male heteronormativity, from birth to college to career to marriage to family to insurance to home ownership. Without these signifiers, there is no masculinity—there is no *there* there. The greatest threat is not that Wyatt and Gary will not be powerful men, but rather that they will be stripped of the external signifiers of masculinity, finding nothing remains.

DESTINATION UNKNOWN

With Lisa now at the wheel, *Weird Science* becomes a kind of magical "road movie," in the style of the popular Dean Martin and Jerry Lewis films of the 1950s. Those films are, of course, so pronounced in their play with queer sexuality that they frequently remade romantic comedies with just the duo (*Living It Up* [1954] and *You're Never Too Young* [1955], for instance). Jerry Lewis would go on to write about their friendship in *Dean and Me: A Love Story*. Indeed, the road movie is in essence a homosocial rom com, a working-through of what male bonding is (or can?) look like in a modern era. Along with homosocial bonding, a key feature of these films is the colonial dominance of White men, knifing through the landscape and commanding every space in which they find themselves. Take *Hollywood or Bust* (1956) for instance: the film follows Martin and Lewis as they embark on a cross-continental "gal chase" on their westward expansion. The film's trailer promises, "Arizona's kick is an Indian chick doing a rock 'n' roll war dance!" as Lewis swing dances with a Native American woman on an Indian reservation. The road movie promises freedom, mobility, and the confirmation that White men still dominate every space that they enter.

Weird Science updates this conceit for the teen sex comedy, presenting the White male domination of subaltern space as a prerequisite for masculinity. In her analysis of this film cycle, Leslie Speed argues that the 1980s vulgar teen comedy foregrounds "young, middle-class men's presumed right to behave hedonistically on other people's territory."[16] Gary and Wyatt are newly outfitted by Lisa, who—like a fairy godmother—transforms their drab garbs into pinstriped suits and conjures a carriage (a new sports car) to take them to the ball. In *Weird Science*, the journey to self-actualization is commensurate with assuming the mantle of White male privilege, to realize, as Steinberg and Kincheloe note, that "young men are entitled to misbehave . . . to destroy, by virtue of who they are: White, male, and middle-upper-class Americans. Hollywood is positioning these youth as the CEOs of tomorrow, the new inductees into the 'Old Boys Club,' these 'new boys' are . . . following in the footsteps of their fathers. They are doing what society, their parents and the audiences expect them to do."[17]

Their first stop is The Kandy Bar, an African American blues bar. The obligatory "record-scratch" sound and the crowd's collective head-turn designates this an antagonistic space, echoed by Gary's high-pitched aside: "Lisa, I don't think we belong here." The boys are clearly emasculated in the presence of Black masculinity, a point underscored when Wyatt escapes to the restroom only to accidentally sit in the lap of a (presumably Black) bar patron on the toilet. Such anal rape jokes are endemic to the homosocial screwball comedy, often presented as the "lowest of low" moment when the White male protagonist (often imprisoned) must fend off the overtures of a Black male rapist. Such jokes belie the precarious and situational nature of masculinity, wherein White masculinity is threatened by the presumed phallic superiority of Black men. This sequence in The Kandy Bar represents Black and Latino masculinity as a kind of *marginalized masculinity*, which Connell describes as masculinities that do not have access to the full privileges of hegemonic masculinity due to racial or class barriers.

To assume their proper role in hegemonic White masculinity, Gary and Wyatt must first colonize Black masculinity. To do so, Gary gets drunk and begins to employ a "jive" accent, a caricatured version of Black masculinity which, though played for laughs, cements his inclusion within this community of Black men. This traffics in fantasies of White mobility and mutability: the ability to selectively "take on" the identity formations of other racial categories. By appropriating and performing Black masculinity, *Weird Science* authenticates the right of White masculinity to assert its might even in marginalized spaces. This White dominance of Black-identified spaces is a notable trope in '80s teenage screwball comedy—what Traub calls the "suburban-in-the-city genre," wherein "blacks recognize the white superior talent."[18] Traub notes a similar blues bar takeover scene in *Adventures in Babysitting* (1987) and the protagonist's command of an all-Black chorus in *Ferris Bueller's Day Off*. *Revenge of the Nerds* seems a noteworthy addition, as the geeky losers gain authority and muscle by joining a Black fraternity, who arrive to lend phallic power to the nerds against the White jocks who threaten to emasculate them.

However, the mechanics of this appropriation in *Weird Science* deserve a closer examination, as they reveal how entry into heterosexual masculinity requires not only a particular performance, but a particular rhetoric. "Last year, I was insane for this crazy little eighth-grade bitch," begins Gary. The crowd of grown Black men draw in for more, as Gary talks about her "big-ass titties." The mood shifts when Gary confesses that "the bitch knee'd my nuts, man!" and the men express their resounding disgust about this 14 year-old "bitch" who symbolically castrated their newfound friend. The scene is constructed as a moment of coalition between White and Black masculinity—misogyny as an alternative form of homosocial bonding that elides differences and dispels homoeroticism through the objectification and denigration of women. Woman-hating circulates as a kind of social currency between men. In "Connell's Concept of Hegemonic Masculinity: A Critique," Demetrakis Demetriou argues that there may be an external and internal hegemony operating simultaneously: one that solidifies men's dominance over women and another that promotes one form of masculinity over another."[19] Here misogyny is the external hegemony that sutures men together; but the film locates that misogyny as something endemic to Black masculinity that White masculinity can commandeer and deploy when necessary.

Later, during the climactic party that will close the film, one of the Black patrons from the bar returns to serve drinks to the White suburban youths. When the two school bullies request a bottle of scotch, the bartender responds, menacingly, "Tell you what. You bend over and I'll shove it straight up your ass." As in *Revenge of the Nerds*, the film deploys colonialism-as-coalition, as Black masculinity serves as the hyperphallic reinforcement to White masculine power.

BURNING DOWN THE HOUSE

The boys' "road trip to masculinity," has detours along the way. Though the boys are able to lay claim to the Black marginal masculinity in The Kandy Bar, they are quickly emasculated by the film's main antagonist, Wyatt's brother

Chet. In a film thick with intertextual references to other contemporary films, Chet seems transported from another film entirely. His hypermasculine sadism recalls the drill sergeants of films like *The Boys in Company C* (1978), *The Deer Hunter* (1978), and *Apocalypse Now* (1979), and he is the only character whose threats of physical violence against the boys seem real and visceral, outside of the terrain of the cartoonish violence of other characters. Upon discovering Gary and his new girlfriend in bed, Chet shoves the barrel of his gun into the mouths of both Gary and Deb (Suzanne Snyder), before moving down the hall to terrorize Wyatt and Hilly (Judie Aronson). Chet's militarized masculinity marks the outer limit of masculinity and anchors the film between two competing polarities: queer homosociality and toxic masculinity. But Chet's intertextual presence as war film masculinity is the first of many Hollywood tropes that the boys will have to unmask.

The film's critique of hypermasculinity comes in the final act, when Lisa arranges for the obligatory teen pic house party at Wyatt's home. Once tormentors, the high school bullies now call upon Gary and Wyatt to share the secrets of their technological prowess. "So what's the deal with Lisa?" Max asks. "Can we borrow her?" The boys demur, but it is clear that their newly elevated masculine status has allowed them access into a new space of masculine privilege: now instead of exchanging misogynist barbs as social currency, they talk of exchanging women themselves. This is of course the apotheosis of woman-as-property: daughters handed from father to husband, trophy wives collected and discarded when no longer useful. "You let us have a crack at Lisa," say the bullies, "and we'll let you have Deb and Hilly."

The scene then cuts to Wyatt and Gary and the bullies recasting the ritual that created Lisa, a tacit endorsement of the exchange of women that seems to betray any critique of hypermasculinity. But as earlier, the film suggests that the outward display of misogyny in homosocial circles is a necessary prerequisite of heterosexual masculinity. More than any other figures, Gary and Wyatt's subjugated masculinity seems to require the rhetoric of misogyny and the exchange of women to compensate for their lack of demonstrative masculinity.

The creation sequence repeats much of the anarchic chaos from before, but with a decidedly more phallic twist: furniture is magically drawn into the fireplace and ejaculated out of the chimney to the yard below. Then, in a sequence that seems sadistically out of place, a blonde woman is stripped naked by an unseen force that recalls the spectral rape scene from *The Entity* (1982) and she is similarly ejected out of the chimney onto the ground below. This difference in tone may be explained by the boys' error: instead of using a Barbie doll as their avatar, the ritual accidentally brings to life an image of the Pershing II, a nuclear-capable missile that served as the United States' primary Cold War threat during the 1980s. Now animated, the hyperphallic missile pushes its way through the floor and upwards, penetrating its head through the roof of Wyatt's family home.

The statement, as directly political as Hughes seems to get in any of his films, is that this nuclear missile—and the Cold War paranoia that it represents—is the hyperbolic manifestation of the Monstrous Masculine. Indeed, it is the omission of femininity that turns artistic energy into warfare: creation becomes destruction. This is a theme, of course, explored by Mary Shelley in *Weird Science*'s source text—how the evacuation of woman from the site of birth leads to catastrophic creation, and how privilege with nothing left to possess can only destroy. Lisa chastises the boys, telling them their peers will love them for who they are, and they don't need to perform masculinity to impress their peers—but this rings hollow, ultimately, since the very narrative of *Weird Science* seems to tout the necessity of these very acts of performative masculinity. Indeed, in the final climax of the film, Lisa will call upon the boys to perform the role of cinema protagonists as she conjures up the antagonists of recent Hollywood blockbuster cinema.

WHIP IT (WHIP IT GOOD)

With a wave of her hand, Lisa brings to life the monsters of horror, action, and sci-fi cinema to terrorize the young partygoers and force the boys into action. The first intertextual villain to arrive is the cannibal Pluto from *The Hills Have Eyes* (1977), in which a clan of savages rape and murder a vacationing family. Actor Michael Berryman, whose ectodermal dysplasia gives him a distinctive Nosferatu-like appearance, reprises his role from the film. Berryman's literal presence makes the intertextuality of the next two characters more apparent: first is a human cyborg, his face ripped to reveal the robotics underneath in a copyright-friendly version of Arnold Schwarzenegger's unstoppable machine from James Cameron's *The Terminator* (1984). The last to arrive is a leather-clad and mohawked Wez from *Mad Max 2: The Road Warrior* (1981), in which settlers must defend themselves from savage marauders in a post-apocalyptic world. As Paul Lester Robertson notes, the *Mad Max* series represents "a reactionary viewpoint [that] appeals to the worst impulses of the Reagan-era America" as "Indian-ness" is used to signify the collapse of White civilization and a regression to the tribal savagery of the settler-colonial imagination.[20] Actor Vernon Wells reprises his role as well, though interestingly, this version de-queers its villainous Wez. In *Mad Max 2*, Wez's sex slave companion is young boy dubbed the "Golden Youth." In *Weird Science*, Wez is accompanied by a female sex slave on a chain-link leash. The combination of these three figures as the final obstacle of *Weird Science* is to defeat the very image of heterosexual hypermasculinity in Reagan-era Hollywood cinema.

Figure 11.3 In one of the film's many contradictory moments, Gary takes up the gun to conquer the toxic hypermasculinity of Hollywood cinema.

The Hollywood villains proceed to mock Gary and Wyatt's fragile masculinity, assault their party guests, and finally, kidnap their girlfriends Deb and Hilly. And again, the performance of masculinity through misogyny and homophobia becomes paramount. First, turning to the female sex slave, Gary quiets her laughter, saying, "Why don't you shut up, bitch?" Then, turning to Wez, he says "You don't come into my house with your faggot friends . . ." This is an interesting rhetoric, as Hughes decides to heterosexualize the character; thus the use of "faggot" here is meant to symbolize effeminacy and submissiveness rather than an actual designation of sexuality. Gary then shoves a gun—that ultimate phallic signifier—into Wez's face, forcing the villains to retreat. But not just retreat—rather, they reveal themselves as charlatans, as actors in an impossible performance of fraudulent masculinity. By the end of the film, Lisa has also transformed the once-threatening Chet into an abject pile of feces. What better transformation for the one character who, above all others, has consumed and digested those images of Hollywood hypermasculinity? The other intertextual arrivals from Hollywood cinema are revealed to be performers, frauds, and shadows, and likewise Lisa reveals Chet to be fraud as well—literally a crock of shit.

So the critique here is complex and contradictory: the boys must reject the false images of Hollywood masculinity, but they must lay claim to the gun-as-phallus to prove their masculinity. They must repudiate hypermasculinity as the relic of a Cold War mentality, but do so through violence, homophobia, and misogyny. Perhaps the film advocates a kind of situational masculinity. Perhaps the goal is to unmask the charlatans of masculine performance and pray that no one does the same to you. Perhaps Hughes understands, as a former advertising executive, the conflicting and contradictory images of masculinity that a young man in 1985 must select from. Indeed, young men may have to hack Hollywood cinema for themselves—like Dr. Frankenstein, they may take the parts that they find useful and discard the elements that they find problematic. This, of course, is a useful metaphor for spectatorship itself, and how a young viewer may consume the conflicting messages of *Weird Science*. Perhaps in 1985, Hughes is unsure how to bring these bits and pieces together.

EVERYBODY WANTS TO RULE THE WORLD

If *Weird Science* is John Hughes working through the question of masculinity in the 1980s, his film *Ferris Bueller's Day Off* is his answer. There are assured echoes of *Weird Science* in *Ferris Bueller's Day Off*. The film features a computer-savvy hero who uses his technological prowess to fool his parents and school administrators as he and his friends play hooky from school. Ferris (Matthew Broderick) brings chaos into the life of his best friend Cameron (Alan Ruck), leading Cameron to destroy his father's car in a fit of youthful rebellion. In many ways, *Ferris Bueller's Day Off* plays out like a continuation of *Weird Science*, in which Ferris functions as the embodiment of the now empowered Wyatt and Gary, whose technological mastery has placed them at the top of the masculine hierarchy. Indeed the boys of *Weird Science* function as first-draft Ferris Buellers. Ferris is the man that Wyatt and Gary long to be. It is appropriate that *Ferris Bueller's Day Off* is set in the town of Northbrook, Illinois—Northbrook was the name given to Shermerville (shortened to Shermer in *The Breakfast Club* and *Weird Science*) after it was incorporated in 1923. As the final draft of the yuppie adolescent in Hughes's Nerd Trilogy, Ferris Bueller is the *incorporated* version of Brian Johnson and Gary Wallace—controlled, autonomous, independent. In essence, Hughes returns to the same character in the same town and in the same high school—freshman year, sophomore year, and junior year—and maps their social and psychological development through high school.

In Ferris, the yuppie nerd has completed his studies to become a hedonistic anarchist hacker with almost magical abilities. He breaks the fourth wall, stops time, commands a Black chorus, and never, ever, gets caught. If Lisa is the unruly woman of screwball comedy who exists to upend structure, rules, and authority, we may say that Ferris serves a similar function. Indeed, his sole purpose seems to be to fortify the subjugated masculinity of best friend Cameron by placing him in more and more precarious situations to force him to rebel. Indeed, there is ample room to read *Ferris Bueller's Day Off* as a fairly conventional romantic comedy, with Ferris taking the role of "manic pixie dream boy" to Cameron's milquetoast bachelor in need of a renewed purpose in life.

In his analysis of shifting rhetorics of masculinity, John Beynon refers to the 1980s as "the hello and goodbye decade, specifically 'hello' to the yuppie and 'goodbye' to the 'old industrial man'."[21] This Oedipal rejection of past formations of hegemonic masculinity saw the previous generation as "the riposte to vilified 'old man,' his father, and a refugee from the hardline masculinity epitomized by the paranoid, macho men with stifled emotions . . . enacted on screen by Wayne, Bogart, Bronson, and Stallone."[22] The new yuppie masculinity was "driven by an excessive desire to spend money. Whether it was property, cars, or personal artifacts, consumption was the dominant feature of the yuppie lifestyle . . . At his heart was conspicuous consumption and a ruthless, cutthroat determination to be seen as successful."[23] In transitioning from what historian Gil Troy calls "the 'Me Decade' to the 'Mine All Mine' decade,"[24] consumerist masculinity became a way for the postindustrial man to access to a different mode of masculine display. These are what Rios and Sarabia refer to as "masculinity-making resources"[25] which offer a compensatory means to compete with more dominant forms of masculinity.

In 1985, *Weird Science* is unsure if yuppie masculinity can ever compete with more demonstrative forms of manhood. By 1986, Ferris Bueller dominates and emasculates authority figures through his mastery of technology. As Traub notes, Ferris Bueller "provides a narrative charter for the consumption ethic and a lesson in the qualities required for a successful bureaucratic career . . . Ferris is a particularly uncompromising version of a new type of ironist hero, whose seeming rebelliousness is in fact what qualifies him for success in the corporate world."[26] In 1985, *Weird Science* is an episodic journey in search of what it means to be a man. In 1986, Ferris Bueller has already arrived, fully formed and unchanging. In 1985, *Weird Science* asks of masculinity: "My creation—is it real?" Do the signifiers of masculinity—the car, the clothes, the girlfriend—amount to anything but the play of surfaces? A year later, Ferris is a creature composed entirely *of* surfaces—a postmodern pastiche of situational identities out to rule the world.

NOTES

1. Gene Siskel, "'Weird Science' Proves Even John Hughes Can Short-Circuit," *Chicago Tribune*, August 2, 1985, https://www.chicagotribune.com/news/ct-xpm-1985-08-02-8502200420-story.html.
2. Raewyn Connell, *Masculinities* (Berkeley: University of California Press, 1995). For further reading on the application of Connell's taxonomy, see Melanie Heath, "Manhood Over Easy: Reflections on Hegemonic, Soft-Boiled, and Multiple Masculinities," in *Exploring Masculinities: Identity, Inequality, Continuity, and Change*, eds. C. J. Pascoe and Tristan Bridges (Oxford: Oxford University Press, 2015), 155–65; or Tony Coles,

"Negotiating the Field of Masculinity: The Production and Reproduction of Multiple Dominant Masculinities" in *Men and Masculinities*, 12, no. 1, 30–44.
3. Connell, 139.
4. Michael A. Messner, "On Patriarchs and Losers: Rethinking Men's Interests," in *Exploring Masculinities: Identity, Inequality, Continuity, and Change*, eds. C. J. Pascoe and Tristan Bridges (Oxford: Oxford University Press, 2015), 199.
5. Donald F. Sabo, "Different Stakes: Men's Pursuit of Gender Equity in Sports," in *Sex, Violence and Power In Sports: Rethinking Masculinity*, eds. M. A. Messner and D. F. Sabo (Freedom, CA: Crossing Press, 1994), 202–13.
6. Connell, 78.
7. Elizabeth Young, "Here Comes the Bride: Wedding Gender and Race in *The Bride of Frankenstein*," in *The Dread of Difference: Gender and the Horror Film*, ed. Barry Keith Grant (Austin: University of Texas Press, 1996), 365.
8. See Timothy Shary, *Generation Multiplex: The Image of Youth in Contemporary American Cinema* (Austin: University of Texas Press, 2002).
9. Connell, 141.
10. In the John Hughes documentary *Don't You Forget About Me* (Matt Austin, 2009, Stay the Course Productions, Canada, DVD), Kelly LeBrock describes her character Lisa as "Mary Poppins with breasts."
11. Julia Kristeva, *Powers of Horror: An Essay on Abjection*, trans. Leon S. Roudiez (New York: Columbia University Press, 1982), 4.
12. Barbara Creed, "Horror and the Monstrous-Feminine: An Imaginary Abjection," in *The Dread of Difference: Gender and the Horror Film*, ed. Barry Keith Grant (Austin: University of Texas Press, 1996), 35–65.
13. Kathleen Rowe, *The Unruly Woman: Gender and the Genres of Comedy* (Austin: University of Texas Press, 1995).
14. "Fort/da" refers to Freud's observation of his 18-month old grandson at play in *Beyond the Pleasure Principle* (The International Psycho-analytical Press, 1920). His grandson would throw away his toy (fort/"gone") and pleasurably sigh upon its retrieval (da/"there"). Freud saw this as one way in which an infant managed the trauma of abandonment by restaging the experience with a manageable signifier.
15. Marianne H. Whatley, "Raging Hormones and Powerful Cars: The Construction of Men's Sexuality in School Sex Education and Popular Adolescent Films," *Journal of Education*, 170, no. 3 (1988), 118.
16. Lesley Speed, "Loose Cannons: White Masculinity and the Vulgar Teen Comedy Film," *Journal of Popular Culture*, 43, no. 4 (2010), 840.
17. Shirley R. Steinberg and Joe L. Kincheloe, "Privileged and Getting Away With It: The Cultural Studies of White, Middle-Class Youth," *Studies in the Literary Imagination*, 31, no. 1 (1998), 110.
18. Elizabeth Traube, "Secrets of Success in Postmodern Society," *Cultural Anthropology*, 4, no. 3 (1989), 281.
19. Demetrakis Demetriou, "Connell's Concept of Hegemonic Masculinity: A Critique," *Theory and Society*, 30 (2001), 355.
20. Paul Lester Robertson, "Indians of the Apocalypse: Native Appropriation and Representation in 1980s Dystopic Films and Comic Books," *The Journal of Popular Culture*, 51, no. 1 (2018), 88.
21. John Beynon, *Masculinities and Culture* (Buckingham: Open University Press, 2002), 99.
22. Beynon, 100.
23. Beynon, 105.

24. Gil Troy, *Morning in America: How Ronald Reagan Invented the 1980s* (Princeton, NJ: Princeton University Press, 2007), 17.
25. Victor Rios and Rachel Sarabia, "Synthesized Masculinities: The Mechanics of Manhood Among Delinquent Boys," in *Exploring Masculinities: Identity, Inequality, Continuity, and Change*, eds. C. J. Pascoe and Tristan Bridges (Oxford: Oxford University Press, 2015), 166.
26. Traube, 284.

CHAPTER 12

"You look good wearing my future:" Social Class and Individualism in the 1980s Teen Films of John Hughes

Robert C. Bulman

I graduated from a suburban public high school in 1985. You might say I'm part of the *Breakfast Club* generation. I vividly recall going to a local movie theater with a high school friend to see the 1985 John Hughes classic about five high school students in a day of Saturday detention. We did not find, as a critic from the *Hollywood Reporter* did at the time, that the film was very much like being in detention itself, "a grim and dull experience."[1] Instead, I was enraptured by its richly drawn characters who spoke directly and honestly to an 18-year-old White, male, middle-class, suburban, high school senior. I identified with the character of Brian (Anthony Michael Hall) in particular. Like Brian, I was an awkward boy in college-preparatory classes and most certainly not a jock or part of the popular crowd. While I didn't take a vocational "shop" class to learn practical skills (which Brian famously fails), I did get a C in badminton and I was, ahem, a virgin. The film stuck with me for many years and became one of those films that you can watch over and over and never grow tired of. By the time I was a young assistant professor in 2000, I was surprised to learn that, 15 years later, many of the students in my sociology courses still found the film to be a personal favorite. This remains the case today—remarkable for a film about teens that is now over three decades old. The cultural power of Hughes's work is strong.

In this chapter I focus on four films John Hughes wrote in the 1980s with a focus on adolescents (two of which he also directed): *The Breakfast Club*, *Pretty in Pink*, *Ferris Bueller's Day Off*, and *Some Kind of Wonderful*. I focus on these examples because the 1980s were the peak of the teen film genre—in part because they were the peak for John Hughes. And to understand teen films in general, we must first understand Hughes's contribution. Hughes's films about adolescents represent the typical features of the entire genre of the suburban school film, as well as the promise of youth and the longing for freedom of expression. They represent the ideas of not conforming, of not joining the rat race, of marching to your own drummer, of living life as you want to live it as a free individual. The adolescent heroes in his films embody the characteristics of most of the heroes in other suburban school films from the era, such as *Can't Buy Me Love* (1987) or *Say Anything . . .* (1989). These student heroes express themselves, make mistakes, experience insight, learn and grow, but with only marginal help, if any, from their schools and other adult authorities.

This chapter is an exploration, in particular, of Hughes's depiction of social class differences among his teenage characters. While Hughes's depiction of poor and working-class students is more nuanced and sensitive than other filmmakers in this genre, I find that rather than making a critique of social class inequality, the way in which Hughes grapples with social class tension ends up reinforcing the dominant theme of American individualism that de-emphasizes class differences.

As a sociologist, I understand social class as a complex measure of one's material condition in life. On the individual level it is measured by educational and occupational attainment, income, and wealth. Social class differences are not natural but are the result of generations of collective conflict over scarce resources. The scars of these conflicts are etched in our economic, political, and social institutions. Nevertheless, in the United States, social class membership is not on the tip of our tongues when we describe our lives. Americans tend to see themselves as unmoored from their class history or origins. We are much more likely to see our race or gender as a salient part of our lived experiences.[2] Nevertheless, class plays an insidious role in our lives. Based on our class origins, we do or do not have access to resources that enable our educational, occupational, and financial achievements. We do or do not have to face obstacles that have been placed in the way of our upward mobility. These pre-existing structures of class inequality are rooted in differences in power and privilege. The exercise of class privilege—admission to the right schools, access to the right jobs, the freedom to take risks—reinforces and reproduces the unequal distribution of material resources. But in part because of our cultural value of individualism, Americans tend to see class differences not through the lens of power, but through the lens of individual qualities and characteristics. We see class inequality as an expression of individual success or failure, rather than as a consequence of pre-existing class inequalities embedded in our society.

Social class for Hughes is a prop to help tell the story of American individualism. For all his sensitivity to social class differences, the social class conflicts in Hughes's films are expressed as romantic tensions, which become the mechanism Hughes uses to tackle social class differences, and through which the characters ultimately express their individuality. Rather than relating to social class as a utilitarian achievement as measured by educational achievement, income, and wealth, Hughes's characters see social class as a barrier to fully expressing their true selves. Social class provides the dramatic tension in his films, but it does not do so with the utilitarian goal of doing well on a test, passing a class, graduating high school, getting into college, or finding a job. Rather, social class is yet another vehicle through which the characters figure out who they are and how they relate to others.

SOCIAL CLASS IN HIGH SCHOOL FILMS

My fascination with Hughes and the cultural resonance he seemed to have (at least among middle-class suburban White kids) piqued my curiosity about other teen films, to see what they could teach us about the American adolescent experience in high school and, more generally, about American culture. As a sociologist of education and culture, I wanted to know not only how real schools operate and how real students experience those schools, but I was curious to know how American culture makes sense of these experiences and how they are represented in the popular media. Not surprisingly, the work of John Hughes became central to this research project and his films feature prominently in my 2015 book *Hollywood Goes to High School: Cinema, Schools, and American Culture*.[3]

That book contrasts the different ways Hollywood films represent students and teachers in three types of schools: struggling urban public schools in low-income neighborhoods (such as *Coach Carter* [2005], *Stand and Deliver* [1988], and *Dangerous Minds* [1995]); well-resourced suburban public schools in middle and upper-income neighborhoods (such as *Project X* [2012], *Easy A* [2010], and *Superbad* [2007]); and elite private high schools that serve a high-income population (such as *School Ties* [1992], *Finding Forrester* [2000], and *The Emperor's Club* [2002]). I argue that when Hollywood tells a story about poor and mostly non-White students in urban public high schools, the hero of the movie is nearly always an adult—specifically, a middle-class teacher, principal, or coach who "saves" the students by teaching them to believe in themselves, work hard, and aspire toward academic achievements. For instance, in the urban school film *Freedom Writers* (2007), the drama revolves around the efforts of Erin Gruwell (Hilary Swank), a young, White upper-middle-class teacher who strives to save her students from their impoverished and gang-infested lives in Long Beach, California. Naive at first, she nearly gives up the difficult job but gradually wins the hearts (and minds!) of her students. She teaches her students lessons about bias and prejudice through the history of the Jewish holocaust, assigns *The Diary of Anne Frank*, and encourages them to chronicle their own lives in diaries. She eventually convinces her students to apply themselves academically and to strive for a better life beyond the dysfunctional problems of the low-income ghetto.

There is nothing wrong, certainly, with a message to work hard in school and to strive for a better and more materially comfortable life. But what I have argued is that such messages, absent of an attempt to depict the very real structural obstacles to upward mobility, feed into a middle-class fantasy that poverty is essentially an individual-level problem, not a structural one. These films tell heart-warming stories, but they let the middle and upper classes off the hook for their share of the responsibility for class inequality.

By contrast, when Hollywood tells a story about middle-class and mostly White students in suburban public high schools, the hero of the movie is nearly always a student—specifically, a middle-class student who successfully struggles to assert their identity against the pressures of conformity by peers, parents, and the school. In the typical suburban school film, the drama revolves around a conflict between students about cliques, dating, parties, and popularity, not academic achievement. For instance, in *Mean Girls* (2004), the hero is Cady Heron (Lindsay Lohan), a new student at her suburban high school. She becomes friends with both the social outcasts and the popular "mean girls" of the school, the "Plastics." After a cynical attempt to infiltrate the popular crowd on behalf of the outcasts, she becomes seduced by the power of her own growing popularity. Soon, she becomes the new "queen bee" of the mean girls. By the end of the film, however, she has learned the error of her ways and, as homecoming queen, makes an impassioned speech about the importance of accepting everyone, regardless of their social clique, and that everyone should be free to be themselves. She breaks her homecoming queen tiara and passes out pieces to the crowd, proclaiming that "everyone looks like royalty tonight."

Of course, *Mean Girls* and *Freedom Writers* are very different sorts of movies with different intents and audiences. *Mean Girls* is a smart and fun comedy about popularity in a suburban high school, aimed at a teen audience. *Freedom Writers* is a serious drama about the obstacles to and hopes for educational success in urban schools. In spite of the difference in genre, these films—both about American high schools and their students—reflect not just the *actual* differences between urban and suburban schools, but they reflect the different cultural ways in which Americans *make sense* of them.

There is a cultural reason that Hollywood tends to portray poor and non-White students in deathly serious dramatic fashion while middle-class White students are more likely to be depicted in light-hearted comedies: dominant middle-class White American culture makes very different sense of adolescents based on their race and social class. American culture has a double standard that finds expression in the high school film, and individualism is at the heart of that double standard. The powerful cultural lens of American individualism colors our perception of inequality. Rather than seeing inequality as the result of historical legacy of economic and political structures, Americans tend to attribute economic success and failure to individual characteristics and abilities. Individualism, however, finds two different—and, at times, contradictory—expressions in American culture. I argue that Americans selectively draw upon these different expressions of individualism depending upon the socio-economic status of the characters depicted.

In the influential *Habits of the Heart* (1985), Bellah et al.[4] argue that there is a tension in American culture between "utilitarian individualism" and "expressive individualism." They argue that the strain of utilitarian individualism has its origins in the Protestant work ethic and the ideas of the early founders like Benjamin Franklin who expressed such advice as, "God helps those who help themselves."[5] It is the idea that one should work hard and strive for material success because individuals are responsible for their own success or failure in life. In contrast, the strain of "expressive individualism" in American culture suggests that the pursuit of material rewards is empty if it means you sacrifice important parts of yourself to conform to the expectations of others. These ideas have their roots in the American transcendentalists such as Henry David Thoreau, who wrote, "If a man does not keep pace with his companions, perhaps it is because he hears a different drummer."[6]

I apply this theoretical understanding of American individualism to the genre of the high school film, arguing that Americans have contradictory class-based understandings of what it means to be an adolescent in American society. In urban high school films such as *Freedom Writers*, poor and mostly non-White students are expected to be utilitarian individuals; in suburban school films such as *Mean Girls*, middle-class and mostly White students are expected to be expressive individuals. This reflects the ways that American culture thinks very differently of poor and middle-class adolescents. We want poor, non-White students in urban environments to solve their own problems by pulling themselves up by their bootstraps. We don't have patience for their struggles with identity or their youthful mistakes. Simultaneously, we allow middle-class White students to make mistakes because it is part of the path they must travel to develop a healthy identity and to feel comfortable expressing themselves. Of course, real students must eventually develop both utilitarian and expressive sides of themselves, but Hollywood denies the full humanity of students in these films because they become caricatures of their social class.

THE BREAKFAST CLUB (1985)

The Breakfast Club is no doubt familiar to readers of this volume by now. Five students from different social situations find themselves unhappily serving a Saturday detention together at Shermer High School: Andrew (Emilio Estevez), the popular "athlete"; Brian, the nerdy "brain"; Allison (Ally Sheedy), the loner "basket case"; Claire (Molly Ringwald), the rich "princess"; and John Bender (Judd Nelson), the working-class "criminal." Their initial suspicion and distrust of each other is eventually replaced with mutual respect and admiration after they bond together by smoking pot and baring their souls to each other. They come to realize that the differences between them as individuals are smaller than the differences between teens and adults. As Allison conveniently sums up the moral of the story, "When you grow up, your heart dies."

While Shermer High School is a suburban high school that seems to serve mostly middle-class kids, the character of John Bender (primarily referred to by his surname) allows Hughes to explore social class differences between the students. Bender is the only student to arrive at school on his own rather than being dropped off by his parents. He is the only one who does not bring a lunch to detention. And he is the primary lightning rod of conflict between the students or with Mr. Vernon (Paul Gleason), their supervising teacher. The other students dismiss Bender almost immediately. As Andrew tells him, "You know, Bender, you don't even count. I mean, if you disappeared forever it wouldn't make any difference. You may as well not even exist at this school."

Over the course of the day, we learn that Bender is physically and verbally abused by his parents. We learn that he is not involved in school activities and not on the academic track. He has all the hallmarks of a working-class "burn-out."[7] Claire, on the other hand, comes from a rich family—she is dropped off in a BMW, she eats sushi for lunch, and she is serving detention for skipping school to go shopping. There could not be a sharper contrast drawn between Claire and Bender, and it is primarily through the tension in their relationship that Hughes explores social class differences. It comes out most explicitly in the following exchange during the students' group confessional:

> Claire [to Bender]: You know, I have just as many feelings as you do and it hurts just as much when somebody steps all over them.
> Bender: God, you're so pathetic! Don't you ever, *ever* compare yourself to me, okay? You got everything and I got shit . . . School would probably fucking shut down if you didn't show up . . . I like those earrings, Claire. Are those real diamonds, Claire? I bet they are. Did you work for the money for those earrings or did your daddy buy those for you? I bet he bought those for you. I bet those were a Christmas gift, right? You know what I got for Christmas this year? It was a banner fucking year at the old Bender family. I got a carton of cigarettes.

This moment of intense class conflict is quickly defused, however, when Andrew asks if they will grow up to be like their parents. Hughes quickly shifts the attention away from the social class differences between the students to the differences between them and adults—putting the teens back together on the same side of a different conflict.

Hughes also explores issues of social class through the character of Carl (John Kapelos), a janitor. A perceptive viewer will notice that in the opening credits there is a photo of Carl as the "Man of the Year" from his senior year at Shermer High School in 1969. We are left to wonder how Carl went from Man of the Year to the school janitor 16 years after graduation. Whatever Carl's backstory, however, we are not meant to feel sorry for him. He is not a symbol of failure or shame. His character is not a cautionary tale as might be expected in an urban school film. Rather, he is man at peace because he is comfortable with who he is. It is Bender, of all people, who tries to shame Carl by asking condescendingly in front of everyone, "How does one become a janitor?" Unflustered, Carl responds with confidence:

> Carl: You guys think I'm some untouchable peasant, serf, peon? Maybe so. But following a broom around after shitheads like you for the last eight years I've learned a couple things. I look through your letters. I look through your lockers. I listen to your conversations. You don't know that, but I do. I am the eyes and ears of this institution, my friends.

Bender offers a knowing smile of appreciation as Carl leaves the room. Carl is also the only adult in the film whom we have any respect for. In contrast to Mr. Vernon, who Carl catches unethically rummaging through the school's confidential files, Carl is the wise sage of the school. He's the only character who knows who he is; he doesn't have a journey to take or a lesson to learn. His position on the lower rung of the class ladder is not used by Hughes as a way of critiquing inequality or encouraging utilitarian achievement—it's used as a way of demonstrating that you need not be upwardly mobile to have found yourself. That may be fine psychologically for adolescents searching for an adult identity, but it doesn't honestly confront the reality of social class inequality. A janitor is much more likely to be an admirable character in middle-class suburban school films because only in such films is the achievement of a personal *identity*, rather than a social class destination, the primary point of the educational journey.[8] If the point of the journey is social class mobility as in urban school films, then the role of the janitor becomes tragic. The best we can hope for the students in Saturday detention is that they come to a place of similar satisfaction in their lives as Carl—that they learn to be comfortable in their own skin regardless of their social or economic status.

The character growth for Bender comes not from any lesson taught by Mr. Vernon, but by his evolving relationship with the other students, Claire in particular. Through their "group therapy" session, Bender is humanized in the eyes of the other students. His humanity is cemented when Claire, a wealthy popular girl, develops a romantic attachment to him (as unlikely as that seemed for most of the film). Claire sneaks her way to Bender, who has been put in an isolated closet by Mr. Vernon, and kisses him on the neck. Bender, it would seem, now "counts." As the students leave for the day, Claire gives Bender one of her diamond earrings, which he had criticized sharply as a symbol of her unearned privilege. In this intimate moment the diamond becomes a symbol of Claire's romantic interest in him. He accepts and wears the earring without cynicism or irony. The expensive earring is both a symbol for unearned wealth and a symbol of romantic love, which resolves the tension between the resentful working-class Bender and the snobbish upper-class Claire. The two find each other by bridging the social class divide to become potential romantic partners, thereby undermining (or at least dispensing with) the nascent class critique Bender expressed earlier.

PRETTY IN PINK (1986)

Andie Walsh (Molly Ringwald) is from a single-parent, low-income home. Her mom left the family, leaving her dad depressed and unmotivated to find work. Andie is a talented student in a class-diverse public high school. There is a lot of tension between the rich and poor students in the school and there is very little social interaction between the two groups. Andie's best friend Duckie (Jon Cryer) is also a low-income student and has a serious but unrequited crush on her. Blane (Andrew McCarthy) is a rich student who develops a crush on Andie from a distance. He visits her in the record shop where she works with her older friend Iona (Annie Potts), and soon Andie has a crush on Blane as well. Andie begins to fantasize about what it would be like to date someone rich. She even cruises wealthy neighborhoods to imagine what it would be like to live in a mansion.

Blane asks her out and they first go to a party at his rich friend Steff's (James Spader) house. Steff had previously propositioned Andie, but his lecherous overture had been rebuffed in no uncertain terms. At the party, Blane's friends are unwelcoming to Andie, so they decide to go to a club where Andie and her friends hang out. Blane is uncomfortable and is treated rudely by Duckie, who is furious that Andie would date someone from such a crowd of arrogant and selfish rich kids whose lives differ so much from his own. Upon learning that Andie is dating Blane, Duckie exclaims, "Blane?! His name is Blane?! That's a major appliance. That's not a name!"

Despite the difficulties of finding a social space where they both feel welcome and comfortable, Blane asks Andie to go to the prom. She excitedly agrees, but Andie is torn by the social class differences between them and has doubts about continuing to pursue the relationship. She has a heart-to-heart conversation with her dad that convinces her to stick with it:

Mr. Walsh: Who is this guy?
Andie: His name's Blane. He's a senior. He's so beautiful. Umm. He's a . . . richie.
Mr. Walsh: A whatie?
Andie: A richie. It's kind of stupid. It's just, his family has a lot of money.
Mr. Walsh: Is that a problem?
Andie: No. It's just weird. His friends have a lot of money. He has a lot of money. He drives a BMW. I am not really sure they can accept me.
Mr. Walsh: What does that mean? You like him. He likes you. What his friends think shouldn't make a difference.
Andie: Yeah, but it's not just his friends. It's my friends, too. It's everybody. I'm not real secure about it.
Mr. Walsh: So take the heat . . . It's worth it.
Andie: Is it?
Mr. Walsh: Well, isn't it?

Blane is also criticized by his friends for crossing class boundaries to date Andie. Steff says, "If you want your piece of low-grade ass, fine. Take it, you know. But if you do, you are not going to have a friend." Blane gives in to the peer pressure and backs out of the prom date. Sad but undeterred, Andie makes a homemade pink prom dress and goes to the dance by herself. She meets Duckie there, but Blane, also there alone and looking sad, approaches Andie and declares his love for her. Ever a romantic at heart, even the lovesick Duckie encourages her to be with Blane. In an ending that shows that love can triumph over class divisions, Andie and Blane embrace and kiss in the parking lot outside the dance.

The original ending had Andie ending up in a romantic relationship at the prom with her social-class peer, Duckie.[9] Test audiences, however, hated that ending—perhaps because Blane is so much dreamier than Duckie. But I suggest that audiences also wanted Andie to experience upward social mobility. Rather than achieving that mobility through the application of a work ethic in school (as we see in many urban school films), we see it here through her choice of a rich boyfriend. If you can't beat them, join them. Andie, as a Cinderella-like character, finds her rich Prince Charming. As Anthony C. Bleach has argued about gender and social class in Hughes's films, Andie plays the role of the "morally upright poor young woman [who] is somehow more worthy of the trappings of the wealthy than the wealthy themselves."[10] Andie gets her cake and eats it, too. She is the moral victor and she is rewarded with riches. Tellingly, Blane loses nothing but an obnoxious friend. His class status was never threatened.

As in *The Breakfast Club*, we see upward mobility achieved in *Pretty in Pink* not through utilitarian effort but through romantic love. The great divide between the rich and the working class is not depicted as one of class exploitation, unearned privileges, power differentials, or unequal structural opportunities. Rather, the great class divide is depicted as a chasm between friendship groups. Again, social class becomes a vehicle through which Hughes shows how adolescents struggle with their identities and express themselves by breaking tradition, crossing boundaries, and being true to themselves. Although, to be fair, there is a hint of utilitarianism in *Pretty in Pink*—Andie explains that the reason she works so hard in school is so she doesn't have to work in a record shop her whole life (although that seems like a perfectly content life for small-business owner Iona). Here, the dramatic social class tension of the film is resolved not in the classroom, but at the prom.

As in *The Breakfast Club*, the blame for cross-class conflict is depicted as one equally shared by the rich and the poor. Blane's rich friends and Andie's poor friends are both obstacles to the expression of true love. Social class differences are not portrayed as the result of inequality in power or privilege, but as idiosyncratic character differences that can be overcome through interpersonal relationships, not structural change. Timothy Shary has argued similarly. In the teen pics of the '80's, he writes, love is depicted "as a delirious solution to working-class limitations and upper-class ignorance." [11] Shary correctly notes that while the rich may be humbled by the moral lessons of the poor, they never have to risk their economic status. The lessons they learned are taught in the currency of love.

SOME KIND OF WONDERFUL (1987)

Some Kind of Wonderful (1987) is somewhat of a retread of *Pretty in Pink*, but with a twist ending. Keith (Eric Stoltz) is a high school student from the wrong side of the very literal train tracks. His working-class dad sells tires for a living and Keith works at a gas station. He has a crush on Amanda (Lea Thompson), who also lives in his working-class neighborhood, but she is dating a rich, arrogant jerk named Hardy (Craig Sheffer). In one of the first scenes of the film, we see Keith gazing upon Amanda from a distance and then, self-consciously, his eyes fall to his greasy hands. Amanda is of his neighborhood, but she has transcended it by dating Hardy and joining the rich and popular social crowd at school. Keith's best friend is the similarly working-class Watts (Mary Stuart Masterson), who secretly has an unrequited crush on Keith. When Keith tells Watts that he has a crush on Amanda, Watts is hurt, but she's also incredulous because Amanda, she says, has joined the "big money, cruel hearts society" now that she "runs with the rich and beautiful."

Keith's dad is determined to get his son into college so he can have a more financially comfortable life than he does. He wishes Keith would pursue utilitarian success and upward class mobility. He urges his son to think seriously about his future because he has "a shot to be the first guy in this family who doesn't have to wash his hands after a day's work." Keith, however, is an artist and doesn't share his dad's utilitarian middle-class dreams of college. To his dad's horror, Keith withdraws all his college savings from the bank to impress Amanda on an expensive date because he wants "to show this girl that I'm as good as anybody else." Furious, his dad says to Keith, "You don't know what's important! You don't know what the hell you are talking about!" Keith replies with a speech that is typical of the expressive individuality celebrated in suburban school films: "I do know what the hell I'm talking about! You just never listen to me. You only hear what you want. Would you listen to me for once? . . . I'm not going to college. It's over. This whole dream. It's not what I wanted . . . when does my life belong to me?"

Apparently, Keith's life finally belongs to him later that night because, notwithstanding his father's objections, he spends his entire college savings on the elaborate date to impress Amanda. Keith's idea of an impressive date is one that apes the styles and tastes of wealthy adults. This high school junior uses his college savings to rent a fancy vintage car (which he asks Watts to chauffeur). He takes Amanda to an expensive gourmet restaurant where he orders caviar. They go to an art museum after hours. They go to the Hollywood Bowl for the romantic and classy atmosphere. And, ultimately, Keith gifts Amanda diamond earrings that cost him thousands of dollars: "In this box is my future. Every cent I've ever earned. It's for you."

Later in the evening, Amanda comes to the realization that she wants to learn to stand on her own—not to be propped up by a man or by the social status of her wealthy friends. Therefore, she returns the earrings and rejects Keith. Belatedly, Keith finally realizes whom he should be with. He chases after Watts, who had left the party in tears. He offers her the expensive diamond earrings and she accepts, saying, "I wanted these. I really wanted these." The movie ends with Keith telling Watts, "You look good wearing my future."

Diamond earrings again. Just as in *The Breakfast Club* when rich Claire is criticized by Bender for wearing the diamonds that her daddy gave her, that she didn't earn with her own money, the diamond earrings in *Some Kind of Wonderful* represent high social status, the closed club of the elite. They represent exclusion and class status. They represent Keith's sacrificed future. And, ultimately, in both films, they represent love. Amanda rejects the earrings as a way of rejecting Keith. Watts accepts them as a way of accepting Keith. She is also poor, but accepts them as a symbol of belonging, perhaps of class striving, but rather than working for them or earning them, she takes them because of their romantic implications.

In Hughes's films, the importance of teen romance trumps the importance of social class, school, work, and utilitarian class mobility. Upward mobility is romantic mobility—achieved only in sexual relationships and expressive individualism, not utilitarian achievement. In an urban school film, an upwardly mobile utilitarian student would have sold the earrings to buy a college education and a more secure material future after being scolded by an adult. Keith, rather, ignores the sensible utilitarian advice of his father. Instead of learning the lesson that you can't buy love or social status, that you need to plan for the future, that you need to invest in yourself, he gifts away his material future in favor of love. It is not irrelevant that Keith is White. Had Keith been a non-White student in one of the urban school films, his choices would never have been painted as romantic and noble. What makes Keith's character different is the unspoken, taken-for-granted privilege of Whiteness that allows for Keith to dismiss the lessons of middle-class suburban utilitarian individualism and still triumph as an expressive individual.

Once again in Hughes's work, diamond earrings become the class-based vehicle for romantic attachment. However, rather than using love as a vehicle to upward mobility as in *Pretty in Pink*, Keith ultimately rejects the higher-status Amanda in favor of the much more conventionally working-class Watts. It is as if Duckie is redeemed! Even though Watts doesn't strive to be part of the rich and popular crowd, she accepts the diamond earrings with glee. These earrings do represent Keith's future—his lost chance at upward mobility. Yet, in the end, they serve as a symbol of Keith's realization about who he is and who he is romantically interested in. The earrings, in other words, become the vehicle through which Keith expresses his individualism, by rejecting a utilitarian path to upward mobility. Coming to terms with one's social class or finding a way to transcend it becomes a sign of growing up—of finding one's self.

FERRIS BUELLER'S DAY OFF (1986)

Social class tension is not as visible in *Ferris Bueller's Day Off*. Here, most of the characters are firmly in the upper middle class (or higher) and there is little dramatic tension explicitly organized around social classes or inequality. Nonetheless, Hughes still offers us lessons in these films about social class, individual identity, and personal growth. Ferris Bueller (Matthew Broderick) and his friends are rich. Ferris is comfortable in his own skin, and comfortable with his privilege, which he takes for granted. His girlfriend Sloane (Mia Sara) and his best friend Cameron (Alan Ruck) are wealthy, but less certain about their identities and less certain about the status of their futures. Between the two,

Cameron's character is more developed. His unhappy home life and abusive father contribute to his own low self-esteem, neuroses, and uncertainty about the future. Cameron is the one character who has some growing to do. Ferris is already fully developed and at ease (and Sloane plays a surprisingly minor role).

Ferris concocts a plan to take the day off from school, and he enlists Sloane and Cameron in his machinations. For Ferris's plan to work, it is crucial for Cameron to borrow his father's priceless 1961 Ferrari, and he reluctantly agrees to do so. The three teens spend the day driving in the Ferrari, eating lunch at a fancy restaurant, going to the Art Institute of Chicago, attending a Cubs game, going to the top of the Sears Tower, and participating in a Von Steuben Day Parade in downtown Chicago. It is a spectacularly carefree day of three privileged youth playing the roles of rich adults after deceiving the school and their parents. It all goes according to plan until the very end, when Cameron accidentally destroys his father's Ferrari.

The destruction of the car offers a moment of clarity for Cameron. He realizes that he now can't avoid a confrontation with his abusive father. He'll have to face him, and he relishes the opportunity. The destruction of the car is not so much a financial concern to Cameron as it is a chance to express anger at his father for loving the car more than he loves his son. Cameron's reaction leaves no doubt about the social class position of his family. Anyone who can feel relatively cavalier about the destruction of a priceless Ferrari because it will be an entrée to an honest discussion with his father certainly doesn't have financial worries. Instead, the expensive car becomes a symbol of personal growth for Cameron. The expensive automobile is neither an aspirational symbol nor a marker of social class. Instead, it is a vehicle (literally) for Cameron to figure out who he is in relationship to his abusive father. It becomes a coming-of-age moment—a chance for Cameron to face his demons by facing his father and standing on his own as an expressive individual.

CONCLUSION

In high school films, adolescence becomes a metaphorical arena in which social class conflict and resolution play out. Americans generally are not adept at talking about class as a social category. Our individualism interferes with our ability to see the advantages and disadvantages of our social class position. Americans like to think that all things are possible for all people of all backgrounds if we work hard enough. If we see our lives affected by social categories at all, we tend to see race and gender rather than class as the identities that define our lives. Nonetheless, social class is there beneath the surface of our individualism and it often finds expression in popular culture whether we easily recognize it or not.

Adolescence is a time of life in which we like to think that all things are possible. It is a time when we struggle to determine our identity, to plan our future, and to negotiate relationships with our peers, parents, and authority. It is a moment in our lives when everything seems possible, but when every choice seems to acutely determine the path our lives will take. Adolescence is a particularly rich and dramatic time of life. As such, adolescence—the promise and the threat—lends itself well to cinematic exploration. It also lends itself well to explorations of how Americans understand social class. The depictions of adolescents in Hughes's 1980s teen films indirectly illustrate how Americans view social class and social mobility through the filter of American individualism.

But adulthood is just around the corner. Conformity, rules, restrictions, expectations, and utility are waiting for us when we "grow up." Adolescence in Hughes's films represents expressive individualism. It represents freedom. It represents Thoreau's ideal of marching to the beat of your own drummer. However, adolescence as freedom is only possible for the middle classes. Expressive individualism—non-conformity—is a luxury of the privileged. Poor, mostly non-White students in high school films must conform to utilitarian ideals within the constraints of the school in order to have a happy ending. Their youthful expressions of individuality are punished. Sex is rarely depicted and, when it is, there is often a threat of pregnancy or disease hanging over it. Drug use often results in prison or death. Hollywood asks urban, poor, and mostly non-White kids to quickly become adults. On the other hand, Hollywood asks suburban, middle-class, and mostly White kids to stay kids a little longer. Illicit drug use brings teens closer together in *The Breakfast Club*. Cutting school is an amusing pastime in *Ferris Bueller's Day Off*.

Social class inequality is not fully analyzed or criticized in Hughes's work. Social class is worn as yet another identity in the complicated social world of high school. The structure of social class is never questioned. It is as if some people are rich or poor, just like some people are men or women, some are jocks, and some are nerds. Social class categories are naturalized, not placed in social context. The problem of social class is depicted primarily as one of miscommunication and misunderstanding between the classes, not as power differences between the classes. The viewer is left to think that solving the problem of class conflict and inequality requires us to merely improve communication. The films suggest that improvement in class conflict requires change by *both* parties—as if the poor and the rich are equally responsible for the inequality between them. It may be asking too much of a teen comedy, but if Hughes was able to describe and critique the cliques that govern the social world of high schools with complexity and sensitivity, then he certainly could have offered more sustained and sophisticated critical commentary about the inequities of social class that undergird such social worlds.

Hughes comes close to a more trenchant critique of social class inequality through Bender's character in *The Breakfast Club*. For instance, Bender contrasts his troubled home life with his perception of Brian's ideal middle-class home life with loving parents. However, we learn later that his perception of Brian's life is biased, and that Brian too has problems at home with his parents—as if there were an equivalence between Bender's working-class problems and Brian's middle-class problems. Furthermore, the potential for any meaningful class critique is lost when Claire gifts Bender her expensive diamond earring, which previously had been the symbol of unearned wealth and privilege. Bender's critique of the earrings is defanged when it becomes the symbol of a budding cross-class teen romance. Bender accepts the earring, and in so doing accepts Claire's status.

But social class has more weight in our lives than does popularity or romantic relationships. Social class patterns our life chances. That is, it lays out for us the game board we are to play our lives on and it doles out the resources with which we navigate the game of life. Social class resources (education, occupation, income, and wealth) reverberate through our lives. They pattern what is possible for us and color how we see the world. By reducing social class status to yet another individual characteristic that influences interpersonal relationships, Hughes missed an opportunity to explain the richness of teens' lives in the social world beyond the high school library.

NOTES

1. Duane Byrge, "Review of *The Breakfast Club*," *The Hollywood Reporter*, February 15, 1985, https://www.hollywoodreporter.com/news/breakfast-club-thrs-1985-review-773357.
2. Martin M. Marger, *Social Inequality: Patterns and Processes*, 3rd edn (New York: McGraw Hill, 2005), 54.
3. Robert Bulman, *Hollywood Goes to High School: Cinema, Schools, and American Culture* (New York: Worth, 2015).
4. Robert Bellah, et al., *Habits of the Heart: Individualism and Commitment in American Life* (Berkeley: University of California Press, 1985).
5. Bellah, 32.
6. Henry David Thoreau, *Walden* (New York: Signet, 1961), 216.
7. Penelope Eckert, *Jocks and Burnouts. Social Categories and Identity in High School* (New York: Teachers College Press, 1989).
8. For other hero janitors in suburban school films see *Disturbing Behavior* (1998), *Not Another Teen Movie* (2001), or *17 Again* (2009).
9. Susannah Gora, *You Couldn't Ignore Me if You Tried: The Brat Pack, John Hughes, and Their Impact on a Generation* (New York: Three Rivers Press, 2010).
10. Anthony C. Bleach, "Postfeminist Cliques? Class, Postfeminism, and the Molly Ringwald–John Hughes Films," *Cinema Journal*, 49, no. 3 (Spring 2010), 42.
11. Timothy Shary, "Buying Me Love: '80s Class-Clash Teen Romances," *Journal of Popular Culture*, 44, no. 3, 565.

CHAPTER 13

The Unbearable Whiteness of Being in a John Hughes Movie

Frances Smith

A brief but significant scene occurs early on in *Sixteen Candles* (1984), the film that began John Hughes's memorable run of teen films in the mid-1980s. The film stars Molly Ringwald as Samantha, a girl who is overlooked and forgotten even by her own parents. In her sympathetic portrayal of the character, Ringwald was cemented as an embodiment of vulnerability and "charismatic normality,"[1] and began a significant triptych of film collaborations with Hughes in the mid-1980s, following up *Sixteen Candles* with *The Breakfast Club* (1985) and *Pretty in Pink* (1986).[2] It is in the first of this film cycle that Sam (Ringwald) and her friend Randy (Liane Curtis) reflect on Sam's ideal sixteenth birthday party:

> Sam: A big party, band, and tons of people.
> Randy: And a big Trans Am in the driveway with a ribbon around it and some incredibly gorgeous guy that you, like, meet in France and you do it on a cloud without getting pregnant or herpes.
> Sam: I don't need the cloud.
> Randy: Just the pink Trans Am and the guy.
> Sam: A Black one.
> Randy: A Black guy?
> Sam: A black Trans Am; a pink guy.

The combination of romantic fantasies, yearning for hi-spec consumer goods, and the ready dismissal of a "Black guy" as an object of desire, speaks to the priorities of Hughes's suburban youth universe.[4] Sam's correction of the "pink guy" instead of the "pink Trans Am" might work to highlight the racial specificity of White people, which, as many scholars of Whiteness have observed, are otherwise constructed as a social norm, without a racial identity.[5] As will become apparent in this chapter Sam's rejection of the very possibility of a "Black guy" as her lover is far from the only problematic element of *Sixteen Candles*. However, at this point it seems clear that the film is engaged in a reification of Whiteness as an unmarked racial category, and as the default mold of desirable masculinity for the two young women.

This chapter investigates the representation of non-White characters throughout Hughes's teen-oriented work. In doing so, it will argue that his films are principally invested in the reification of Whiteness as a norm and as an ideal model of social life. Further, I suggest that by displaying the heterogeneity of White identities in the tropes for which Hughes's youth films are admired, the films also show the variety and dominance of Whiteness. Hughes has been widely praised for his sensitive portrayal of teenage life, and in particular, owing to his 1980s collaborations with Molly Ringwald, for his construction of girlhood in 1980s teen cinema.[6] Notably, Jonathan Bernstein argues that female characters in Hughes's films are exceptions to their 1980s contemporaries, who, rather than merely displaying "good-natured tolerance in the face of stalking, voyeurism, or fumbled attempts at seduction,"[7] were instead calling attention to the acute social divisions that were increasingly apparent during that decade. Nonetheless, Hughes's construction of racial identity has been subject to far less attention, with critics only now starting to come to terms with the films' overwhelming Whiteness.[8] In this chapter I first examine instances in which non-White characters appear in his films, before moving on to consider how Whiteness is reified and nuanced precisely through Hughes's well-documented attention to social class and gender roles.

DEFENDING THE UNBEARABLE WHITENESS OF HUGHES'S WORK

One reason for which the construction of racial identity in Hughes's work has remained largely free from scholarly scrutiny is surely the almost monoracial universes that Hughes creates. Yet as Phil Chidester argues, it is a mistake to presume that, if texts do not overtly grapple with questions of race, that such matters are not present rhetorically, in their very absence.[9] This chapter aims to uncover some of the effects of the rhetorical absences. It should be acknowledged, of course, that John Hughes is far from the only filmmaker to have provided such an overly White depiction of an environment that is presented as universal. Yet, perhaps as a result of their popularity, longevity, and ability to stand in for the teen genre as a whole, Hughes's films have been the subjects of particularly vociferous criticisms, more than other 1980s films with similar problems.

One paradox within popular and scholarly discussion of Hughes is critics' praise of what they deem to be his authenticity, while that same authenticity provides Hughes with his key defense of the overwhelming Whiteness in his films. He argued that, "I think it's wise for people to concern themselves with the things they know about . . . I'd really like to do something on gangs, but to do that, I've got to spend some time with gang members. I'd feel extremely self-conscious writing about something I don't know."[10] In Hughes's logic, since the North Shore Chicago suburbs in which his films are located, and where he grew up, are largely White and middle class, then the films ought to follow suit. Significantly, that same construction of authenticity is key to the ongoing cultural currency of Hughes's teen output.

Hadley Freeman's study of 1980s Hollywood is nostalgic for the relative progressiveness, diversity and, perhaps surprisingly for a decade of filmmaking principally associated with mainstream genres and blockbusters, the individuality of American films made in the 1980s in comparison with the present day. One significant area in which the individuality and authenticity of Hughes's films comes into play is in the reported input of his teenage cast. Indeed, Freeman reports that Hughes encouraged his young actors to wear their own clothes in the films, and discussed his films' music with them.[11] Perhaps the most obvious fruit of Hughes's conscious effort to portray contemporary teenage culture on screen was his use of the Psychedelic Furs song "Pretty in Pink" as the title track for the film of the same name, which was recommended to him by Molly Ringwald.[12] It is this construction of authenticity that allows Hughes to create a narrowly White vision of adolescence. Nonetheless, I argue that authenticity does not license Hughes's sole focus on White adolescence. As Klein argues, one does not require first-hand experience of "gangs," themselves a cipher for a particular idea of racialized, alienated youth, in order to include one or two characters of color in a high school drama.[13] Further, Hughes's teen tales do not merely exclude non-White characters,[14] but, as I demonstrate, actively belittle and undermine them as well. As a result, I argue that Hughes's claims to authenticity do not excuse his work from criticism.

The claim that including non-White characters would disrupt the creator's unique creative vision remains an argument put forward by many contemporary filmmakers. Consider Lena Dunham, who, in defending her show's notable absence of people of color from her Brooklyn-based TV show, *Girls* (2011–17), claims that she wrote "something that was super-specific to [her] experience." Channeling Hughes, she then goes on to say that she would always "want to avoid rendering an experience [she] can't speak to accurately."[15] More recently still, filmmaker Sofia Coppola defended her decision to omit the only African American character from her 2017 adaptation of Thomas Cullinan's novel, *The Beguiled*, on the basis that including Hallie, the household's slave, would have significantly altered the film's dynamic. Indeed, Coppola argues that including Hallie would itself be problematic, claiming that "young girls watch my films and this was not the depiction of an African American character that I would want to show them."[16] Despite Don Siegel's 1971 film managing to include Hallie (played by Mae Mercer), and give the character some limited agency, Coppola's film begins with a simple omission: "the slaves left." As a result, the question of race relations in the Antebellum South during the American Civil War is conveniently elided. In all these examples, the limitations of the (White) creators' own experiences are constructed as allowing them to ignore the presence of those around them of other ethnicities.

This same type of erasure is also apparent in the existing scholarship on John Hughes, and the teen movie more generally. In my own work, I have argued that many Hollywood teen movies possess complicated racial politics, before turning my attention elsewhere.[17] Similarly, Christina Lee's study of the cultural afterlife of John Hughes and the brat pack acknowledges the Whiteness of those 1980s films, yet argues that her own work will not be the place where these are addressed.[18] However, Richard Dyer persuasively argues that race is never *not* a factor in considering representation and the construction of identity in visual culture.[19] This chapter therefore serves not only to highlight those instances of erasure such as in the opening excerpt, but also to consider what is at stake in the unbearable Whiteness of—or rather, the rhetorical absence of racial discourses in—Hughes's teen movies. When the director is so firmly associated with a nuanced take on suburban teenage life, and "took teenagers as seriously as they took themselves,"[20] what does this say about the construction of Whiteness on screen?

STEREOTYPING AND APPROPRIATION IN THE HUGHES OEUVRE

This piece began with an excerpt from *Sixteen Candles*, a film that as a whole probably provides the most overt racial stereotyping of Hughes's entire oeuvre. Researching Hughes's background while reflecting on her own experience working on his films, Molly Ringwald unearthed material from Hughes's *National Lampoon* days, and was unpleasantly surprised by their crassness. For instance, in the "Hughes Engagement Guide," the director offers "how to determine if a woman has ancestors of different races based on what her relatives look like."[21] If he were able, Hughes might well respond that such material was produced in jest, and not intended to be taken as a serious manual for the curious bachelor. Just as in *Sixteen Candles*, though, the unspoken norm is one of Whiteness. Any humor that might be derived from these jokes is squarely aimed at the prospect of inadvertently marrying a woman of mixed racial heritage. The narrowness of Whiteness does not permit racial ambiguity of the type described here.

A further illustration of the types of crass racial stereotyping present in *Sixteen Candles* occurs in the form of Long Duk Dong, a Chinese exchange student played by Japanese American actor, Gedde Watanabe.[22] Dong is a temporary resident in Sam's family home, and is presented paradoxically as a sexual threat, but one that lacks real menace, while also as an individual that is wholly undesirable. Consider his move upside down from his top bunk bed to accost Sam with "What's up, hot stuff?" and her swift rejection of him. The scene is capped with the sound of a comical gong, recalling Mickey Rooney's woeful outing as Mr. Yunioshi in *Breakfast at Tiffany's* (1961). In this, Dong is squarely in line with the coarse caricatures of the *National Lampoon* franchise.

Significantly, through Long Duk Dong, *Sixteen Candles* also provides a space in which abject racial identity is used to delineate what counts as abject gender and sexual identity as well. The character's unusually small stature is made apparent in his relationship with a larger girl with an unflattering moniker, "the lumberjack" (Debbie Pollack), who looms over him when they embrace, and who works out on an exercise bike with Dong perched on her lap. Dong is thus both feminized through his diminutive size, but also expressly defined as heterosexual through both his harassment of Sam and his subsequent relationship. It is through the construction of racial stereotyping that Dong embodies these contradictions, that is, as a sexual lothario who in fact presents no sexual or physical threat, without the possibility that he might be coded as homosexual. As Kat Chow observes, Long Duk Dong's character tapped into and reified for a new generation stereotypes surrounding Asian Americans, namely "the socially inept mute; the lecherous but sexually inept loser."[23] Hughes uses racial stereotypes in order to represent his disquiet over non-normative gender and sexual identity.

The selective deployment of non-White racial identities provides a means through which Hughes might portray non-normative gender and sexual identities within a mainstream teen film. As I have argued elsewhere, the teen movie, whose conventions Hughes's films helped to coalesce into a coherent genre, is generally devoted to depicting sexual coming-of-age on screen.[24] The portrayal of Duckie (Jon Cryer), a White character in *Pretty in Pink* provides a significant example of the type of mediation of gender and sexual identity that Hughes undertakes through appropriation of non-White identity. In the film, Duckie shares Andie's (Molly Ringwald) multi-layered, post-punk style, which combines elements from older, respectable clothing styles of the past to excessively create what the character himself describes as a "volcanic ensemble." He thus combines smart shirts with bolo ties, elaborate jewelry, and mismatching jackets and trousers. Despite Duckie's pursuit of Andie throughout the film, the former's frequently frenzied, parodic dialogue, such as his suggestion to two girls in the bathroom that "either one, or the both of you, could be pregnant by the holidays. What do you say?" is not to be taken seriously despite its latent sexual aggression. Ringwald says she makes sense of Duckie's indeterminacy through her belief that the character is based on a gay friend of hers.²⁵ While an intriguing idea, I do not believe that the film lends itself well to that conclusion, not least because *Pretty in Pink* was reportedly to conclude with Andie and Duckie as a couple.²⁶ For the purposes of this chapter I want to assess how Duckie's indeterminate gender and sexual identity is mediated through his appropriation of race.

In one notable scene, Duckie turns up unexpectedly as Andie and Iona (Annie Potts) are closing up the record shop Trax. As they complete their tasks, Iona puts on an Otis Redding record, "Try a Little Tenderness," in a knowing bid to aggravate her "yuppie" neighbors who don't care for the track's introductory gunfire sound effects. It is at this point that Duckie unexpectedly appears, suddenly lip-synching and dancing to the song in order, it appears, to seduce Andie. In this, the character takes on—albeit briefly—the persona of this iconic, Black artist, whose words and music Duckie believes will have the power to seduce Andie more effectively than he ever could alone. As such, the appropriation of non-White identity provides a means for a White man to assert his distinction and worth.

Duckie's performance is presented as ludicrous, both to Andie and Iona, and to the extra-diegetic audience alike. Howard Deutch, who cut his teeth as a director of music videos, and was therefore no stranger to the art of choreographing lip-synching and dance on screen, here uses cinematography precisely in order to undermine Duckie's seduction. Discordant framing makes the dance look absurd: medium close-ups fill the frame with the character's intense facial expression, while cuts to his feet—often the locus of expertise when deployed in the Hollywood musical—conversely display the lack of artistry in his movements. In turn, crosscuts to Iona and Andie's bemused expressions inform the extra-diegetic audience that the characters are not enjoying the performance. Rather, it is a source of irritation for the pair. When the dance develops further, Duckie's ever more expansive movements are obscured by the merchandise and shop displays so that we only occasionally see his head move up and down behind the stands. Shown in long shot, the moments show the unsuitability of the shop as a place for seduction, and by extension the inappropriateness of Duckie's actions themselves. When Duckie moves to the crux of the song, at which he lies back and thrusts in the air, the scene's cinematography ensures that the dance is taken as comical, rather than seductive. Indeed, by this point, he has become so absorbed in the performance that he has not registered his love interest's evident exasperation. This performance of seduction has unequivocally failed.

It seems significant that Duckie's excessive performance intersects with a song that, for a paean to tenderness, is itself unduly forceful. As Black popular music specialist Emily Lordi observes, Redding's song is "distinctly untender," with its ever-building crescendo, strong brass tones, and Redding's powerful vocal style itself.²⁷ For Lordi, Redding's forcefulness is connected with the song's revolutionary potential, which would have been apparent to listeners at the time of its 1966 release. It's undeniably a stretch to consider Duckie channeling the African American civil rights movement in the scene. Yet it should be acknowledged that "Try a Little Tenderness" provides the only track by an African American in a film otherwise dominated by (White) post-punk. Further, the internal contradictions inherent to Redding's track, which advocates tenderness in a vigorous way, provides a vehicle through which Duckie's own indeterminacies might be mirrored. Indeed, he is a character who claims to adore Andie, yet whose suggestions of love continue to ring hollow. While Ringwald believes that the character is gay,[28] the sly look to the camera when he pairs off with an attractive blond student in the final scenes at the prom appears to dispute that assertion. Once again, Hughes uses the selective deployment of non-White identities precisely to layer and add complexity to his White characters.

As I have demonstrated above, Duckie's performance of Otis Redding's song presents a failure to embody seductive, heterosexual, and White norms of masculinity. This failure is made all the more apparent through the character's evident distance from the masculinity embodied by Otis Redding. Elsewhere in *Pretty in Pink*, Duckie's lack of coherence is made apparent. Steff (James Spader) cattily refers to him as "the most *interesting* prom date" that Andie could have chosen for the event, and is typically scathing of the character's lack of access to markers of class status. In contrast to Duckie, who bears a chippy vulnerability throughout the film, Ferris Bueller, played by Matthew Broderick in *Ferris Bueller's Day Off* (1986), comically epitomes White, upper-middle-class masculinity. For Shirley Steinberg and Joe L. Kincheloe, Ferris is the exemplar of Hughes's "maverick" characters, whose positioning as White, male, and upper middle class permits their deviations from authority, which in turn is shown to be slow, ineffective, and immoral by comparison.[29] Ferris continually succeeds in outwitting various figures of authority during his extravagant day off in Chicago, to the obvious delight and disbelief of his friends. In contrast to the presentation of Duckie in *Pretty in Pink*, which never gives us much insight into the character except through the eyes of Andie, in *Ferris Bueller* the titular character is permitted moments of direct address which work to draw the audience into his point of view. It is the coherence of the White, upper-middle-class identity that allows Ferris to perform in a similar manner to Duckie, and that allows it to be successful.

The film culminates in a parade, which Ferris first hijacks and eventually leads. While Duckie's interruption in Trax was perceived as a tiresome disruption to the two women closing the shop, Ferris's infiltration into the dance routine is received with delight. The German dancers are initially taken aback by his sudden appearance, but soon warm to him as the performance goes on. The music style changes and The Beatles' "Twist and Shout" starts to play, at which point the parade suddenly finds itself accompanied by a group of African American dancers, who make their way down a flight of steps to join the parade.

The racial dynamics of the bodies that are allowed to be seen and heard are significant here. The Beatles, of course, were a group of four White men from Liverpool. Yet this song, which appeared on their first album, *Please Please Me*, in 1963, notably takes up the scratchy qualities of the Stax/Volt records used principally by soul artists, including Otis Redding. Indeed, while "Twist and Shout" was originally recorded in 1961 by a Black group, The Top Notes, the song remains best known as a Beatles track. Here, then, we have the complex politics of cultural appropriation throughout the history of popular music and cinema. While the music and style may have initially been made famous by African American performers, it is through their charismatic, White mouthpieces that their work has become well known. We might consider here who is allowed to count as rebellious, and under what terms in Hughes's films. Ferris is normative, charismatic, and upper middle class, unlike his earlier equivalent who is positioned as working class, and possessing a somewhat incoherent gender and sexual identity. Nonetheless, what unites Duckie and Ferris is their Whiteness. And in both *Ferris Bueller's Day Off* and *Pretty in Pink*, "black elements are acknowledged and disavowed"[30] in order to highlight the complexities and strengths of these male characters. The following section examines how the very absence of racial discourses and stereotypes works to reify the boundaries of Whiteness.

NOT QUITE WHITE? INTERSECTIONS OF RACE AND CLASS

In his study of Whiteness, Richard Dyer persuasively argues that in order for it to appear as a racialized category, and thus to dislodge Whiteness from its positioning as a social norm, or shorthand for "human" itself, it too must be made strange.[31] One especially potent moment of Whiteness being made strange occurred in *Get Out* (2017), a horror/satire of American racial politics. In the film's final scenes, by which time the monstrousness of the White family at its center has become clear, Rose (Allison Williams) is shown in medium shot sipping milk from a striped straw, while listening to the *Dirty Dancing* (1987) soundtrack. In this instance, she presents an image of Whiteness that is both comedic and horrifying in its quotidian banality.

I want to suggest that Hughes achieves something equivalent in the specificities of his references to contemporary youth culture in his 1980s films especially. That is, Hughes does not render Whiteness horrifying. Rather, he delineates its contours so precisely that his films enable his audiences to see how White adolescence is constructed in the particular time and place in which he operates. While Hughes has used authenticity as a defense against representing multiple adolescent experiences in his films, I contend that the very construction of authenticity that Hughes espouses both shows the specificity of White adolescence, and conversely, demonstrates that his teen movies are invested in the delineation and reification of Whiteness as a norm.

And to that end, this section turns its attention to the most influential of Hughes's teen films, *The Breakfast Club*. Many scholars of the teen movie have noted the ways in which Hughes took the template established by "the princess, the brain, the athlete, the basket case and the criminal" and simply reapplied it elsewhere.[32] *The Breakfast Club*, of course, does not feature the type of racial stereotyping or appropriation delineated elsewhere in this piece. On the contrary, it is a hermetically sealed space of Whiteness that takes place almost entirely shut off from the outside world. Nonetheless, from the outset, the film is keen to demonstrate that despite the characters all being held in detention during this particular Saturday, they all inhabit strikingly different worlds from one another. Indeed, Claire (Molly Ringwald) confirms Brian's (Anthony Michael Hall) suspicion that upon their return to school, the film's "princess" and "athlete" characters will not associate with the likes of him. The film is concerned with finding commonalities between these angst-ridden teens, despite their surface distinctions.

Phil Chidester suggests that in narratives in which Whiteness is reinforced through the rhetorical absence of racial discourse, or the literal absence of non-White characters, that a circle is used to create boundaries that are not to be transgressed. In proscenium staging such as that used in the three-camera sitcom, the audience is invited to fill the gap created by those three walls.[33] In *The Breakfast Club*, the students are seated firstly at desks all facing one direction, before the characters' movements become much freer, moving not only around the library, but reappropriating other spaces throughout the school. The camera position moves from a broad overview of the scene, to one that reflects that of another student sitting among the characters, either at a nearby desk, or among them in the mezzanine. In this, the film creates a closed circle of Whiteness that interpellates the viewer into its rhetorical exclusion of other races.

What is at stake in Claire and Andy's (Emilio Estevez) rejection of Allison (Ally Sheedy), Brian, and Bender (Judd Nelson) is inarguably social class. This being a teen movie, representation of social class is filtered through the characters' participation, or lack thereof, in groups that emphasize status within the high school, like the prom committee (not academic clubs, like those in math and physics, Brian's hangouts of choice). Nonetheless, the cars driven by their parents, and the lunches that the characters have had prepared for them, bring social class more acutely into focus through conventionally adult markers of status. Indeed, the lingering shot of the BMW badge on Claire's father's car leaves us in no doubt of the character's social class. On the opposite end of the spectrum, Bender must walk into school himself. Apparent from the film's very opening scenes then, *The Breakfast Club* draws class differences, and the consequences for adolescent life, into sharp focus.

Matt Wray's study of the term "white trash" teases out the liminality in such a construction. For Wray, designating a particular group of people "white trash" is concerned with creating "boundaries, symbolic and social" around Whiteness itself.[34] As he observes, the term both demonstrates that Whiteness, in contrast to much of the scholarship on the term, need not necessarily be dominant (since this group is demonstrably constructed as abject), yet the use of "white" as a modifier suggests that White people being part of the abject is an unusual phenomenon.[35] In this, those deemed to be "white trash" might be considered "not-quite-white," to use Anahid Kassabian's description of those who possess a more complicated relationship to White identity, such as people of Irish, Italian, or Latinx descent.[36] *The Breakfast Club* plays with this liminality, showing that most of the characters are unquestionably privileged, and their angst is no less valid for that, while Mr. Vernon (Paul Gleason) cruelly implies that Bender meets the designation of "white trash." *Pretty in Pink*, a film that features no non-White characters, likewise plays with the boundaries of Whiteness through the lens of social class. Andie is dubbed a "mutant" by the preening Steff, on whom the tables are turned by the end of the film when Blane (Andrew McCarthy) tells Steff that Andie "thinks you're shit. And deep down you know she's right." In both films, the assertion of the abject, whether in the form of trash, mutant, or shit, works to police the boundaries of Whiteness.

Among the most appealing elements of these films are the ways in which those boundaries are made porous. *Pretty in Pink* concludes with the cross-class couple of Andie and Blane, while *The Breakfast Club* not only sees Claire hand a diamond earring to Bender as a token of their brief romance, but Allison and Andy also transcend the boundaries of their school social roles as well. Taking up Jorie Lagerwey and Taylor Nygaard's recent work on what they call "Horrible White People" television shows, I want to suggest that Hughes's focus on the plight of young White people in his 1980s work might contribute to a narrative that shores up White supremacist narratives around White suffering. Lagerwey and Nygaard's study calls attention to a recent wave of 30-minute television comedies, among them, *Catastrophe* (2015–2019), *Broad City* (2014–present), and *Fleabag* (2016–2019), which center on the plight of well-meaning White people. They argue that these shows have worked to reposition White suffering on contemporary television, and in so doing, have shored up the preferred causes of the American far right.[37] These television shows, marketed and aired on both sides of the Atlantic, present White characters' loss of access to markers of middle-class status, notably home ownership and job security. Clearly, Hughes's teen films take place in a rather different context to these contemporary, prestige television shows. Yet given the near universal focus on White characters, and the ways in which non-White identities are instrumentalized and stereotyped, it is also undeniable that Hughes draws attention to the sadness and angst experienced by White characters alone, thereby reinforcing their plight.

CONCLUSIONS

This chapter has examined a number of Hughes's youth films made in the 1980s to argue that, taken together, his work provides a construction of on-screen adolescence that largely excludes non-White characters in a number of distinct ways. Examining *Sixteen Candles*, in which some of Hughes's most overt racial stereotyping occurs, I argued that Chinese exchange student Long Duk Dong was an example of where his crass *National Lampoon* style of comedy had leaked into his teen films, which are generally regarded as being rather more sensitive in tone. Further, this gross racial stereotyping enabled Hughes to create an abject representation of gender and sexuality through Long Duk Dong.

Other Hughes teen films featured White characters providing the mouthpieces for Black culture. In *Pretty in Pink*, that took the form of Duckie's absurd lip-synching to Otis Redding's music. In turn, *Ferris Bueller's Day Off* saw the eponymous character take over a parade, and lead a group of Black dancers. In the disparate fortunes of the two performances, one of which is deemed ridiculous, the other a sign of the character's infallibility, can be found the differences in the characters' social class status. Turning to *The Breakfast Club*, I demonstrated that Hughes is principally invested in portraying small differences between the statuses of characters attending the same school. Arguing that absence of overt referencing from the film does not mean that it has nothing to say about race, I observed the ways in which the film tacitly polices the boundaries of Whiteness. This occurs through exclusive attention to the plight of the all-White characters, through aesthetic decisions that unify the characters into a circle and interpellate viewers into its hold, and through attention to the abject in the evocation of "white trash."

The Breakfast Club is undoubtedly Hughes's most revered work. It is the only one, for instance, to have earned the considerable cachet of the Criterion Collection. It is the one most associated with the director's ear for dialogue and attention to how teenagers perceive the world. Yet it is also the film that, perhaps unwittingly, has the most invested in a multifaceted portrayal of Whiteness, and thereby in reifying Whiteness as a social norm. Of course, after *Some Kind of Wonderful* (1987) just two years later, Hughes changed direction and began to work on family-oriented films, most often in the capacity of writer or producer. Although these films differed substantially in tone and content, their preoccupation with White middle-class suburban characters remained. Indeed, Steinberg and Kincheloe spot a continuation between Ferris Bueller and Kevin McCallister (Macaulay Culkin in *Home Alone* [1990]), and perhaps even Dennis Mitchell (Mason Gamble in *Dennis the Menace* [1993]). It is perhaps unfair to single out John Hughes for his representation of non-White characters, and his seemingly exclusive preoccupation with Whiteness. As I have demonstrated, the contemporary film and television industries must still reckon with these matters. There is also the question of what validity there might be in judging the cultural products of some 30 years previously by the values of present. Yet it is perhaps the rearview perspective that provides the necessary critical distance from the films required to interrogate their construction of youth. When *The Breakfast Club* concluded with the Simple Minds song "Don't You (Forget About Me)," Hughes may just have got what he bargained for.

NOTES

1. Pauline Kael, *Hooked: Film Writings 1985–1988* (New York: Marion Boyers Publishers, 1992), 133.
2. Readers may question why, if John Hughes is not the director, that I include *Pretty in Pink* as an example of Hughes's works. Questions of Hughes's authorship are covered more fully in the introduction to this volume. However, here it suffices to note that Hughes wrote the script for *Pretty in Pink* and produced the film. It is widely acknowledged as a "Hughes film" by scholars of his work. See Anthony Bleach, "Postfeminist Cliques: Class, Postfeminism, and the Molly Ringwald-John Hughes Films," *Cinema Journal*, 49, no. 3 (2010), 44; and Frances Smith, *Rethinking the Hollywood Teen Movie: Gender, Genre and Identity* (Edinburgh: Edinburgh University Press, 2017), 97.
3. Transcription is my own. As of June 22, 2020, the Chicago Manual of Style moved to a preferred use of the capitalized term *Black* in reference to "racial and ethnic identity," and "as a matter of editorial consistency, *White* and similar terms may also be capitalized when used in this sense." We have followed this style accordingly, capitalizing both terms when referring to human races with noun or adjective forms.
4. See Bleach for a thoughtful analysis of the ways in which consumerism is valorized in Hughes's teen texts.
5. Richard Dyer, *White: Essays on Race and Culture* (London: Routledge, 1997); Raka Shome, "Outing Whiteness", *Critical Studies in Media Communication*, 17, no. 3 (2000), 366–71. The reference to a "pink guy" recalls the frequent insult "gammon," which has recently been leveled at a particular type of old White men. See Yasmeen Serhan, "Pork legs are shaking up British politics," *The Atlantic*, May 17, 2018, https://www.theatlantic.com/international/archive/2018/05/is-gammon-racist/560507/.
6. There have also been exceptions to the widespread adulation of Hughes's teen films, notable among them Ann De Vaney, who is particularly vehement in her criticism that the director's portrayal of girls restricts them to the roles of wives and mothers. See "Pretty in Pink? John Hughes Reinscribes Daddy's Girl in Homes and Schools," in *Sugar, Spice and Everything Nice: Cinemas of Girlhood*, eds Frances Gateward and Murray Pomerance (Detroit: Wayne State University Press, 2002), 203.
7. Jonathan Bernstein, *Pretty in Pink: The Golden Age of Teenage Movies* (New York: St. Martin's Griffin, 2007), 173–4.

8. See in particular the following for their thoughtful reflections on Hughes's work: Maulud Sadiq, "Loving John Hughes Movies while Black," Medium, January 24, 2017, https://medium.com/the-brothers/loving-john-hughes-movies-while-black-1c4acba2e628; Kat Chow, "What's So Cringeworthy about Long Duk Dong in Sixteen Candles?" *National Public Radio*, 2017, https://www.npr.org/sections/codeswitch/2015/02/06/384307677/whats-so-cringe-worthy-about-long-duk-dong-in-sixteen-candles?t=1531756678520; Amanda Ann Klein, "'The Breakfast Club' 30 Years Later: A Conversation Across Generations," RogerEbert.com, March 26, 2015, https://www.rogerebert.com/mzs/the-breakfast-club-30-years-later-a-conversation-across-generations.
9. Phil Chidester, "May the Circle Stay Unbroken: Friends, the Presence of Absence, and the Rhetorical Reinforcement of Whiteness," *Critical Studies in Media Communication*, 25, no. 2 (2008), 158.
10. Hughes, quoted in Klein.
11. Hadley Freeman, *Life Moves Pretty Fast: The Lessons We Learned from Eighties Movies* (London: Fourth Estate, 2015), 63.
12. Freeman, 65.
13. Klein.
14. I use the term "non-White" here somewhat reluctantly, since, as Richard Dyer argues, it seems foolish to define swathes of the public by something which they are demonstrably not (1997, 11). Nonetheless, the types of behavior I describe here occur to a number of different demographic groups, none of whom are White. Consequently, the term non-White seems to be the most concise way of expressing this reality.
15. Tambay A. Obenson, "Lena Dunham addresses *Girls* diversity criticism, and why I just don't care," Indiewire, May 8, 2012, http://blogs.indiewire.com/shadowandact/2c060de0-993b-11e1-bcc4-123138165f92.
16. Coppola quoted in Corey Atad, "Lost in Adaptation," Slate, June 20, 2017, http://www.slate.com/articles/arts/culturebox/2017/06/sofia_coppola_s_whitewashed_new_movie_the_beguiled.html?via=gdpr-consent.
17. Smith, 4.
18. Christina Lee, *Screening Generation X: The Politics and Popular Memory of Youth in Contemporary Cinema* (Aldershot: Ashgate, 2010), 19.
19. Dyer, 15.
20. Freeman, 61.
21. Molly Ringwald, "What About 'The Breakfast Club'?: Revisiting the Movies of My Youth in the Age of #MeToo," *The New Yorker*, April 6, 2018, https://www.newyorker.com/culture/personal-history/what-about-the-breakfast-club-molly-ringwald-metoo-john-hughes-pretty-in-pink.
22. Presumably "Duk" is meant to sound like "duck," in which case Jon Cryer's later role as Duckie in *Pretty in Pink* forms a further example of a wrong Anatid partner for Molly Ringwald.
23. Chow.
24. Smith, 30.
25. Ringwald.
26. See Timothy Shary, "Buying Me Love: '80s Class-Clash Teen Romances," *Journal of Popular Culture*, 44, no. 3 (2011), 563–82.
27. Emily Lordi, "Hearing Otis Redding's 'Try a Little Tenderness' as a Song of Resistance," *The Atlantic*, December 20, 2017, https://www.theatlantic.com/entertainment/archive/2017/12/otis-reddings-try-a-little-tenderness-as-a-song-of-resistance/547655/.
28. Ringwald.

29. Shirley L. Steinberg and Joe L Kincheloe, "Privileged and Getting Away with It: The Cultural Studies of White, Middle-Class Youth," *Studies in the Literary Imagination*, 31, no. 1 (1998), 108. We might also think of Kevin McCallister (Macaulay Culkin) in the *Home Alone* films (1990; 1992), which Hughes wrote and produced.
30. Richard Dyer, "White Enough?" in *The Time of Our Lives: Dirty Dancing and Popular Culture*, eds Yannis Tzioumakis and Sian Lincoln (Detroit: Wayne State University Press, 2013), 77.
31. Dyer (1997), 10.
32. Holly Chard observes how Hughes continued to apply narrative templates to his later family-oriented films, which she argues allowed him to be more responsive to the demands of the market. See "'Give People What They Expect': John Hughes' Family Films and Seriality in 1990s Hollywood," *Film Studies*, 17, no. 1 (2017), 111–27.
33. Chidester, 166.
34. Matt Wray, *Not Quite White: White Trash and the Boundaries of Whiteness* (Durham, NC: Duke University Press, 2006), 14.
35. Wray, 3.
36. Anahid Kassabian, *Hearing Music: Tracking Identifications in Contemporary Hollywood Film Music* (London: Routledge, 2001), 78.
37. Jorie Lagerwey and Taylor Nygaard, "Catastrophe and Horrible White People Shows," unpublished conference paper, presented at the National Cultures of Television Comedy Symposium, London, November 8, 2017.

Other Films and Television Shows Cited in this Collection

Adventures in Babysitting (Chris Columbus, 1987)
American Graffiti (George Lucas, 1973)
An American Werewolf in London (John Landis, 1981)
Animal House (John Landis, 1978)
A Nightmare on Elm Street (Wes Craven, 1984)
Annie (John Huston, 1982)
Annie Hall (Woody Allen, 1977)
A Patch of Blue (Guy Green, 1965)
Apocalypse Now (Francis Ford Coppola, 1979)
The Arsenio Hall Show (Paramount, 1989–94)
Baby Talk (ABC, 1991–92)
Back to the Future (Robert Zemeckis, 1985)
Bad Boys (Rick Rosenthal, 1983)
Bagdad Café (CBS, 1990–91)
Batman (Tim Burton, 1989)
The Beguiled (Don Siegel, 1971)
The Beguiled (Sofia Coppola, 2017)
Beverly Hills, 90210 (Fox, 1990–2000)
Beverly Hills Cop (Martin Brest, 1984)
Bikini Beach (William Asher, 1964)
Bill and Ted's Excellent Adventure (Steven Herek, 1989)
Bill and Ted's Excellent Adventures (CBS 1990–91)
Birdy (Alan Parker, 1984)
Blue Collar (Paul Schrader, 1978)
The Blue Lagoon (Randal Kleiser, 1980)
Blue Velvet (David Lynch, 1986)
The Boys in Company C (Sidney J. Furie, 1978)
Boyz N the Hood (John Singleton, 1991)
Breakfast at Tiffany's (Blake Edwards, 1961)

Breakin' (Joel Silberg, 1984)
Bride of Frankenstein (James Whale, 1935)
Bringing Up Baby (Howard Hawks, 1938)
Broad City (Amazon, 2014–present)
Buffy the Vampire Slayer (Fran Rubel Kuzul, 1992)
Buffy the Vampire Slayer (The WB, 1997–2003)
The 'Burbs (Joe Dante, 1989)
Caddyshack (Harold Ramis, 1980)
Can't Buy Me Love (Steve Rash, 1987)
Carrie (Brian De Palma, 1976)
Catastrophe (Channel 4, 2015–19)
Cheers (NBC, 1982–93)
Class of 1984 (Mark L. Lester, 1982)
Clueless (Amy Heckerling, 1995)
Coach Carter (Thomas Carter, 2005)
The Cosby Show (NBC, 1984–92)
Cry-Baby (John Waters, 1990)
Dances with Wolves (Kevin Costner, 1990)
Dangerous Minds (John N. Smith, 1995)
The Dark Crystal (Jim Henson, Frank Oz, 1982)
The Darkest Minds (Jennifer Yuh Nelson, 2018)
Dawson's Creek (The WB, 1998–2003)
Deadly Friend (Wes Craven, 1986)
Degrassi: The Next Generation (CTV, 2002–09)
Diary of a Mad Housewife (Frank Perry, 1970)
Die Hard (John McTiernan, 1988)
Dirty Dancing (Emile Ardolino, 1987)
Divergent (Neil Burger, 2014)
Don't You Forget About Me (Matt Sadowski, 2009)
The DUFF (Ari Sandel, 2015)
Easy A (Will Gluck, 2010)
Easy Rider (Dennis Hopper, 1969)
Eddie Dodd (ABC, 1991)
Eerie, Indiana (NBC, 1991–92)
The Emperor's Club (Michael Hoffman, 2002)
Endless Love (Franco Zefirelli, 1981)
Fame (Alan Parker, 1980)
Fargo (Joel Coen, Ethan Coen, 1996)
Fargo (FX, 2014–present)
Fast Times (CBS, 1986)
Fast Times at Ridgemont High (Amy Heckerling, 1982)
Father of the Bride (Charles Shyer, 1991)
The 5th Wave (J. Blakeson, 2016)
Finding Forrester (Gus Van Sant, 2000)
Firestarter (Mark L. Lester, 1984)
Flashdance (Adrian Lyne, 1983)
Fleabag (BBC, 2016–19)

Footloose (Herbert Ross, 1984)
Foul Play (Colin Higgins, 1978)
Frankenhooker (Frank Henenlotter, 1990)
Frankenstein (James Whale, 1931)
Freedom Writers (Richard LaGravenese, 2007)
Friends (NBC 1994–2004)
The Fresh Prince of Bel-Air (NBC, 1990–96)
Friday Night Lights (Peter Berg, 2004)
Friday Night Lights (NBC, 2006–11)
Friday the 13th (Sean S. Cunningham, 1980)
Friday the 13th Part 2 (Steve Miner, 1981)
Get Out (Jordan Peele, 2017)
Girls (HBO, 2011–17)
The Godfather (Francis Ford Coppola, 1972)
Going Berserk (David Steinberg, 1983)
The Goldbergs, (ABC, 2013–present)
Gone With the Wind (Victor Fleming, 1939)
GoodFellas (Martin Scorsese, 1990)
The Graduate (Mike Nichols, 1967)
The Great Muppet Caper (Jim Henson, 1981)
Gremlins (Joe Dante, 1984)
Halloween (John Carpenter, 1978)
The Hangover (Todd Phillips, 2009)
Hard to Hold (Larry Peerce, 1984)
The Heart is a Lonely Hunter (Robert Ellis Miller, 1968)
Heathers (Mark Lehmann, 1989)
Herbie Goes Bananas (Vincent McEveety, 1980)
The Hills Have Eyes (Wes Craven, 1977)
The Hired Hand (Peter Fonda, 1971)
Hollywood or Bust (Frank Tashlin, 1956)
Honey, I Shrunk the Kids (Joe Johnston, 1989)
The Host (Andrew Niccol, 2013)
Hull High (NBC, 1990)
The Hunger Games (Gary Ross, 2012)
The Hunger Games: Catching Fire (Francis Lawrence, 2013)
The Hunger Games: Mockingjay Part 1 (Francis Lawrence, 2014)
The Hunger Games: Mockingjay Part 2 (Francis Lawrence, 2015)
I Dream of Jeannie (NBC, 1965–70)
It Happened One Night (Frank Capra, 1934)
It's a Wonderful Life (Frank Capra, 1946)
The Jerk (Carl Reiner, 1979)
The Karate Kid (John G. Avildsen, 1984)
Kramer vs. Kramer (Robert Benton, 1979)
The Last Movie (Dennis Hopper, 1971)
The Last Starfighter (Nick Castle, 1984)
Late Night With David Letterman (NBC, 1982–93)
The Learning Tree (Gordon Parks, 1969)
Leave It to Beaver (CBS, 1957–58; ABC, 1958–63)
Little Darlings (Ron Maxwell, 1980)

Living It Up (Norman Taurog, 1954)
Look Who's Talking (Amy Heckerling, 1989)
Mad Max (George Miller, 1979)
Mad Max 2: The Road Warrior (George Miller, 1981)
Malcolm X (Spike Lee, 1992)
Married . . . with Children (Fox, 1986–97)
Mary Poppins (George Stevenson, 1964)
M*A*S*H (Robert Altman, 1970)
M*A*S*H (CBS, 1972–83)
Mean Girls (Mark Waters, 2004)
Minnie and Moskowitz (John Cassavetes, 1971)
Modern Problems (Ken Shapiro, 1981)
Mrs. Doubtfire (Chris Columbus, 1993)
My Fair Lady (George Cukor, 1964)
My Own Private Idaho (Gus Van Sant, 1991)
My Science Project (Johnathan R. Betuel, 1985)
1941 (Steven Spielberg, 1979)
Not Another Teen Movie (Joel Gallen, 2001)
Old School (Todd Phillips, 2003)
Ordinary People (Robert Redford, 1980)
The Outsiders (Francis Ford Coppola, 1983)
Pajama Party (Don Weis, 1964)
Parenthood (Ron Howard, 1989)
Parenthood (NBC, 1990–91)
Parker Lewis Can't Lose (Fox, 1990–93)
Pennies from Heaven (Herbert Ross, 1981)
Porky's (Bob Clark, 1981)
Porky's II: The Next Day (Bob Clark, 1983)
Pretty Woman (Garry Marshall, 1990)
The Princess Diaries (Garry Marshall, 2001)
Private Lessons (Alan Myerson, 1981)
Project X (Nima Nourizadeh, 2012)
Purple Rain (Albert Magnoli, 1984)
Real Genius (Martha Coolidge, 1985)
Rebel Without a Cause (Nicolas Ray, 1955)
Red Dawn (John Milius, 1984)
Revenge of the Nerds (Jeff Kanew, 1984)
Risky Business (Paul Brickman, 1983)
Rocky (John G. Avildsen, 1976)
Rocky III (Sylvester Stallone, 1982)
Rocky IV (Sylvester Stallone, 1985)
The Rocky Horror Picture Show (Jim Sharman, 1975)
Roxanne (Fred Schepisi, 1987)
Saturday Night Live (NBC 1975–present)
Say Anything . . . (Cameron Crowe, 1989)
School Ties (Robert Mandel, 1992)
SCTV (Global 1976–84)
She's All That (Robert Iscove, 1999)
Silence of the Lambs (Jonathan Demme, 1991)
Silent Running (Donald Trumbull, 1972)

60 Minutes (CBS, 1968–present)
The Skin I Live In (Alejandro Almodóvar, 2011)
Smokey and the Bandit (Hal Needham, 1977)
Splash (Ron Howard, 1984)
Splendor in the Grass (Elia Kazan, 1961)
Square Pegs (CBS, 1982–83)
Stand and Deliver (Ramón Menéndez, 1987)
The Stepford Wives (Bryan Forbes, 1975)
The Stepford Wives (Frank Oz, 2004)
Stranger Things (Netflix, 2016–present)
Streets of Fire (Walter Hill, 1984)
Stripes (Ivan Reitman, 1981)
Summer Rental (Carl Reiner, 1985)
Superbad (Greg Mottola, 2007)
Superman (Richard Donner, 1978)
Taking Off (Milos Forman, 1971)
Taps (Harold Becker, 1981)
Tea and Sympathy (Vincente Minnelli, 1956)
Ten Things I Hate About You (Gil Junger, 1999)
The Terminator (James Cameron, 1984)
Three O'Clock High (Phil Joanou, 1987)
Tomorrowland (Brad Bird, 2015)
Top Gun (Tony Scott, 1986)
Two-Lane Blacktop (Monte Hellman, 1971)
2001: A Space Odyssey (Stanley Kubrick, 1968)
Unforgiven (Clint Eastwood, 1992)
Valley Girl (Martha Coolidge, 1983)
WarGames (John Badham, 1983)
Warm Bodies (Jonathan Levine, 2013)
We Need to Talk About Kevin (Lynne Ramsay, 2011)
Westworld (Michael Crichton, 1972)
Westworld (HBO, 2016–present)
The Wild Life (Art Linson, 1984)
Working Girl (NBC, 1990)
You're Never Too Young (Norman Taurog, 1955)

Bibliography

Ahmed, Sara. "The Happiness Turn." *New Formations*, 63 (2007), 7–14.
Ahmed, Sara. *The Promise of Happiness*. Durham, NC: Duke University Press, 2010.
Allen, R. C. "Home Alone Together: Hollywood and the 'Family Film'." In *Identifying Hollywood's Audiences: Cultural Identity and the Movies*, edited by Melvyn Stokes and Richard Maltby, 109–34. London: British Film Institute, 1999.
Almond, Steve. "John Hughes Goes Deep: The Unexpected Heaviosity of *Ferris Bueller's Day Off*." In *Don't You Forget About Me: Contemporary Writers on the Films of John Hughes*, edited by Jaime Clarke, 5–14. New York: Simon Spotlight, 2007.
Altman, Rick. "A Semantic/Syntactic Approach to Film Genre." In *Film Genre III*, edited by Barry Keith Grant, 27–41. Austin: University of Texas Press, 2003.
Andreeva, Nellie. "'Uncle Buck' Series: John Hughes & John Candy Families Displeased." Deadline Hollywood, October 10, 2014, https://deadline.com/2014/10/uncle-buck-series-john-hughes-john-candy-disapprove-849424/.
Ansen, David. "Goofing Off in Grand Style." *Newsweek*, June 16, 1986, 75.
Antunes, Filipa. "Attachment Anxiety: Parenting Culture, Adolescence and the Family Film in the US." *Journal of Children and Media*, 11, no. 2 (2017), 214–28.
Appelo, Tim. "John Hughes' View from the Top." *Entertainment Weekly*, December 2, 1994, http://ew.com/article/1994/12/02/john-hughes-view-top/.
Associated Press. "President's Joke About Bombing Leaves Press in Europe Unamused." *New York Times*, August 14, 1984, https://www.nytimes.com/1984/08/14/world/president-s-joke-about-bombing-leaves-press-in-europe-unamused.html.
Atad, Corey. "Lost in Adaptation." Slate, June 20, 2017, http://www.slate.com/articles/arts/culturebox/2017/06/sofia_coppola_s_whitewashed_new_movie_the_beguiled.html?via=gdpr-consent.
Atkinson, Tracy. "Pop Art and the American Tradition." In *Pop Art: The Critical Dialogue* edited by Carol Anne Mahsun, 157–73. Ann Arbor, MI: UMI Research Press, 1989.
Austin, Matt. *Don't You Forget About Me*. DVD. Stay the Course Productions, Canada, 2009.
Bailey, Steve, and James Hay. "Cinema and the Premises of Youth: 'Teen Films' and Their Sites in the 1980s and 1990s." In *Genre and Contemporary Hollywood*, edited by Steve Neale, 218–36. London: British Film Institute, 2002.
Bakhtin, Mikhail. *Rabelais and His World*, trans. Hélène Iswolsky. Bloomington: Indiana University Press, 1984.
Barth, Jack. "John Hughes: On Geeks Bearing Gifts." *Film Comment*, 20, no. 2 (1984), 46.

Barth, Jack. "Kinks of Comedy." *Film Comment*, 20, no. 2 (1984), 44–7.
Bellah, Robert, et al., *Habits of the Heart: Individualism and Commitment in American Life*. Berkeley: University of California Press, 1985.
Belton, John. "Introduction." In *Movies and Mass Culture*, edited by John Belton, 1–22. London: Athlone, 1996.
Belton, John. *American Cinema/American Culture*. New York: McGraw, 1993.
Benfer, Amy. "The 'Sixteen Candles' Date Rape Scene?'" *Salon*, August 11, 2009, https://www.salon.com/2009/08/11/16_candles/.
Berardinelli, James. "Sixteen Candles (United States, 1984)." *Reelviews*, May 16, 2009, http://www.reelviews.net/reelviews/sixteen-candles.
Bernstein, Jonathan. *Pretty in Pink: The Golden Age of Teenage Movies*. New York: St. Martin's Griffin, 1997.
Best, Joel. *Threatened Children: Rhetoric and Concern about Child-Victims*. University of Chicago Press, 1990.
Beynon, John. *Masculinities and Culture*. Buckingham: Open University Press, 2002.
Biskind, Peter. *Easy Riders, Raging Bulls: How the Sex-Drugs-and-Rock-'N'-Roll Generation Saved Hollywood*. New York: Bloomsbury, 1998.
Bleach, Anthony C. "Postfeminist Cliques? Class, Postfeminism, and the Molly Ringwald-John Hughes Films." *Cinema Journal*, 49, no. 3 (2010), 22–44.
Bobbin, Jay. "Once is Not Enough." *Santa Ana Orange County Register*, August 26, 1990, TV Section, 6.
Borrelli, Christopher. "'The Breakfast Club' 30 Years Later: Don't You Forget About Them," *Chicago Tribune*, February 17, 2015, http://www.chicagotribune.com/entertainment/movies/ct-the-breakfast-club-30th-anniversary-20150217-column.html.
Brickman, Barbara. *New American Teenagers: The Lost Generation of Youth in 1970s Film*. New York: Bloomsbury, 2012.
Brinkema, Eugenie. *The Forms of the Affects*. Durham, NC: Duke University Press, 2014.
Brown, Bill. "How to Do Things with Things (A Toy Story)." *Critical Inquiry*, 24, no. 4 (1998), 935–64.
Bulman, Robert. *Hollywood Goes to High School: Cinema, Schools, and American Culture*. New York: Worth, 2015.
Bush, Barbara. "Commencement Address." Wellesley College, June 1, 1990, https://www.wellesley.edu/events/commencement/archives/1990commencement/commencementaddress.
Byrge, Duane. "Review of *The Breakfast Club*." *The Hollywood Reporter*, February 15, 1985, https://www.hollywoodreporter.com/news/breakfast-club-thrs-1985-review-773357.
Caillois, Roger. *Man, Play and Games*, trans. Meyer Barash. Chicago: University of Illinois Press, 2001.
Carroll, Noel. *Philosophy of Horror: Or, Paradoxes of the Heart*. New York: Routledge, 1990.
Carter, Bill. "Hear About a Film That Became a Hit TV Series? You're Not Alone." *New York Times*, December 17, 1990, C11.
Carter, Bill. "Him Alone." *New York Times*, August 4, 1991, http://www.nytimes.com/1991/08/04/magazine/him-alone.html.
Cerone, Daniel. "Stylized Reality? Not a Problem. Fox's *Parker Lewis* Combines Imaginative Dubb, Creative Sound Effects." *Los Angeles Times*, TV Times, March 17, 1991, 3.
Chard, Holly. "Mainstream Maverick? John Hughes and New Hollywood Cinema." PhD dissertation, University of Sussex, 2014.
Chard, Holly. "'Give People What They Expect': John Hughes' Family Films and Seriality in 1990s Hollywood." *Film Studies*, 17, no. 1 (2017), 111–27.

Chidester, Phil. "May the Circle Stay Unbroken: Friends, the Presence of Absence, and the Rhetorical Reinforcement of Whiteness." *Critical Studies in Media Communication*, 25, no. 2 (2008), 157–74.

Chow, Kat. "What's So Cringeworthy about Long Duk Dong in Sixteen Candles?" *National Public Radio*, 2017, https://www.npr.org/sections/codeswitch/2015/02/06/384307677/whats-so-cringe-worthy-about-long-duk-dong-in-sixteen-candles?t=1531756678520.

Cieply, Michael. "John Hughes obituary." *New York Times*, August 4, 2009, 20.

Clark, Jaime. *Don't You Forget About Me: Contemporary Writers on the Films of John Hughes*. New York: Simon Spotlight Entertainment, 2007.

Connell, Raewyn. *Masculinities*. Berkeley: University of California Press, 1995.

Considine, David. *The Cinema of Adolescence*. Jefferson, NC: McFarland, 1985.

Cook, David A. *Lost Illusions: American Cinema in the Shadow of Watergate and Vietnam, 1970–1979*. Berkeley: University of California Press, 2002.

Coontz, Stephanie. *The Way We Never Were: American Families and the Nostalgia Trap*. New York: Basic Books, 1992.

Cooper, T. "You Look Good Wearing My Future, or The Sexually Ambiguous Best Friend." In *Don't You Forget About Me: Contemporary Writers on the Films of John Hughes*, edited by Jaime Clarke. 47–58. New York: Simon Spotlight, 2007.

Cooper Albright, Ann. "Strategic Abilities: Negotiating the Disabled Body in Dance." In *Moving History/Dancing Cultures: A Dance History Reader*, edited by Ann Dils and Ann Cooper Albright, 56–66. Middletown, CT: Wesleyan University Press, 2001.

Corliss, Richard. "Well, Hello Molly!" *Time*, May 26, 1986, http://www.time.com/time/magazine/article/0,9171,1101860526-144177,00.html.

Crafton, Donald. "Pie and Chase: Gag, Spectacle and Narrative in Slapstick Comedy." In *Cinema of Attractions Reloaded*, edited by Wanda Strauven, 355–64. Amsterdam: Amsterdam University Press, 2006.

Creed, Barbara. "Horror and the Monstrous-Feminine: An Imaginary Abjection." In *The Dread of Difference: Gender and the Horror Film*, edited by Barry Keith Grant, 35–65. Austin: University of Texas Press, 1996.

de Certeau, Michel. *The Writing of History*, trans. Tom Conley. New York: Columbia University Press, 1988.

De Vaney, Ann. "Pretty in Pink? John Hughes Reinscribes Daddy's Girl in Homes and Schools." In *Sugar, Spice and Everything Nice: Cinemas of Girlhood*, edited by Frances Gateward and Murray Pomerance, 201–16. Detroit: Wayne State University Press, 2002.

Dellio, Phil. "Some Candy Talking!" *Graffiti*, January 1986, 45.

Demetriou, Demetrakis. "Connell's Concept of Hegemonic Masculinity: A Critique." *Theory and Society*, 30 (2001), 337–61.

Deming, Caren. "Locating the Televisual in Golden Age Television." In *A Companion to Television*, edited by Janet Wasko, 126–41. New York: Wiley-Blackwell, 2009.

Denby, David. "Happy Birthday, Sweet Sixteen." *New York*, May 1984, 96.

Dennis, Jeffery. *Queering Teen Culture: All-American Boys and Same-Sex Desire in Film and Television*. New York: Harrington Park Press, 2006.

Diamond, Jason. *Searching for John Hughes: Or, Everything I Thought I Needed to Know About Life I Learned from Watching '80s Movies*. New York: William Morrow Paperbacks, 2016.

Doherty, Thomas. *Teenagers and Teenpics: The Juvenilization of American Movies in the 1950s*. Philadelphia: Temple University Press, 2002.

Donelan, Loretta. "15 Movies You Didn't Realize Were Sexist." Bustle, January 22, 2017, https://www.bustle.com/p/15-movies-you-didnt-realize-were-sexist-30553.

Driscoll, Catherine. *Teen Film: A Critical Introduction*. Oxford: Berg, 2011.

Duscha, Julius. "The Problem of Living Up to L'eggs." *New York Times*, March 5, 1978, F5.
Dyer, Richard. "White Enough?" In *The Time of Our Lives: Dirty Dancing and Popular Culture*, edited by Yannis Tzioumakis and Sian Lincoln, 73–86. Detroit: Wayne State University Press, 2013.
Dyer, Richard. *White: Essays on Race and Culture*. London: Routledge, 1997.
Eberstadt, Mary. *Home-Alone America: The Hidden Toll of Daycare, Behavioural Drugs, and Other Parent Substitutes*. New York and London: Sentinel, 2004.
Ebert, Roger. "John Hughes: When You're 16, You're More Serious than You'll Ever Be Again." RogerEbert.com, April 29, 1984, https://www.rogerebert.com/rogers-journal/john-hughes-when-youre-16-youre-more-serious-than-youll-ever-be-again.
Ebert, Roger. "Review: Sixteen Candles," *Chicago Sun-Times*, May 4, 1984, https://www.rogerebert.com/reviews/sixteen-candles-1984.
Ebert, Roger. "Some Kind of Wonderful," RogerEbert.com, February 27, 1987, https://www.rogerebert.com/reviews/some-kind-of-wonderful-1987.
Ebert, Roger, "Gimmicks Distract in 'Having a Baby'." *Chicago Sun-Times*, February 5, 1988, 25.
Eckert, Penelope. *Jocks and Burnouts. Social Categories and Identity in High School*. New York: Teachers College Press, 1989.
Edgerton, Gary. "The Film Bureau Phenomenon in America and Its Relationship to Independent Filmmaking." *Journal of Film and Video*, 38, no .1 (1986), 40–7.
Faludi, Susan. *Backlash: The Undeclared War Against American Women*. New York: Crown, 1991.
Foucault, Michel. *Discipline and Punish: The Birth of the Prison*. New York: Vintage Books, 1995.
Freeman, Hadley. *Life Moves Pretty Fast: The Lessons We Learned from Eighties Movies (and Why We Don't Learn Them from Movies Any More)*. New York: Simon and Schuster, 2015.
Friedan, Betty. "The Sexual Sell." In *The Consumer Society Reader*, edited by Juliet B. Schor and Douglas B. Holt, 26–46. New York: The New Press, 2000.
Gad, Josh. "Ferris Bueller's Day Off." *Reunited Apart with Josh Gad*, June 29, 2020, https://www.youtube.com/watch?v=dOaa3Znh75w.
Genzlinger, Neil. "A Nostalgia Fix of the Eerie Kind." *New York Times*, July 15, 2016, C4.
Gilbey, Ryan. "John Hughes: Director, Screenwriter and Producer Who Was One of the Most Prolific Independent Film Makers in Hollywood History." *The Guardian*, August 7, 2009, https://www.theguardian.com/film/2009/aug/07/john-hughes-film-director-dies1.
Glass, Ira. "Is This What I Look Like?" This American Life, May 23, 2014, https://www.thisamericanlife.org/526/is-that-what-i-look-like.
Gleiberman, Owen. "Bittersweet Sixteen: Burning the Candles at Both Ends." *Boston Phoenix*, May 8, 1984, C4.
Goldberg, Tod. "That's Not a Name, that's a Major Appliance: How Andrew McCarthy Ruined My Life." In *Don't You Forget About Me: Contemporary Writers on the Films of John Hughes*, edited by Jaime Clarke, 86–95. New York: Simon Spotlight Entertainment, 2007.
Goldstein, Patrick. "John Hughes in the Pink at MCA." *Los Angeles Times*, March 1, 1987, http://articles.latimes.com/1987-03-01/entertainment/ca-6707_1_john-hughes.
Goldstein, Patrick. "John Hughes' Imprint Remains." *Los Angeles Times*, March 24, 2008, http://www.latimes.com/entertainment/news/movies/la-et-goldstein25mar25,0,3535882.story.
Gora, Susannah. *You Couldn't Ignore Me if You Tried: The Brat Pack, John Hughes, and Their Impact on a Generation*. New York: Three Rivers Press, 2011.
Grady, Constance. "The Rape Culture of the 1980s, Explained by Sixteen Candles." Vox, September 27, 2018, https://www.vox.com/culture/2018/9/27/17906644/sixteen-candles-rape-culture-1980s-brett-kavanaugh.
Greenberg, Joshua. "Universal Signs Hughes to 3-Year Pact." *Variety*, May 2, 1984, 19.

Grindon, Leger. "1986: Movies and Fissures in Reagan's America." In *American Cinema of the 1980s: Themes and Variations*, edited by Stephen Prince, 145–66. New Brunswick, NJ: Rutgers University Press, 2007.

Hamad, Hannah. *Postfeminism and Paternity in Contemporary US Film: Framing Fatherhood*. London: Routledge, 2014.

Harbidge, Lesley. "Audienceship and (Non)Laughter in the Stand-up Comedy of Steve Martin." *Participations: Journal of Audience and Reception Studies*, 8, no. 2 (2011), 128–44.

Hark, Ina Rae. "Fear of Flying: Yuppie Critique and the Buddy-Road Movie in the 1980s." In *The Road Movie Book*, edited by Steven Cohan and Ina Rae Hark, 204–31. London: Routledge, 1997.

Harris, Mark. "*Parker Lewis Can't Lose!*" *Entertainment Weekly*, August 31, 1990, https://ew.com/article/1990/08/31/parker-lewis-cant-lose/.

Harvey, Sylvia. "Woman's Place: The Absent Family of Film Noir." In *Movies and Mass Culture*, edited by John Belton. London: Athlone, 1996.

Harwood, Sarah. *Family Fictions: Representations of the Family in 1980s Hollywood Cinema*. Basingstoke: Macmillan, 1997.

Heath, Melanie. "Manhood Over Easy: Reflections on Hegemonic, Soft-Boiled, and Multiple Masculinities." In *Exploring Masculinities: Identity, Inequality, Continuity, and Change*, edited by. C. J. Pascoe and Tristan Bridges, 155–65. Oxford: Oxford University Press, 2015.

Hill, Michael. "Fox's *Parker Lewis* Gets It Right." *Hutchinson News*, September 9, 1990.

Honeycutt, Kirk. *John Hughes: A Life in Film*. New York: Race Point Publishing, 2015.

Hughes, John. "Vacation '58 / Foreword '08." *All-Story*, 12, no. 2 (2008), https://web.archive.org/web/20080731165748/http://www.all-story.com/issues.cgi?action=show_story&story_id=389.

Huizinga, Johan. *Homo Ludens: A Study of the Play-Element in Culture*. Boston: Routledge, 1949.

Jeffers McDonald, Tamar. *Romantic Comedy: Boy Meets Girl Meets Genre*. London: Wallflower, 2007.

Jeffords, Susan. *Hard Bodies: Hollywood Masculinity in the Reagan Era*. New Brunswick, NJ: Rutgers University Press, 1994.

Jenkins, Claire. *Home Movies: The American Family in Contemporary Hollywood Cinema*. London: I. B. Tauris, 2015.

Jenkins, Henry, and Kristine Brunovska Karnick. "Introduction: Funny Stories." In *Classical Hollywood Comedy*, edited by Henry Jenkins and Kristine Brunovska Karnick, 63–86. New York: Routledge, 1995.

Johnson-Yale, Camille. *Runaway Production: A History of Hollywood's Outsourcing Debate*. Lanham, KY: Lexington Books, 2017.

Jubera, Drew. "In Front of TV 12 Hours a Day: Is Marathon Television Viewing as Dangerous as Some Claim?" *San Francisco Chronicle*, August 9, 1991, F7.

Kael, Pauline. *5001 Nights at the Movies*. New York: Holt, Rinehart, and Winston, 1985.

Kael, Pauline. *Hooked: Film Writings 1985–1988*. New York: Marion Boyers, 1992.

Kaklamanidou, Betty. *Easy A: The End of the High-School Teen Comedy?* London: Routledge, 2018.

Kamp, David. "Sweet Bard of Youth." *Vanity Fair*, March 2010, http://www.vanityfair.com/hollywood/features/2010/03/john-hughes-201003.

Kapur, Jyotsna. *Coining for Capital: Movies, Marketing and the Transformation of Childhood*. Piscataway, NJ: Rutgers University Press, 2005.

Kassabian, Anahid. *Hearing Music: Tracking Identifications in Contemporary Hollywood Film Music*. London: Routledge, 2001.

Kaveney, Roz. *Teen Dreams: Reading Teen Film and Television from Heathers to Veronica Mars*. New York: I. B. Tauris, 2006.

Keefe, Terry. "The Hollywood Interview: Anthony Michael Hall." The Hollywood Interview, November 30, 2008, http://thehollywoodinterview.blogspot.com/2008/11/anthony-michael-hall-hollywood.html.

Keeley, Pete. "*Parker Lewis Can't Lose* at 25: Co-Creators Clyde Phillips and Lon Diamond on Creating a Cult Classic." *The Hollywood Reporter*, June 13, 2018, https://www.hollywoodreporter.com/live-feed/parker-lewis-cant-lose-are-they-now-creators-interview-1119715.

Kehr, Dave. "*Pretty in Pink*." *Chicago Reader*, 1986, https://www.chicagoreader.com/chicago/pretty-in-pink/Film?oid=1686089.

Kehr, Dave. "'Some Kind of Wonderful.'" *Chicago Tribune*, February 27, 1987.

Kelly, Maura. "John Hughes: The Films He Created in the Decade of Greed Made Adolescent Angst Funny and Bearable Without Romanticizing It." Salon, July 17, 2001, http://www.salon.com/2001/07/17/john_hughes_2/.

Kempley, Rita. "*Uncle Buck*." *Washington Post*, August 16, 1989, https://www.washingtonpost.com/wp-srv/style/longterm/movies/videos/unclebuckpgkempley_a0c9a1.htm.

Kempley, Rita. "*National Lampoon's Christmas Vacation*." *Washington Post*, December 1, 1989, http://www.washingtonpost.com/wp-srv/style/longterm/movies/videos/nationallampoonschristmasvacation.htm.

Keveney, Bill. "Strangest Thing: '80s Ardor Just Keeps Growing." *USA Today*, August 27, 2017, 2D.

Kincheloe, Joe. "The New Childhood: Home Alone as a Way of Life." In *The Children's Culture Reader*, edited by Henry Jenkins, 159–76. New York University Press, 1998.

Kincheloe, Joe L. "*Home Alone* and Bad to the Bone: The Advent of a Postmodern Childhood." In *Kinderculture: The Corporate Construction of Childhood*, 3rd edn, edited by Shirley R. Steinberg, 265–89. Boulder, CO: Westview Press, 2011.

Kinder, Marsha. "Home Alone in the 90s: Generational War and Transgenerational Address in American Movies, Television and Presidential Politics." In *In Front of the Children: Screen Entertainment and Young Audiences*, edited by Cary Bazalgette and David Buckingham, 75–91. London: British Film Institute, 1995.

King, Andrea. "John Hughes: An Exclusive on the Ordinary." *The Hollywood Reporter ShoWest Producer of the Year Special Report* (1991), S16.

King, James. *The Ultimate History of the '80s Teen Movie*. New York: Diversion, 2019.

Klein, Amanda Ann. "'The Breakfast Club' 30 Years Later: A Conversation Across Generations." RogerEbert.com, March 26, 2015, https://www.rogerebert.com/mzs/the-breakfast-club-30-years-later-a-conversation-across-generations.

Kristeva, Julia. *Powers of Horror: An Essay on Abjection*, trans. Leon S. Roudiez. New York: Columbia University Press, 1982.

Krutnik, Frank. "The Clown-Prints of Comedy." *Screen*, 25, no. 4/5 (1984), 50–9.

Krutnik, Frank. "A Spanner in the Works? Genre, Narrative and the Hollywood Comedian." In *Classical Hollywood Comedy*, edited by Kristine Brunovska Karnick and Henry Jenkins, 17–38. New York: Routledge, 1995.

Krutnik, Frank. "General Introduction." In *Hollywood Comedians: The Film Reader* edited by Frank Krutnik, 1–18. London: Routledge, 2003.

Krutnik, Frank. "Mutinies Wednesdays and Saturdays: Carnivalesque Comedy and the Marx Brothers." In *A Companion to Film Comedy*, edited by Andrew Horton and Joanna Rapf, 87–110. Malden, MA: Wiley-Blackwell, 2012.

Lagerwey, Jorie, and Taylor Nygaard. "Catastrophe and Horrible White People Shows." Unpublished conference paper, presented at the National Cultures of Television Comedy Symposium, London, November 8, 2017.

Lalich, Richard. "Big Baby." *Spy*, January 1993, 66–73.

Landers, Ann. "The Problem of 'Date Rape' Is an Ambiguous One." *San Bernardino Sun*, July 29, 1985, https://cdnc.ucr.edu/cgi-bin/cdnc?a=d&d=SBS19850729.1.12&e.

Landers, Ann. "A Male Viewpoint on Date Rape." *St. Louis Post-Dispatch*, August 4, 1991, 11C.

Lee, Christina. *Screening Generation X: The Politics and Popular Memory of Youth in Contemporary Cinema*. Aldershot: Ashgate, 2010.

Lev, Peter. "Regional Cinema and the Films of Texas." *Journal of Film and Video*, 38, no. 1 (1986), 60.

Levy, Emanuel. *Cinema of Outsiders: The Rise of American Independent Film*. New York: New York University Press, 1999.

Little, Daniel. "Philosophy of History." In *The Stanford Encyclopedia of Philosophy*, 2017, edited by Edward N. Zalta, https://plato.stanford.edu/archives/sum2017/entries/history/.

Lordi, Emily. "Hearing Otis Redding's 'Try a Little Tenderness' as a Song of Resistance." *The Atlantic*, December 20, 2017, https://www.theatlantic.com/entertainment/archive/2017/12/otis-reddings-try-a-little-tenderness-as-a-song-of-resistance/547655/.

Lupton, Deborah and Lesley Barclay. *Constructing Fatherhood: Discourses and Experiences*. London: Sage, 1997.

Manzoor, Sarfraz. "More than a Quintessential Eighties Teen Film." *The Independent*, March 24, 2004, http://www.independent.co.uk/arts-entertainment/films/features/more-than-a-quintessential-eighties-teen-film-65704.html.

Marger, Martin M. *Social Inequality: Patterns and Processes*, 3rd edn. New York: McGraw Hill, 2005.

Martin, Adrian. "Teen Movies: The Forgetting of Wisdom." In *Phantasms: The Dreams and Desires at the Heart of our Popular Culture*. Ringwood, Vic: McPhee Gribble, 1994.

Maslin, Janet. "'16 Candles,' A Teen-Age Comedy." *New York Times*, May 4, 1984, https://www.nytimes.com/1984/05/04/movies/screen-16-candles-a-teen-age-comedy.html.

Maslin, Janet. "Film: John Hughes's 'Pretty in Pink.'" *New York Times*, February 28, 1986.

Maslin, Janet. "'Some Kind of Wonderful.'" *New York Times*, February 27, 1987.

Maslin, Janet. "Film View: Marching toward Maturity." *New York Times*, March 15, 1987, https://www.nytimes.com/1987/03/15/arts/film-view-marching-toward-maturity.html.

Matthews, Nicole. *Comic Politics: Gender in Hollywood Comedy After the New Right*. Manchester: Manchester University Press, 2000.

McLane, Betsy. "Domestic Theatrical & Semi-Theatrical Distribution and Exhibition of American Independent Feature Films: A Survey in 1983." *Journal of University Film and Video Association* 35, no. 2 (1983), 17–24.

McLellan, Dennis. "Ned Tanen dies at 77; Former President of Universal, Paramount." *Los Angeles Times*, January 8, 2009, http://articles.latimes.com/2009/jan/08/local/me-tanen8.

Messner, Michael A. "On Patriarchs and Losers: Rethinking Men's Interests." In *Exploring Masculinities: Identity, Inequality, Continuity, and Change*, edited by C. J. Pascoe and Tristan Bridges, 196–208. Oxford: Oxford University Press, 2015.

Modleski, Tania. *Feminism Without Women: Culture and Criticism in a "Postfeminist" Age*. London: Routledge, 1991.

Moran, Kathleen, and Michael Rogin. "'What's the Matter with Capra?': *Sullivan's Travels* and the Popular Front." *Representations*, 71 (2000), 106–34.

Mulvey, Laura. "Visual Pleasure and Narrative Cinema." In *Feminism and Film*, edited by E. Ann Kaplan, 34–47. New York: Oxford University Press, 2000.

Nadel, Alan. *Flatlining on the Field of Dreams: Cultural Narratives in the Films of President Reagan's America*. New Brunswick, NJ: Rutgers University Press, 1997.

Nelson, Elissa H. "Teen Films of the 1980s: Genre, New Hollywood, and Generation X." Dissertation, University of Texas at Austin, 2011.

Nelson, Elissa H. "The New Old Face of a Genre: The Franchise Teen Film as Industry Strategy." *Cinema Journal*, 57, no. 1 (2017), 125–33.

Nelson, Elissa. *The Breakfast Club: John Hughes, Hollywood and the Golden Age of the Teen Film*. London: Routledge, 2019.

O'Connor, John J. "TV: Incongruities of Steve Martin." *New York Times*, February 14, 1980, C27.

O'Connor, John. "When Boys Will, of Course, Be Boys." *New York Times*, October 8, 1990, 43.

O'Connor, Thomas. "John Hughes: His Movies Speak to Teen-Agers." *New York Times*, March 9, 1986, http://www.nytimes.com/1986/03/09/movies/john-hughes-his-movies-speak-to-teen-agers.html.

Obenson, Tambay A. "Lena Dunham addresses *Girls* diversity criticism, and why I just don't care." Indiewire, May 8, 2012, https://www.indiewire.com/2012/05/lena-dunham-addresses-girls-diversity-criticism-why-i-just-dont-care-145804/.

Paul, William. *Laughing Screaming: Modern Hollywood Horror and Comedy*. New York: Columbia University Press, 1994.

Pearlman, Alison. *Unpackaging Art of the 1980s*. Chicago: University of Chicago Press, 2003.

Popular Memory Group. "Popular Memory: Theory, Politics, Method." In *Making Histories: Studies in History-Writing and Politics*, edited by Richard Johnson et al., 205–52. Minneapolis: University of Minnesota Press, 1982.

Puig, Claudia. "TV & Video." *Los Angeles Times*, December 13, 1990, F2.

Rettenmund, Matthew. *Totally Awesome 80s: A Lexicon of the Music, Videos, Movies, TV Shows, Stars, and Trends of That Decadent Decade*. New York: St. Martin's Griffin, 1996.

Reyes, Sonia. "Talkboy: *Home Alone 2* Toy Is Hot, Hot, Hot." *New York Daily News*, December 16, 1993, https://archive.seattletimes.com/archive/?date=19931216&slug=1737234.

Reynolds, Rachel and David Jefferson, "The Crime Few Victims Will Report; Rapes Committed by Acquaintances Called Epidemic." *San Diego Union-Tribune*, August 26, 1985, A1.

Rhodes, John David. *Spectacle of Property: The House in American Film*. Minneapolis: University of Minnesota Press, 2017.

Richmond, Ray. "Check Out 'Parker Lewis' and You Can't Lose." *Orange County Register*, August 31, 1990, P46.

Ridgway, Shannon. "25 Examples of Rape Culture." Everyday Feminism, March 10, 2014, https://everydayfeminism.com/2014/03/examples-of-rape-culture/.

Ringwald, Molly. "Molly Ringwald Interviews John Hughes." *Seventeen*, March 1986, 239.

Ringwald, Molly. "The Neverland Club." *New York Times*, August 12, 2009, http://www.nytimes.com/2009/08/12/opinion/12ringwald.html.

Ringwald, Molly. "What About 'The Breakfast Club'? Revisiting the Movies of My Youth in the Age of #MeToo," *The New Yorker*, April 6, 2018, https://www.newyorker.com/culture/personal-history/what-about-the-breakfast-club-molly-ringwald-metoo-john-hughes-pretty-in-pink.

Rios, Victor and Rachel Sarabia. "Synthesized Masculinities: The Mechanics of Manhood Among Delinquent Boys." In *Exploring Masculinities: Identity, Inequality, Continuity, and Change*, edited by C. J. Pascoe and Tristan Bridges, 163–78. Oxford: Oxford University Press, 2015.

Roberts, Soraya. "A Diamond and a Kiss: The Women of John Hughes." Hazlitt, July 5, 2016, http://hazlitt.net/longreads/diamond-and-kiss-women-john-hughes.

Robertson, Paul Lester. "Indians of the Apocalypse: Native Appropriation and Representation in 1980s Dystopic Films and Comic Books." *The Journal of Popular Culture*, 51, no. 1 (2018), 68–90.

Rodkin, Dennis. "John Hughes: A True Friend of Chicago." *The Hollywood Reporter ShoWest Producer of the Year Special Report* (1991), S20.
Rogers, Stephanie. "'Sixteen Candles,' Rape Culture, and the Anti-Woman Politics of 2013." Btchflcks, July 8, 2013, http://www.btchflcks.com/2013/07/sixteen-candles-rape-culture-and-the-anti-woman-politics-of-2013.html#.XUdkW-hKiM8.
Rosenberg, Howard. "NBC's *Ferris Bueller* Premieres Tonight." *Los Angeles Times*, August 23, 1990, F11.
Roush, Matt. "This *Ferris* Should Be in Detention." *USA Today*, August 23, 1991, 3D.
Rowe, Kathleen. *The Unruly Woman: Gender and the Genres of Comedy.* Austin: University of Texas Press, 1995.
Russo, Mary. "Female Grotesques: Carnival and Theory." In *Feminist Studies/Critical Studies*, edited by Teresa de Lauretis, 213–29. Basingstoke: Macmillan, 1988.
Sabo, Donald F. "Different Stakes: Men's Pursuit of Gender Equity in Sports." In *Sex, Violence and Power in Sports: Rethinking Masculinity*, edited by M. A. Messner and D. F. Sabo, 202–13. Freedom, CA: Crossing Press, 1994.
Sadiq, Maulud. "Loving John Hughes Movies While Black." Medium, January 23, 2017, https://medium.com/the-brothers/loving-john-hughes-movies-while-black-1c4acba2e628.
Sanday, Peggy Reeves. *A Woman Scorned: Acquaintance Rape on Trial.* Berkeley: University of California Press, 1997.
Sarris, Andrew. "Anodynes for Adolescents." *Village Voice*, June 17, 1986, 56.
Sarris, Andrew. *The American Cinema: Directors and Directions 1929–1968.* Boston: Da Capo Press, 1996.
Schatz, Thomas. "The New Hollywood." In *Film Theory Goes to the Movies*, edited by Jim Collins, Hillary Radner, and Ava Preacher Collins, 8–36. New York: Routledge, 1993.
Schwartz, Danielle B. "'You Look Good Wearing My Future': Resisting Neoliberalism in John Hughes's *Pretty in Pink* and *Some Kind of Wonderful*." *The Journal of Popular Culture*, 51, no. 2 (2018), 379–98.
Scott, A. O. "An Appraisal: The John Hughes Touch." *New York Times*, August 8, 2009, http://www.nytimes.com/2009/08/08/movies/08appraisal.html?fta=y.
Segal, Lynne. *Slow Motion: Changing Masculinities, Changing Men.* New Brunswick, NJ: Rutgers University Press, 1990.
Seidman, Steve. *Comedian Comedy: A Tradition in Hollywood Film.* Ann Arbor, MI: UMI Research Press, 1981.
Sensei, Seren. "Should Sofia Coppola stay in her white lane? Sure. But that means acknowledging her racism." Medium, June 23, 2017, https://medium.com/@seren.sensei/should-sofia-coppola-stay-in-her-white-lane-sure-but-that-means-acknowledging-her-racism-56a29d1d9109.
Serhan, Yasmeen. "Pork legs are shaking up British politics." *The Atlantic*, May 17, 2018, https://www.theatlantic.com/international/archive/2018/05/is-gammon-racist/560507/.
Shary, Timothy. *Teen Movies: American Youth on Screen.* New York: Wallflower, 2005.
Shary, Timothy. "Buying Me Love: '80s Class-Clash Teen Romances." *Journal of Popular Culture*, 44, no. 3 (2011), 563–82.
Shary, Timothy. *Generation Multiplex: The Image of Youth in American Cinema since 1980*, rev. edn. Austin: University of Texas Press, [2002] 2014.
Sherwood, Rick. "TV's Blackboard Bungle." *Los Angeles Times*, October 27, 1990, F1.
Shome, Raka. "Outing Whiteness." *Critical Studies in Media Communication*, 17, no. 3 (2000), 366–71.
Simmons, Matty. *If You Don't Buy This Book, We'll Kill This Dog: Life, Laughs, Love and Death at National Lampoon.* New York: Barricade Books, 1994.

Simpson, Mark. "The Straight Men of Comedy." In *Because I Tell A Joke Or Two: Comedy, Politics and Social Difference*, edited by Stephen Wagg, 132–45. London: Routledge, 1998.
Siskel, Gene. "'Weird Science' Proves Even John Hughes Can Short-Circuit." *Chicago Tribune*, August 2, 1985, https://www.chicagotribune.com/news/ct-xpm-1985-08-02-8502200420-story.html.
Siskel, Gene. "Teenage Life Gets Touching New Portrayal." *Chicago Tribune*, February 15, 1985, http://articles.chicagotribune.com/1985-02-15/entertainment/8501090715_1_breakfast-club-sixteen-candles-film.
Siskel, Gene. "The John Hughes Magic Missing in 'Pretty in Pink,'" *Chicago Tribune*, February 28, 1986.
Sklar, Robert. *Movie-Made America: A Cultural History of American Movies, Revised and Updated*. New York: Vintage Books, 1994.
Smith, Frances. *Rethinking the Hollywood Teen Movie: Gender, Genre and Identity*. Edinburgh: Edinburgh University Press, 2017.
Smith, Sean M. "Teen Days that Shook the World." *Premiere*, December 1999.
Smokler, Kevin. *Brat Pack America: A Love Letter to '80s Teen Movies*. Los Angeles: Vireo, 2016.
Sofer, Andrew. *The Stage Life of Props*. Ann Arbor: University of Michigan Press, 2003.
Speed, Lesley. "Loose Cannons: White Masculinity and the Vulgar Teen Comedy Film." *Journal of Popular Culture*, 43, no. 4 (2010), 820–41.
Spence, Sharon Lloyd. "Chicago Screenwriter Makes His Directorial Debut." *Back Stage*, August 12, 1983, 54.
Stein, Ellie. "John Hughes: How National Lampoon led to 'The Breakfast Club' and 'Ferris Bueller'." Salon, June 24, 2013, https://www.salon.com/2013/06/24/john_hughes_how_national_lampoon_led_to_the_breakfast_club_and_ferris_bueller/.
Steinberg, Shirley R. and Joe L. Kincheloe, "Privileged and Getting Away With It: The Cultural Studies of White, Middle-Class Youth." *Studies in the Literary Imagination*, 31, no. 1 (1998), 103–26.
Stockton, Kathryn Bond. *The Queer Child, or Growing Sideways in the Twentieth Century*. Durham, NC: Duke University Press, 2009.
Stuever, Hank. "'Real Men Can't Hold A Match to Jake Ryan Of 'Sixteen Candles'." *Washington Post*, February 14, 2004, https://www.washingtonpost.com/archive/lifestyle/2004/02/14/real-men-cant-hold-a-match-to-jake-ryan-of-sixteen-candles/df1fc4ca-bfba-4396-8a4b-345498840759/.
Svetkey, Benjamin. "*Ferris Bueller* Super Bowl Ad: All the Easter Eggs in One Basket." *Entertainment Weekly*, February 6, 2012, https://ew.com/movies/2012/02/06/ferris-bueller-super-bowl-ad-easter-eggs/.
Taft, Larry. "My Vagina, as told to John Hughes." *National Lampoon*, April 1979, http://www.tgfa.org/fiction/MyVagina.htm.
Tasker, Yvonne. "Perfectly Perfect People: Postfeminism, Masculinity and Male Parenting in Contemporary Cinema." In *A Family Affair: Cinema Calls Home*, edited by Murray Pomerance, 175–88. London: Wallflower, 2008.
Thomas, Bob. "He's Still Chevy Chase and You're Not." *Associated Press*, January 4, 1983.
Thoreau, Henry David. *Walden*. New York: Signet, 1961.
Thulin, Lila. "The 97-Year-History of the Equal Rights Amendment." *Smithsonian Magazine*, November 13, 2019, https://www.smithsonianmag.com/history/equal-rights-amendment-96-years-old-and-still-not-part-constitution-heres-why-180973548/.
Tincknell, Estella. *Mediating the Family: Gender, Culture and Representation*. London: Hodder Arnold, 2005.
Traube, Elizabeth G. "Secrets of Success in Postmodern Society." *Cultural Anthropology*, 4, no. 3 (1989), 273–300.

Traube, Elizabeth G. *Dreaming Identities: Class, Gender, and Generation in 1980s Hollywood Movies*. Boulder, CO: Westview Press, 1992.
Tropiano, Stephen. *The Prime Time Closet: A History of Gays and Lesbians on TV.* New York: Applause Books, 2002.
Tropiano, Stephen. *Rebels & Chicks: A History of the Hollywood Teen Movie*. New York: Back Stage Books, 2006.
Troy, Gil. *Morning in America: How Ronald Reagan Invented the 1980s*. Princeton, NJ: Princeton University Press, 2007.
Truffaut, François. "A Certain Tendency of the French Cinema (1954)." In *Movies and Methods: Volume 1*, edited by Bill Nichols, 224–36. Berkeley: University of California Press, 1976.
Tzioumakis, Yannis. "'Indie Doc': Documentary Film and American 'Independent', 'Indie' and 'Indiewood' Filmmaking." *Studies in Documentary Film*, 10, no. 2 (2016), 1–21.
Tzioumakis, Yannis. "From Independent to Indie: The Independent Feature Project and the Complex Relationship between American Independent Cinema and Hollywood in the 1980s." In *A Companion to American Indie Film*, edited by Geoff King, 233–56. Oxford: Wiley Blackwell, 2017.
Vavrus, Mary. "Domesticating Patriarchy: Hegemonic Masculinity and Television's 'Mr. Mom'." *Critical Studies in Media Communication*, 19, no. 3 (2002), 352–75.
Velvet Light Trap, "The 1980s: A Reference Guide to Motion Pictures, Television, VCR, and Cable." *Velvet Light Trap*, no. 27 (1991), 79–80.
Vice, Sue. "Bakhtin and Kristeva: Grotesque Body, Abject Self." In *Face to Face: Bakhtin and Russia in the West*, edited by Carol Adlam et al., 160–74. Sheffield: Sheffield Academic Press, 1997.
Villarejo, Amy. *Film Studies: The Basics*. New York: Routledge, 2013.
Wahlberg, Adam. "Don't You Forget About John Hughes." *Today*, March 17, 2008, https://www.today.com/popculture/don-t-you-forget-about-john-hughes-wbna23677561.
Weiss, Michael. "Some Kind of Republican." Slate, September 21, 2006, http://www.slate.com/articles/arts/dvdextras/2006/09/some_kind_of_republican.html.
Whalley, Jim. *Saturday Night Live, Hollywood Comedy, and American Culture*. London: Palgrave, 2010.
Whatley, Marianne H. "Raging Hormones and Powerful Cars: The Construction of Men's Sexuality in School Sex Education and Popular Adolescent Films." *Journal of Education*, 170, no. 3 (1988), 100–21.
Wheatley, Karen. "My Penis, as told to John Hughes." *National Lampoon*, November 1978, http://www.tgfa.org/fiction/MyPenis.htm.
Willman, Chris. "*Uncle Buck:* John Hughes' Valentine to Teenhood." *Los Angeles Times*, August 16, 1989, http://articles.latimes.com/1989-08-16/entertainment/ca-376_1_uncle-buck.
Wilson, Emma. *Cinema's Missing Children*. London, Wallflower, 2003.
Wojcik, Pamela Robertson. *Fantasies of Neglect: Imagining the Urban Child in American Film and Fiction*. New Brunswick, NJ: Rutgers University Press, 2016.
Wood, Robin. *Hollywood from Vietnam to Reagan . . . and Beyond*. New York: Columbia University Press, 2003.
Wray, Matt. *Not Quite White: White Trash and the Boundaries of Whiteness*. Durham, NC: Duke University Press, 2006.
Wren, Celia. "A Bath of Déjà vu: 'Stranger Things'." *Commonweal*, 143, no. 15 (September 2016), 22.
Wyatt, Justin. "Independents, Packaging and Inflationary Pressure in 1980s Hollywood." In *A New Pot of Gold: Hollywood Under the Electronic Rainbow 1980–1989*, by Stephen Prince, 142–59. Berkeley: University of California Press, 2002.
Yasui, Todd Allan. "Corin Nemec: Trying Anything in *Parker Lewis*." *Washington Post*, January 27, 1991, Y8.

Young, Elizabeth. "Here Comes the Bride: Wedding Gender and Race in *The Bride of Frankenstein*." In *The Dread of Difference: Gender and the Horror Film*, edited by Barry Keith Grant, 359–87. Austin: University of Texas Press, 1996.

Zoglin, Richard. *Comedy at the Edge: How Stand-up in the 1970s Changed America*. New York: Bloomsbury, 2009.

Index

101 Dalmatians (1996), 6, 23
1941 (1979), 164
5th Wave, The (2016), 17n
60 Minutes TV series, 75
'80s culture, 3, 8–12, 21, 27, 33, 37, 73, 76, 83, 85, 109, 120, 143–5, 156, 180, 199, 214, 218; *see also* Reagan '80s

A&M record label, 52
abandonment of children, 102–5, 118–34, 140, 191, 219n
ABC television network, 65, 67, 68, 76
abuse, 32, 104–9, 113–14, 187, 226
academic pressure, 38, 188, 223–4
Academy Awards, 6
adaptations, 15, 50, 66, 76, 203, 207–9, 238; *see also* television
adolescence, 3, 8, 21, 29, 34, 83, 85–98, 103–4, 199, 202, 221–34, 244–6
adulthood, 3, 82–3, 95–8, 120–4, 189, 234
Adventures in Babysitting (1987), 213
advertising, 4, 7, 21, 49–50, 134, 139, 142–5, 149–50, 154–7; *see also* marketing, TV commercials
African Americans, 105, 108, 148, 173, 175, 201, 212, 238–43
Ahmed, Sara, 114, 116n, 140
Allen, Dede, 53
Allen, R. C., 125, 131
Altman, Rick, 7, 63n
American Graffiti (1973), 52, 86
angst, 83, 93, 202, 244–6

Animal House (1978), 32, 49, 65
Aniston, Jennifer, 69
Annie Hall (1977), 162
anti-Semitism, 147
Antunes, Filipa, 120
anxiety of youth, 56, 91–8, 108, 111, 120; *see also* angst
Apatow, Judd, 34
Apocalypse Now (1979), 214
archetypes of youth, 8–9, 27, 58–9
art *see* modern art, pop art
Art Institute of Chicago, 68, 99
Asians, 30, 35, 240
At Ease TV series, 22, 65
athletes, 89, 93, 188, 204, 213; *see also* sports
audience, 8–9, 33–4, 64, 67, 125, 147, 153, 161–76, 181, 200, 224, 229, 241–4; *see also* youth audience
auteurism, 11, 21, 24–40, 143–4
automobiles *see* cars

babies, 14, 120–4, 129–30, 159n
Baby Talk TV series, 67
Baby's Day Out (1994), 18n, 120–4, 129–30
babysitting, 68, 126, 165
Bad Boys (1983), 81
Bagdad Café TV series, 67
Bailey, Steve, 189
Baker, Blanche, 30, 86
Bakhtin, Mikhail, 90, 140, 168, 174, 177n
Barbie doll, 28, 154, 155, 214

INDEX

Barron, Dana, 170, 183
beer, 172, 173, 183, 186, 188
Beethoven (1992), 6, 17n, 82, 119, 121–4, 126, 130–3, 139, 143, 149, 155
Beethoven TV series, 65, 77n
Beethoven's 2nd (1993), 143
Beethoven's 3rd (2000), 143
Beethoven's 4th (2001), 143
Beethoven's 5th (2003), 143
Beguiled, The (2017), 238
Belton, John, 132
Berardinelli, James, 36
Bernstein, Jonathan, 9, 17n, 104, 109, 115n, 116n, 237
Best, Joel, 120
Beverly Hills, 90210 TV series, 74, 75
Beynon, John, 218
Big (1988), 67
Bill and Ted's Excellent Adventure TV series, 76
Birdy (1984), 7
birthdays, 7, 30, 32, 53, 56, 57, 71, 86–7, 104, 118, 169, 172, 185, 236
Black actors, 30, 68
Blackness, 35, 201, 212–13, 217, 236–47; *see also* African Americans
Bleach, Anthony, 9, 229
blockbusters, 11, 21, 44, 50–2, 144, 156, 215, 238
Blue Velvet (1986), 46
bodily excess, 9, 164, 168–9, 176, 177n, 210
body images for youth, 85–8, 94, 204
Bono, Sonny, 74
bourgeoisie, 111, 124, 128, 164, 168, 172
Bowie, David, 56, 92
box office, 24, 29, 33, 44, 51–3, 55, 61n, 65, 66, 163
Boyz N the Hood (1991), 83
Bracken, Eddie, 134, 167, 192
Brat Pack, 4, 22
Breakfast at Tiffany's (1961), 240
Breakfast Club, The (1985), 2, 4, 8–9, 24–38, 52–4, 81–6, 91–4, 98–100, 104, 114, 115n, 117n, 180, 186, 194, 200, 202, 217, 221, 230–4, 244–7
Breakin' (1984), 55
Brewton, Maia, 72
Brickman, Barbara, 15, 82

Bride of Frankenstein (1935), 206
Bringing Up Baby (1938), 210
Brinkema, Eugenie, 93
Brinkley, Christie, 158n, 166, 184
Broad City TV series, 245
Broderick, Matthew, 22, 29, 64, 70, 76, 84, 109, 141, 188, 201, 217, 232, 242
Bruckheimer, Jerry, 45
Buffy the Vampire Slayer (1992), 67
Buffy the Vampire Slayer TV series, 67, 73
Bullock, Sandra, 67
bullying, 34, 74, 94, 140
Bulman, Robert, 16, 200
'Burbs, The (1989), 46
Bush, Barbara, 64
Bush, George H.W., 181

Caddyshack (1980), 163
Caillois, Roger, 94–5, 97
California, 48, 66, 69, 183
camera movement, 73–4, 82, 84, 86, 89, 93–4, 99, 159n, 187, 192, 244; *see also* crane shots, tracking shots
Canby, Vincent, 143–4
Candy, John, 11, 13, 17n, 68, 139, 140, 161–76, 180
Cannon studio, 55
capitalism, 116n, 120–2, 132–5, 143, 146, 149; *see also* late capitalism
Career Opportunities (1991), 144, 153–4
Carrie (1976), 81, 206
cars, 9, 12, 31, 58, 69, 76, 86–8, 96–8, 108, 113–14, 117n, 144, 146–9, 158n, 166–9, 172, 183, 185, 189–90, 210, 212, 217–18, 231, 233, 244; *see also* Ferrari, Porsche, station wagon
casting, 11, 22, 24, 54–60, 64, 67, 77, 140
Catastrophe TV series, 245
Cates, Phoebe, 58, 204
Channel Productions, 49–54, 58, 60
Chard, Holly, 16, 57, 140, 157n, 249n
Chartoff, Melanie, 72
Chase, Chevy, 11, 12, 52, 139–40, 147–8, 161–3, 166, 176, 180, 201
Cheers TV series, 65
Chicago, 3–4, 6, 13, 22, 48–9, 54, 68–9, 77, 95–9, 105–10, 164–5, 174, 182, 199, 202, 233, 238, 242; *see also* Illinois

Chicago Board of Trade, 95, 96
Chidester, Phil, 237, 244
child consumers, 119, 157
childcare, 11, 13, 139–40
children, 2, 3, 6, 14, 33, 51, 68, 82–3, 84–5, 87, 91–2, 97–9, 105–7, 110, 113–14, 116n, 118–35, 139, 170–4, 179–94; *see also* preteens
choreography, 76, 163, 241; *see also* dance
Chow, Kat, 240
Christmas, 123, 128–9, 132–4, 163, 170–6, 192–4, 226
Christmas Vacation, National Lampoon's (1989), 33, 161, 163, 167, 170–6
cinemas *see* movie theaters
cinematography, 74, 85, 241; *see also* deep focus shots, framing, mise-en-scène, point-of-view shots
Class of 1984 (1982), 81
class, 5–6, 9–10, 12, 14–16, 25, 27–8, 35, 81–2, 84–7, 91–6, 99–100, 106, 115n, 119–23, 128–9, 132, 143, 149, 151, 163, 171–5, 181, 199–201, 206, 209, 212, 221–35, 237–8, 242–7; *see also* bourgeoisie, rich kids, upper class, working class, white trash
Class Reunion, National Lampoon's (1982), 4, 21, 50, 85
Clinton, Bill, 193–4
cliques, 34, 158n, 224, 234
Clueless (1995), 9, 34
Coach Carter (2005), 223
Coca-Cola, 147
Cold War, 21, 214–16
college, 51, 108, 223, 231–2
Columbus, Chris, 6
comedians, 49, 68, 139–40, 161–76
comedy *see* humor, role-reversal comedies, satire, screwball comedies, sex comedies, slapstick, vaudeville
coming of age, 8, 11, 35, 199, 233, 240
computers, 68, 89, 97, 155, 199, 206–8, 217
Connelly, Jennifer, 153
conservatism, 23n, 29, 31, 57, 73, 106–9, 115n, 119, 129, 134, 162, 172, 176, 180–1
consumer goods, 9, 133, 139–40, 144–56, 236; *see also* shopping
Coontz, Stephanie, 125, 131–2

Coppola, Sofia, 238–9
Cosby Show, The TV series, 65
costuming, 10, 76, 130, 147, 163, 189, 229; *see also* earrings; make-up styles, underpants
cousins, 172–5, 193
Crafton, Donald, 145–6
crane shots, 9, 89–91
credits (opening or end), 77, 98, 190, 227
Creed, Barbara, 210
crime, 90, 104–5, 121–4, 130–4; *see also* imprisonment, police, violence
Crowe, Cameron, 7
Cry-Baby (1990), 46
Culkin, Kieran, 193
Culkin, Macaulay, 13, 17n, 104–5, 118, 133, 139, 149, 185, 190, 247
Curly Sue (1991), 6, 33, 45, 123, 131, 133, 149
Cusack, Joan, 56

dance, 38, 76, 87, 94–5, 108, 168, 184, 201, 212, 229, 241–3
Dances with Wolves (1990), 83
D'Angelo, Beverly, 149, 166, 170, 172, 183
Dangerfield, Rodney, 49
Dangerous Minds (1995), 223
Dantès, Edmond (pseudonym for John Hughes), 6
Darkest Minds, The (2018), 17n
date rape *see* rape
dating, 7, 31, 71, 99, 102, 228–31, 242; *see also* romance
Dawson's Creek TV series, 73
de Certeau, Michel, 36
De Vaney, Ann, 8, 115n, 247n
Deadly Friend (1986), 208
Dean, James, 109, 116n
deep focus shots, 94, 98
Degrassi: The Next Generation TV series, 73
delinquency, 69, 188; *see also* crime, rebellion
Delta House TV series, 4, 21, 22, 50, 65
Demetriou, Demetrakis, 213
Denby, David, 55
Dennis the Menace (1993), 6, 33, 82, 142, 247
Dennis, Jeffery, 109
Deutch, Howard, 4–5, 24, 34, 98–9, 241
dialogue, 2, 81, 159n, 166, 170, 240, 246; *see also* screenplays

Diamond, Lon, 73–5
Diary of a Mad Housewife (1970), 52
Die Hard (1988), 13
DiGaetano, Michael, 73
Dirty Dancing (1987), 46, 243
Disneyland, 182
Disturbing Behavior (1998), 235n
Divergent franchise (2014–19), 17n
documentaries, 34, 47, 158n, 219n
dogs, 90, 122, 126, 165, 186
Doherty, Thomas, 8
Dolenz, Ami, 69
domesticity, 11–14, 120, 123–7, 139, 180, 182, 185, 191, 205–8
Don't You Forget About Me (2009), 34, 158n
Douglas, Brandon, 69
Downey, Robert Jr., 204
Drillbit Taylor (2008), 6
drinking (alcohol), 31–2, 56–7, 75, 87–8, 115n, 122, 164, 172–3, 188, 212–13; *see also* beer
drugs *see* marijuana
DUFF, The (2015), 9
Dunham, Lena, 238
Dyer, Richard, 239, 243, 248n
dysfunctional families, 119, 125, 129–32, 173

earrings, 200, 226, 228, 231–2, 235, 245
Easy A (2010), 63n, 223
Easy Rider (1969), 52
Eberstadt, Mary, 119–20
economic issues *see* class
Eddie Dodd TV series, 67
Edgerton, Gary, 47, 48
editing, 6, 34, 53, 60, 73, 88, 99, 112, 170, 187; *see also* freeze frames, montage, shot/reverse-shot
education *see* schooling
Eerie, Indiana TV series, 75
effeminacy, 106, 205, 216
Elvira, 74
Emperor's Club, The (2002), 223
Endless Love (1981), 81
Epps, Mike, 68
Equal Rights Amendment, 21, 23n
Estevez, Emilio, 2, 4, 93, 115n, 186, 226, 244
European Vacation (1985), 167
Every Which Way But Loose (1978), 51
existential conflict, 111–12, 119, 123, 133

Fame (1980), 81
family films, 12–14, 23, 33, 44, 83, 118–35, 144, 149, 180–1, 193–4, 246, 249n
family life, 2, 3, 6, 7, 12–14, 16, 21, 29, 53, 57, 81–3, 86–8, 99, 103–6, 114, 116n, 118–35, 139–41, 146–51, 161–76, 179–94, 201, 226–33; *see also* babies, children, domestic duties, dysfunctional families, incest, marriage, nuclear family, relatives, siblings
family values, 16, 29, 119–20, 128–33, 169–72, 179–81
fantasy, 10, 30, 37, 71, 82, 86, 89, 105–6, 114, 115n, 127, 153–4, 170, 199, 204–5, 209–12, 228, 236
Fargo (1996), 67
Fargo TV series, 67
Fast Times at Ridgemont High (1982), 7, 28, 52, 55, 76, 203–4
Fast Times TV series, 76
father figures, 12, 140, 149, 175, 179, 186, 190, 194, 200
Father of the Bride (1991), 12
fatherhood and fathers, 11–16, 77, 82, 96–9, 104, 108–9, 113, 117n, 124–34, 139–41, 170–5, 179–94, 231–3
female objectification, 57, 89–90, 203, 210
feminism, 11, 12, 85, 139, 180, 193, 204–8; *see also* Equal Rights Amendment, postfeminism, second-wave feminism, women's rights
Ferrari, 96, 109, 113, 166, 184, 189–90, 233
Ferris Bueller TV series, 22, 64–77
Ferris Bueller's Day Off (1986), 4, 15, 24, 27, 29, 31–2, 38, 44, 64, 81–2, 84, 89, 91–2, 95–100, 103–10, 141, 142, 179–80, 186–92, 199, 201–2, 213, 217–18, 221, 232–4, 242–7
Finding Forrester (2000), 223
Firestarter (1984), 55
Fleabag TV series, 245
Flintstones, The TV series, 174
Flubber (1997), 6, 23
Fonda, Peter, 52
food, 168–9, 185
Footloose (1984), 55
Forman, Miloš, 52
fort/da game, 210, 219n

Foul Play (1978), 163
Fox Network, 66, 73–5
Fox studio, 50, 55
framing, 82, 84–100, 105, 159n, 193, 241
Frankenhooker (1990), 208
Frankenstein (1931), 89, 91, 199, 203, 207
Freedom Writers (2007), 223–5
Freeman, Hadley, 8, 27, 238
freeze frames, 98, 184, 195n
Fresh Prince of Bel-Air, The TV series, 65–6
Freud, Sigmund, 210, 219n
Friday Night Lights (2004), 67
Friday Night Lights TV series, 67
Friday the 13th (1980), 81
Friedan, Betty, 149–50

Gad, Josh, 76
Ganz, Lowell, 67
Garr, Terry, 149, 182
gay youth, 73, 106–9, 116n, 206, 240, 242; *see also* closeted teens, homoeroticism, homophobia, homosociality, lesbian identity, queerness
gender conformity, 107, 112, 116n, 205
gender identity, 5, 12, 31, 102, 116n, 150, 199, 201, 205–10, 237, 240–3
gender stereotypes, 2, 37, 179, 182, 240 *see also* effeminacy
Generation X, 22, 35, 36
genre, 7–11, 21, 26–39, 44–5, 50–60, 85, 103, 106–7, 120, 124–5, 165, 169, 171, 221–5, 240; *see also* comedy, fantasy, road movies, romance, sex comedies, science fiction, teen films
Get Out (2017), 243
Girls TV series, 238
Gleason, Paul, 31, 41n, 93, 140, 180, 226, 245
Gleiberman, Owen, 55
Glenbrook North high school, 59
globalization, 85
Going Berserk (1983), 164
Goldbergs, The TV series, 76
Gone With the Wind (1939), 32
GoodFellas (1990), 83
Graduate, The (1967), 3, 52
Grady, Constance, 37
Great Outdoors, The (1988), 33

Gremlins (1984), 55
Grey, Jennifer, 31, 68, 84, 109
Grodin, Charles, 126
guns, 148, 167, 183, 191, 214, 216
Gyllenhaal, Jake, 76

Hall, Anthony Michael, 4, 24, 27, 30, 34, 56, 57, 87–9, 92, 114, 116n, 154, 183, 188, 199, 202, 203, 204, 221, 244
Halloween (1978), 7, 28, 81
Hamad, Hannah, 180
Hangover, The (2009), 75
Harbidge, Lesley, 163–4
Hard to Hold (1984), 55
Hark, Ina Rae, 171
Harvey, David, 151
Harwood, Sarah, 123, 128
Hay, James, 189
Heard, John, 13, 140, 191
Heart is a Lonely Hunter, The (1968), 3
Heathers (1989), 17n, 117n
Heckerling, Amy, 7, 52
hegemony, 213
Hellman, Monte, 52
Hepburn, Katherine, 210
heteronormativity, 15, 82, 107, 115n, 211
heterosexuality, 82, 86, 103–14, 116n, 117n, 128–33, 154, 171, 189, 205–16, 240, 242
high school *see* schooling
high-concept films, 7, 14, 22, 45, 48, 51–5
Hill, Michael, 75
Hills Have Eyes, The (1977), 215
Hired Hand, The (1971), 52
HIV, 120
Hoffmann, Gaby, 169, 185
holidays *see* Christmas, Thanksgiving
Hollywood movies, 3, 8, 21, 26, 32–4, 44–60, 125, 162–8, 180, 189, 203, 215–17, 223–5, 238–9
Hollywood or Bust (1956), 211
Home Alone (1990), 6, 13–15, 22, 33, 44, 82, 86, 103–4, 118–35, 140, 142, 144, 149, 154, 179, 181, 190–5, 247, 249n
Home Alone 2: Lost in New York (1991), 13, 82, 119, 131, 133–4, 139, 157, 190, 192–3
Home Alone 3 (1997), 14
Home Alone 4: Taking Back the House (2002), 135n

Home Alone: The Holiday Heist (2012), 135n
home video, 8, 21, 28, 61n, 145, 153; *see also* VHS
homoeroticism, 108–9, 117n, 207, 213
homophobia, 30, 106, 117n, 171, 216
homosociality, 205–14
Honey, I Shrunk the Kids (1989), 12
Honeycutt, Kirk, 3, 4, 36
Hope, Bob, 161
Hopper, Dennis, 52
horror movies *see* slasher films
Host, The (2013), 17n
Howard, Ron, 67
Hughes Music, 28
Hughes, John (biography), 1–16, 17n, 21, 24–9, 33–4, 44–61, 65, 81, 99, 120, 139, 144, 157, 159n, 161, 165, 167, 170, 199, 202, 217, 238–9, 246; *see also* Dantès, Edmond, screenplays, visual style
Huizinga, Johan, 95
Hull High TV series, 66
humor, 2, 4, 16, 21, 25, 31–3, 38, 50, 56, 74, 83, 103, 140, 143, 148, 163–76, 239
Hunger Games, The franchise (2012–15), 17n
hypermasculinity, 207, 214–16
hyphenate filmmaking, 45, 54, 58

I Dream of Jeannie TV series, 203, 209
Illinois, 4, 29, 44, 48–9, 55, 59–60, 90, 101n, 143, 217
Illinois Film Office, 48
I'm Gonna Git You Sucka (1988), 67
Imagine Entertainment, 46, 67
imprisonment, 95, 96, 98, 192, 212, 234
improvisation, 53, 60, 162, 164, 165
incest, 170, 173
Independent Feature Project, 46
independent film, 44–61; *see also* regional filmmaking
intertextuality, 146, 203, 207, 209, 214–16
It Happened One Night (1934), 174
It's a Wonderful Life (1946), 124

Jarmusch, Jim, 54
Jaws 2 (1978), 51
Jeffords, Susan, 180
Jerk, The (1979), 164

Joanou, Phil, 74
jocks *see* athletes
Jones, Jeffrey, 68, 97, 180
Just Visiting (2001), 6

Kael, Pauline, 24
Kapelos, John, 188, 227
Kapur, Jyotsna, 122, 124, 128
Karate Kid, The (1984), 28, 55
Kassabian, Anahid, 245
Kavanaugh, Brett, 37
Kaveney, Roz, 17n, 103, 109, 115n, 116n
Keaton, Michael, 12, 150, 181
Kelly, Jean Louisa, 13, 165, 185
Kempley, Rita, 18n, 173
Kincheloe, Joe, 120, 122, 124, 132, 191, 212, 242, 247
Kinder, Marsha, 181
King, Stephen, 55
kissing, 31, 88, 112, 117n, 173, 189, 228, 229
Kramer vs. Kramer (1979), 180
Kristeva, Julia, 177n, 210
Krutnik, Frank, 162, 167

Lacan, Jacques, 159n
laddism, 13
Lalich, Richard, 7, 14, 17n
Last Movie, The (1971), 52
Last Starfighter, The (1984), 7, 55
late capitalism, 134, 143
Late Night With David Letterman TV series, 165
Latinx, 212, 245
Learning Tree, The (1969), 81
Leave It to Beaver TV series, 74
LeBrock, Kelly, 28, 90, 154, 199, 203, 209, 211, 219n
Lee, Christina, 239
Leppert, Alice, 16, 140
lesbian identity, 73, 116n
Levy, Emanuel, 48
Levy, Eugene, 147, 164
Lewis, Jerry, 161, 203, 211–12
LGBT issues *see* gay youth, lesbian identity, queerness
Life board game, 211
liminality, 81, 85, 90–2, 98, 101n, 169, 171, 174, 199, 245

Little Darlings (1980), 28
Living It Up (1954), 211
Longo, Tony, 87
Look Who's Talking (1989), 12, 67
Lucas, George, 4, 52

M*A*S*H (1970), 67, 253
M*A*S*H TV series, 67, 253
McCarthy, Andrew, 10, 41–2, 99, 200, 228, 245
McClurg, Edie, 188
McGovern, Elizabeth, 149
Mad Max (1979), 203, 215
Mad Max 2: The Road Warrior (1981), 215
magical realism, 71, 73
Maid in Manhattan (2002), 6
Malcolm X (1992), 83
male gaze, 88, 100, 203–4
Mandel, Babaloo, 67
Manhattan *see* New York City
manhood *see* masculinity
Manning, Michelle, 52–3
marijuana, 188
marketing, 50, 135n, 153, 159n, 164, 174
marriage, 97, 133, 142, 166, 170–2, 185–6, 211
Married . . . with Children TV series, 74
Martin, Adrian, 9, 17n, 85, 100
Martin, Dean, 203, 211
Martin, Steve, 139, 161–4. 167, 175, 177n
Marx Brothers, 161, 177n
Mary Poppins character, 210, 219n
Mary Poppins (1964), 199, 203, 209–10
masculinity, 11–13, 16, 100n, 171, 179, 182, 188–9, 194n, 199–200, 202–3, 205–6, 208, 210–20, 237, 242, 257n, 259; *see also* father figures, fatherhood, hypermasculinity; male gaze; patriarchy; toxic masculinity
Masius, John, 65, 68–71
Maslin, Janet, 17, 30, 41n, 101n
Masterson, Mary Stuart, 99, 107, 230
materialism, 119, 132–3, 189; *see also* child consumer, consumer goods
Mattel, 139, 157
MCA, 28, 41n, 50
Mean Girls (2004), 9, 224–5
Meaney, Kevin, 68

MeToo and TimesUp movements, 2, 16n, 25, 37, 40n, 116n, 248n
MGM/UA studio, 55
military, 22, 65
mimicry, 28, 95–7
Minnie and Moskowitz (1971), 52
Miracle on 34th Street (1994), 23, 82, 119, 121–2, 127, 130–3
mise-en-abîme, 89
mise-en-scène, 85, 87, 151, 154, 190
misogyny, 35, 38, 145, 213–14, 216
missing children, 120–1, 135n
Mitchell-Smith, Ilan, 29, 88, 155, 199, 203–4
mobility, 81–2, 84–9, 91, 93, 95, 98–9, 115n, 158n, 212, 222, 224, 227, 229–32, 234; *see also* social mobility
modern art, 160n, 164
Modern Problems (1981), 163
Modleski, Tania, 14, 18n
monsters, 91, 101n, 134, 155, 209–10, 215, 219n, 243
monstrousness *see* monsters
montage, 76, 86, 92, 99, 142, 153–5, 174, 182, 184, 193
moral panic, 180
Moranis, Rick, 164
Morris, Haviland, 14, 31, 87
motherhood and mothers, 13–14, 82, 102, 104, 111, 121, 124, 126–7, 129–30, 132, 134, 140, 184–6, 191, 209–10; *see also* working mothers
movie theaters, 221
Mr. Mom (1983), 4, 12, 21–2, 50, 52, 65, 85, 139, 142, 144, 149–51, 154–5, 159n, 179, 181–2, 185, 191
Mr. Mom TV pilot, 22, 65
Mrs. Doubtfire (1993), 12
MTV network, 12, 89
Mull, Martin, 149
Mulvey, Laura, 100n
Murray, Bill, 65
music, 21, 28, 34, 42n, 50, 53, 55–6, 66, 89, 126, 201, 238, 241–3, 246, 249n
My Fair Lady (1964), 209
My Own Private Idaho (1991), 107
My Science Project (1985), 208
mythology, 15

Nadel, Alan, 179, 185, 190, 194–5n
National Lampoon magazine, 4, 21, 38, 49, 51, 56, 62n, 176–7, 239–40, 246
Native Americans, 212
NBC television, 64–6, 68, 73, 75, 164
neglect of children, 9, 15, 82, 102–6, 108, 113–14, 115n, 119–20, 133
Nelson, Elissa, 8, 15, 17n, 21–2, 24, 41n, 43n, 49, 61–2n
Nelson, Judd, 2, 4, 25, 93, 104, 186, 200, 226, 244
Nemec, Corin, 66, 72, 78n
neoconservative, 35, 115, 139, 193
nerds, 93, 114, 116n, 202, 205, 217
New Man, 11, 13
New Port South (2001), 6
New York City, 6, 13, 193
Nightmare on Elm Street, A (1984), 7
Northbrook, Illinois, 217
nostalgia, 8, 37, 115n, 125, 131, 135n, 153
Not Another Teen Movie (2001), 34, 235n
nuclear family, 13–14, 82, 103, 119, 121–2, 125, 133, 148, 161–2, 169–70, 174–5, 189
nudity (female), 57, 170

O'Connor, John, 24, 71, 78n, 177n
O'Hara, Catherine, 13, 127, 140, 191
Ode to Billy Joe (1976), 116n
Oedipal tensions, 218
Oingo Boingo, 155, 205
Old School (2003), 75
Oliver-Powell, Melissa, 15, 82, 115n, 118
Ordinary People (1980), 180
Ortega, Kenny, 76
Osbourne, Ozzy, 74
Outsiders, The (1983), 28, 81
outsiders, 28, 61n, 172

Pajama Party (1964), 3
Paramount studio, 4, 54–5, 62n
Parenthood (1989), 12, 46, 164
Parenthood TV series, 67
parental neglect *see* neglect of children
parents, 15, 27, 38, 66, 68–9, 72, 81–4, 86, 95–8, 104–5, 108, 114–15, 118–20, 122, 124–5, 127–8, 130–4, 170, 179–80, 183, 185–6, 188–9, 191, 194, 212, 217, 224, 226–7, 233–6, 244; *see also* Oedipal tensions

Parker Lewis Can' t Lose TV series, 22, 66, 71–5, 77–8
parties, 3, 27, 56, 70, 81, 86, 89, 152–5, 172, 185, 203, 213–14, 216, 224, 228, 231, 236
Patch of Blue, A (1965), 3
patriarchy, 123, 141, 179, 181–3, 185, 189–94, 206, 210; *see also* fatherhood and fathers
Paul, Alice, 23n
Paul, William, 101n, 166, 176n
Paxton, Bill, 90, 206
Pearlman, Alison, 151, 159n
penis jokes, 49
Pennies from Heaven (1981), 164
Pepsi, 150–2, 159n
Pesci, Joe, 122, 190
Petersen, Christina, 15, 81, 84
pets *see* dogs
Phillips, Clyde, 73–5, 78n
Phillips, Todd, 75
Pickett, Cindy, 68, 76
Planes, Trains and Automobiles (1987), 11, 13, 142, 149, 161, 164–5, 167–9, 171–2, 174–6, 185
play, 92, 94–8, 101n, 110, 152–3, 211, 217–18, 219n; *see also* computers, Life board game, sports, toys, video games
Playboy magazine, 49, 89
Plaza Hotel, 192–3
point-of-view shots, 96–7, 99, 130
police, 76, 124, 129, 173, 184, 191, 193
Porky's (1981), 7, 28, 32, 51, 203
Porsche, 146–7, 149, 158n
postfeminism, 12, 17n, 42n, 194n, 201n, 235n, 247n
post-punk *see* punk
pot *see* marijuana
Potts, Annie, 31, 228, 241
pregnancy, 90, 172, 234, 236, 240
preteens, 118–20, 125, 128, 131, 133–5
Pretty Woman (1990), 209
Priestley, Jason, 74
Princess Diaries, The (2001), 209
Private Lessons (1981), 51
Project X (2012), 223
prom, 7, 9, 107, 206, 229–30, 242, 244
Promise Keepers, 180
props, 16, 76, 139, 142–5, 148, 152, 156–8

Pryor, Richard, 30
Psychedelic Furs, 238
punk, 91, 187, 240, 242
Purple Rain (1984), 55
Pygmalion, 199, 203, 208–9
Pygmalion (1913), 209

Quaid, Randy, 172
queerness, 82, 102–3, 105–10, 112–17, 171, 205–7, 211, 214

racial identity, 199–201, 237, 240; *see also* African Americans, Asians, Blackness, Latinx, Native Americans, Whiteness
racism, 2, 30, 145
Ramis, Harold, 52, 65, 159n, 170, 173
Ramones, The, 183
Ramsay, Lynne, 82
rape, 31–3, 35, 37, 41–3n, 209, 212, 214–15
Reach the Rock (1998), 6
Reagan '80s, 116n, 144, 181, 193, 207, 215
Reagan, Ronald, 9, 21, 81, 117n, 142–4, 149, 153–4, 156–7, 160n, 180–1, 193–5, 207, 220n
Real Genius (1985), 208
Rebel Without a Cause (1955), 81, 109, 114, 116n
rebellion, 22, 66, 71, 76, 93, 217
Red Dawn (1984), 55
Redding, Otis, 201, 241–3, 246, 248n
regional filmmaking, 22, 45, 47–9, 59–61n
regression, 83, 98, 167, 215
Reitman, Ivan, 45
relatives, 172, 239; *see also* cousins, parents, siblings
Revenge of the Nerds (1984), 32, 55, 203, 208, 213
revenge porn, 32
Rhodes, John David, 143, 158n
rich kids (richies), 4, 99, 200, 226, 228–32
Riehle, Richard, 69–70
Riney, Hal, 142–3, 157n
Ringwald, Molly, 1–4, 9–10, 16–17n 24–5, 29–31, 34, 37–8, 40–3n, 53, 56–8, 62n, 86, 93, 99, 104, 106, 115–16n, 139, 146, 199–201, 226, 228, 235n-40, 242, 244, 247–8n
Rivers, Joan, 49

road movies, 167, 169, 171, 177n, 202–3, 211–12
road trips, 149, 163, 169, 181–2, 213
Roberts, Soraya, 37, 43n
Robertson, Paul Lester, 215, 219n
Rocky (1976), 21, 182
Rocky Horror Picture Show, The (1975), 208
Rocky III (1982), 182
Rocky IV (1985), 54
role-reversal comedies, 179, 182
romance, 2, 10, 37, 57, 109, 114, 128–9, 153–4, 158n, 183, 200–1, 232, 235, 245, 248n
Rosenberg, Howard, 70, 78n
Roush, Matt, 71, 78n
Rowe, Kathleen, 210, 219n
Roxanne (1987), 164
Ruck, Alan, 38, 68, 76, 95, 103–4, 179, 217, 232
Russo, Mary, 168, 177n

Sabo, Don, 206, 219n
Sadiq, Maulud, 37, 43n, 248n
salesmen, 11–12, 147, 164, 183
Santa Claus, 122, 127, 130–1, 192–3
Sara, Mia, 32, 68, 76, 95, 108, 189, 232
Sarris, Andrew, 25, 40n, 109, 115–16n
satire, 38, 167, 243
Saturday Night Live TV series, 162, 175–6
Savage Islands (1983), 50
Say Anything . . . (1989), 222
Sayles, John, 54
Scahill, Andrew, 16, 100n, 199–202
Schlatter, Charlie, 64, 70
Schoeffling, Michael, 25, 56–7, 86, 146
school bus, 56, 86, 98, 190
school principals *see* teachers
School Ties (1992), 223
schooling, 3–4, 7, 9–10, 22, 27, 33, 36, 57, 66, 68–9, 72–4, 76–7, 85–7, 89–95, 99, 118, 158n, 169, 182, 186, 188, 200, 202–3, 206, 217, 221–35, 238, 244–6; *see also* teachers
Schwarzenegger, Arnold, 11, 215
science fiction, 4, 55, 88, 199
screenplays, 4, 6, 11–12, 27, 30, 50, 52, 54, 60, 65, 144, 161, 163, 168, 170–1, 173, 175, 177n, 179, 202; *see also* adaptations

screwball comedies, 171, 174–5, 203, 209–10, 212–13, 217
scripts *see* screenplays
SCTV TV series, 162, 164–5, 175
second-wave feminism, 11–12, 85, 139
Sedgwick, Eve Kosofsky, 207
Segal, Lynne, 180, 194n
Seidman, Steve, 162, 176n
Seventeen magazine, 29, 40n
sex comedies, 7, 57, 202, 212
sexism, 2; *see also* female objectification, misogyny
sexual assault, 2, 37; *see also* rape
sexuality, 16, 25, 35, 37, 106–7, 170, 246
  of youth, 28, 106–7, 116n, 206, 209–11, 216, 219n; *see also* dating, effeminacy, heteronormativity, heterosexuality, kissing, nudity (female), queerness, virginity
Shafer, Leah, 16, 139
Shales, Tom, 71
Shary, Timothy, 41n, 57, 63n, 100n, 107, 115–17n, 188, 194–5n, 201n, 219n, 230, 235n, 248n
She's All That (1999), 209
She's Having a Baby (1988), 33, 45, 142, 144, 149, 152, 159n
Sheedy, Ally, 4, 28, 93, 104, 226, 244
Sheen, Charlie, 76
Sheffer, Craig, 31, 230
Shermer, Illinois, 29, 89–90, 92, 101n, 143, 202, 217, 226–7
Shermerville, 217
Shields, Brooke, 58
shopping, 7, 9, 128, 191–2, 226
shopping malls, 7, 28
shot/reverse-shot, 87, 99, 102, 111, 130, 186–7
showers, 89, 166, 174, 203, 209
siblings, 29, 129, 185–6, 191
Silence of the Lambs (1991), 83
Silent Running (1972), 52
Simple Minds, 92, 247
Simpson, Don, 45
Singer, Lori, 58
Siskel, Gene, 24, 40, 101n, 202, 218n

Sixteen Candles (1984), 2, 4, 7–9, 24–5, 27, 29–31, 33, 35–8, 40–1n, 43–4n, 52–3, 55, 57–60, 77, 81, 84–6, 88–91, 96, 100, 104, 118, 142, 144, 146, 153, 155, 158n, 236–7, 239–40, 246, 248n
Skin I Live In, The (2011), 208
Sklar, Robert, 24, 40n
slapstick, 120, 145–6, 150, 154, 158n, 163, 167, 170–1, 175–6, 185, 188
slasher films, 7, 28, 81
Smith, Frances, 100n, 200–1
Smith, Kevin, 34
Smith, Will, 65
Smiths, The, 110, 112, 117n
social class *see* class
social mobility, 82, 85, 88–9, 91, 99, 229, 234
Sofer, Andrew, 146, 158n
Some Kind of Wonderful (1987), 5–6, 11, 24, 29–31, 33, 84, 98–101, 114, 116n, 158n, 199, 221, 230–1, 246
Sonnenfeld, Barry, 74
sound, 71, 73–4, 78n, 85–6, 98, 160n, 173, 183, 212, 240–1
soundtracks, 28, 41n, 53, 127, 157, 171, 183, 204, 243; *see also* music
Spader, James, 10, 155, 228, 242
Speed, Leslie, 212, 219n
Spicer, Bryan, 74
Spielberg, Steven, 4, 45
Splash (1984), 164
Splendor in the Grass (1961), 81
sports, 208, 212, 219n
Square Pegs TV series, 73
St. Elsewhere TV series, 70
Stallone, Sylvester, 11, 54, 218
Stand and Deliver (1988), 223
Stanton, Harry Dean, 14, 99, 140
Star Wars (1977), 21
station wagon, 86, 142–3, 147–9, 154, 183
Stein, Ben, 76
Stepford Wives, The (1975, 2004), 208
Stern, Daniel, 122, 190
Stockton, Kathryn, 105–6, 113, 115–16n
Stolz, Eric, 230
Stranger Things TV series, 102–3, 115n
Streets of Fire (1984), 53, 55
Stripes (1981), 65, 164

suburbs, 3–4, 6, 10, 29, 59, 77, 85–6, 90, 98, 101n, 105–6, 115n, 121, 123–4, 126–7, 131–2, 134, 142–4, 147, 152, 155, 162–3, 165, 167, 170–1, 173–4, 176, 180, 199, 208, 213, 221–7, 231–2, 234–5, 236, 238–9, 247
Summer Rental (1985), 164
Sundance Institute, 46
Superbad (2007), 223
Superman (1978), 21, 51
supernatural, 102, 108, 126, 131

Taking Off (1971), 52
Talkboy, 139, 157, 160n
Tanen, Ned, 15, 22, 29, 49–50, 52–4, 58, 62n
Target store, 153–4
Tasker, Yvonne, 180, 194n
Tea and Sympathy (1956), 107
teachers, 3, 41n, 66, 68–70, 72–3, 75–7, 141, 169, 179–80, 186, 200, 205, 223, 233, 235–6
technology, 89, 97, 203, 205–8, 218
teen films, 1–2, 4–5, 7–11, 17n, 21, 24–30, 33–6, 39–43n, 46, 50, 54–5, 57–8, 60–1, 63n, 76, 81–2, 84–5, 91, 98, 100n, 103–4, 106–7, 110, 112–17, 118, 120, 144, 154, 158n, 179–80, 186, 193–5, 199–201, 221, 223, 234–6, 239–40, 244–7
teenagers, 3, 7–9, 11, 15, 17n, 21–4, 26–7, 29, 33, 35, 39, 45, 51–2, 55, 58–60, 65–6, 75–6, 81–3, 91–5, 97, 103–5, 107, 114, 116n, 140, 153, 155, 157, 172, 179–81, 193–4, 199–200, 202, 208, 221, 226–7, 233–5, 239, 244, 246; *see also* preteens
television, 15, 17n, 22–3, 48, 50, 62, 64–9, 71, 73–8n, 89, 109, 116n, 134–5, 139, 143–5, 151–3, 155, 158–9n, 162, 165, 179–80, 194, 245–7, 249n; *see also individual show titles*
Ten Things I Hate About You (1999), 9
Terminator, The (1984), 215
Thanksgiving, 11, 127, 164
Thompson, Lea, 31, 99, 114, 230
Thoreau, Henry David, 225, 235n

Three Men and a Baby (1987), 14
Three O'Clock High (1987), 74
Tiger Electronics, 133–4
Tincknell, Estella, 12–13, 18n
Tomorrowland (2015), 17n
Tortorici, Peter, 67–8
toxic masculinity, 214, 216
toys, 123, 131–5, 139, 157, 160n, 192–3, 219n
tracking shots, 89, 93–4
Traube, Elizabeth, 116, 172, 177n, 190, 195n, 219–20n
trauma, 102–4, 107–8, 219n
Tropiano, Stephen, 15, 22, 180, 194n
Troy, Gil, 218, 220n
True Believer (1989) *see Eddie Dodd* TV series
Turley, Myra, 70
TV commercials, 74–6, 142, 144–5, 153–4, 157, 159n, 207–8
Two-Lane Blacktop (1971), 52
Tzioumakis, Yannis, 15, 22, 249n

Uncle Buck (1989), 6, 11, 13, 18n, 22, 33, 68, 78n, 140, 142, 149, 161, 165, 168–9, 172, 176–7, 180–1, 185, 191–2, 195n
Uncle Buck TV series, 65, 67–8, 77n
Underwood, Jay, 13, 165, 185
Unforgiven (1992), 83
Uni Records, 50, 53
Universal Pictures, 4, 46, 49–50, 52–5, 58–9, 62n, 68
University of Arizona, 4
upper class, 10, 82, 86–7, 95, 200, 212, 224, 228, 230
USA Network, 23

Vacation, National Lampoon's (1983), 4, 11, 50–2, 85, 103, 139, 142, 144, 147, 149, 155, 158–9n, 161, 163, 174–5, 177n, 179
Vacation '58, 42n, 49–50, 163, 176n
vacations, 21, 124, 163, 167; *see also* road trips
Valley Girl (1983), 81
vaudeville, 162–3
Vavrus, Mary, 179, 194n
Vernon, Kate, 32
Vestron, 46

VHS, 8, 21, 28, 131, 153, 157
video games, 74
Vietnam War, 21
violence, 32, 81–2, 103, 108, 120, 146–7, 151, 155, 185, 191, 203, 214, 216
virginity, 31, 87, 210, 221
visual style, 48, 60, 66, 73–4, 157n; *see also* camera movement, cinematography, editing, mise-en-scène
Von Steuben Day Parade, 68, 95, 110, 233
voyeurism, 9, 203–5, 237

Walley World, 163, 182–4
Wang, Wayne, 6, 54
Ward, Lyman, 68, 189
WarGames (1983), 51, 81, 208
Warhol, Andy, 150
Warm Bodies (2013), 17n
Warner Bros. studio, 50, 55, 159n
Watanabe, Gedde, 30, 240
Watergate, 21
Waters, John, 46
Watley, Marianne H., 210
We Need to Talk About Kevin (2011), 82
weddings, 53, 86
WeeGee, 153, 159n
Weinstein, Harvey, 2, 37
Weird Science (1985), 4, 16, 24, 28–31, 38, 65, 81, 84–5, 88–91, 100–1n, 104, 144, 154, 158n, 199, 202–8, 210–13, 215, 217–18

Weird Science TV series, 23, 65, 77n
West, Mae, 210
Westworld (1972), 67
Westworld TV series, 67
Whaley, Frank, 153–4
white trash, 172–5, 245–6
Whiteness, 12, 16, 21, 30, 106, 114–15n, 129, 142, 146, 148–9, 161, 172–5, 180, 199–201, 211–13, 221, 223–5, 232, 236–9, 242–8n
Wild Life, The (1984), 55
Willis, Bruce, 11, 13
Wilson, Mara, 127
Wojcik, Pamela, 82, 105–6, 114–15n, 117n
women's rights, 21, 32, 179
Wood, Natalie, 114
Wood, Robin, 189, 194–5n
Working Girl TV series, 67
working mothers, 127, 180
working class, 5, 10, 16, 93, 122, 174–5, 181, 200, 208, 222, 226, 228, 230, 232, 235, 243
World War II, 3, 8, 25–6, 105, 115n
Wyatt, Justin, 45–6, 61n

You're Never Too Young (1955), 211
Young, Elizabeth, 207, 219n
youth audience, 7–8, 24, 26, 28, 50–1, 57, 61n, 66, 105
yuppies, 241, 164, 167, 171, 173, 175, 177n, 205, 217–18

EU representative:
Easy Access System Europe
Mustamäe tee 50, 10621 Tallinn, Estonia
Gpsr.requests@easproject.com